T0302099

Innovating for the Middle of the Pyramid in Emerging Countries

The transformation of emerging markets in recent decades has generated a new, growing, and very large middle-class market, also known as the middle of the pyramid. This market segment, which is middle by the standards of emerging markets yet low by the standards of advanced economies, is extremely attractive for firms, but still poorly understood and underserved. This volume presents detailed analyses of exemplary firms that have innovated products, services, and business models to fulfill the needs and desires of these new middle classes. It provides useful insights for managers, consultants, researchers, and students interested in emerging economies, and actionable lessons on how to innovate for a new and expanding market segment.

ALVARO CUERVO-CAZURRA is Professor of International Business and Strategy at Northeastern University, AIB Fellow, and coeditor of *Global Strategy Journal*. He studies the internationalization of firms, particularly emerging market multinationals; capability upgrading, mainly technological capabilities; and governance issues, especially corruption in international business. He received a PhD from MIT and an honorary doctorate from Copenhagen Business School.

MIGUEL A. MONTOYA is Full Professor and was the Director of the Graduate School at Tecnológico de Monterrey, Mexico. He is country representative at AIB-LAC and a founding member of the Fudan Latin America University Consortium. He has published on international business and economics, particularly emerging market multinationals, trade, and investment between China and Latin America. He coedited the book *Mexican Multinationals* (Cambridge University Press). He received a PhD from Universitat Autonoma de Barcelona, Spain.

Innovating for the Middle of the Pyramid in Emerging Countries

Edited by

ALVARO CUERVO-CAZURRA
Northeastern University

MIGUEL A. MONTOYA
Tecnologico de Monterrey

CAMBRIDGE
UNIVERSITY PRESS

CAMBRIDGE
UNIVERSITY PRESS

University Printing House, Cambridge CB2 8BS, United Kingdom

One Liberty Plaza, 20th Floor, New York, NY 10006, USA

477 Williamstown Road, Port Melbourne, VIC 3207, Australia

314–321, 3rd Floor, Plot 3, Splendor Forum, Jasola District Centre,
New Delhi – 110025, India

79 Anson Road, #06–04/06, Singapore 079906

Cambridge University Press is part of the University of Cambridge.

It furthers the University's mission by disseminating knowledge in the pursuit of
education, learning, and research at the highest international levels of excellence.

www.cambridge.org
Information on this title: www.cambridge.org/9781108480192
DOI: 10.1017/9781108647731

© Cambridge University Press 2021

First published 2021

A catalogue record for this publication is available from the British Library.

Library of Congress Cataloging-in-Publication Data
Names: Cuervo-Cazurra, Alvaro, editor.
Title: Innovating for the middle of the pyramid in emerging countries / edited by
  Alvaro Cuervo-Cazurra, Miguel A. Montoya, Monterrey Tec, Guadalajara.
Description: New York, NY : Cambridge University Press, [2021] | Includes
  bibliographical references and index.
Identifiers: LCCN 2020040530 (print) | LCCN 2020040531 (ebook) |
  ISBN 9781108480192 (hardback) | ISBN 9781108727136 (paperback) |
  ISBN 9781108647731 (epub)
Subjects: LCSH: Technological innovations–Developing countries. | Basic needs–
  Developing countries. | Middle class–Developing countries.
Classification: LCC HC59.72.T4 I5253 2021 (print) | LCC HC59.72.T4 (ebook) |
  DDC 338/.064091724–dc23
LC record available at https://lccn.loc.gov/2020040530
LC ebook record available at https://lccn.loc.gov/2020040531

ISBN 978-1-108-48019-2 Hardback

Sebastian Cuervo, the future

*Celi Zaragoza, Lupita Bayardo, Andrea, Migue,
and Nacho Montoya*

Contents

Figures

Tables

Contributors

Jorge L. Alcaraz is Professor of International Business at Pontificia Universidad Javeriana Cali in the Management Organizations Department. He holds a PhD in International Business and was a visiting scholar at Columbia University. His main research interest is in the different factors affecting the global strategy of enterprises from emerging economies, particularly those from Latin America.

L. Arturo Bernal is Professor of International Finance at Tecnologico de Monterrey (Mexico), where he also received a doctoral degree. He studies risk management using derivatives. He also analyzes real options valuation. He has published articles in academic journals.

Mauricio Cervantes is Professor of International Strategy at Tecnologico de Monterrey (Mexico). His research interests are Microfinance, Base of the Pyramid, and Cultural Finance. He is the executive director of the Asia Pacific Institute of Monterrey Tec. He is a consultant in the areas of International Finance, Portfolio Theory, Risk Coverage, and Business in China. He has been a visiting professor at University of International Business and Economics in Beijing, China; Portland State University, USA; Universidad San Francisco de Quito, Ecuador; ESAN, Graduate School of Business, Peru. He holds a PhD in Finance from UT-Austin/Tecnologico de Monterrey (Mexico), an MBA, and a Bachelor's degree in Electronic Engineering.

Alvaro Cuervo-Cazurra is Professor of International Business and Strategy at Northeastern University. He studies the internationalization of firms, particularly emerging market multinationals; capability upgrading, focusing on technological capabilities; and governance issues, especially corruption in international business. He is Fellow of the Academy of International

Business and coeditor of the *Global Strategy Journal*. He received a PhD from the Massachusetts Institute of Technology and an honorary doctorate from Copenhagen Business School.

Eileen Daspro, DBA, is Clinical Professor of International Business at the University of San Diego School of Business. Her research interests include the international competitiveness of firms and internationalization strategies in emerging markets. She has published in the *Latin American Business Review*, the *Journal of Business Ethics* and Cambridge University Press. She is a NASBITE Certified Global Business Professional and Trainer.

Mario Adrián Flores-Castro is a regional vice president of Tecnologico de Monterrey (Mexico). He currently leads the team representing Mexico in the Global Entrepreneurship Monitor (GEM). He has done research in the United Kingdom, the United States, and Latin America. Before joining the academic world, he worked for over ten years at companies such as The Goodyear Tire and Rubber Company and Continental Tires. He holds a PhD in Business Administration with specialization in Operations. He also holds an MS in Industrial Engineering and is a mechanical engineer.

Isaí Guízar is Professor of Finance and Economics at Universidad de Guadalajara. Guizar's primary research field is development economics and finance. His current research areas include financial services in developing countries, interest rate restrictions, and the effects of credit rationing on microenterprises. He holds a PhD from The Ohio State University.

Daniel Lemus-Delgado is Professor of International Relations at Tecnologico de Monterrey (Mexico). He studies the national and regional innovation system, specifically in emerging countries. He also analyzes the relationship between building innovation capacities and culture, with a special interest in East Asia. He is a member of the National System of Researchers in Mexico. He received a PhD from Colima University, Mexico.

Jasenko Ljubica, PhD, is Associate Professor at National Research University, Higher School of Economics, St. Petersburg, Russia. His research lies at the intersection of Organizational Behavior, Organizational Psychology, and Human Resources in International Business where he studies Expatriate Management and Global Leadership as well as Organization and Management Theory where he studies Business Models. He also specializes in Research Methods in Management Sciences.

Miguel A. Lopez-Lomelí has a PhD in Entrepreneurship and Management with specialization in Marketing from the Universidad Autonoma de Barcelona (UAB), Spain. He had a professional career for twenty years in sales and sustomer marketing at the Procter & Gamble Company in Mexico, United States, and the Latin America Region, holding positions from sales representative to director of customer marketing for Latin America. He teaches courses in sales and marketing strategy in the Undergraduate and Executive Education programs at Tecnologico de Monterrey (Mexico). He has published articles in various academic journals, as well as book chapters.

Miguel A. Montoya is Professor of International Economics and Business at Architecture, Art, and Design School at Tecnologico de Monterrey (Mexico). He studies multinational companies of Latin America. He also analyzes innovations at Base of the Pyramid in emerging markets. He has published articles in various academic journals and book chapters. He received a PhD from the Autonomous University of Barcelona.

Jose F. Moreno has a PhD in Finance from the University of Texas Pan-American. He is Associate Professor of Finance at the University of the Incarnate Word in San Antonio, Texas.

Edgar Muñíz-Ávila is Professor of Business Creation and Director of the Entrepreneurship and Innovation area at Tecnologico de Monterrey (Mexico). He studies entrepreneurship with special interests in social entrepreneurship, creation and development of enterprises, and family businesses. For the last nine years, he directed the Business Incubator and the Enterprise Acceleration program. He received a PhD from University of Antonio de Nebrija.

Ana Belén Perdigones is Director of Master Programs and a professor at ESIC Business & Marketing School in Madrid, Spain. She has a Master's in Marketing by ESAN in Lima, Perú and a Master's in Marketing Science by ESIC. She is a specialist in market research, business intelligence, and consumer behavior in emerging markets. She is Fellow of the Higher Education Academy (FHEA) – AdvanceHE.

Otto Regalado-Pezúa is Professor and Chair of Marketing Department at ESAN Graduate School of Business, Peru. He received his PhD degree in Organizations Sciences from the Université de Nice-Sophia Antipolis, France. His research interest areas include services marketing, higher education, and tourism systems.

Lucía Rodríguez-Aceves is Professor of Entrepreneurship at Tecnologico de Monterrey (Mexico). She studies knowledge management and strategy, with a special interest in using social network analysis to measure collaboration in knowledge-based networks. She participates in the Global Knowledge Research Network and the Iberoamerican Knowledge Systems Community. She received a PhD in Business Administration from the EGADE Business School of Tecnologico de Monterrey (Mexico).

José Manuel Saiz-Álvarez has a PhD in Economics and Business Administration from Autonomous University of Madrid, Spain, and a PhD in Sociology from Pontifical University of Salamanca, Spain. He has been the academic director of Business Administration Doctoral Studies, Nebrija University, Spain, and a member of the Scientific Research Council, Professor Edward Lipinski School of Economics, Law and Medical Sciences at Kielce, Poland. He is a member of the editorial board and referee of numerous national and international journals and appears in Who's Who in the World.

Francisco J. Valderrey is a professor at Tecnologico de Monterrey (Mexico). His research focuses on strategy in the tourism industry, as well as marketing in China and negotiation strategy in multicultural environments. He has published several articles on Asia Pacific topics, and most recently he started a research group analyzing technology and global business. He has coauthored two textbooks on fundamentals of marketing. He earned a PhD in Administration and Marketing from the University of Valencia in Spain.

Xiomara Vázquez is an associate professor at Tecnologico de Monterrey (Mexico). She has published in the Microfinance field. She has been a speaker at international academic events in the United States, Canada, Brazil, Argentina, and Spain. She had been the Accounting and Finance Department director and Master in Finance director. She received a PhD in Economics and Management Sciences from the Universidad de Guadalajara in 2011, as well as a Master's in Finance (Honors), a Master of Business Administration, and a Bachelor of Accounting (Honors) from Tecnologico de Monterrey (Mexico).

Preface

Innovation is at the core of the development of countries and the advantage of firms. Much attention has been paid to how companies in advanced economies innovate to serve the needs of demanding and wealthy consumers who are willing to pay premium prices for novel products and services. Additionally, these companies benefit from a sophisticated innovation system at home that supports their ability to create new products and services. Recently, the topic of frugal innovation has emerged to acknowledge that companies in emerging economies do develop new products and services to address the needs of people with extremely low levels of income, i.e., the based of the income pyramid. These innovations are designed to provide the first access to very basic goods and services for individuals who have very little money to pay for them.

However, this leaves individuals that are middle-income by emerging economy standards, even if they are low income by advanced economy standards, underserved. Such customers do not have the income to pay for the latest highly innovative products, but already have some basic products that cover their essential needs and some money to splurge on new products. These middle-income customers in emerging economies are the ones we are analyzing in this book, aiming to understand how companies have developed innovations that address their more sophisticated needs without attaching the premium prices that normally accompany their latest products.

The idea for the book came from a research project on innovations for low-income consumers in emerging markets that started at Tecnologico de Monterrey in Guadalajara, Mexico in 2012. This project resulted in a number of academic research papers. As the research progressed, it became apparent that the innovations we were identifying and the consumer needs we were studying were not quite what the literature was discussing. Consumers in Mexico had much higher levels of income than those studied in other countries. They already had their basic needs covered and were looking for better products and services rather than first-time access to products and services. As a result, we started considering developing a collaborative volume to deepen the understanding already gained about innovations and extend it to analyzing innovations for the new middle classes in emerging markets. Hence, at a meeting in May 2015, we decided to bring the ideas into a book format that would facilitate the dissemination of the insights gained beyond the academic community. We met with potential coauthors to discuss the core idea of the book and the structure of its arguments, identifying the initial challenges and cases. From June to October 2015, the authors of each chapter gathered secondary data on the cases and the innovations created to solve particular challenges and outlined some of the themes that they thought could be relevant to the study. In September 2015, we obtained a grant from the Mexican nongovernmental organization Promotora Social Mexicana (www.psm.org.mx) to fund the research project. This generous grant enabled us to go deeper into the analysis and gave us the freedom to explore what we considered were relevant issues. A conference on October 15–16, 2015 helped consolidate the arguments, reorganize the structure of the book, and ensure progress. Once the chapters were created using secondary data, the authors of each chapter conducted interviews with current and past managers of the companies to understand in more detail the reasons behind the actions taken and gather additional data that were not publicly available. On March 9, 2016, a second conference ensured progress. At this meeting, the authors of the chapters agreed on the common framework and structure for the chapters to ensure the identification of insights and the drawing of conclusions across chapters. The authors of the chapters continued working on refining the arguments and ideas, incorporating suggestions for improvement from 2017 to 2019.

This lengthy process of gestation resulted in a book that is both timely and deep in its arguments. We hope that the conclusions that we draw from the analysis are useful for other academics analyzing the topic of innovation, as well as for managers of companies interested in better understanding how to innovate to serve the needs of the growing middle classes in emerging markets. To facilitate this, we asked the authors to write their chapters in an accessible manner, moving all the academic discussions into endnotes to facilitate the reading of the cases and the understanding of the conclusions.

We are grateful to many people for their support in helping create this book. Of course, our first thanks go to the authors of the chapters for diligently working on them and incorporating the suggestions for improvement from the group, going deep into the topics and providing useful insights. We also are grateful to the managers of the many companies that we analyze for providing a candid explanation of the innovation process and sharing both the ups and downs of serving the needs of middle-income consumers. We appreciate all the logistics and research of the staff at Monterrey Tec in Guadalajara, in particular Omar Robledo, S. Raúl Silva, and David Roque. We are grateful to Promotora Social Mexicana for providing funding for this research project and their continued support in this large venture. We also benefited from funding coming from Tecnologico de Monterrey in Guadalajara and Northeastern University that enabled us to travel and meet face-to-face to discuss ideas and coordinate the project. Finally, we thank our families for their support and patience, especially during the long hours that we could not be with them.

I Innovating for the Middle of the Pyramid in Emerging Countries

Alvaro Cuervo-Cazurra

INTRODUCTION

The middle of the pyramid, i.e., the middle-income classes, in emerging countries are increasingly becoming a large consumer market but one that is little understood.[1] This increasingly growing middle-of-the-pyramid group is the result of the recent economic progress of many emerging economies. Individuals who until recently were very poor, and commonly ignored as consumers by most companies, are no longer so. They have become entrepreneurs or are employed in jobs that provide them with higher and more stable income. As a result, their consumption patterns have shifted, becoming an attractive but underserved and in most cases misunderstood market.

The middle of the pyramid in emerging markets differs significantly from the middle classes in advanced economies that most companies are used to serving, especially multinationals from advanced economies. One reason is that the middle of the pyramid in emerging economies has much lower levels of income. Although they are middle class in the emerging markets in which they live, they would be considered poor in advanced economies by their level of income alone. Another reason is that their consumption patterns differ markedly. Up until recently, the middle of the pyramid in emerging economies was very poor and just able to purchase necessities. As their income has grown, they are not just replacing older, basic products with upgraded ones but rather buying new products and services that fulfill previously unmet needs. At the same time,

---

[1] See *The Economist* 2009 for an accessible overview of middle classes in emerging markets. For a discussion on how to identify middle classes, see Kharas 2011.

they are still demanding low prices because their residual income is nonetheless limited and they still have remnants of a frugal mentality from when they were poor. However, they have high aspiration needs in their consumption and are willing to splurge on some products.

This rise of the middle of the pyramid in emerging economies challenges our understanding of innovation. Most of the studies of innovation have focused on how innovations in advanced economies are created to serve the needs of sophisticated and wealthy customers there.[2] However, these studies have implicit assumptions that limit their applicability to the reality of the middle of the pyramid in emerging economies. First, these studies tend to presuppose that customers are highly sophisticated and discerning, and willing and able to pay premium pricing for advanced technologies and innovations that address their needs better than previous products did. The customers seek novelty and advanced features and are used to replacing products periodically. Second, the studies also take for granted that companies operate in advanced economies and can rely on sophisticated suppliers to obtain new technologies and collaborate with them in creating innovations. These firms benefit from a highly sophisticated innovation system that supports their ability to produce and use new technologies in creative ways.[3] When considering emerging markets, firms sell the innovations developed in advanced countries to the elites of emerging economies. These elites have the income to afford luxuries, as well as knowledge about these products, because they commonly take trips to advanced economies and shop there.

However, recently studies have started analyzing a different type of innovation: innovations to address the needs of the very poor

---

[2]   For overviews of studies on innovation, see the chapters in the handbooks edited by Dodgson, Gann, & Phillips 2014, Fagerberd, Mowery, & Nelson 2005, Hall & Rosenberg 2010, and Stoneman 1995.

[3]   For a review of national systems of innovation, see the entries in the book edited by Lundvall 2010 and the overview by Edquist 2005.

in emerging economies, which are called frugal innovations,[4] and how some of these innovations may eventually be sold in advanced economies, becoming what is termed as reverse innovations.[5] These innovations that serve the poorest consumers of emerging economies, which have been called the bottom or base of the income pyramid,[6] require a different approach. The poorest in emerging economies have extremely low levels of income. They tend to purchase simple, inexpensive products and services to cover basic needs, in many cases for the first time. Innovations created for these customers are sold primarily on the basis of a low price point at which poor customers can buy them. Companies can make money from serving the poor via the repeated sale of low-priced single-serve units; poor consumers in general cannot afford to buy large packages because they do not have sufficient cash to buy in bulk. Firms can also serve the poor profitably by redesigning packaging and the distribution system to reach these consumers in small neigborhood retailers that tend to keep a low inventory and require continuous replenishment.

The expectations regarding the products of middle-of-the-pyramid consumers differ from other groups. These new middle classes already had experience with basic products and services when they were poor and are now looking to replace those products with more sophisticated ones that match their higher levels of income and expectations. Thus, innovations for the base of the pyramid no longer meet their aspirational needs. At the same time, the middle of the pyramid in emerging markets still has relatively low levels of income and still purchase products based on price. Innovations designed with advanced economy consumers in mind are mostly out of their reach.

---

[4] There is a multiplicity of terms, as I discuss later, but for an overview of the topic see *The Economist* 2010 and Zeschky, Widenmayer, & Gassmann 2011.

[5] For a discussion of the process of creation of frugal innovation in emerging economies and transfer to advanced countries, see Immelt, Govindarajan, & Trimble 2009, Govindarajan & Trimble 2012, and Govindarajan & Ramamurti 2011.

[6] The concept of the base of the pyramid was popularized in the management field by C. K. Prahalad (Prahalad & Hammond 2002; Prahalad 2005).

As a result, these middle-of-the-pyramid customers require new ways of thinking about how to innovate to fulfill their needs and desires. The traditional approach of taking products created for middle classes in advanced economies, stripping them of extra features to lower production costs, and selling them in emerging economies at a low price no longer works. Thanks to their exposure to mass media and access to the Internet, the new middle classes in emerging economies know about the products that consumers in advanced economies are purchasing, and resent being sold second-level products that make them feel like not-good-enough consumers.[7] At the same time, the new middle classes are able and willing to pay more for products that are better than the traditional products they used to buy when they were poor to make them feel like they are progressing in life. Hence, managers need to rethink how they serve these new middle classes, developing products and services that are creative in the ways that fulfill the new needs of these middle classes but are also inexpensive enough that they can be enticed to purchase them.

These innovations are the topic that we analyze in this book: how companies create new products and services that serve the needs of the middle of the pyramid in emerging economies. The analyses reveal a large diversity of companies creating the innovations. Some firms have a long and distinguished history of addressing the needs of nascent middle classes in emerging economies. Others have only very recently focused on creating innovations for this market segment. The chapters also reflect the diversity of innovations created by the firms in solving government and market failures that are common in emerging economies. In some cases, the innovations were created because of government failures in the provision of public goods and services, such as quality and affordable education or health care.

---

[7] For example, consumers in Eastern Europe were furious about what they thought were lower quality versions of the same products being sold in their countries while better products were sold across the border in Western Europe (*The Economist* 2017).

Companies were able to find creative ways to address these challenges, both satisfying the needs of new customers and addressing the inability of the government to meet these needs. In other cases, there were significant market failures from inefficiencies in the allocation of goods and services that limited the customers' access despite their willingness to pay for them. Some companies developed resourceful ways of producing and delivering products to solve the consumption needs of the middle of pyramid while reducing market failures. In all cases, firms created new products and services to address the unmet needs of the middle of the pyramid in emerging economies in ways that had not been done before.

THE MIDDLE OF THE PYRAMID IN EMERGING ECONOMIES

A traditional view of consumer markets in emerging economies is that they are composed of two main segments: one that is wealthy and cosmopolitan and has the income to purchase luxury imported products, and another that is poor and local and barely covers its needs with domestic products. This was neatly summarized by the Brazilian economist Edmar Bacha in 1974, with the metaphor of Brazil being "Belindia," i.e., a wealthy Belgium-like economic core within a larger India-like poor periphery.[8]

As a result, the interest of many foreign multinationals was to sell to the elite consumers who had the money and were willing to pay for imported products, even if in many cases products were more expensive than in advanced countries because of tariffs. Some foreign multinationals produced locally to get around tariffs and transportation costs, selling their products as aspiration ones at a high price point. Domestic companies were left to create products for the rest of the market and sell them at a lower price. In many cases, these were products of inferior quality that could only be sold locally.

---

[8]   This two-way grouping seems to still apply to the companies, with a few world-class, highly efficient, and technologically advanced multinationals and many domestic and inefficient domestic firms, according to *The Economist* 2015.

In the early 2000s, the concept of the fortune at the bottom of the pyramid changed this view by pointing out that the poor in emerging economies could be a profitable market for multinationals from advanced countries, if only these firms redesigned the products to sell them at the low price points at which these poor consumers could buy them.[9] The challenge was not that the poor were not consumers. On the contrary, they are heavy consumers in the sense that much of their income is spent on daily consumption products such as food and beverages. Moreover, because of inefficiencies in distribution and access, and their inability to buy in bulk, they tend to pay more than wealthy consumers for the same products. For example, in a comparison of prices in a slum and a middle-class neighborhood in Mumbai, poor consumers were shown to be paying several times more than middle-class consumers. The price multiples ranged from ten times more for diarrhea medication to thirty-seven times more for municipal-grade water to fifty-three times more for credit.[10]

The concept of the bottom of the pyramid became very appealing to managers and consultants, and companies rushed to create new products and services that would serve the needs of poor consumers in emerging markets. Among them, microcredit became one of the main new products that targeted these consumers.[11] New financial institutions, many of them nonprofit organizations, loaned very small sums of money to groups of individuals who would use the funds to create new entrepreneurial ventures and then repay the money loaned. Consumer product firms redesigned their offering for this market segment, for example, by selling shampoo in single-use

---

[9]   This is discussed in more detail in Prahalad & Hart 2002, Hammond et al. 2007, and Prahalad 2005. The latter presents many examples of the products and services that multinationals from advanced economies, and some domestic firms, have created to serve the needs of the poor in emerging economies.

[10]   See Prahalad & Hammond 2002 for more detail.

[11]   See Yunus 2007 for a history of how the Grammen Bank started the microlending segment.

sachets instead of the traditional bottle or selling simple-to-use water filtration systems.[12]

However, in the 2000s, the middle-of-the-pyramid market in emerging economies started to become noticed. It was both very large and different from other segments.[13] The transformation of emerging economies with the implementation of pro-market reforms in the 1980s and 1990s led to the renovation of income segments in emerging countries in the 1990s and 2000s. To the traditional two segments of very wealthy consumers and very poor consumers, a new segment was added: the middle of the pyramid.

This new middle of the pyramid is rapidly becoming the largest segment of the population in many emerging economies. Thus, the old view of emerging economies as consisting of a pyramid with a large base of poor people, those with less than USD 1500 a year; a small middle-income segment, those with between USD 1500 and USD 20000 a year; and a tiny elite, those with more than USD 20000, has changed.[14] In many countries, the shape of the pyramid is no longer a pyramid but has become more of a rhomboid, with a small segment of poor people, a very large middle-income segment, and a small segment of high-income individuals. In advanced economies, in contrast, there is an inverted pyramid, with a tiny segment of very poor individuals, a smallish middle-income sector, and a large segment of high-income people. Figure 1.1 illustrates the different shapes of the income pyramid in emerging economies in four geographic regions: Africa, America, Asia, and Europe.

The new middle classes in emerging markets are different. They were poor until very recently and had a very limited ability to consume. With their rise in income, they are able to consume more and consume new categories of products and services. They also change their attitude toward consumption and savings; instead of living

---

[12]   See some examples in Hammond et al. 2007.
[13]   See the special report in *The Economist* 2010.
[14]   These were 2000 prices, discussed in Prahalad & Hammond 2002 and Prahalad 2005.

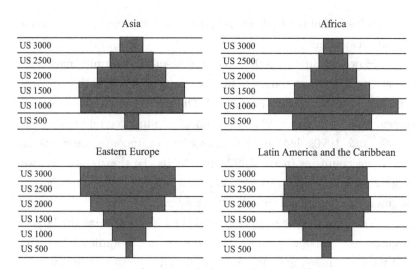

FIGURE I.I Market size in the base on the pyramid by income segments.
Source: Created using information from Hammond et al. (2007)

paycheck to paycheck, they start saving and investing some of their income to ensure a better future. They are also able to think about the products they consume and begin considering them not only by the needs covered but also by the status provided. They are, in many cases, purchasing their first durable, sophisticated products, such as appliances, computers, motorcycles, and even cars.

Identifying the middle of the pyramid in emerging economies is difficult, unfortunately, because there is no fixed definition of what middle class is. The middle class seems to be more an attitude toward consumption and savings than a level of income. The attributes that are commonly associated with middle classes are people who do not have all their material needs fully covered (as the rich do), but who are able and willing to postpone consumption to improve their lives (unlike the poor who do not have enough income to save). Thus, middle classes have a level of discretionary income available (usually about a third of their income, after paying for housing and food) that enables them to buy consumer durables such as refrigerators and cars as well as services such as health care and education.

Nevertheless, most analyses of middle classes rely on income to identify them because it is easier to measure. In this regard, there are two distinct approaches to identifying middle classes: one relative and another absolute. The relative approach considers middle classes to be those that have incomes in a bracket; for example, those in the 20% to 80% range of income.[15] This measurement of middle classes takes into account the differences across nations in the distribution of income. At the same time, it limits comparisons because income levels vary from one country to another. Thus, a person considered middle class in an emerging economy by income would likely be considered poor in an advanced country.

The alternative is to use an absolute approach and consider middle classes to be those segments of the population that have a daily income above the poverty level but below what can be considered wealthy. The challenge with this definition is deciding which are the appropriate cutoff points. Depending on the level that one chooses, the differences are stark.[16]

First, we have a distinction between emerging market middle classes and global middle classes. Emerging market middle classes are people who are no longer poor in emerging markets but are still not able to afford global products and brands, while the global middle classes of emerging markets can. This classification is usually based on the level of income, with the middle classes in emerging

---

[15] This is the approach taken by, for example, Easterly (2000). There are alternative levels such as between 0.75 and 1.25 times the median of income per capita, as done by Birdsall, Graham, & Pettinato (2000).

[16] There is a wide disparity in preferred levels across authors. For example, Banerjee & Duflo (2007) identify middle classes as those with daily incomes of USD 2 to USD 4, as well as those with daily per capita expenditures between USD 6 and USD 10. Ravallion (2009) identifies two middle classes: an emerging market middle class as those with incomes between the median poverty line of developing countries and the poverty line of the USA (USD 2 to USD 13 daily in 2005 PPP), and a global middle class as those with incomes above the US poverty level. Milanovic & Yitzaki (2002) measure (global) middle classes as those with incomes between the average income in Brazil and Italy, or about USD 12 and USD 50 in 2000 PPP.

economies defined as those with incomes between USD 2[17] and USD 10 in power purchasing parity (PPP) per day, and the global middle classes identified as those with incomes between USD 10 and USD 50 PPP per day.

Second, an alternative is to be more fine-grained in the analysis, considering the dynamics of income and how individuals move from one level to another.[18] With this approach, we can identify three levels of income, using the cutoff points of USD 4 and USD 50 as the levels at which we have a transition from lower to middle to upper class. Thus, we can consider the lower class to be those who have incomes below USD 4 PPP per day, which is about USD 6000 per year for a family of four. Within this segment we have two sub-segments: abject poverty, or individuals with an income below USD 2 PPP per day; and plain poor, or those individuals with an income between USD 2 and USD 4 PPP per day. This is roughly equivalent to incomes of about USD 3000 to USD 6000 per year for a family of four. The middle class is those individuals who have incomes between USD 4 and USD 50 PPP per day. Within this segment, we have two sub-segments: the vulnerable middle class, or individuals with an income between USD 4 and USD 10 PPP per day; and the solid middle class, or individuals with an income of USD 10 to USD 50 PPP per day. The term vulnerable middle class acknowledges that these people are no longer considered poor but are still at risk of falling back into poverty. These segments correspond roughly to a family of four with an annual income of USD 6000 to USD 15000 for the vulnerable middle class, and USD 15000 to USD 73000 for the solid middle class. The upper

---

[17] The World Bank used the level of US$1, later revised to USD 1.25 and since 2016 to USD 1.9, as the level of income below which individuals are considered poor (Ferreira, Jollifee & Prydz 2015). In its classification of countries, it uses the level of 2018 per capita income of USD 1025 (roughly USD 2.8 a day) or less to classify countries as low-income; USD 1026 to USD 3995 (USD 2.8 to USD 11 a day) as lower middle-income; USD 3996 to USD 12375 (USD 11 to USD 347 a day) as upper middle-income; and above USD 12376 (US 34 a day) as high-income (World Bank 2020).

[18] This follows the approach of Lopez-Calva & Ortiz-Juarez (2011), who identify middle class as those who are less vulnerable to falling back into poverty, using income surveys from Chile, Mexico, and Peru.

class is comprised of those individuals with incomes above USD 50 PPP per day.

Table 1.1 illustrates the use of this classification in the largest twenty countries in the world by population. The countries are grouped into three types based on the shape of the distribution of income: pyramid, rhomboid, and inverted pyramid. Pyramid countries are those with a very large proportion of the population with very low income. These are countries in Asia and Africa, which conjure the typical image of emerging countries with very large segments of poor people. Rhomboid countries are nations in which the segment of poor is still significant, but most of the population falls into the middle classes. These are countries in Latin America, Eastern Europe, the Middle East, and parts of Asia, which until recently were pyramid countries, and whose new middle classes offer a largely untapped market opportunity. Inverted pyramid countries are those in which there is an insignificant proportion of the population that can be considered very poor and a large segment of the population with a high income. These are advanced countries in Europe, America, Asia, and Oceania. Within each group of countries, there are significant variations in the distribution of income. For example, within the inverted pyramid group, Japan has 29.6% of the population earning more than USD 50 PPP a day, while the United States has 52.8%.

The relevant characteristics for companies are not only the sizes of these growing middle classes in emerging economies but also their differing patterns of behavior. They are no longer considered poor, and they do not consider themselves poor. Their consumption has shifted significantly. They not only have more income but use some of this income for products and services that were out of their reach before, such as leisure and some conspicuous consumption. They replace household goods with new ones that incorporate the latest technologies and can impress neighbors. They start to save for the future and buy goods on credit because they have relatively steady incomes that, even if low, are somewhat predictable. They exert pressure on companies to create new and better products that meet their needs, as

Table 1.1 *Income distribution in the largest twenty countries by population*

Income distribution	Country	Percentage of population living on				
		less than USD 2/day PPP	USD 2–4/day PPP	USD 4–10/day PPP	USD 10–50/day PPP	more than USD 50/day PPP
Pyramid	Bangladesh	17.8	50.7	28.4	3.1	0.0
	Congo, Democratic Republic	78.5	16.3	4.8	0.4	0.0
	Egypt, Arab Republic of	4.2	41.1	47.9	6.7	0.1
	Ethiopia	34.2	46.9	16.6	2.2	0.0
	India	24.5	49.3	22.9	3.2	0.1
	Indonesia	31.8	47.2	15.2	0.2	5.7
	Nigeria	56.5	28.6	13.1	1.8	0.0
	Pakistan	5.4	47.7	40.8	5.9	0.2
	Philippines	9.4	36.2	41.0	13.2	0.2
Rhomboid	Brazil	4.8	7.7	28.3	51.3	8.0
	China	0.7	10.5	45.8	42.1	0.9
	Iran, Islamic Republic	0.3	4.2	31.9	59.8	3.8
	Mexico	9.4	44.5	41.8	2.4	2.0
	Russian Federation	0.0	0.6	17.6	75.7	6.1
	Thailand	0.0	1.9	37.8	58.2	2.1
	Turkey	0.2	3.0	27.7	63.6	5.6
	Vietnam	2.2	10.1	49.0	38.2	0.5
Inverted pyramid	Germany	0.0	0.2	1.0	54.0	44.8
	Japan	0.7	0.2	1.7	67.8	29.6
	United States	1.3	0.3	2.0	43.8	52.8

Source: Computed using estimates from PovcalNet (2020)

they can try alternative suppliers and compare their offerings. They become more demanding from the government. They are beginning to pay income tax, and this shifts their mindset in requiring better services out of the government in exchange for these taxes.

INNOVATING FOR THE MIDDLE OF THE PYRAMID IN EMERGING MARKETS

Innovating for the middle of the pyramid in emerging economies requires a different approach than the one used for innovations for the top and bottom of the pyramid. The latter two types, which have been called lavish and frugal, respectively, have relatively well-identified characteristics. Innovations for the middle of the pyramid seem to combine aspects of both but are sufficiently different from either type. Table 1.2 summarizes their differences.

Table 1.2 *Lavish and frugal innovation*

	Innovations for the top of the pyramid: Lavish innovation	Innovations for the middle of the pyramid	Innovations for the bottom of the pyramid: Frugal Innovation
Context	Advanced country	Emerging country	Emerging country
Target income level	High income	Middle income	Low income
Initial user	Lead user	Laggard user	Laggard user
Need	Unmet dispensable needs	Unmet status needs	Unmet life needs
Logic	Satisfy	Upgrade	Solve
Solution of	Novelty	Desire	Limitation
Key driver	Functions/ features	Status	Cost
Lifetime	Short term	Medium term	Long term

Source: Adapted and extended from Asakawa, Cuervo-Cazurra, & Un (2015)

Innovations for the top of the pyramid, i.e., lavish innovations, are the traditional innovations that individuals in advanced economies are accustomed to experiencing. Companies aim to find new solutions for new needs and use the latest technologies in creative ways to generate products and services with many additional new features. The targeted consumers are high-income individuals who are open to and even desire new technologies, i.e., lead users of new technologies. Consumers prefer novelty and appreciate additional features they did not encounter in previous versions of the product. The lifetime of the product tends to be relatively short, i.e., products have planned obsolescence, as high-income consumers tend to replace the products with new products that have additional features even if the products are still fully functional. These innovations are sold later as aspirational products to consumers with mid-level incomes. As the products become commoditized, new versions appear, and prices drop.

In contrast, frugal innovations[19] are created for very poor consumers in emerging economies. They are designed to meet needs that

[19]   Frugal innovation is known by a multitude of different and related terms: "innovation for the bottom of the pyramid," or innovation "focused on the unique requirements of the poor" (Prahalad & Hart 2002: 12); "catalytic innovation" or the ability of a firm to challenge industry incumbents by offering simpler, good-enough alternatives to an underserved group of customers (Christensen et al., 2006); frugal innovation, or innovations that "reduce costs to reach more customers, resulting in thin profit margins to gain volume" (*The Economist* 2010) or "good-enough, affordable products that meet the needs of resource-constrained consumers" (Zeschky, Widenmayer, & Gassmann 2011); "Ghandian innovation," or innovation focused on "affordability and sustainability, not premium pricing and abundance" (Prahalad & Mashelkar 2010: 134); "resource-constrained innovation," or innovations that are affordable and locally sustainable products (Ray & Ray 2010); "Indovation" (Lamont 2010) and "*jugaad* innovation" (Radjou, Prabhu, & Ahuja 2012) or innovations created using *jugaad*, the ability to solve constraints by creatively improvising solutions, to solve the needs of poor people; "inclusive innovation" or the "development and implementation of new ideas which aspire to create opportunities that enhance social and economic wellbeing for disenfranchised members of society" (George, McGahan, & Prabuh 2012). Finally, a related but different term is "reverse innovation," or innovations that "lower costs, increase access, and improve quality ... were developed for markets in emerging economies ... and are now being sold in the United States" (Immelt, Govindarajan, & Trimble 2009); reverse innovations are a subset of

poor consumers, because of the very low levels of income, have not been able to fulfill yet. The focus of innovation is to find ways to reduce the costs of production and distribution to the point that poor people can afford the products. The technologies do not have to be the latest, as poor consumers tend to be laggards in the use of new technologies and are more focused on finding solutions to their essential needs. Frugal innovations tend to have limited features, as their main selling point is their low price. They are used over the long term, because poor consumers tend to use and reuse them repeatedly, and only replace the products when they can no longer be repaired.

In between these two types of innovation, we have innovations for the middle of the pyramid in emerging markets. These innovations are neither lavish innovations that are stripped of their additional features to reduce their price nor frugal innovations to which additional features are added to fulfill more sophisticated needs. They are designed for the new middle classes who, with their aspirational needs, are upgrading and replacing products. The innovations need to help them show their newly found status and be sufficiently durable, but they are likely to be replaced periodically.

Adapting lavish and frugal innovations and marketing them as innovations for the middle of the pyramid is unlikely to work well and may result in consumer backlash. Lavish innovations that are stripped of features might result in middle-income consumers creating a negative perception of the products and the company. They realize they are paying a premium for products they consider superior but are getting second-level products. Frugal innovations that have additional features might, be sold at the price point that middle-of-the-pyramid consumers can afford.[20] However, they may not fulfill their aspirational desires.

frugality-based innovations, those that are eventually transferred from emerging to advanced economies.

[20]   Analyses of frugal innovations have been usually based on the experiences of firms in India and in some cases China, and reflected in books discussing innovation for the bottom of the pyramid (Prahalad 2005), frugal innovation (Leadbeater 2014; Radjou & Prabhu 2014), jugaad innovation (Radjou, Prabhu, & Ahuja 2012), or reverse innovation (Govindarajan & Trimble 2012), among others. However, the experiences of

CONTENT OF THE BOOK

Hence, in this book, we explain how firms have created these innovations for the middle of the pyramid. To do so, we focus on companies in Latin American countries. The historical, cultural, economic, and political similarities among these countries enable a better comparison of how innovations are developed to address the needs of the middle of the pyramid, and how some of these innovations can be transferred across countries. Local experts wrote each of the chapters, using their deep contextual knowledge to explain how the characteristics of the middle of the pyramid and the conditions of operation in the country led to the development of particular innovations. The project benefited from a grant by the Mexican nongovernmental organization Promotora Social Mexico, which provided complete freedom of operation.

The book is organized into twelve chapters organized by the issues that the innovations solve. They illustrate the range of innovations that companies have created to satisfy the particular needs of middle-income consumers in emerging economies.

Chapter 2 presents a more detailed overview of the middle of the pyramid in emerging countries. It summarizes the debate on how to identify these consumers around the world and the growing importance of this segment for companies. It then discusses variations within and between countries in terms of the distribution of income. Its analysis then moves to an overview of Latin America and the characteristics of its consumers, and how these consumers differ from those in other countries that have been traditionally analyzed in the literature on innovations for the base of the pyramid, namely India and China.[21]

firms in India and China may not translate well to other emerging countries that enjoy higher levels of income and have fewer people in extreme poverty. The base of the pyramid does not seem to be as relevant in Latin America and Eastern Europe, which although emerging have higher levels of average income.

[21]   For an overview of the similarities across Latin American countries and the transformation of domestic firms into successful multinationals, see Aguilera et al. 2017 and Cuervo-Cazurra 2007, 2008.

The core of the book is a series of comparative analyses of solutions that address the needs of middle-income consumers in emerging countries. The chapters follow a common structure to facilitate comparisons across solutions and the drawing of conclusions. Each chapter provides an overview of the challenge addressed, how the challenge can become an opportunity for firms, and how some companies have generated the innovations to take advantage of it.

The book is organized around the needs of middle-of-the-pyramid consumers in emerging markets and the solutions found for such needs: lower health care provision (Chapter 3); lower quality education (Chapter 4); poorer housing (Chapter 5); lower access to durable goods (Chapter 6); reduced consumption (Chapter 7); fewer entertainment options (Chapter 8); less developed access to credit (Chapter 9); poorer risk coverage (Chapter 10); and weaker distribution (Chapter 11). Although the innovations discussed in each chapter are market solutions with potential profit generation, they nevertheless have a social impact. These market solutions to social problems neither involve charity on the part of the company nor government subsidies of public goods or investments in redistribution and social development.

Chapter 12 presents the conclusions and lays out a comparison of the insights gained from the study of a variety of innovations. It reflects on the process for identifying the needs, the process for creating the innovations and implementing them in the marketplace, the impact on the lives of middle income consumers, and the expansion of innovation across markets (trickle up innovations to consumers with higher levels of income, or trickle down innovations to the base of the pyramid). It ends with a discussion of the lessons for managers, consultants, and academics.

The answers to these questions provide valuable and novel insights to managers of emerging economies who want to sell to the growing middle classes, who until recently were commonly being served in the informal economy. They also provide useful ideas to managers of multinationals from advanced countries who may find that the expanding middle classes in emerging economies are a profitable market segment to serve.

REFERENCES

Aguilera, R., Ciravegna, L., Cuervo-Cazurra, A., & Gonzalez-Perez, M. A. 2017. Multilatinas and the Internationalization of Latin American firms. *Journal of World Business* 52(4): 447–460.

Asakawa, K., Cuervo-Cazurra, A., & Un, C. A. 2015. Frugality-Based Advantage. Paper presented at the Academy of Management Annual Meeting.

Banerjee, A. & Duflo, E. 2007. What Is Middle Class about the Middle Classes around the World? MIT Department of Economics Working Paper 07-29, Cambridge, MA.

Birdsall, N., Graham, C., & Pettinato, S. 2000. Stuck in the Tunnel: Is Globalization Muddling the Middle? Working Paper 14, Brookings Institution, Washington, DC.

Christensen, C. M., Baumann, H., Ruggles, R., & Sadtler, T. M. 2006. Disruptive Innovation for Social Change. *Harvard Business Review* 84(12): 94–101.

Christensen, C. M., Hang, C.-C., Chai, K.-H., & Subramanian, A. M. 2010. Editorial: Managing Innovation in Emerging Economies: An Introduction to the Special Issue. *IEEE Transactions on Engineering Management* 57: 4–8.

Cuervo-Cazurra, A. 2007. Sequence of Value-Added Activities in the Internationalization of Developing Country MNEs. *Journal of International Management* 13(3): 258–277.

Cuervo-Cazurra, A. 2008. The Multinationalization of Developing Country MNEs: The Case of Multilatinas. *Journal of International Management* 14(2): 138–154.

Cuervo-Cazurra, A. 2011. How Context Matters: Non-Market Advantages of Developing-Country MNEs. *Journal of Management Studies* 48(2): 441–445.

Cuervo-Cazurra, A. 2012. How the Analysis of Developing Country Multinational Companies Helps Advance Theory: Solving the Goldilocks Debate. *Global Strategy Journal* 2: 153–167.

Cuervo-Cazurra, A. & Montoya, M. 2014. Building Chinese Cars in Mexico: The Grupo Salinas–FAW Alliance. *Innovar* 24(54): 219–230.

Cuervo-Cazurra, A. & Ramamurti, R. 2014. *Understanding Multinationals from Emerging Markets*. Cambridge: Cambridge University Press.

Cuervo-Cazurra, A., Newburry, W., & Park, S. 2016. *Emerging Market Multinationals: Solving Operational Challenges in Internationalization*. Cambridge: Cambridge University Press.

Dodgson, M., Gann, D. M., & Phillips, N. 2014. *The Oxford Handbook of Innovation Management.* New York: Oxford University Press.

Easterly, W. 2000. The Middle Class Consensus and Economic Development. Policy Research Working Paper 2346, World Bank: Washington, DC.

Edquist, C. 2005. Systems of Innovation: Perspectives and Challenges. In J. Fagerberg, D. C. Mowery, & R. R. Nelson (eds.), *Oxford Handbook of Innovation*: 181–208. New York: Oxford University Press.

Fagerberg, J., Mowery, D. C., & Nelson, R. R. (eds.). 2005. *The Oxford Handbook of Innovation.* New York: Oxford University Press.

Ferreira, F., Jolliffe, D. M., & Prydze, E. B. 2015. The International Poverty Line Has Just Been Raised to $1.90 a Day, But Global Poverty Is Basically Unchanged. How Is That Even Possible? World Bank Blogs. Accessed May 17, 2020. https://blogs.worldbank.org/developmenttalk/international-poverty-line-has-just-been-raised-190-day-global-poverty-basically-unchanged-how-even

George, G., McGahan, A. M., & Prabhu, J. 2012. Innovation for Inclusive Growth: Towards a Theoretical Framework and a Research Agenda. *Journal of Management Studies* 49(4): 661–683.

Govindarajan, V. & Ramamurti, R. 2011. Reverse Innovation, Emerging Markets and Global Strategy. *Global Strategy Journal* 1: 191–205.

Govindarajan, V. & Trimble, C. 2012. *Reverse Innovation: Create Far from Home. Win Everywhere.* Boston: Harvard Business Review Press.

Hall, B. H. & Rosenberg, N. 2010. *Handbook of the Economics of Innovation.* Volume 1 and 2. Amsterdam: North Holland.

Hammond, A. L., Krammer, W. L., Katz, R. S., Tran, J. T., & Walker, C. 2007. *The Next 4 Billion.* Washington, DC: International Finance Corporation.

Immelt, J. R., Govindarajan, V., & Trimble, C. 2009. How GE Is Disrupting Itself. *Harvard Business Review* 87(10): 56–65.

Karnani, A. 2007. The Mirage of Marketing to the Bottom of the Pyramid: How the Private Sector Can Help Alleviate Poverty. *California Management Review* 49(4): 90–111.

Kharas, H. 2011. The Emerging Middle Class in Developing Countries. OECD Development Center, Working Paper no. 285. OECD: Paris. Accessed May 17, 2020. www.oecd.org/dev/44457738.pdf

Lamont, J. 2010. The Age of "Indovation" Dawns. *Financial Times*, June 14, 2010. Accessed September 13, 2011. www.ft.com/cms/s/0/6762f77a-77de-11df-82c3-00144feabdc0.html#axzz1dFlmeTlW

Leadbeater, C. 2014. *The Frugal Innovator: Creating Change on a Shoestring Budget.* New York: Palgrave MacMillan.

Lopez-Calva, L. F. & Ortiz-Juarez, E. 2011. A Vulnerability Approach to the Definition of the Middle Class. World Bank Policy Research Working Paper 5902. Accessed May 17, 2020. https://core.ac.uk/download/pdf/6258575.pdf

Lundvall, B.-A. (ed.). 2010. *National Systems of Innovation: Towards a Theory of Innovation and Interactive Learning.* London: Anthem Press.

Milanovic, B. & Yitzhaki, S. 2001. Decomposing World Income Distribution: Does the World Have a Middle Class? World Bank: Washington, DC.

PovcalNet. 2020. PovcalNet: The on-line tool for poverty measurement developed by the Development Research Group of the World Bank. Accessed May 17, 2020. http://iresearch.worldbank.org/PovcalNet/povOnDemand.aspx.

Prahalad, C. K. 2005. *The Fortune at the Bottom of the Pyramid: Eradicating Poverty through Profits.* Philadelphia: Wharton Business School Press.

Prahalad, C. K. & Hammond, A. 2002. Serving the World's Poor, Profitably. *Harvard Business Review* 80(9): 48–57.

Prahalad, C. K. & Hart, S. L. 2002. The Fortune at the Bottom of the Pyramid. *Strategy + Business* 26: 1–14.

Prahalad, C. K. & Mashelkar, R. A. 2010. Innovation's Holy Grail. *Harvard Business Review* 88(7/8): 132–141.

Radjou, N. & Prabhu, J. 2014. *Frugal Innovation: How to Do More with Less.* London: Profile Books.

Radjou, N., Prabhu, J., & Ahuja, S. 2012. *Jugaad Innovation: Think Frugal, Be Flexible, Generate Breakthrough Growth.* San Francisco: Jossey-Bass.

Ravallion, M. 2009. The Developing World's Bulging (But Vulnerable) "Middle Class." World Bank: Washington, DC.

Ray, P. K. & Ray, S. 2010. Resource-Constrained Innovation for Emerging Economies: The Case of the Indian Telecommunications Industry. *IEEE Transactions on Engineering Management* 57: 144–156.

Stoneman, P. (ed.). 1995. *Handbook of the Economics of Innovation and Technological Change.* Cambridge, MA: Blackwell.

The Economist. 2009. Special Report: The New Middle Classes in Emerging Markets. *The Economist,* February 12. Accessed September 13, 2015. www.economist.com/node/13063298

The Economist. 2010. Easier Said than Done. Emerging-Market Consumers Are Hard to Reach. *The Economist,* April 15. Accessed September 13, 2011. www.economist.com/node/15879299

The Economist. 2015. Brazil's Business Belindia. *The Economist,* February 26. Accessed September 13, 2017. www.economist.com/news/business/21645214-why-country-produces-fewer-world-class-companies-it-should-brazils-business-belindia

The Economist. 2017. Eastern Europeans Think Western Food Brands Are Selling Them Dross. *The Economist,* June 29. Accessed May 17, 2020. www.economist .com/news/europe/21724408-dual-foods-furore-hints-eastern-mistrust-west-east ern-europeans-think-western-food

WDI. 2015. World Development Indicators. Poverty. Accessed May 10, 2015. http://data.worldbank.org/topic/poverty

World Bank. 2007. *Global Economic Prospects 2007: Managing the Next Wave of Globalization.* World Bank: Washington, DC.

World Bank. 2020. World Bank Country and Lending Groups. Accessed May 17, 2020. https://datahelpdesk.worldbank.org/knowledgebase/articles/906519-world-bank-country-and-lending-groups

Yunus, M. 2007. *Banker to the Poor: Microlending and the Battle against World Poverty.* New York: Public Affairs.

Zeschky, M. B., Winterhalter, S., & Gassmann, O. 2011. Frugal Innovation in Emerging Markets: The Case of Mettler Toledo. *Research Technology Management* 54: 38–45.

2 New Middle Classes in Medium-Income Countries

Miguel A. Montoya and Francisco J. Valderrey

INTRODUCTION

In recent years, the world has witnessed unparalleled shifts in income distribution at a country, industry, and personal level. Changes have been remarkable, with unmatched adjustments in India and China. Those two nations, in fact, have been profusely analyzed in the literature covering the base or bottom of the pyramid (BoP). Another important transformation in our societies, neglected in the managerial literature, is the one concerning changes in the middle classes. Whereas in advanced societies middle-income groups struggle to maintain their position, in many emerging nations entire segments of the population are prospering and reaching the middle of the pyramid (MoP). For instance, Latin America has witnessed the advance of a large part of its population, with many people leaving deep poverty behind. The new middle class, though, is still settling, amid economic pressures and perhaps at the mercy of international trends. Nevertheless, reforms recently carried out in the most prominent markets, along with a younger population, promise to be the blueprint for reaching higher levels of development.

In this chapter, we discuss the advance of middle classes in the Latin American region. First, we take a glance at India, China, and other emerging economies and present statistical data before we look at the transformation taking place in Latin America. We underline the heterogeneous nature of some of the main developing markets and the uniqueness of the Latin American demographic pyramid, which is more diamond shaped. Countries in that region carry different weight and, therefore, we examine those differences, pointing at those nations that are splitting apart from the mainstream. Presently, Brazil, Mexico, Argentina, Chile, Colombia, and Peru are the most attractive countries for investors and dwarf the others due to their larger size and population. We then analyze the underlying data of those markets with a mention of some examples to attest to the value of innovation conducted in this region. In fact, a main theme throughout the book is how products, services, and business models generated in this geographical area may be fully functional in similar or even more advanced economies. In the end, we unveil how the time is ripe for those enterprises that are prepared to bet on innovation, either for capturing local market share or for expanding into upward markets. The aim is to explain the characteristics of this new emerging market in different economies in the world, and predominantly in Latin America, to present an opportunity for investment in this area throughout different sectors.

Swimming with Sharks

After Prahalad and other scholars, India and China are at the center of academic discussion for their untapped markets at the BoP.[1] In fact, such a concept originated in India, rapidly extending to the other Asian colossus. The number of people living within that income bracket (under USD 10) finds no match across the world. Indeed, sometimes statistical data includes China as a region in itself, and comparisons of both nations with Latin America are more reasonable when considering this last region as a whole. China is leading a profound change in prosperity on the planet, as shown in Table 2.1. Data on the same table also points at significant shifts in wealth distribution among major regions of the world. Such rearrangement demonstrates the emergence of the middle class worldwide. There are five different categories or classes, which consider daily income

---

[1] According to Prahalad 2005, if the distribution of wealth and capacity to generate income in the world was represented in the form of an economic pyramid, the top would represent the wealthy people with abundant opportunities to generate high levels of income, while the bottom would represent the 4 billion people in the world who live with less than USD 2 per day. Even if the people in the BoP have a very low income, they represent one of the largest groups of the world's population and a potential to do business and promote innovation.

Table 2.1 *Percentage of wealth, divided by social class and selected region measured by daily income and adjusted by Purchasing Power Parity* (PPP)

	Lower (%)	Vulnerable (%)	Low Middle (%)	Upper Middle (%)	Upper (%)
Latin America	27	37	21	11	4
South East Asia	71	23	4	1	1
East Europe	4	40	38	16	2
Middle East	49	41	7	2	1
Sub Saharan-Africa	88	8	2	1	1
China	58	32	6	3	1

Source: Own elaboration, based on Penfold & Guzmán 2014, with data from The World Bank.

measured according to Purchasing Power Parity (PPP). Those categories are as follows: *Low, Vulnerable, Low Middle, Upper Middle,* and *High*. Individuals in each category have earnings of less than USD 4, between USD 4 and 10, between USD 10 and 20, between USD 20 and 50, and more than USD 50, respectively. In this section, we present a comparison among some of the leading emerging economies, including a brief profile of their consumers to understand the purchasing differences in products and services they have.

The emergence of middle-income groups is changing the rules of the game for international trade, production of goods, wealth creation, and many other aspects of emerging markets. Competition for the Latin American region, though, is not limited to India and China. Other nations are entering with full force into the economic rankings, each one with a different profile. China and India dominate by the number of potential consumers. Regarding GDP, China is the clear leader, while India and Russia have similar numbers to each other, and all other economies fall behind. Russia and Turkey are better off; or at least in nominal terms, since the purchasing power parity comparison is much more favorable as compared to India. When considering the well-being of the population, as measured by the Human Developing Index, results are not encouraging: Only Russia and Turkey occupy modest places in international rankings, while the other emerging economies score poorly. The literacy rate is relatively high for most nations, except for India. China outpaces the other countries in international trade, but all others have significant numbers for imports and exports. The number of households varies largely between The Philippines, South Africa and Turkey, on one side, and Russia, India, and China on the other hand. The last three nations have some households that are larger than the population of most countries in the world. The case of China is surprising, as the Asian nation combines a relatively low number of persons per household with more than 400 million family units, while Russia has the lowest number and India far exceeds any international average. Finally, the average consumer expenditure changes dramatically for India, as opposed to South Africa, Russia, and Turkey. Results from Table 2.2 indicate the diversity found among the selected nations, especially when considering markets such as Indonesia or The Philippines. Those results are also evident if including every one of the so-called emerging economies.

A VIEW OF LATIN AMERICA

The Latin American region is the geographical area of the Americas embracing nations where Spanish and Portuguese are spoken, from the southern border of the United States to the Patagonia peninsula. Those vast territories, over 7 million square miles, share a common heritage, and cultural cohesiveness is relatively evident. The region has a highly concentrated urban population, which prevails near the coast. From an economic standpoint, Latin America has a common denominator: the abundance of resources. Natural deposits, raw materials, and commodities, indeed, have dictated the fate of the region during centuries, especially in countries such as Chile, Peru, Ecuador, Venezuela, and Bolivia. Overall, in South America dependency on production and export of staple goods and undifferentiated

Table 2.2 *Comparison among selected emerging economies*

	India	China	S. Africa	Russia	Turkey	Indonesia	Philippines
Population (million people)	1,353	1,393	58	144	82	268	107
Area (thousand Km²)	3,287	9,563	1,219	17,098	784	1,911	300
GDP (USD bn)	2,936	14,140	359	1,638	744	1,112	357
GDP per capita (USD)	2,172	10,099	6,100	11,163	8,958	4,164	3,294
Medium age (years)	24	33	24	37	27	27	22
Literacy rate (%)	61	91	93	96	87	96	93
Urban population (%)	34	59	66	74	75	55	47
Human development index	130	90	116	50	72	110	115
Households (million)	194	402	16	55	18	56	17
Size of household (people)	5.3	3.5	3.4	2.7	4.2	4.0	5
Household consumer expenditure (USD)	1,608	3,154	4,580	6,203	8,835	2,373	2,140

Source: Own elaboration, with data selected from Santander Trade.

products has contributed to the noticeable concentration of wealth in the hands of a few, with limited incentives for progress or modernizing efforts. Latin American political parties bitterly opposed each other under the effect of extreme ideologies. Except for a few exceptions, not many changes have happened regarding income distribution. For centuries, the elites have been renewed, with little advance for most of the population.

Breaking with the Past

Throughout history, Latin America has invariably been an example of social inequality. When the Europeans set foot on the continent, they established plantations and mining operations and carried out activities that favored prosperous minorities at the expense of an impoverished population. Slavery made matters worse for workers, while independence from the colonial powers did not reverse the unfair treatment to the local people.

The first major social transformation in Latin America happened in the mid-twentieth century, because of agrarian reforms. Those changes targeted poor peasants, the overwhelming majority of the population, in an attempt to fight extreme poverty and create a new social class, standing halfway between large landowners and those in need.[2] In recent decades, neoliberal governments paved the road to massive exploitation of natural resources by Western multinationals. The consequences are social transformation, urbanization, and industrialization in many countries throughout the region.

In most cases, the neoliberal period has led to modernization – at a price, however, of inflationary crises and the worsening of the gap between the wealthy and the have-nots. Depending on the historical–political background, this has led to almost all countries in the South American continent to the establishment of social democratic (Brazil, Argentina) or Bolivarian or indigenous socialist governments

[2]   García 1970.

(Venezuela, Bolivia, and Ecuador). Although between the first and the latter there is a substantial difference in foreign policy choices, especially in moving away from American interests, the proposals of the new governments targeted a more equitable redistribution of wealth and nationalization of the country's key resources. It is noticeable that the stability and redistribution policies implemented by these governments have led to more development and equality and consequently to the growth of the middle class. Latin America presents an attractive outlook, and its democratic institutions are not generally in question across its territory.

Above all, the region offers fast-growing consumer markets, an appetite for a wide variety of products, and a young population eager to find new opportunities. Although problems persist, this part of the world is leaving behind some of the major obstacles to prosperity. The 2015 review of the Millennium Development Goals[3] shows encouraging results.[4] Indeed, for many companies, the region is now a land of opportunity.

A Promising Market

This region is moving forward, and the general increase in the standard of living relies on economic, political, sociocultural, and technological improvements. Key drivers, such as economic growth and stability, poverty reduction, social mobility, and access to credit, are making a difference.[5] Income disparity is still an important issue, but the upsurge of a substantial segment representing the MoP[6] stands against all the odds. For instance, when the concept of the middle-

---

[3]   The Millennium Development Goals were the targets of an unprecedented global effort coordinated by the United Nations to fight poverty and bring less prosperous nations to new stages of social development. More information can be found at www.un.org/millenniumgoals.

[4]   ECLAC 2015.   [5]   Robles, Wiese, & Torres-Baumgarten 2015.

[6]   According to Birdsall's (Birdsall et al. 2010) absolute approach, the middle class embraces individuals with annual incomes exceeding USD 3900 in purchasing power parity (PPP) terms or with daily per capita expenditures between USD 6 and 10.

income trap[7] appeared in the last decade, many scholars anticipated Latin America's ill-fated destiny. On the contrary, the middle class in Latin America has grown steadily over the years, without severely hindering progress and innovation. Data from the World Bank shows the rapid expansion of intermediate segments of the population across the region, mainly in Argentina, Brazil, Mexico, Chile, Colombia, and Peru. In those countries, a more affluent upper middle class is also stabilizing and, according to the previously mentioned institution, by the year 2030 the segment of the population earning between USD 10 and USD 50 a day will outpace the BoP and MoP.[8] Other analysts share an even more optimistic picture, such as in the case of the consultancy firm Frost & Sullivan. To them, the creation of the so-called "middle bulge" is imminent, with 69% of the population falling into that category by the year 2025.[9] The interesting thing to note from such analysis is the rise of a segment of the population made up of those people with yearly incomes between USD 32000 and USD 60000.[10] In any event, we can estimate the total size of the combined poor and vulnerable sections of the pyramid, the so-called "majority market," at about USD 759 billion.[11]

To Eat or Not to Eat, That Is the Question

A breakdown of the majority market by categories shows the importance of satisfying necessities. In the majority market, the need for food (USD 200 billion) prevails, along with housing (USD 184 billion) and transport (USD 82 billion). Food services (USD 44 billion), clothing (USD 42 billion), others (USD 40 billion), and energy (USD 38 billion) have similar market value. Health (USD 29 billion), education (USD 29 billion), and ICT (USD 25 billion) also represent similar percentages, while recreation (USD 14 billion), financial (USD 11 billion), and water (USD 10 billion) are the least important categories

---

[7]   The concept of middle-income-trap simply states that countries, after reaching a certain level of wealth, will start losing international competitiveness.

[8]   Ferreira et al. 2012.   [9]   Rajan 2014.   [10]   Rajan 2014.

[11]   Azevedo et al. 2015.

in value.[12] Although those figures are quite appealing, it is important to evaluate the real market potential considering the difference between essential and discretionary goods and services, even within those ranges. Financial services and recreation are included in the discretionary category while leaving food services halfway between necessity and aspiration. After that, the demand for water, education, health, energy, clothing, transport, housing, and food become a necessity. Purchases of those goods take a higher spending share and demand becomes less elastic.[13] It is imperative to understand that the public sector in Latin America has historically addressed many of the basic needs, leaving little room to private enterprises for providing products or services in some areas of the broad categories included in the majority market.

New reforms are opening the door to private companies, but many businesspeople prefer to stay away from industries that are more prone to face restrictions from the local government or even risk nationalization. Therefore, we focus on those needs that might be appropriately satisfied by private individuals and enterprises. Companies offering solutions to those problems deal with complex scenarios while targeting a constantly changing customer base. Thus, the proposed ideas have many chances to work for people in similar situations, regardless of the distance or the different cultural background.

A Brighter Future

The Latin American market is indeed promising. The reasons are many, including the size of the national markets, a population close to 600 million people, and a young generation with disposable income and the desire to acquire a vast array of products and services. Still, there are some perils of prosperity, as pointed out by the Economic Commission for Latin America and the Caribbean (ECLAC). The rise of Latin America has brought some other positive aspects, such as a

[12]   Azevedo et al. 2015.   [13]   ECLAC 2014.

significant improvement in market infrastructure or a better business climate. Businesspeople traveling throughout the region, especially to the vibrant megacities, may witness the construction of new airports, a variety of means of transportation, modern facilities, state of the art communication, and other attractive conditions often like those found in more advanced nations. Poverty belts are still a reality around the major cities, but at the very least those developments are encouraging signs for times to come.

FINDING THE MIDDLE OF THE PYRAMID

Middle-income groups are a reality in many countries, although their presence has been fragile and rather weak and permanently exposed to civil wars and revolutions, unexpected changes, and frivolous political decisions, or perhaps only sharing the uncertain economic destiny of their home countries. Between 1990 and 2007, 56 million Latin American families joined the MoP, with approximately 128 million individuals. Over the past two decades, decreasing fertility, greater participation of women in the workforce, and the resulting change in the family structure favored higher income, new consumption patterns, and the overall shifting of families toward the middle class. Additionally, liberal governments further encouraged a better income. Presently, millions of people have abandoned extreme poverty and now belong to the central part of the pyramid. The reasons behind the new prosperity may vary by state but, in general terms, Latin America has profited from external factors, such as the insatiable demand of minerals, agricultural goods and commodities from China and other Asian economies, or the demand for manufactured goods from North America and Europe. Governments also deserve recognition for economic and political reforms, improvement of educational systems, and public actions addressing the most neglected segments of the population. Furthermore, local people have been fundamental in reshaping society: In fact, public intervention and the previously mentioned external factors also required the talent of individuals that changed static

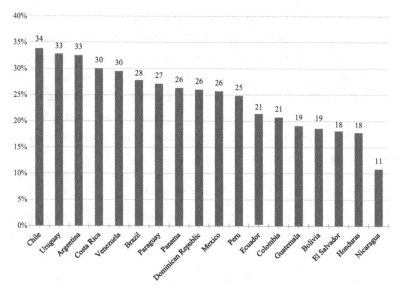

FIGURE 2.1 Middle-income population share, Latin American countries. Source: Elaborated with information from the Pew Research Report 2015

communities through innovation. Thus, the standards of living have risen substantially: Except for a few deeply troubled countries, this is a new constant throughout Latin America. Nowadays 222 million people belong to the so-called *vulnerable* sector, earning between USD 4 and USD 10 a day, although there are 183 million individuals in the so-called *poor* group, or making less than USD 4 a day. When combined, the two segments account for roughly 70% of the total population.[14] According to the same source, the movements between both areas of the pyramid are quite significant: during the first decade of this century, the total market value for the poor decreased to USD 174 billion. Meanwhile, the vulnerable sector grew by 39% in total market value, reaching USD 585 billion.[15] Figure 2.1 shows an overview of middle-income population share in Latin American countries.

[14]   Azevedo et al. 2015.   [15]   Azevedo et al. 2015.

Where Is the Middle of the Pyramid?

Despite the positive news, the MoP in Latin America is quite undefined. When given the opportunity to specify their social status, people throughout the region respond differently, often with an apparent deviation from statistical definitions. Individuals may admit being part of the middle class according to their view, even when their income is substantially higher or lower than the accepted range. Latin Americans, indeed, share values such as uncertainty avoidance and low individualism,[16] and those values make them feel more comfortable in the "one size fits all" middle-income group. Most people in Latin America will not identify themselves with conceptual definitions solely related to income. For instance, in Mexico, the scale most frequently used, AMAI,[17] adds to income some factors such as the educational level of the head of the household, the number of rooms in the house, or even ownership of a vacuum cleaner or a microwave oven. Additionally, other countries try to figure out their statistical scales. Undoubtedly, a more precise definition of the middle class should include income, wealth, consumption, or demographic factors, but then international comparisons would become unattainable. Other experts prefer to stick to a rule of thumb of considering aggregate family income and deduct two-thirds used for necessities. Then, the remaining third will account for truly disposable income, which will give access for ordinary families to a better quality of life. Although this previous description of the middle class is appealing in its simplicity, it seems to fit better with more advanced economies.

In this part of the world, the task of collecting reliable data is next to impossible. Therefore, we use the statistical measurement from the leading international organizations, such as The World Bank, The United Nations Commission on Trade and Development (UNCTAD), or the Inter-American Bank, to analyze and compare the

---

[16]   Hofstede 2011.   [17]   AMAI 2016.

Table 2.3 *Latin America, regional data and middle classes*

Regional Data		Middle Class Profile	
Population (Million)	641	Middle Class (as a % of total population)	41.1%
GDP (USD bn)	$5,819	Daily Household income per capita (USD) $ PPP	$45
GDP per capita (PPP$)	$9,574	Years of education, adults 25–65	8.6
Real GDP growth	0.6%	Age of household head	50.3
CPI Inflation	3.1%	Age of children (0–17)	9.4
Gini coefficient	0.47	Household size (persons)	3.5
Trade openness as % of GDP	47%	Children per household	0.6
Accumulated external debt as % of GDP	52%	Climbers from poor to Middle Class 2002-2017	2.3%
Poverty rate (% population)	4.4%	Climbers from vulnerable to Middle Class 2002-2017	19.3%

Source: Own elaboration, with data from ECLAC and The World Bank

Latin American socioeconomic pyramid. It seems appropriate to use the population earnings breakdown of the United Nations Development Program and identify the MoP for Latin American countries with those people making between USD 4 and USD 10 a day. This segment is often called the vulnerable sector.[18] Table 2.3 shows general data for Latin America and a general profile of the middle-income group in the region.

An Elusive Consumer

Defining the Latin American consumer is an exceedingly difficult task. In addition to the variety of tastes and preferences, purchasing power by itself prevents a proper description of the average consumer.

[18]   The term vulnerable sector seems to be more adequate to indicate the MoP in Latin America, because it represents a wider and more stable group of people and is also closer to international standards used to compare income in emerging countries.

Is it possible to portrait the Latin American consumer? Admitting that results would be questionable, such a person would be about twenty-eight years old, with seven years of formal education, predominantly urban and most probably sharing his home with two or three more members of the family. Most likely he will own the house, equipped with a TV set, a refrigerator, and a telephone line. His chances of acquiring a washer will be one out of three and possessing a computer one out of five. On the positive side, he will be covered regarding some general services, such as electricity, running water, and sanitation.[19] In summary, that is the portrait of the Latin American consumer according to statistics, although reality may be quite different. Additionally, even if the average consumer could indeed exist, that person would constantly be changing shape. After all, mutability is a regional trademark.

Some consumer trends seem to be common all over the region, such as the growing number of elderly customers, an increase in disposable income associated with the lower size of families, concern for health issues, and the new role of women in the economy.[20] This last factor, known as the "she economy," may bring significant changes in the labor market, income distribution by gender, and consumer habits. Another important factor also comes from demographic changes: the mobility of broad sectors of the population across countries, either because of pressing needs or looking for a land of opportunity. The inclusion of immigrants into other societies is a distortion factor, and their foreign remittances are bringing profound changes in some of the markets while creating cultural bridges across nations. Finally, connectivity is bringing forth changes that today are incommensurable.

The market research firm Gallup tried a different approach from standard procedures by analyzing urban consumers and categorizing them by formal education, occupation, age, housing, and marital status. The study found the following eight segments of almost

[19]   Azevedo et al. 2015.   [20]   Capizzani, Ramirez, & Rocha 2012.

similar size: *emerging professional elite, traditional elite, progressive upper MC (middle class), self-MC, skilled MC, self-skilled MC, industrial working class,* and *struggling working class.* The sample comprised more than 17,000 households, with data gathered in five countries, not including marginal populations. The results favored the view of one single market, instead of the more traditional view of separating the region into individual national entities. The study also recommended concentrating all marketing efforts in fifteen major cities. Those urban areas are Mexico City, Monterrey, and Guadalajara, in Mexico; Sao Paulo, Rio de Janeiro, Salvador, and Porto Alegre, in Brazil; Buenos Aires, Rosario, and Cordoba in Argentina; Bogota, Medellin, Cali, and Barranquilla, in Colombia; and Santiago in Chile. Furthermore, the researchers advised to be cautious about official data and to rely on real disposable income for the different socioeconomic groups.[21]

A survey conducted by Kantar Worldpanel provides us with a more recent picture of the evolution of the Latin American consumer. The Shopper & Retail Dynamics Latam study seeks to showcase opportunities for companies in the region. Based on Latin American habits of consumption, the research highlights a variety of styles. Customers are looking for a promise of life and others who are interested in interaction with the brands through different experiences. Time-savings, proximity, and convenience represent an aggregate value for the consumers. Six trends seem to characterize the Latin American customer: selective growth, a changing buying rhythm, importance given to proximity, quality–price ratio, sales, and down-trading.[22] Despite the previous findings, it seems that differences among consumers are undeniable. A fundamental proposition, therefore, is to profile customers on a country basis, specifically for the more robust economies, such as Argentina, Brazil, Chile, Colombia, Mexico, and Peru. Table 2.4 displays data for the middle class for the previously mentioned countries.

[21]   Gonzalez-Molina 2001.   [22]   Kantar Worldpanel 2015.

Table 2.4 *Middle class in Latin America, selected countries*

	Argentina	Brazil	Chile	Colombia	Mexico	Peru
Population (million)	45	210	19	50	126	32
Area (Km²)	2,780,400	8,515,770	756,096	1,141,749	1,964,380	1,285,220
GDP (US$ bn)	$446	$1,847	$294	$328	$1,274	$229
GDP per capita (US$)	$9,899	$8,797	$15,339	$6,508	$10,118	$7,047
Human Development Index	40	75	42	97	74	84
Middle Class as % of population	47.5%	51.7%	58.4%	49.5%	26.2%	52.0%
Population in MC (million)	21.38	120.12	11.10	24.75	33.01	16.64
Climbers from Lower to MC between 2002 and 2017	29.1%	20.1%	30.9%	18.8%	2.6%	23.3%
Middle Class Employer	n.a.	7.4%	3%	6.4%	6.9%	8.6%
Middle Class Employee	n.a.	66.7%	70.7%	54.6%	76.3%	56.3%
Middle Class Self-Employed	n.a.	20%	21.9%	31.6%	12.9%	28.1%
Middle Class Working without salary	n.a.	3.4%	0.4%	1.9%	2.2%	4.2%
Middle Class Unemployed	n.a.	2.5%	4%	5.4%	1.8%	2.8%

Source: Own elaboration, with data selected from Santander Trade and ECLAC

Neighbors, Not Brothers

Among the most prominent economies, we selected the countries based on GDP, per capita income, the robustness of the economy, and development trends.

Brazil stands alone by total surface and population. The country has been the regional leader and capable of opposing powerful nations across the whole continent. Brazil, though, is the quintessence of Latin America, at times the economic miracle, right before plummeting into uncontrollable crisis. Its international trade mix is unique since it keeps a steady foreign trade with neighboring countries of Mercosur, the United States, China, and the European Union. Mexico has been its real competitor, especially in geopolitical matters. After NAFTA, though, Mexican governments have separated themselves from South America, entirely depending on their new trade partners. This nation has an extraordinary dependency on the United States, which usually brings economic benefits and stability, although new political developments in its neighboring country may bring forth notable changes. Nowadays, Mexico is gaining leadership over most Central American countries and is the regional superpower, with its vast territory and growing population, ensuring a leading position for many years to come. Argentina, with a large population and much larger area, has been in deep economic and political trouble for decades. As happens with Brazil, Argentina may appear as a rising star of international commerce and immediately fall from heaven. Though Argentinians enjoy a human development index, per capita income, level of economic growth, and quality of life among the most developed in Latin America, its high inflation and commodity export-oriented economy makes of Argentina a volatile country, with frequent political disputes. Peru has not been a major player in modern times, but lately it seems to have awakened from lethargy. Peru is deeply dependent on mining and export of commodities, although a new wave of reforms and political stability is bringing prosperity to the growing population. The Andean country had in recent years a remarkable level of growth, which made Peru one the highest-growing economies of the region. Colombia has a territory of similar size, although more densely populated. Even if the country faces internal conflicts and problems related to illegal drug trade, its institutions are stable, and its economy is robust and open to international trade. Colombia is the fourth richest economy of the region, with an economy that depends on 34% from oil exportation. Lastly, Chile is a nation smaller in size and population. Anyhow, the country is probably the most reliable and advanced in the region. Over the years, Chile has reduced its dependency on exports of copper and commodities, thus diversifying the product offering and markets.

As already seen, consumer behavior changes across the zone. Despite the similarities found within the same socioeconomic segment, differences are evident in each country. To that purpose, Banco Santander, a leading financial institution in the region, provides valuable insights about consumers from some of those countries. According to their research, the Argentinian consumer is "rational and conservative, selective, reticent to regard new products and not very loyal to brands." The Brazilian consumer is "more demanding and selective, aware of quality, prices of goods and special offers, while attached to foreign products as exterior signs of wealth." Chileans are "more conscious consumers, with better access to credit, not limiting their purchases to essential goods and considering a wider spectrum of factors before buying a product or service." Finally, Mexican consumers are "influenced by family and friends, and most of the time the buyer is the housewife." They "are very loyal to their favorite brands, demand proper customer service, individual attention, and a fair deal regarding cost and benefit." The Peruvian consumer "is optimistic about the future, but also strict, rational, well informed and ready to take advantage of promotional pricing," while the Colombian consumer is also "sensible, looking for bargains and less confident about the future."

FINAL REMARKS AND CONCLUSIONS

The challenge of satisfying the needs of many and providing them with a better lifestyle imposes much pressure on society. Governments alone cannot meet those demands and participation from private enterprises is most needed. On the positive side, Latin America is a breeding ground for innovation and an attractive opportunity for companies to extend their markets. There are numerous examples in the region demonstrating the role of innovation in the social and economic betterment of society. Unfortunately, Latin America is lagging in technological and business improvements, as compared to other emerging markets. Recently the *InnovaLatino* survey recognized the efforts of many countries in the region but also showed many weaknesses regarding innovation.[23] The main criticism pointed at the lack of global scope of innovation in the area. The survey included only manufacturing firms, but results were disappointing, despite some positive signs coming from private enterprises in product, process and organization, marketing, and business model innovation. Apparently, this region is moving forward, although not at a speed imposed by other countries. In the first category, the report reviewed the case of VASIMIR, a Costa Rican-designed electromagnetic thruster for spacecraft propulsion. The example for the second type came from changes in process and organization at Embraer, the Brazilian aircraft manufacturer. In the third category Havaianas flip-flops, produced in Brazil, demonstrated innovation in marketing by turning a simple product into a fashionable footwear, sold across the globe. The Mexican company Cinepolis is the example for the fourth category, with new entertainment alternatives in an already decaying market.

Latin America presents many business opportunities for multi-national corporations, smaller size companies, or even for the individual entrepreneur. They will have access to the land of the majority

---

[23]   Fundación Telefónica 2011.

market, with an estimated value of USD 759 billion by the Inter-American Development Bank. There are millions of people prospering and willing to purchase products and services that were previously unavailable to them. Furthermore, a sizable market will be there for many years to come; the socioeconomic pyramid is subject to many changes, but presumably the majority market will continue growing in purchasing power over the next few decades. Astute investors might keep alert for local developments of products, services, or business models addressing the majority market. In fact, creative individuals continually devise products that could become a world-wide success; frequently, though, they lack the financing or the organizational resources. Those products might also be exported to other emerging countries or even commercialized in the most advanced markets.

The estimated size of the majority market for Latin America nears USD 759 billion; this is plenty of money, but lower than the assessed value of Apple. Emerging markets offer the chance to tap unparalleled business opportunities, but is necessary to look, first and foremost, at potential growth. It is also wise to monitor innovation as the source of new opportunities; in Latin America innovation goes beyond the public effort, through the examples provided by start-ups, multilatinas, and companies already born global. There is also a learning experience from the volatile nature of Latin American markets, which continually foster new solutions to deal with change.

Emerging markets represent a challenge for companies addressing the needs of BoP and MoP. As described by Prahalad, companies need to carry out innovation to reach consumers of limited means.[24] In the process, those innovative efforts lead to business opportunities, market expansion, and economic growth. Increasingly, multinational corporations are looking for those low-income consumers, adapting their product offerings to the local buying capacity. Companies with an understanding of the majority market in Latin America will also be

---

[24]   The Wharton University of Pennsylvania 2017.

able to evaluate business opportunities within their national boundaries. After all, the world is shrinking, and large segments of the population of advanced markets are falling into the BoP and MoP in their societies.

The middle of the pyramid is a new emerging market, posing new challenges, but also generating new opportunities to innovate products and services addressing their specific needs and aspirations. Multinationals have started to notice this opportunity, with innovations that target this majority market in order to expand into the middle classes and tap into the business opportunities arising in the emerging economies. This segment of the population is underserved and on the rise; therefore, dedicating efforts toward understanding and attending their needs is becoming an attractive business option to expand or to start new ventures in emerging economies.

REFERENCES

AMAI. 2016. Official Web Page. *AMAI.* Accessed March 22, 2016. www.amai.org

Azevedo, V., Balgun, A., Bouillon, C., Duke, D., & Gallardo, M. 2015. Un mercado creciente de US $750 mil millones. Inter-American Development Bank. Accessed February 12, 2016. http://publications.iadb.org

Birdsall, Nancy. "The (Indispensable) Middle Class in Developing Countries." Equity and Growth in a Globalizing World 157 (2010).

Capizzani, M., Ramirez, F., & Rocha, P. 2012. *Retail in Latin America: Trends, Challenges, and Opportunities.* Barcelona: IESE Business School–University of Navarra.

Economic Commission for Latin America and the Caribbean (ECLAC). 2014. *Anuario Estadístico de América Latina y el Caribe* (Statistical Yearbook for Latin America and the Caribbean). United Nations Publications.

Economic Commission for Latin America and the Caribbean (ECLAC). 2015. *Latin America and the Caribbean: Looking Ahead after the Millennium Development Goals. Regional Monitoring Report on the Millennium Development Goals in Latin America and the Caribbean.* United Nations Publications.

Economic Commission for Latin America and the Caribbean (ECLAC). 2019. Social Panorama for Latin America.

Ferreira, F. H., Messina, J., Rigolini, J., López-Calva, L. F., Lugo, M. A., Vakis, R., & Ló, L. F. 2012. *Economic Mobility and the Rise of the Latin American Middle Class*. World Bank Publications.

Fundación Telefónica. 2011. *InnovaLatino: Fostering Innovation in Latin America*. Fundación Telefonica.

García, A. 1970. *Dinámica de las reformas agrarias en América Latina (Vol. 6)*. Editorial La Oveja Negra.

Gonzalez-Molina, G. 2001. Latin America: Consumers Without Borders. *Gallup*. Accessed February 12, 2016. www.gallup.com/businessjournal/190/latin-amer ica-consumers-without-borders.aspx

Hofstede, G. 2011. Dimensionalizing Cultures: The Hofstede Model in Context. Online Readings in Psychology and Culture. http://scholarworks.gvsu.edu/cgi/ viewcontent.cgi?article=1014&context=orpc

Kantar Worldpanel. 2015. Six Key Trends in LatAm in Shopper Behaviour. (n.d.). Accessed September 07, 2017. www.kantarworldpanel.com/global/News/Six-key-trends-in-LatAm-retail-and-shopper-behaviour

Penfold, M. & Guzmán, G. R. 2014. La creciente pero vulnerable clase media de América Latina: Patrones de expansión, Valores y preferencias. Serie Políticas Públicas y Transformación Productiva (17).

Prahalad, C. K. 2005. *The Fortune at the Bottom of the pyramid: Eradicating Poverty through Profits*. Philadelphia, PA: Wharton School Publishing.

Rajan, B. 2014. Innovations in Emerging Economies – Latin America (Technical Insights). Technology Innovations That Can Shape and Impact the Latin American Economy. *Frost*. Accessed February 12, 2016. www.frost.com/reg/ people-finder result.do?id=2792384&backlink=ref

Robles, F., Wiese, N., & Torres-Baumgarten, G. (2015). *Business in Emerging Latin America*. New York and London: Routledge.

The Wharton University of Pennsylvania. 2017. La base de la pirámide como fuente de innovación. Universia Knowledge Wharton. Accessed April 22, 2017. www .knowledgeatwharton.com.es/article/la-base-de-la-piramide-como-fuente-de-innovacion

UNCTAD. 2016. World Investment Report. Investor Nacionality: Policy Changes. Geneva: UNCTAD. Accessed June 17, 2020. https://unctad.org/en/ PublicationsLibrary/wir2016_en.pdf

3   Innovation That Saves Lives

Miguel A. Montoya and Francisco J. Valderrey

INTRODUCTION

The literature centered on the base (BoP) and middle of the pyramid (MoP) covers an ample spectrum of unfulfilled needs for most of the world population. Few of these requirements are as essential as those related to health. In fact, proper nutrition, prevention of diseases, or basic sanitation may well epitomize the starting point for leaving poverty behind. The quality of health care is one of the issues that highlights the great divide between advanced and less developed societies. Many emerging countries still face uncertainties regarding health care services and struggle to cover the needs of middle and lower classes. The biggest problems concern health education, environmental factors, and the lack of effective universal coverage by health services. Long waiting lists, inadequate facilities, and an insufficient number of doctors are also a reality.

In this chapter, we present a view of the health care industry, with particular reference to Latin America, as well as a glance at innovation and significant trends. Five exemplary cases serve the purpose of illustrating how companies and individuals are bringing new solutions to the market, thus fostering change and improving the quality of life for many people. Three of the companies are in Mexico, one in Argentina, and one in Peru, although the lessons may suit neighboring nations. In all selected cases, audacious entrepreneurs and innovative enterprises are showing the way to those looking for opportunities in emerging markets. The cases related to Mexico include dental health with *Clínica Dental La Zapopana*, protective care with *Clínica del Azúcar*, and the supply of pharmaceutical products with *Farmacias Similares*. The Argentinian example of *Benestare* focuses on home and outpatient care centers, while the

Peruvian case of *Hospital de la Solidaridad* targets general medical and surgical hospitals.

As we will see in the cases presented, there is no single malady and no single remedy in Latin America. Day after day the industry is showing a smiling face to attract the many millions looking for miracles, and fulfilling basic needs is becoming a remembrance of the past, just as seen in other rising economies. Nowadays the middle class demands better medical attention, not simply the healing of traditional ailments. The cry for quality and individual attention is fostering innovation within the many subsectors of the industry.[1] Foreign companies with proven management procedures, financial resources, and superior technologies may find in Latin America an open field for expansion of their domestic or multinational operations.[2] The small business also has a chance to succeed in specialized areas, and, as happens all across the region, entrepreneurs may benefit from the local creativity by taking a closer look at business models developed in site. We consider some of those models in the accompanying cases, although there are others unaccounted for in the managerial literature for the health care sector. What can be understood from the analysis in this chapter is that the new middle classes have more disposable income; as a result, they seek to obtain better products and services, looking for real innovations that are suited for their new status. Therefore, attending to their needs and desires through tailored innovations – especially related to the health care industry, where the government cannot fulfill the needs of the whole population and public–private partnerships – can be beneficial for both the lower and middle classes and the firms that are creating the products they need.

A HEALTHY INDUSTRY

Health care goes beyond the mere task of healing the sick; as pointed out by a report from IBM India,[3] a broader view of health care unveils needs at different levels. The model takes the shape of a pyramid, with

---

[1]   De Jong 2015.   [2]   Cuervo-Cazurra 2016.   [3]   IBM 2008.

a framework inspired by Maslow's hierarchy of needs diagram,[4] with five various stages before attaining complete wellness: the environment, preventive actions, treatment of ailments by doctors, improving personal appearance, and holistic health. The environment is at the very bottom, as clean surroundings, drinkable water, and low pollution create the basis for a healthy society. On a second level are preventive actions, since those activities may give the population of a particular geographical area the opportunity to avoid some diseases that are no longer life threatening somewhere else. In wealthy societies, malaria or tuberculosis are no more than horror stories from the past, but those diseases still take the lives of millions in less developed nations. The third step leads to the treatment of ailments by doctors, much in line with a general vision of health care. The fourth step presents an opportunity to improve the personal appearance of someone who is not in real need of medical intervention, as may be the case with cosmetic surgery. Finally, the fifth step involves holistic health and wellness; this is the area for those looking for longevity, a better quality of life, or enough time and resources to dedicate full attention to themselves.

The model places at the third step the crossroad for the wealthy and the have-nots, an area more equitable among societies. In fact, a patient with advanced-stage cancer stands a better chance for survival in state-of-the-art clinics in Switzerland, but the odds of losing the battle are not extraordinarily different from a patient in similar circumstances in an impoverished country. The third step is also the upper limit on the right to health for the disadvantaged and is the lower limit for the endless needs of the privileged. Traditionally, the wealthy address those needs with private offerings, while the needy rely on governmental support. Recently, prosperous middle

---

[4]   Abraham Maslow conceived the concept of "Hierarchy of Needs." In the book *Motivation and Personality* (1954), he explains how this scale of needs is divided into five different levels, from basic needs (necessary for the survival of the individual) to more complex (social) needs. Individuals are able to develop their lives through various stages, which have to be met progressively.

classes in developing countries are pressing for better medical assistance and a wider set of options to reach wellness; this fact alone
protects the business interest of the all-powerful health care industry
for the foreseeable future.

Where Are the Boundaries?

The health care industry is particularly hard to define due to the
blend of medical care, pharmaceutical products, and hospital or
outpatient treatments, among other fields, but can be summed up
by stating that the health care industry is the products and services
directed toward the improvement or maintenance of physical and
mental well-being. Those areas, nowadays, are complemented with
biotechnology, advanced equipment, or entirely new professions.
The complexity of the sector is even more startling when looking
at the number of actors, both public and private, the entities
involved, and its wide array of occupations. Those players fit into
four groups: *producers, care providers, regulators and influencers,*
and *plans and payers.*[5] The previous classification is standard in the
United States, and obviously there might be variations regarding the
importance given to each group in other countries. For instance,
physicians, administrators, regulatory agencies, or insurance claim
adjusters are identified as part of the health care industry in some
nations, not in others, and the status of each profession varies
widely. There are also some gray areas, such as research and
development, prescription drugs production and distribution, or consumer products, among many other areas occasionally taken as a
part of the industry. Ultimately, the fact of the matter is that millions of people are part of this thriving sector.

Health care industry covers five major areas.[6] Those areas are
*specialist doctors, emergency and other outpatient care centers, phar-
macies and drug stores, home care providers,* and *hospitals.*[7] The five

[5]   Vitalary 2012.   [6]   Montoya & Cervantes 2014.
[7]   Mazzone & Associates 2015.

selected cases represent each subsector and provide background information about the local market involved.[8] The industry numbers are
truly astonishing, even when leaving some core activities out of the
statistics. Table 3.1 provides insight into those figures, showing aggregate and per capita spending data in selected OECD advanced countries[9] that represent some of the world most prominent economies.
There is a lack of a universally accepted definition of the industry, and
some of the statistics are subject to further interpretation, but the big
figures convey the importance of health care activities in every
country.

Leaving aside total spending from the United States, nearing
3-1/2 trillion dollars, we can see the exorbitant monetary resources
dedicated to health care among this group of advanced economies.
When taken to the level of the hypothetical average individual,
those figures give us a reference point to understand the real magnitude of the cost of health care. In fact, total spending per capita
has an OECD median of USD 3994, although most developed
countries have figures considerably higher, with the United States
on the top, with a per capita spending of USD 10586. The global
health care industry is also changing at great speed regarding
expenditures from developed vs. emerging economies. The former
group accounted for 90% of the total health outlay in 1995,
decreased its percentage to 79% in 2010, and is expected to lower
the participation on total spending to 67% by 2020. By that year,
emerging countries will be responsible for approximately one-third
of total expenditures in those services.[10]

---

[8]   Except for the pharmaceutical field, the aforementioned partition of the health industry is close to the US Standard Industry Classification and matches the view of leading
consultancy firms. Indeed, this is a conceptualization of the sector more intended to
suit a business analysis.

[9]   For our purpose we selected the following OECD countries among the most prominent economies: Japan, The Netherlands, New Zealand, Norway, Switzerland, United
Kingdom, United States.

[10]   SIEMENS 2015.

Table 3.1 *Health care industry per capita expenditure. Selected countries, OECD*

	Total health spending (USD bn)	Total health spending as % of GDP	Total health care spending p.c. (USD)	Public current health care spending as % of total (USD)	Private out of pocket current health care spending p.c. (USD)	Other current health care spending p.c. (USD)	Life expectancy at birth
Japan	$541	10.9%	$4,776	9%	13%	78%	84.2
The Netherlands	$91	9.9%	$5,288	6%	11%	83%	81.8
New Zealand	$19	9.3%	$3,923	69%	14%	17%	81.9
Norway	$44	10.2%	$6,187	85%	14%	1%	82.7
Switzerland	$86	12.2%	$7.317	22%	29%	49%	83.6
United Kingdom	$280	9.8%	$4,070	79%	16%	5%	81.3
United States	$3,492	17.0%	$10,586	26%	11%	63%	78.6
OECD median	$54	8.8%	$3,994	36%	21%	43%	80.7

Source: Own, adapted from The Commonwealth Fund with additional data from OECD health statistics, 2019

Industry Trends and Innovation

The industry is going through a profound transformation, even to the extent of questioning the traditional method of providing direct, face-to-face health care services. For instance, telecommunications technology allows providing "in absentia" health care services (through email, video call, or any other telematic means). Another major shift is the quest for the optimal coverage of health care cost.

The health care industry is far from being static, and its intricacies moderate the value of predictions about future developments in the different subsectors. Nevertheless, many firms specialize in data gathering at all levels of the market, searching for laboratories with new treatments and drugs, breakthrough technologies, procedures for minimizing costs, newer consumer preferences, or changes that may give companies a competitive edge. At the forefront of those changes, trends are gearing versus the so-called "new health economy." Those trends include more mobility for consumers and clinicians along with accessibility and connectivity; high preferences for best solution providers and willingness to travel distances or use their own resources to get the best possible treatment; and new financial alternatives for coping with medical expenses and lowering costs.[11] There are many other developments in the making, especially related to the appearance in the market of new business models. There is also plenty of room for improvement since the health care sector still lacks transparency in the monetary transactions and clarity about the outcome of the service provided.[12] As proposed by Michael Porter a decade ago, the health care industry needs to create value based on delivering results to the patient.[13]

Among the different trends emerging, cost reduction is probably prevailing. Administrators in this sector are looking for a complete array of solutions in response to rising costs. Technology and cutting-edge software are reducing management costs significantly. For

---

[11]   PWC 2015.   [12]   PWC 2016.   [13]   Porter & Teisberg 2006.

instance, Smith & Nephew, a medical equipment manufacturing company, developed Sycera, software used by surgeons with considerable cost savings.[14] Those efforts are part of the new health economy that promotes treating patients as "co-creators" of health decisions, willing to allocate their resources according to the expected outcome. Medical attention is far away from being an average service, but standardization is probably one of the directions for lowering cost. Another significant trend comes from the demands of better-informed customers. In fact, customers' demands seem to drive the new debate in public vs. private offering of medical care. Despite the outcry for universal care coverage, many advanced economies in the world are opening the door for private participation, either sharing major areas of the industry with enterprises or leaving final decisions up to the individual consumer.[15]

Although the previously mentioned trends become more evident for the leading economies of the world, some of those adjustments are valid, as well, for other countries. Initially those changes stay within the upper social classes with access to treatments in foreign countries, or with those receiving medical attention in leading local facilities, but eventually the novelties reach other segments of the population. It is also important to be on alert for progress made in emerging markets since some significant improvements have recently surfaced in India or China. Above all, the industry requires a more flexible ecosystem structure, placing consumers at the center.[16] That is the view from the consumer end, although from the service providers' perspective the critical issue is to "engage consumers to manage health care demand."[17] Obviously, the debate is open about who pays for the ever-increasing cost of medical attention and so will be for many years to come.

Innovation is a primary driver for this industry. It comes in different forms and shapes, from technological advances in equipment

[14]   EY 2016.   [15]   Kelly & Son 2013.   [16]   Vitalary 2012.
[17]   Dixon-Fyle & Kowallik 2010.

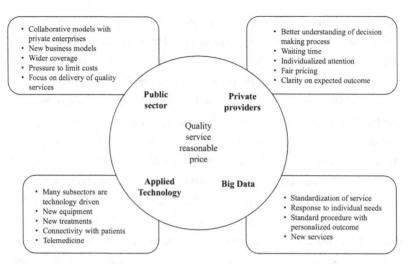

FIGURE 3.1 Drivers of innovation in business models in the health care industry.
Source: Own creation

to much simpler business models that are effectively changing the dynamics of this sector. At the center of innovation is the need to increase the quality of expected outcome, while containing escalating prices, as seen in Figure 3.1. There must be a way to get closer to well-being using reasonable resources. We have not reached that point yet, but innovations large and small are taking us closer. In particular, there are some areas where breakthroughs are turning into medical advances, such as in the treatment of HIV, specific types of cancers, hepatitis C, and, in general, the treatment of illness according to a person's genome. Big data is bringing the computer support needed for testing proposed solutions with unseen rapidity. Data and analytics are creating areas that are entirely new to the industry, such as *tele-health*,[18] *health, electronic medical records*, and *wearables*. Developments in business models are already bringing under scrutiny their administrative procedures, approaching value-based payment models and shared services.[19]

---

[18]   Anta et al. 2009.   [19]   Deloitte 2015.

A revolution is underway in the health care industry, covering several areas. One of these is the accessibility of medical information. In the United States, the public sector is promoting transparency, releasing electronic databases containing the results of many years of research and development in the field. Experts now have access to "big data," which will allows them to identify optimal alternatives to clinical issues, to monitor the reactions to prescription drugs and treatments, or eventually prevent diseases.[20] New technologies in the realm of the Internet of Nano Things (IoNT) are bringing to the market a diversity of solutions, such as sensors that monitor internal changes in the patient, therefore anticipating the eventual formation of pathologies.[21] The challenges for innovation are many, and everything points to unforeseeable scenarios supported by technological breakthroughs that are barely surfacing. In the future, the process will also probably become more inclusive, bringing patients closer to developers of new solutions.

GAUGING LATIN AMERICA'S HEALTH

Middle classes in Latin America commonly complain about the poor quality of medical attention offered by public institutions, but their grievance needs further proof. Therefore, in the following we present an overview of the major indicators that will gauge the health situation in the region. For businesspeople, such an assessment means opportunities.[22] Table 3.2 provides an extract of indicators from the World Health Organization (WHO),[23] covering six of the largest countries in the region: Argentina, Brazil, Chile, Colombia, Mexico, and Peru. The information includes statistical data about health systems and expenditure per country, along with some demographic indicators.

Median age does not vary widely across countries and nears the average for the world population, with Chile on the positive end and

[20]   Groves et al. 2013.   [21]   World Economic Forum 2016.   [22]   GHI 2016.
[23]   Bosset et al. 2014.

Table 3.2 *Selected health indicators for major Latin American countries*

	Argentina	Brazil	Chile	Colombia	Mexico	Peru	World
Median age	32	33	36	31	29	29	31
Life expectancy at birth	73	72	78	74	72	74	70
Crude birth rate per 1000 population	17	14	12	15	18	18	18
Physicians per 1,000 population	4	2.2	2.4	2.1	2.4	1.3	1.6
Total spending on health as % of GDP	9.1%	9.5%	7.2%	6.8%	5.5%	5.0%	9.9%
Total spending on health, P.P. average (USD)	$1,917	$1,472	$1,039	$530	$1,036	$681	$1,409
Government spending on health, P.P. average (USD)	$1,388	$617	$705	$402	$534	$432	$832
Private spending on health as % of total	27.7%	58.1%	32.2%	24.2%	48.5%	36.4%	40.3%

Source: Own creation with data from WHO Statistics 2020

Mexico and Peru at the opposite extreme. Regarding life expectancy, the figures are relatively homogeneous. Once again, Chile presents more positive numbers, and all selected countries show a much higher life expectancy at birth, while statistics for crude birth rate tell a different story, with half of the countries below global average. The range is ample regarding health expenditures as a percentage of GDP. All other nations spend below the global average, with Peru being the worst performer. Regarding per capita total expenditure, Chile, Brazil, and Argentina are above international standards, but Mexico and Colombia score below the international average, while Peru falls below one-half of per capita worldwide expenditures. Prominent Latin American nations perform below standards regarding public spending on health, except for Argentina, while Peru shows even more deceptive figures. Finally, Brazil, Chile, and Mexico show private spending above global standards, while Peru, Argentina, and Colombia show values significantly below the world average.

The table conveys a favorable picture of the general health indicators from Latin America, although the selected nations are among the most advanced in the region. There are some noticeable deviations from standard figures, but it seems like local governments are dedicating a percentage of their resources according to international guidelines. An additional tool for measuring the advance of Latin America is the Millennium Development Goals (MDG). Those are the eight development goals set by the United Nations at the beginning of the century to cope with the most pressing social issues by the year 2015. The goals encompass: poverty eradication, reaching universal primary education, promotion of gender equality, reduction of child and maternal mortality, fighting several diseases, ensuring environmental sustainability, and creating a global partnership for development.[24]

Many Latin American nations have met most of their Millennium goals, but some countries have been left behind from

---

[24]   ECLAC 2015.

those accomplishments. In fact, the report highlights that over 50% of the population is within the vulnerability threshold. As for income distribution, the positive trend recorded will be difficult to sustain during economic downturns. Also, employment remains precarious and productivity is lagging as compared to OECD members. Illiteracy is still a significant challenge that compromises the economic and social inclusion of large segments of the population. The report further mentions the challenges from infant and maternal mortality rates, as well as pregnancies among teenagers. Altogether, inequality is a primary concern, and it undermines the success achieved fighting extreme poverty, hunger, undernourishment, child mortality, and insufficient access to sanitation facilities and clean water.

The new goals set for the 2030 Agenda are targeting some of the unmet objectives, although the vision for the revised project goes far beyond satisfying basic human needs.[25] Interestingly enough, the third goal set under the new agenda is "reaching good health and well-being for the whole population." Not included in either of the reports is the discussion about the role of public and private actors in health care. The debate is of utmost importance for most economies, and the consequences may put high pressure on countries, according to the model accepted. There are five major models: *Free Market, Bismark, Hybrid, Beveridge,* and *Ex-Shemashko.* The Free Market, or American system,[26] is at one end of the spectrum, calling for as little intervention as possible from the government, while the Beveridge system is the paradigm of universal free medical support, and is in place in Spain, Italy, Portugal, the United Kingdom, and the Scandinavian countries.[27] The other systems fall in between the two extremes and are less attractive options to decision makers. Most governments in this region are switching from being the leading providers of health care services to alternative models, mainly

25   Barcena 2015.
26   The American System is undergoing profound changes after the approval and criticism of the so-called Obamacare. Presently, the fate of such a program is not clear.
27   SIEMENS 2015.

attempting to mirror the American system, although a long tradition from the public sector being at the center of essential health coverage is becoming an obstacle to those efforts.

A World Bank report[28] reveals that the Latin American middle class has grown at high rates, equaling the proportion of the poorest. The report explains the benefits of such growth and identifies middle-class members as those with an income ranging between USD 10 and 50 per capita per day. Disposable income in this bracket provides greater resilience to unforeseen events and reflects a lesser likelihood of falling into poverty. The analysis, however, reports that 38% of the population belongs to the vulnerable sector. Located at a hierarchical level between the middle class and the poorest sector, it has a daily income of between USD 4 and 10 and still does not rely on a stable economy. The document highlights a fundamental aspect: The lack of a social contract in several Latin American countries continues to spread the perception among the vulnerable sectors of the population of a mismanagement of public resources.

The health care sector is growing in Latin America and, consequently, business opportunities. There is room for investors since the needs are abundant; additionally, an aging population is showing an insatiable appetite for new services. Physicians address immediate needs of patients, although medical interventions are increasingly targeting aesthetical needs instead of lifesaving procedures. Furthermore, the role of governments as providers of health care is undergoing deep changes, thus creating an opportunity for entrepreneurs and companies of all sizes. Also, in the next four years, pharmaceutical sales in Latin America are expected to grow by 119%, representing the third biggest regional growth after the Middle East and Africa.[29] As frequently happens in this industry, innovators reach overlapping fields, despite the widely shared view of medical activities as carried out by either highly specialized practitioners or entirely driven by a unified state system, with principal actors being

[28] Ferreira et al. 2013. [29] Davies & Mazza 2011.

at the center of unconnected activities. Emerging economies have a widespread necessity in fulfilling needs of different areas of the health care industry. Product and service shortage, insufficient infrastructure, and low public investment, joined with expensive innovation practices, cause the majority market to be underserved. Additionally, there is not a culture of well-being, which leaves the health care industry aside until there is an imminent need for it, when there is no time to look for the best option possible and they end up getting the only one they can find and afford. Therefore, firms can innovate and tap into these needs, providing health care solutions aimed at fair pricing and profit through economies of scale, getting benefits from the volume and the aspirational goals the middle of the pyramid has gained due to their increased income.

CASE STUDY ANALYSIS

Following are the cases of individuals and organizations that have found an opportunity in some of the areas where governments are opening the door to enterprises.[30] Each case is presented separately since they target different needs. All cases portrayed show a world of possibilities for business people to succeed in the health care industry while helping others, since health care is an industry normally financed by the public sector, but not being sufficient in some emerging economies.

Clínica Dental La Zapopana: A Sweet Tooth for Success

Health care has overlapping activities, which, joined with the ambiguous boundaries between public institutions and private enterprises, make the industry hard to grasp, but among its fields is dental health. A point of divergence between medical services covered by the public sector and those offered by private providers lies in dentistry. At best, public institutions offer basic consultation, attention to related emergencies, and a limited array of specialized services – but through

---

[30]   Llumpo et al. 2014.

appointments with long waiting periods, only acceptable to those in extreme need or protected by incomparable endurance. Despite widespread acceptance of the correlation between oral and overall health, dentistry is still an out-of-pocket payment for many people. Also, insurance companies often exclude or limit reimbursements for dental visits. Patterns of consumption for medical services are evident in many circumstances, not so with dentistry. Various reasons inhibit people from taking a dental check-up, such as fear of unpleasant experiences. A closer inspection reveals further concerns: the time-consuming experience, distrust of pricing, lack of clarity about the expected outcome, and limitations coming from a highly individualized service in a world where standards prevail. Those obstacles foster proposals, ranging from cutting costs to the bone, creating franchises, or using highly specialized clinics, among others.

In Mexico, a potential market composed by the needs of more than 120 million people coupled with the great availability and the resourcefulness of new dentists have created a sub-industry, by providing low-cost cross-border dental services. One of those young dentists, Dr. Alfonso Mendoza, faced the same challenges as his new colleagues during the nineties: competing with well-respected dentists. At that time, people with dental problems would go unequivocally to trusted dentists, frequently the same ones treating the entire family. However, a changing economic climate helped him, inadvertently, when the country was approaching its most severe downturn in many years. Pressured by his landlord, Dr. Mendoza was forced to move out and reestablish his practice in a more affordable neighborhood.

The opportunity arrived disguised as people of limited means. This was not a distinguished clientele, but it outnumbered patients from the previous location. Dr. Mendoza took the chance to develop a successful business under the name of Clínica Dental La Zapopana, which started rather small, offering prices well below competitors.[31]

---

[31]   Clínica Dental La Zapopana 2014.

Low prices, membership cards (serving as a loyalty card), and breaking the traditional distance between dentist and patient were the key factors for his success. The growing demand pressured Dr. Mendoza into widening the specialized support offered, followed by adding a dental deposit and a dedicated lab. By 2005 the clinic grew through a franchise system of twenty-four units in different geographical locations. The company added unexpected benefits, such as 24/7 operation, free transportation for the elders and people with disabilities, night transportation in rural and unsafe areas, free initial consultation, and a one-year warranty on the service performed. Customer trust was on the rise, making Clínica Dental La Zapopana the preferred choice for the intended target, with the unexpected inclusion of upscale clientele from other urban areas.

As previously mentioned, Clínica Dental La Zapopana offered dental support, and rapidly it extended geographically in the Guadalajara area. The enterprise developed a new business model: fast dental health,[32] with four pillars: efficiency, standardization, economies of scale, and time. Further analysis of the model shows how efficiency improves through doctor specialization, which is entirely dedicated to high-added-value activities and moving around the patient's location. Standardization, on the other hand, relies on performing the same services with accuracy, at fixed prices, maintaining the same quality. Bulk purchase of supplies and consolidated distribution of ancillary services through the network create economies of scale.[33] Finally, the time dimension is key to the customer, who benefits from the added time coming from the convenience of location, flexibility for scheduling appointments, avoidance of price negotiation, 24/7 operation, and transportation. The model creates a unique bond with the customer, an engagement built on trust. The proposal is not difficult to replicate, as proven by the growing number of units added under the Clínica Dental La Zapopana brand, but it is also dependent on continuous efforts to adapt to new markets and the

---

[32]   Montoya 2014.   [33]   Ebel et al. 2013.

needs of patients. The model is also successful to the point of providing opportunities for vertical growth and trickle-up innovation across market segments.

High Blood Sugar? Leave It to Clínicas del Azúcar

Diabetes may be the illness of the twenty-first century, and all indications point to this condition as one of the most pervasive diseases on the economic side of medical services. Diabetes compromises the well-being of more than 400 million people at this very moment and heading to 500 million in the next decade. This illness is also the malady of prosperity, a non-life-threatening disease to chronic patients but an uncontainable drain of resources for health care providers. Average treatment for this illness changes so widely among countries, or even within the same nation, that is complicated to arrive at a plausible number. Figures coming from the American Diabetes Association placed the yearly cost of treating the illness at about USD 245 million for the nation, with USD 7900 of direct cost per patient.[34] The cure for the disease only extends the life of patients in further need of expensive additional procedures, and the number of cases can be expected to increase due to the levels of obesity found in some of the emerging economies' populations, such as Mexico.

Diligent public health administrators are making provisions to combat the silent enemy, but the humongous resources needed are hard to find. Many institutions are actively seeking the final cure, but the contribution from individuals and small organizations is becoming crucial in those efforts. Such is the case of the Clínicas del Azúcar in Mexico, founded by a few MIT and Harvard graduates who returned to Mexico with the purpose of solving health issues that were heavy burdens for their fellow citizens.[35] Their expertise in diabetes and health-related technologies led them to look for a model that could alleviate the suffering of many in their country and other emerging economies. Mexico has more than 14 million diabetic patients, with

---

[34] American Diabetes Organization 2013.   [35] Clínicas del Azúcar 2015.

more than 80,000 deaths every year, and the illness is "the number one cause of death, and a leading cause of amputations, blindness, kidney failure and suicides in Mexico."[36]

Since the basic premise for the founders was to design a business model that would not rely on charity or public resources, they took a holistic approach for both the business model and the medical support offered. The name itself of Clínica del Azúcar, which in Spanish stands for Sugar Clinic, goes to the root of the health issue involved. Clínicas del Azúcar saw patients as people under siege by a common enemy, with the need for full emotional support from specialists and fellow sufferers as well. The main goal was to create a sound formula for investors and entrepreneurs through a scheme that would appeal to those with the desire to combine moneymaking with social responsibility. Clínicas del Azúcar managed to offer a unique blend of solutions to the diabetic patient. The idea was clear: Clients should be those in the MoP, on the outskirts of the industrial city of Monterrey. Additionally, the model, if successful, could be extended to any similar socioeconomic segment of the population. The clinic met with immediate success and soon opened four more branches in Monterrey. Current plans include the opening of more clinics in other cities.

Clínicas del Azúcar offers a model that shows a way to do sound business while increasing the well-being of many people. The company demonstrates the reversal of the model centered in the services provider, addressing customer's convenience both in location and time. Patients are clients in one-stop-shops where they find general advice, free education and training, medical attention by a team of specialists, a dedicated laboratory, and an array of products for the diabetic patient. Family involvement with the individual patient is also appreciated. The price range of services is attractive, with a yearly policy that covers, free of charge, monitoring and nutritional guidance throughout the same period. The clinics now have programs suited to

---

[36]   Schwab Foundation 2010.

corporations, with various benefits offered to employees at a reduced cost to the organization. Products from the store are sold individually to the diabetic patient, although prices are affordable and remain within a reasonable range.[37] According to Javier Lozano, the managing director, specialization and high technology allow for pricing far below the competition.[38] Marketing is used efficiently, with a precise profiling of the customer base. Also, in this case timesaving is of utmost importance to the patient, and so is the engagement with a trustworthy organization. Clínicas del Azúcar has been capable of reducing the cost of treating diabetes to approximately USD 200 a year.[39]

Farmacias Similares: An Empire Far from Being Generic

Until recently, a way to stop the skyrocketing cost of health care on all fronts was hard to imagine. While costs for any other input in the industry were on the rise, the surge of generic pharmaceutical products provided an alternative to high-priced prescription drugs. Soon they became the object of controversy, involving intellectual property rights, quality control, or unfair advantage, among other pressing concerns. The view on the issue has been evolving, taking the initial blunt opposition to a less antagonistic position of the general public, especially after resulting in lowering prices for people in need or attractive discounts for the consumer.

While the discussion centered in India, Canada, and a few other countries that either initiated or embraced the commercialization of those products, a visionary in Mexico saw a golden opportunity with generics. Victor González Torres, better known in his home country as "Doctor Simi," fought a continuing battle with the local government for reducing the cost of pharmaceutical products and passing the savings to the Mexican people. His idea was to manufacture products with expired legal protection in his facilities, therefore reaffirming his commitment to providing affordable quality medication. By 1997 he

[37] Villafranco 2016.   [38] Ocaranza 2015.   [39] Paniagua and Zafra 2012.

opened a pharmacy in Mexico City entirely dedicated to offering generic products, which was a tug of war to the establishment. He received attacks from many sides, but his low pricing and personal attention to his clientele made bulletproof his outlet, named Farmacias Similares.[40] In a short time, he expanded the small facilities into a chain, growing daily in some units, revenues, profits, and the acceptance of his customer base. From then on, Farmacias Similares was unstoppable, despite adversarial actions from government, large laboratories, and direct competitors. Among the reasons for the success of Farmacias Similares, probably the most significant is innovative marketing tools and communication strategies, including full control of a television channel, public relations activities, and permanent sales promotions. Doctor Simi is an icon in his country, counting with hundreds of thousands of devoted followers. In fact, at one time he was an independent candidate for the Mexican presidency, challenging well-established political parties.

Presently, there are more than 6,000 pharmacies from the chain scattered throughout the country, with additional presence in Guatemala (86 pharmacies), Chile (237), and Peru (4).[41] Farmacias Similares created a sub-industry and competitors are trying to imitate its business model. Nowadays, people commonly ask for the generic variant of a prescribed drug. The company has evolved into an influential group called "Por Un País Mejor" (Spanish for "For a Better Country") with political connotations and containing five not-for-profit organizations and four with a commercial interest under its umbrella. Those four companies included manufacturing activities through Laboratorios Best, distribution and sales of pharmaceutical products through Farmacias Similares, clinical testing through Análisis Clínicos del Dr. Simi, and specialized transportation of industry specific products through Transportes Farmacéuticos Similares. The four companies are fully integrated and sustain the philanthropic

[40] Chu & Garcia-Cuellar 2011. [41] Pallares 2017.

work of several institutions with a different scope, either related to health issues or fighting corruption in Mexico.

Some factors stand out about Farmacias Similares: pricing, vertical integration, marketing, standardization, loyalty, and expanded service. At the cornerstone of the business model stands low pricing, while vertical integration allows for quality control, suppression of intermediaries, efficient procurement, and gains from logistics. Marketing is also of utmost importance; at the very start of the company, a massive advertising campaign shocked the competitors. Ever since, Farmacias Similares has positioned its pharmacies as a price leader, matching competitors' prices. Through the use of mass media, the company reaches an audience loyal to the brand and the company's values. Standardization of products also came as a surprise to the local customer, who was used to depending on the individual service provided by each outlet. Since some remedies were unlabeled, Farmacias Similares had to face customers' initial distrust. Victor Gonzalez made decision making easier for customers, satisfying many of their basic health care needs and rewarding them for their loyalty. He also gained allegiance from his collaborators through a compensation system based on performance bonuses for employees at the counter. Dr. Gonzalez made a similar move with his doctors, by offering them a small medical office adjacent to most of his pharmacies. Those facilities allowed FS to change the traditional pharmaceutical outlet into a one-stop service provider for minor health problems.

Benestare: Your Home Is My Business

Due to price escalation of extended stays, public health systems and insurance companies are looking for new alternatives to keep the patient away from the hospital. Home staying is then the only option, although home care providers do not enjoy equal treatment to colleagues at medical clinics, due to the lack of adequate training or the absence of essential equipment to assist patients. Advances in technology, new professions, and standardized procedures are giving new life to this type of support. It is hard to evaluate the monetary size of the home care providers' sub-industry since much of the activity is carried out by family members, friends, or generous volunteers.

The cost of the facilities is equally difficult to analyze, and some of the estimates place a value of about USD 75 billion for this sector in the United States alone. The subindustry of home care providers keeps growing, allowing for unmatched opportunities for investors, especially because it is deeply fragmented, with the absence of clear leaders. Home care presents additional advantages for those capable of creating standardized procedures and business models since the industry is almost "artisanal." In fact, roughly half of aggregate industry revenue comes from wages. Home care is an area with plenty of room for new consolidating initiatives and business models, as demonstrated by the number of companies in this sector – more than 300,000 in the United States.[42]

Few entrepreneurs envisioned the business possibilities standing in the home care industry. One of them was a young entrepreneur from a rural area of Argentina, Dr. Diego Cingolani. He analyzed how business innovation could bring forth new remedies to people suffering severe illness and eventually his proposal attracted enough attention from investors to his company, Benestare.[43] The young physician understood the principle that complex situations needed a well-defined methodology, a holistic approach, and the necessary flexibility for constant adaptation to the changing environment. Furthermore, Dr. Cingolani profiled patients and divided them into three segments, addressing their individual needs. Fees were different, according to the disposable income of the patient, and the risk of random emergency procedures. At the highest level, he placed people at greater risk, as defined by their pathologies and a careful statistical review of similar cases. At the intermediate level, Dr. Cingolani left patients with a manageable degree of risk, and at the lowest level those patients who primarily needed personalized attention, not so

[42]   Kelly & Son 2013.   [43]   Benestare SA 2014.

much monitoring from a physician. Independent of the group, it was necessary to obtain family involvement and ensure their full cooperation with Benestare specialists. Right from the start, Dr. Cingolani saw the need to bring the hospital to the patient, instead of doing it the other way around. To fulfill such purpose, he leased easily transported equipment and ensured the highest possible rotation of the machines among his clients. He also brought laboratory services to the patient, as well as a full list of highly specialized doctors who will perform repetitive tasks.

The uniqueness of Benestare lies in its organization: a holding group, with three different companies targeting home health care from different angles. Benestare is the jewel in the crown, providing steady revenues, but Fledomex adds higher growth rates by offering similar services to corporate clients. Sometimes Fledomex serves public entities, a new segment of the market with a potential multiplier effect. ESEM, the third company, delivers radiological and laboratory services to customers from both Fledomex and Benestare. A common denominator to the three companies is the use of specialized software for decision making, both in the service offered to outpatients and as a managerial tool. In fact, Benestare uses technology extensively in its methodological approach in evaluating business scenarios, as a way to standardize services and as a means to include a financial review of every step of the process. Although the enterprise does not offer direct financing, it provides third-party alternatives to suit the needs of individual customers. Benestare successfully engages with the customer base and the network of medical service providers, offering the flexibility required in an industry where services are tailor-made. Above all, the company offers the patient a clear view of the expected outcome, leaving little room for the unexpected.

Hospital Solidaridad: Who Can Compete with Those Prices?

Multiple actors are involved in the health care business, many of them offering highly specialized assistance. The industry also needs infrastructure, specifically hospitals. Those facilities vary in size, with the purpose of satisfying a wide array of requirements. Some are neighborhood units providing multipurpose attention within a limited scope, while on the other extreme there are traditional over-sized buildings, offering full attention to patients and the possibility to carry out surgical procedures. Size and functions of those clinics have come under the scrutiny of experts for a variety of reasons, but mainly due to the massive investment needed to raise each building, manage the operation, and meet expected results.

Despite the capital investment required, hospitals are a lucrative business. The average daily cost at the hospital for the American patient nears USD 3949, and the mean stay costs approximately USD $15734, with global aggregate revenues of more than USD 1 trillion.[44] Technology, new procedures, and a breakthrough in the delivery of service, among other factors, keep adding pressure to the administration of a hospital. Furthermore, once more advanced equipment becomes available, it becomes compelling for management to replace the older devices. Making continuous investments is simply part of the business of saving lives, an area where patients and their families are not prepared to go through cost–benefit analysis before committing their resources. Usually, there is a little negotiation for the price tag involved when facing the possibility of extending the life of the patient or moderating pain.

The hospital industry is thriving, but the future is not that bright since it is becoming harder to carry out successful projects. Hospitals have been at the center of the well-renowned case studies in India, where innovation mainly comes from standardization of medical procedures in specially designed facilities. The business model, which allows for marginal pricing, is supported by the astonishing number of patients, something that only India and China may offer in those quantities. Latin America has also provided different alternatives, one of which is Hospital Solidaridad in Peru. The founder, Dr. Luis Castañeda, witnessed during his practice in the

---

[44]   Fay 2019.

public sector the worsening conditions of many people, with limited medical attention to patients and decreasing coverage. He contemplated how sound administration could eventually lead to better assistance, finding a way to help patients while obtaining an economic reward for himself and those who eventually joined his project. His proposal addressed the MoP in Lima, the capital city with more than 7 million people. He also considered all the key concerns from the potential customers, such as price, time, transportation to the clinic, clear pricing policies, and personalized attention. Dr. Castañeda had insufficient resources, but he made his first clinic out of abandoned trailers, buses, and containers. After his initial success, he also obtained from the municipal authorities some abandoned buildings and structures that he skillfully transformed into medical facilities. As of today, he keeps opening new hospitals, with plans for going international.

The reasons for the success of the Hospital Solidaridad business model lie in clear communication, truth on telling prices, and unprecedented personalized attention offered to patients. The clinics were not luxurious, but treatment at more prestigious places was about ten times more expensive. Behind the scenes, there was a well-thought-out plan that made Hospital Solidaridad a unique offering. First, Dr. Castañeda looked for partners, instead of employees. He needed enthusiastic collaborators with a better attitude than the one prevailing at public hospitals. Consequently, he formalized individual agreements with each one of them, offering participation in the business; the arrangement resembled a franchise contract, with doctors earning a set percentage of the revenues while paying a monthly fee for the rental of the facilities, furniture, and essential equipment. The percentage of income accrued was generous to them, with 85% to be kept by doctors. Dr. Castañeda intended to make his money from volume sales, not by squeezing compensation from his partners. In fact, he also established deals with vendors and became the sole supplier to the twenty-nine different clinics. After a few years, he reached 10,000 collaborators, with 1,000 medical doctors and 9,000 employees performing administrative tasks or general support. In the end, Dr. Castañeda created a model somehow similar to the Indian hospitals.

FINDINGS AND LESSONS

There have been advancements in medical practices in upsurging economies. Those examples come primarily from the use of large solutions to fight common ills in overpopulated countries with serious poverty issues. The situation in Latin America is quite different, due to its fragmented markets, lower population density, and higher average income. Nevertheless, since the turn of the century, middle classes are coming up with newer demands for better medical attention; in fact, several governments failed to ensure universal coverage of health services, even where explicitly laid down by national laws. In most Latin American countries, a limited number of hospitals and physicians available creates trouble-free operating times for the wealthy and long waiting lists for those in need, with the consequent perception of an ever-greater gap between the "top" and "bottom" of the pyramid. Fortunately, there is hope that innovation will provide solutions to satisfy those needs, as proven by the enterprises reviewed.

Following the same reasoning, we tried to identify those innovations that address the MoP. In fact, the middle class is made up of people who start to demand quality, fast services, and low prices. Also, the middle class feels perceptibly neglected by an economic system, which solutions address mostly the Top of the Pyramid. The five companies that we choose for our case study analysis aim at different health care needs. True, Clínica Dental La Zapopana targets dentistry; Clínicas del Azúcar helps patients with diabetes; Farmacias Similares sells medicines; Benestare is in the business of outpatient assistance; and Hospital Solidaridad provides hospitals services—but a closer look reveals that those organizations are in fact breaking paradigms in the local health care industry. Table 3.3 compares important aspects of the business models and strategies from the selected companies. We analyze changes in the Latin American

Table 3.3 *Comparative of business models and strategies for selected companies*

	La Zapopana CDZ	Clínica del Azúcar CDA	Farmacias Similares FS	Benestare BE	Hospital Solidaridad HS
Segmentation	BoP & MoP	MoP	BoP & MoP	MoP	BoP & MoP
Product and service	Standard quality Full-service Specialization	High quality Full-service Specialization Dedicated store	Standard quality Full-service Specialization Own pharmacy	High quality Full service Specialization	Standard quality Full-service Specialization
Price	Price leadership Economies of scale	Price leadership	Price leadership Economies of scale	Economies of scale	Price leadership Economies of scale
Market communication	Local promotion Direct marketing	Local promotion Direct marketing Public relations	Mass media Public relations	Local promotion	Local promotion Public relations
Collaboration	Vertical integration (third parties) Franchise	Vertical integration (third parties) Holding group	Vertical integration Partnership with doctors Holding group	Horizontal integration (third parties) Public sector Holding group	Vertical integration Partnership with doctors Public sector
Value proposition	One-stop-shop Low price Easy financing Time saving Clear outcome	One-stop-shop Low price Easy financing Technology Time saving Clear outcome	One-stop-shop Low price Time saving Clear outcome	Home service Fair price Technology Clear outcome	One-stop-shop Low price Easy financing Time saving Clear outcome

Table 3.3 (cont.)

	La Zapopana CDZ	Clínica del Azúcar CDA	Farmacias Similares FS	Benestare BE	Hospital Solidaridad HS
Customer engagement	Personalized attention Clarity in outcome	Personalized attention Clarity in outcome	Personalized attention Clarity in outcome	Personalized attention Clarity in outcome	Personalized attention Clarity in outcome
Growth of business model	Regional One-stop-shop for dental services	Regional One-stop-shop for diabetic patients	National and international One-stop-shop for minor health care services	National Home diagnosis	National and international One-stop-shop for hospital services
Social impact	High	High Philanthropy	High, Philanthropy Political activism	Medium	High Philanthropy Political activism

Source: Own creation

context, but the needs addressed are universal, and so might be the alternatives offered for the betterment of health care.

All companies target the MoP, while Clínica Dental La Zapopana, Farmacias Similares, and Hospital Solidaridad cover both the BoP and MoP, the vulnerable sector. Those three companies offer standardized service, while Clínicas del Azúcar and Benestare aim for higher quality. In all cases, full service and specialization are of great importance. The five organizations strive for price leadership, mainly based on economies of scale, except for Benestare, which offers fair pricing, if not necessarily the lowest. Regarding communication with the market, the selected companies rely on local promotion, except for Farmacias Similares, which approaches customers through mass media and public relations, backed by a generous budget. Public relations is also an important tool for Clínicas del Azúcar and Hospital Solidaridad.

There are differences on the value proposition across those companies, but a common denominator is the one-stop-shop. Their models incorporate different activities that allow customers to save time, have clear outcomes, and get prices, either fair or low. Through this approach, it becomes easier for the majority market to fulfill their needs in a timely and complete manner. In many cases, easy financing is appealing to the clientele, as it shortens the time for the medical procedure and clarifies total prices to pay. Undoubtedly, clarity in the outcome and personalized attention are at the cornerstone of customer engagement, since it creates a feeling of belonging and being heard as their desires and necessities are met. Finally, all the selected companies have different key partners, but main collaboration efforts go through vertical integration, their own or through third parties, and case specific collaborative agreements with specialized service providers. Indeed, agreements with doctors avoid the cost of hiring highly trained and well-paid specialists, while other employees are not part of those deals. Three of the companies are under the umbrella of a holding group, while the remaining two are expected to grow and create a holding of their own. Clínica Dental La Zapopana already has a franchise network, while some of the remaining organizations might soon consider such a formula for further expansion. Clínica Dental La Zapopana, Clínicas del Azúcar, and Benestare grew regionally, while Hospital Solidaridad had a national scope and Farmacias Similares aimed at the domestic market with a direct presence in several markets in Central and South America. In all cases, the turning point came after transforming each company into a one-stop-shop, with important gains in time, perceived value, and price. Finally, all businesses had a social impact, certainly higher with Clínicas del Azúcar and Farmacias Similares, through their philanthropic programs. Clínica Dental La Zapopana, Benestare, and Hospital Solidaridad generated positive actions by lowering market prices and setting standards of expected service.

All five companies have different innovation actions, as shown in Table 3.4. It is important to note that those changes happened in unsophisticated markets with severe limitations to private competition. Indeed, the innovative actions presented from the different cases may seem modest as compared to those well debated in the literature, but such is the nature of those markets.

Table 3.4 summarizes the innovative actions coming from selected companies. Regarding the product, all the selected companies offer a standardized service: Zapopana and Hospital Solidaridad focus on fast service and Farmacias Similares on the sale of generic drugs and the presence of a doctor in the pharmacy. Clinica del Azucar has a dedicated store, while Benestare provides the state-of-the-art equipment at home. With regard to the process, Zapopana relies upon the presence of a general dentist at the place and rotating specialist, in addition to a free transport service. Zapopana, Clinica del Azucar, and Farmacias Similares are a one-stop-shop. The latter also offers an incentive program for its employees. Partnership with doctors and vertical integration are key elements of Benestare and Hospital Solidaridad. All companies, except Benestare, aspire to price leadership. Zapopana, Benestare, and Hospital Solidaridad provide a financing system while Clinica del Azucar offers a membership system for

Table 3.4 *Innovative actions as per time and market from selected companies*

	La Zapopana CDZ	Clínica del Azúcar CDA	Farmacias Similares FS	Benestare BE	Hospital Solidaridad HS
Product/ Service	Fast service 24/7 Service Warranty in dental services Standardized service	Dedicated store Standardized service	Product standardization Sale of generic drugs Doctor in pharmacy Standardized service	Standardized service Home service State of the art equipment at home	Fast service Standardized service
Process	General dentist in place Rotating specialists Free transportation One-stop-shop	One-stop-shop for diabetic patients	Incentive program to collaborators One-stop-shop for minor health services	Customer classification Rotating specialists Leased equipment Partnership with doctors Vertical integration	Partnership with doctors Vertical integration (third parties)
Price/ financing	Price leadership Set pricing 24/7 Financing (third parties)	Price leadership Set pricing Membership for discounts and coverage	Price leadership	Financing (third parties) Mutual payment	Low price Financing (third parties)
Other	Trickle-up to higher income	Social scope	Mass media campaign Political activism	Specialized software for decision making	Public sector cooperation

Source: Own creation

discounts and coverage of its services. All innovations coming from selected companies affect the market and the society where they operate: Zapopana experiences a trickle-up effect on higher income markets; Clinica del Azucar pursues social goals, just as Farmacias Similares favors millions of people by extending the use of generic drugs. Benestare's innovation gears around a specialized software for decision making, while Hospital Solidaridad proposes a model of mixed public–private cooperation.

FINAL REMARKS

This chapter presented an overview of the health care industry in Latin America, its economic importance, and the wide range of needs addressed through different activities. There is no shortage of challenges; after all, health care targets one of the most important desires of human beings: their well-being. The rise of middle classes in the world is bringing new demands for quality and service from patients that see themselves as entitled to the best possible treatment available. Therefore, developing nations are adding pressure to the industry, already under siege by skyrocketing costs and fierce competition. On the positive side, such pressure is inducing innovative proposals, many of those coming from countries that are no longer satisfied by basic compliance of targets set decades ago.

Latin American people have inadvertently reached new prosperity, partially through simple actions that went unnoticed to many experts. Individual innovative efforts may be low profile but are contributing to the economic and social progress sustained in those countries during the last decade. Creativity and resourcefulness seem to be a part of the inner personality of the local people, and it appears that economic growth and indigenous innovation will continue to rely on the individual and the small enterprise, rather than on larger organizations. Technology-driven innovation is out of reach for local companies that have limited access to capital. In fact, costs are notoriously high for developing a new drug, bringing a new medicine to the market, building a hospital, or developing state of the art equipment.

When reviewing the health care situation for emerging economies, regardless of the continent, something becomes obvious: Educated middle classes from emerging markets are no longer satisfied with "plain vanilla" medical care. They have the resources and the desire for better medical attention, just as happens with entertainment, transportation, or any other area of concern. Their demands eventually lead to innovation, the passport for new generations to a more prosperous world. Innovation, by itself, does not solve the needs of the population but certainly can provide business opportunities and keep the vibrancy of those economies.

What can be learned from these examples is that innovation for the middle of the pyramid in emerging economies must come from their particular needs and aspirations. Simply downgrading versions for the upper classes or adding features to those for the lower classes is not enough for these new middle classes. It is necessary to discover the areas underserved in their lives and the adjacent limitations, such as pricing, time, and accessibility, among others. New proposals should address the health care industry and the well-being of the population in a way that attends their personal characteristics. After all, there is real money to be made while doing good for others.

REFERENCES

American Diabetes Organization. 2013. Economic Costs of Diabetes in the U.S. in 2012. American Diabetes Organization. Accessed March 12, 2016. www.diabetes .org/advocacy/news-events/cost-of-diabetes.html?referrer=https%3A%2F%2Fwww .google.com.mx%2F

Anta, R., El-Wahab, S., & A. Giuffrida. 2009. Salud Movil El potencial de la telefonía celular para llevar la salud a la mayoría. Inter-American Development Bank (IBD).

Barcena, A. 2015. Agenda for Sustainable Development in LAC: The Territory Matters. Economic Commission for Latin America and the Caribbean (ECLAC).

Benestare S. A. 2014. Servicios. *Benestare*. Accessed March 9, 2016. www.benestare .com.ar

Bosset, T., Blanchet, N., Sheetz, S., Pinto, D., Cali, J., & Perez-Cuevas, R. 2014. Comparative Review of Health System Integration in Selected Countries in Latin America. Inter-American Development Bank (IBD).

Chu, M. & Garcia-Cuellar, R. 2011. *Farmacias Similares: Private and Public Health Care for the Base of the Pyramid in Mexico.* Cambridge, MA: Harvard Business School.

Clínica Dental La Zapopana. 2014. Brackets La Zapopana. *Dentistas-Clínica Dental La Zapopana.* Accessed March 11, 2016. http://dentallazapopana.com

Clínicas del Azúcar. 2015. Clínica de Diabetes en Monterrey-About us. *Clínicas del Azúcar.* Accessed March 11, 2016. www.clinicasdelazucar.com

Cuervo-Cazurra, A. 2016. Multilatinas as Sources of New Research Insights: The Learning and Escape Drivers of International Expansion. *Journal of Business Research* 69(6): 1963–1972.

Davies, J. & Mazza, O. 2011. *The Pharmaceutical & Healthcare Industry in Latin America.* Citi's Online Academy.

De Jong, H. 2015. *How Can Latin America Provide Quality Healthcare to All?* Geneva: World Economic Forum.

Deloitte. 2015. *2015 Global Health Care Outlook: Common Goals, Competing Priorities.* New York: Deloitte.

Dixon-Fyle, S. & Kowallik, T. 2010. *Engaging Consumers to Manage Health Care Demand.* Seattle: McKinsey & Company.

Ebel, T., Larsen, E., & Shah, K. 2013. *Strengthening Health Care's Supply Chain: A Five-Step Plan.* Seattle: McKinsey & Company.

ECLAC. 2015. Latin America and the Caribbean: Looking Ahead after the Millennium Development Goals Regional Monitoring Report on the Millennium Development Goals in Latin America and the Caribbean, 2015. Economic Commission for Latin America and the Caribbean (ECLAC).

EY. 2016. Pulse of the Industry. Medical Technology Report 2016. EYGM Limited.

Fay, B. 2015. Hospital and Surgery Cost. American Debt Organization. Accessed June 30, 2020. www.dineroenimagen.com/2015-02-09/50618

Ferreira, Francisco H. G. et al. 2012. *Economic Mobility and the Rise of the Latin American Middle Class.* Washington DC: World Bank Publications.

GHI. 2016. Opportunities in Latin America's Healthcare Sector 2016. Global Health Intelligence (GHI). Accessed April 14, 2016. www.globalhealthintelligence.com

Groves, P., Kayyali, B., Knott, D., & Kuiken, S. V. 2013. *The "Big Data" Revolution in Healthcare. Accelerating Value and Innovation.* Seattle: McKinsey & Company.

IBM. 2008. *Healthcare in India.* New York: IBM Institute for Business Value.

Kelly, D. & Son, A. 2013. *Healthcare Reform Opens Up Middle-Market Opportunities*. Los Angeles: IBIS World.

Llumpo, A., Montagu, D., Brashers, E., Foong, S., Abuzaineh, N., & Feachem, R. 2015. Lessons from Latin America: The Early Landscape of Healthcare Public-Private Partnerships. Healthcare Public–Private Partnership Series, No. 2. San Francisco: Global Health Sciences.

Mazzone & Associates. 2015. *2015 Healthcare Industry Report*. Atlanta: Mazzone and Associates, Inc.

Montoya, M. 2014. *Fast Dental Health*. Guadalajara: Tecnológico de Monterrey Campus.

Montoya, M. & Cervantes M. 2014. *M. Business Models for the Base of the Pyramid*. Guadalajara: Tecnológico de Monterrey Campus Guadalajara.

Ocaranza, P. 2015. La diabetes le dio a este emprendedor su misión. *Dinero en Imagen*. Accessed April 2, 2016. www.dineroenimagen.com/2015-02-09/50618

OECD. 2015. Health at a Glance 2015 OECD Indicators. Organization for Economic Cooperation and Development. Accessed March 2, 2016. http://apps.who.int/medicinedocs/documents/s22177en/s22177en.pdf

OECD. 2019. Health at a Glance 2019: OECD Indicators. Organization for Economic Cooperation and Development. OECD Publishing, Paris.

Pallares, M. 2017. Similares va por más de 7 mil unidades. *El Universal*. September 9th, 2017. Accessed November 22, 2019. www.eluniversal.com.mx/cartera/negocios/similares-va-por-mas-de-7-mil-unidades

Paniagua, E. & Zafra, E. 2012. Tratamiento integral de la diabetes para comunidades con pocos recursos. *Espacio Crítico 23*. February 13th, 2014. Accessed March 03, 2016. https://espaciocritico23.wordpress.com/2014/02/14/javier-lozano-tratamiento-integral-de-la-diabetes

Porter, M. & Teisberg, E. 2006. *Redefining Health Care: Creating Value-Based Competition on Results*. Boston: Harvard Business School Press.

PWC. 2015. *Global Health's New Entrants: Meeting the World's Consumer*. London: PricewaterhouseCoopers (PWC).

PWC. 2016. *Top Health Industry Issues of 2016: Thriving in the New Health Economy*. London: Pricewaterhouse Coopers (PWC).

Schwab Foundation. 2010. Javier Lozano. The Schwab Foundation for Social Entrepreneurship. Accessed March 2, 2016. www.schwabfound.org/content/javier-lozano

SIEMENS. 2015. Thinking Healthcare Ahead. SIEMENS.

The Commonwealth Fund. 2010. *The Commonwealth Fund*. Accessed May 6, 2016. www.commonwealthfund.org

Villafranco, G. 2016. Clínicas del Azúcar: ¿cómo tratar la diabetes a bajo costo? *Forbes México*. Accessed May 2, 2016. www.forbes.com.mx/clinicas-del-azucar-como-tratar-la-diabetes-precios-accesibles

Vitalary, N. 2012. A Prospective Analysis of the Future of the US Health Care Industry. Center for Digital Transformation. University of California-Irvine. Accessed April 2, 2016. http://merage.uci.edu/ResearchAndCenters/CDT/Resources/Documents/N%20Vitalari%20A%20Prospective%20Analysis%20of%20the%20Healthcare%20Industry.pdf

WHO. 2015. World Health Statistics 2015. World Health Organization (WHO).

World Economic Forum's Meta-Council on Emerging Technologies. 2016. *Top 10 Emerging Technologies of 2016*. Geneva: World Economic Forum.

4 Education for Everyone

Otto Regalado-Pezúa and Daniel Lemus-Delgado

WHAT WE MEAN WHEN WE SAY "EDUCATION"

Education for everyone is an extremely important and laudable goal. As the Organization of Latin American States asserts, a relevant, equitable, and quality education is the key to development. It can therefore be said that the real wealth of nations resides in a good education.[1]

According to Yoka Brandt, UNICEF deputy executive director, education can make a lasting difference in children's lives. From Brandt's perspective, "School is not just good for kids; it is also good for nations. Investing in education is not only the right thing to do, but it is also smart economics. Education can put people on a path towards good health, empowerment, and employment. It can help to build more peaceful societies. And the benefits of educating girls extends to their children, who are often healthier and more educated themselves because their mothers went to school. Evidence shows that, on average, each additional year of education boosts a person's income by 10% and increases a country's GDP by 18%."[2]

The challenge of education for everyone is a problem even for middle-income countries around the world. It is a universal challenge, not limited to a region or a small set of nations. In fact, education has been considered an essential tool for boosting a high standard of life. Nowadays, it is common to affirm that it is impossible to think of a formula for development that doesn't include a massive effort toward good education. For example, the experiences of Singapore, Taiwan, South Korea, and Hong Kong, four countries that are recognized as Asian tigers, showed how education was a critical factor toward

[1]   OEI 2014a.   [2]   Brandt 2015.

development. From 1965 to 1990, the countries' dramatic economic growth, improved human welfare, and more equitable income distribution were the result of a set of public policies that included the promotion of education.[3]

In the case of Latin America, there is a documented link between poverty and lack of education, with the most economically disadvantaged having lower levels of educational achievement. In consequence, "Educational opportunities are the key to providing Latin American citizens access to knowledge, the chance to participate in the creation of wealth, and the opportunity to prosper. As the economy becomes more global and knowledge-based, those with the greatest access to knowledge will benefit the most from the possibilities resulting from the integration into the world economy."[4]

Education is a prime means of reducing inequality in Latin America, with different educational levels having different objectives. If we want education to be a powerful instrument to transform social and economic structures in Latin America, it is necessary to build an innovation model to increase the opportunities to offer education for everyone. Specifically, education for everyone demands that we think of new ways for universities and schools to establish strong links with society to provide access to elementary, secondary, and tertiary education. This issue is not only about the number of people that can obtain an education, but also about the quality of it. This means that private efforts can contribute to the task. In this way, education in Latin America is at the same time a route to development and a business opportunity.

LATIN AMERICA FACING THE CHALLENGE

In Latin America, the economic and political development of some countries in the region has had a positive impact on many macro- and microeconomic areas. The middle class in Latin America comprises almost 200 million people; in this sense, it is the second most

---

[3]   Birdsall et al. 1993.   [4]   Reimers 1999.

significant proportion among developing regions, just after Eastern Europe.[5] In the last two decades, most Latin American countries have experienced a period of profound social transformation. A prolonged commodity boom powered above-average growth in the region during the 2000s, which contributed to the expansion of the middle class. In fact, this phenomenon is shaping how governments cope with new social demands, specifically education. The growth in the middle class has incentivized investment in various sectors, such as education, which accounts for an average of 5% of the regional GDP. However, there are multiple challenges in this area.

First, there is a rise in the educational level of students graduating that is not matched by a corresponding increase in the same level of primary education. Second, there is a lack of government leadership or follow-up of processes to help ensure a high-quality universal education. Third, there is a lack of government leadership in the formation of quality teaching professionals who enjoy competitive salaries, the development of which would give recognized status to the profession of instruction and would help to attract the best candidates. For example, higher education has expanded dramatically in the last fifteen years, as the average gross enrollment increased from 21% to 43% between 2000 and 2013. At present, the system includes approximately 20 million students, 10,000 institutions, and 60,000 programs.[6] However, the rapid and massive growth of the systems, the characteristics of the new students, and the lax regulation of some higher education institutes have led many to question the quality of their programs and the possibility of all students gaining access to a high-quality option. Fourth, there is a need to lower the dropout rate, both at the secondary and higher-education level. Fifth, there is a slow labor-market entry for young people. Sixth, there are non-standardized educational levels that are inadequate for admission to post-secondary or tertiary education for those young people who do complete secondary school. Finally, there is the "neet" phenomenon

[5]   Penfold & Trinkunas 2015.   [6]   Ferreyra et al. 2017.

("not in education, employment, or training"), and the problem of
how to ensure the incorporation of young people from the most
marginalized communities into work or study programs.

The specific situation and educational challenges in Latin
America vary from country to country, but it is possible to identify
a common issue: how to guarantee students access to a quality
education.[7]

Education is a prime means of reducing inequality in Latin
America, with different educational levels having different objectives.
The first level is the initial stage (sometimes referred to as "pre-
primary"), which encompasses the child's early years (ages 0–6).
This first stage is crucial in the development of a child as it influences
the development of physical and psychological abilities and foments
creativity as well as teaches the child to be autonomous and confident. Initial education is not considered obligatory in the majority of
countries until the age of five years, but this level creates the basis for
the education of the child. Primary education follows this initial stage
and takes place from the age of six to eleven or twelve; at this stage,
the child will learn basic mathematics as well as reading and writing
and various cultural concepts that are considered essential. The
primary stage is followed by the secondary, the purpose of which is
to prepare the student for higher education. Finally comes tertiary
education, which is the term used by such international organizations
such as UNESCO, the OECD, and the World Bank for the majority of
post-secondary studies such as university or technical studies.

Taking these factors into account, one of the most common
means of measuring access to education is by analyzing the number
of students who successfully finish each level. There has been a
noticeable rise in students graduating in Latin America in recent
years, specifically in the elementary school, a situation that has been

---

[7]   Latin America is a region classified as middle income. The principal problems of the
countries are the quality, not the quantity, of education. The challenge is very different
in comparison with other regions, such as South Asia and Africa, with large illiterate
populations.

Table 4.1 *Selected indicators related to participation and completion*

	Primary	Low secondary	Upper secondary	Primary	Low secondary	Upper secondary	Primary	Low secondary	Upper secondary
Caucasus and Central Asia	3	6	19	0.2	0.4	0.6	*	*	*
Eastern and South-Eastern Asia	4	10	22	7	8	18	95	79	57
Europe and North America	3	2	8	2	1	3	*	98	87
Latin America and the Caribbean	5	8	24	3	3	7	90	79	59
North Africa and Western Asia	11	15	33	5	4	9	80	60	33
Pacific	7	2	34	0.3	0	0.5	*	99	85
Southern Asia	6	19	49	11	20	68	83	69	31
Sub-Saharan Africa	21	36	57	33	26	34	59	38	25
Low Income	19	38	38	20	19	25	50	27	13
Low middle income	10	19	19	31	34	91	83	68	37
Upper middle income	4	8	8	8	8	22	95	82	60
High income	3	1	7	2	0.6	3	*	96	84
World	**9**	**16**	**37**	**61**	**62**	**141**	**83**	**69**	**45**

Source: UNESCO Global Education Monitoring Report. http://unesdoc.unesco.org/

made possible by the substantial increase in access to education for children in the region. In Latin America, in general, an average of 75% of students graduate annually, with this varying from 41% in Guatemala to 95% in Brazil. Conversely, however, the dropout rate has also increased, particularly in the secondary education level.

Regarding the access to education available in Latin America, there is still great room for improvement. Secondary school in the region is only available to 74% of the population, while tertiary education is only accessible to 42%.[8] It is indispensable, therefore, to broaden the offering of professional technical education, which would permit students from the middle class who finish secondary school to continue studying. Recent progress in the enrollment of students in education up until the age at which attendance is no longer obligatory has not been as impressive as previously; the most likely reason for this is the lack of qualified teaching staff.[9]

The most accurate measurements of educational quality are those taken by the Program for the International Evaluation of OCDE Students, also known as PISA. According to the PISA scale, the results obtained at the regional level are extremely low when compared to similar regions in other parts of the world and remain well below the average. For example, 50% of students in Brazil, Argentina, Panama, and Peru fail to reach even level 2, considered the minimum reading standard. In contrast, 90% of students in Finland, South Korea, Hong Kong, and Shanghai reach this level. Latin America and the Caribbean consistently obtain worse results than those predicted by level of income per person or level of education spending.[10] In practical terms, this translates to a difference in the development of Latin American students that is equivalent to almost two years of school.[11]

There is also an inherent educational inequality between poor children and those who come from the middle and upper classes, a fact that is thrown into stark relief when comparing geographical

---

[8]   OECD 2014.   [9]   OEI 2014b.   [10]   OCDE 2009.   [11]   OECD 2014.

regions. Peru is a good example of a nation where significant differences in the quality of education and even infrastructure is evident when making comparisons based on geographic location. An example would be the rural zones of Moquegua and Loreto, where the latter benefits from the local mining industry and contributions to the community from private enterprises, both of which have had beneficial effects on educational levels. It is a fact that access to educational opportunities in the higher socioeconomic echelons is directly related to greater family income. Similarly, Regalado highlights "the lack of integration between the business and tourism sectors and institutes of higher education in Latin America."[12] He points out that in Peru specifically, in response to industry demand for qualified tourism professionals, the number of universities offering these courses at a low educational level has increased. The reason behind this is believed to be the failure to take into account the actual needs of the labor market. As a consequence, there is a training gap between graduate capability and industry requirements.[13]

The root of the problem is the vast inequality that is present in Latin America. For example, in 2014 the average GDP per capita compared to Purchasing Power Parity (PPP) for Latin America was USD 12443. However, a more detailed study of the regional results reveals a much larger disparity. For example, Uruguay enjoys the highest GDP in real terms per capita of USD 17343. The lowest values registered were in Nicaragua with USD 4111, Honduras with USD 4349 USD, and Bolivia with USA 5557 USD.[14] A second way of appreciating the inequality between Latin American countries is by way of the Gini index.[15] According to this index, Latin American countries make up six of the fourteen countries in the world with

[12]   Regalado-Pezúa 2013   [13]   Regalado-Pezúa 2013.   [14]   CEPAL 2014.
[15]   This index measures the extent to which income distribution between individuals or households in an economy varies from an entirely equitable distribution. In the Gini index, a score of 0 represents perfect equality, while an index of 100 represents perfect inequality. According to data from the World Bank, in 2012 Argentina had a Gini index of 42.3; Peru, 44.7; Mexico, 48.1; Chile, 50.5; Brazil, 52.9; Colombia, 53.5; and Honduras, 53.7. Banco Mundial 2016.

the highest income disparity. Honduras is in sixth place, Colombia in seventh, Brazil in eighth, Guatemala in ninth, Panama in tenth, and Chile in fourteenth.[16] These inequalities also become evident in public expenditure per student at the tertiary level as a per-capita percentage of GDP. For example, in 2010, Peru spent 10% and Cuba 63%.[17]

In conclusion, there is a huge challenge regarding strengthening the teaching profession in terms of basic teacher training, particularly regarding responsibility toward communities, status, and financial remuneration, in addition to increasing public funding per student. The salaries quoted in the PPP show marked differences between Latin American countries and those countries that comprise the OECD and the EU. Despite the most recent educational reforms that have taken place in the region over the last decade, a study carried out by the McKinsey consulting group revealed that the quality of the school system is still directly linked to the quality of the teaching body. Consequently, investment in education should concentrate on selecting, evaluating, motivating, and adequately rewarding teachers, instead of being used for infrastructure.[18] This challenge is even greater if we consider the unprecedented growth in tertiary education, which has doubled or in some cases nearly tripled in all Latin American countries over the last two decades. Table 4.2 shows the evolution of the gross tertiary enrollment rate in Latin America from 1990 to LYA (last year available).

The aforementioned factors are prejudicial not only to regional competitiveness but also to the possibility of improving the quality of life for the Latin American population. The Program for the Promotion of Education Reform in Latin America and the Caribbean indicates that Latin American workers continue to lag behind their counterparts in Eastern Europe and East Asia in educational level, and the gap continues to widen.[19]

---

[16]   Banco Mundial 2016.   [17]   UNESCO 2016.   [18]   Jabonero 2014.
[19]   Programa de Promoción de la Reforma Educativa en América Latina y el Caribe 2005.

Table 4.2 *Evolution of the gross tertiary enrollment rate in Latin America*

Country	1990	2000	2010	LYA
Argentina	38.4	53.1	74.8	79.9
Bolivia	s/d	34.9	37.7	37.7
Brazil	10.8	16.0	s/d	46.4
Chile	21.0	37.2	65.9	86.6
Colombia	14.2	23.9	39.0	51.21
Costa Rica	26.4	25.6	44.5	53.1
Cuba	21.1	22.0	82.4	40.9
Dominican Republic	s/d	33.3	46.4	58.8
Ecuador	19.8	18.8	40.5	40.4
El Salvador	15.3	20.7	23.4	28.8
Guatemala	8.2	9.5	18.7	18.3
Honduras	8.9	13.8	20.6	21.1
Mexico	14.8	19.3	26.7	29.9
Nicaragua	7.7	17.0	s/d	17.2
Panama	20.9	41.1	43.9	38.7
Paraguay	8.3	15.7	34.5	34.5
Peru	30.3	34.4	40.6	40.6
Uruguay	29.9	34.3	63.2	63.2
Venezuela (BR)	27.8	28.3	77.9	77.9

Source: UNESCO http://data.uis.unesco.org. Chile, Colombia, Costa Rica, Dominican Republic, El Salvador, Honduras, and Mexico, year 2014; Argentina, Brazil, Guatemala, and Panama, year 2013; Bolivia, Peru, Uruguay, and Venezuela, year 2010; Nicaragua, year 2002.

In this context, it is evident that the schooling offered in the tertiary sector, whether higher technical education or university, cannot adequately provide the training required by the Latin American population, particularly in areas associated with the lowest income percentiles.

In Latin America, the state faces multiple challenges. Problems such as corruption, the absence of the rule of law, insufficient tax collection, increased inequality, and systematic and generalized violence mean that the State assumes education as a political approach rather than as leverage for development. Thus, governments seek to prevent education from becoming a political problem. For this reason, politicians boot the massification of education. However, in the absence of quality, parents seek other higher quality options that allow their sons to graduate with more skills and better employability. In this regard, Mexico is a good example. In 2017, Universidad Nacional Autónoma de México, the best public university in the country, admitted only 8.6% of those who applied. More than 131,000 students were rejected.[20] Many of these students could be admitted to other public universities that are located in the interior of the country, but in many cases parents want to pay for a private university because they think that quality of education is better. It is not always that way. Logically, the inability of Latin American governments to offer a relevant, quality education in the tertiary sector is a business opportunity with a social focus, offering the possibility of improving society as a whole through education. The lack of educational opportunities of this type for all population segments is the cause of the "neet" ("not in education, employment, or training") phenomenon.

The term "neet" has its origins in the late 1990s, although it did not come into widespread use until the world financial crisis of 2008–2009. It is used to refer to those young people who are outside the formal system and who are not participating in either education or formal employment. The term covers young people between the ages of fifteen to twenty-four; in Latin America, there are 108 million individuals in this age range. The "neet" percentage of the population, according to CEPAL,[21] had grown to 22% in 2012.

According to the most recent data from the World Bank and La Tercera in Chile, there are 20 million "neets" in the fifteen countries that comprise Latin America, a number that is steadily increasing. In fact, there was an increase of 4 million from just 1992 to 2013.

---

[20]   Regeneración 2017.   [21]   CEPAL 2012.

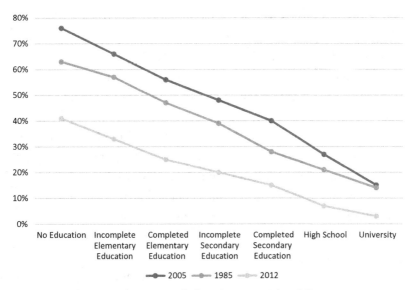

FIGURE 4.1 The impact of education on social mobility – Peru.
Source: Undergraduate Scholarship Office – PRONABEC with own updated data

To better understand the composition and profile of these 20 million "neets," it has been estimated that 70% live in cities and have a low educational level. Sixty percent come from poor or vulnerable homes located in the bottom 40% in terms of household income, and six of the nine countries in the region have approximately 28% of their population of African descent. Along with indigenous communities, these are the groups that are the most educationally marginalized.[22] In the case of Peru, the likelihood of poverty lessens considerably as the educational level rises (see Figure 4.1).

According to recommendations from CEPAL and the UN, in order for the gap in educational attainment to be diminished, policies need to be put in place that address the needs of these groups. Those requirements include, for instance: a flexible educational cycle and flexible payment terms more in tune with the lived experience of

22   CEPAL 2012.

these communities, as well as the use of examples and cases related to the indigenous population and the realities of the geographical area.

According to Jorge Familiar, Vice President of SM for Latin America and the Caribbean, "Neets help to perpetuate generational inequality... Confronting the challenge ... will involve taking advantage of their tremendous potential to work together to contribute to the future of the region." In the document "Neets in Latin America: 20 million young people in search of opportunities," the World Bank clearly outlines the steps that need to be taken to reduce this number by helping young people to stay in school and helping them to subsequently make the transition to stable employment.[23]

States have an obligation to generate conditions that guarantee children and adolescents access to a quality education that is inclusive, multicultural, and that foments democracy and diversity, as well as ensuring that they stay in the system and complete their formal education. These problems are becoming increasingly severe, particularly in vulnerable and rural populations.[24]

THOSE WHO CHALLENGED THE SITUATION

Secondary Education: The Beginning of the Working Age

High school has an extremely high dropout rate and a poor quality in terms of PISA evaluations. The most recent studies agree that on average, about the year 2010, between 64% and 68% of upper secondary school-age adolescents attended school in the countries in the region, and graduation rates from this level reached between 45% and 48%.[25] Those who do graduate from high school in Latin America have a uniformly low academic level that is inadequate to allow them to access tertiary education. Such low-level academic preparation is one of the reasons why young people find it so difficult to continue studying, along with a lack of stable and sufficient income.

---

[23]   SOURCE: https://openknowledge.worldbank.org/bitstream/handle/10986/22349/K8423.pdf?sequence=5&isAllowed=y

[24]   OEI 2014a.   [25]   Bentaouet Kattan & Székely 2015.

Innova Schools, Perú. In Peru, government investment in education has gone hand-in-hand with the country's recent economic growth. The budget allocated to the school sector in 2015 represents 3.5% of GDP, an increase from 2014, although other nations in the region invest an average of 5% of GDP.

The lack of investment in education and the growth in the mean income in Peru in recent years has in turn driven demand for private schools and colleges. The Intercorp Group, owned by Carlos Rodriguez-Pastor, has become involved in investment in the education field due to its strategy of diversifying into different economic sectors with a view to improving the education of Peruvian children. Today the company participates in the Universidad Tecnológica del Perú (UTP), IDAT institutes, and Innova Schools.

The following example will focus on the case of Innova Schools, one of the thirteen most innovative educational institutions in the world, according to TECH Insider magazine. In 2014, Innova Schools received the international AdvancED prize, the only Peruvian entity ever to win this distinction. The Innova Schools Network has also received praise from both *Fortune Magazine* and the Business Creativity Organization for its use of innovative teaching methodology.

According to Ana Teresa Angulo, Human Resources Manager at Innova Schools, "The biggest challenge is the teachers, since their numbers are steadily declining because fewer young people want to study education, and at the same time, many universities close the education faculty for lack of students. Fewer faculties which teach education and those which remain are of poor formative quality."

The idea behind Innova Schools was to bring innovative, high-quality educational methodology to Peru. Based on internationally successful educational models, Innova developed its methodology through collaborating and co-working with different institutions. Innova began by focusing on pre-primary education (comprised of pupils between the ages of three and six years), developing a methodology in conjunction with the University of Berkeley. For both primary and secondary education, they developed the blended method, which alternates between individual and group work, in collaboration with IDEO. Secondly, the entire model draws on the development of two concepts: space and people. The result was the development of a whole learning plan: curriculum, teaching strategies, infrastructure, operating plans, and finally the financial model for setting up the network of colleges.

However, the project could not be carried out without qualified teachers who are the facilitators of the subject matter and who know these innovative teaching methods.

A significant challenge is the faculty. For this education system to continue advancing and growing in both schools and students, it is vital to build a team of highly motivated teachers who are dedicated to their field and open to new ideas. They should take the challenge to increase their knowledge, through methodologies beyond this one or any other.

"We seek teachers who are young or highly adaptable to change, since it is necessary to change their mindset. Teachers become frustrated, and for that reason it is important to identify their profiles accurately. The universities teach how to teach in the traditional way: whiteboard, write and dictate. To this must be added a lack of ideas about the subject being taught, to the point that it is necessary to teach mathematics to the mathematics teacher," emphasizes Angulo with regard to the importance not only of the design of the training process, but also of the correct selection of teachers.

"We begin the selection process in May and it concludes in October. The selection process is very arduous; of every 11 teachers who enter the process, I hire only 1 teacher. 50% fail the reading comprehension test; that is our reality. I have to ensure that I have the best teachers in the market, and this year we are hiring 550 teachers after the filtering process, from among more than 5,000 teachers. The subjects are related to reading comprehension, group dynamics, subject proficiency test, among others," specifies Angula with regard to the selection process of teachers.

Once the teacher has been selected, his process within Innova begins. First with the training, followed by the assignment of a coach who will give him personalized monitoring and with a contract that specifies the minimum training that he must follow in order to continue in the institution. This is followed by the continuous assessment of the teacher, in order to determine his performance and motivation.

"The training process begins in October, an online training from their current jobs (before going to Innova) and during the entire month of February they only receive training, their contract begins on February 1. They start work in March and continue to receive training during the entire cycle," comments Angulo with regard to the training process. It must be taken into account that in Peru the course starts in March and finishes in December of each year, therefore with this training system the teachers do not lose a training course, and at the same time they prepare for the start of classes in March.

"We carry out formal performance evaluations twice a year. This consists of a 360-degree evaluation, involving the parents, the students, the peer group, the principals ... by means of this they obtain benefits, salary increase or promotions. Objective measurement is sought," concludes Angulo, regarding the method of evaluation of teachers.

The education model was designed to enable the students to be more independent and take charge of their learning. Aurelia Alvarado, director of innovation, outlines the innovative vision of this teaching methodology, which consists of creating an interest in the theme in the student (motivation), identification of and information about the subject (construction), and the undertaking of practicing and relating learned concepts to other topics (closing). Each phase is combined in the blended method, which means a progression from group work to working with a partner, and then on to individual work.

The national Student Assessment Census carried out in 2014 measured the impact of the Innova school's methodology on the development of student ability. The report showed that Innova students achieved a development level of 71% in mathematics and 85% in reading comprehension, as opposed to the 26% and 57%, respectively, obtained by students from other private educational institutions.

An outstanding pedagogical methodology and an innovation in professor selection and learning development is what differentiates Innova Schools, but how can the school deal with the challenges described at the beginning of the chapter? Given the lack of qualified teachers, they are contacting universities, specifically the Faculty of Education, so as to support the faculty and thus have the first option to hire. In this sense, private schools are their direct competition, above all because they offer a higher salary to already trained teachers, and the state also appears as a competitor, since it presents proposals "with fine print" to teachers, without so many obligations concerning formation and constant training.

On the other hand, having the income required to fund tuition fees is important to guarantee access. Tuition fees for Innova College average USD 130, which means that the institution is affordable for a significant number of families when compared with the average income for the target demographic, who have a monthly income on average of USD 1500. Most private educational institutions charge a monthly fee similar to the standard in Peru, which ranges from USD 500–1100.

There is also a scholarship system. Innova Schools has partnered with Peru Champs, a charitable organization, in order to help children who have the ability but whose families do not have the capacity to pay the school fees required for an international standard private college. There is also a system of discounts in place depending on how many children from the same family enroll in Innova Schools.

In the face of such adversity, what was the motivation behind the founding of the Innova School project? "With the surge in growth that the country is experiencing, this is a daunting task, and, as a result, the corporation was drawn to work in education. If profit were the motivation behind Innova Schools, we would be focusing on other areas. We are certainly a company motivated by profit making, but education is the guiding purpose. Eventually, without such motivation, millions of students who fail to learn to read and write correctly will have their life chances curtailed. There are a lot of challenges, but the final result provides the motivation behind the project. On the way, the results that we achieve and the exposure this gives us feeds this motivation." Ana Teresa Angulo asserts that the incentive is not meeting annual targets or growth but becoming a contributing factor in the country's advancement.

By 2015, the network of colleges had 29 locations at the national level and 19,000 students in total, divided between the cities of Lima, Piura, Chimbote, Chiclayo, Chincha, Huacho, Tacna, and Arequipa, with a goal of 100 colleges by the year 2025. A high-level teacher-training college is also planned for the future.

Tertiary Education: The Purpose of Building and Following Your Path

The tertiary or higher education sector in Latin America is both diverse and complex. On the one hand, the traditional model of higher education is heterogeneous and fragmented. On the other hand, several new institutions, all with different levels and perspectives, have come into being.[26]

The gross tertiary enrollment rate worldwide has grown from 19% in the year 2000 to 29.2% in 2010. In Latin America, access to higher education in the year 2000 was a little more than 22.6% of young people aged 18–22, increasing to 40.5% in 2010. According to data from the World Bank, this is in line with the average growth rate in the tertiary education sector in other regions, as can be seen in Table 4.3.

The number of students registered in higher-education institutions in Latin America has risen from 18,481,481 in 2005 to 24,945,111 in 2011. It has increased by almost 35% in only six years

[26]   Didriksson 2008.

Table 4.3 *Gross enrollment ratio, tertiary, both sexes (%) by region*

Region	Percent
East Asia and the Pacific	39.14
European Union	67.71
Latin America and the Caribbean	44.66
The Middle East and North Africa	37.91
Sub-Saharan Africa	8.59
BRIC	
Brazil	49.3
Russia	78.7
India	26.9
China	39.4
South Africa	19.4
Other emerging economies in Latin America	
Mexico	29.9
Chile	88.6
Colombia	55.7
Argentina	82.9

Source: World Bank, 2017

and the sector continues to expand. Figure 4.2 shows the growth in student enrollment from 1970 to the year 2011.

While coverage has increased and access has improved in most countries in the region, this growth has benefited the higher socio-economic quintiles most; for example, as of 2010 Mexico has enrollment rates of 43.8% in quintile 5 and 15% in quintile 1; Chile has rates of 61.6% in quintile 5 and 21.2% in quintile 1.[27] There is an opportunity to increase both the public and private offerings for the least-privileged segments. In this sense, the growth of students in higher-education institutions is similar to that of other regions in the world in

[27]   SOURCE: Higher education policies in Latin America 2009–2013 – a study undertaken by the Center for Comparative Education Studies (CPCE) of the Diego Portales University and the UNESCO Chair for Comparative Higher Education Studies – Santiago de Chile.

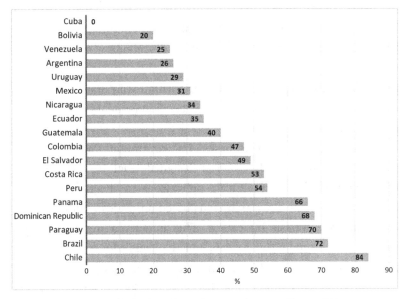

FIGURE 4.2 Latin America: private tertiary enrollment (%).
Source: Self-elaborated with data from the UIS Database

the last two decades. Beyond this comparison, the most important thing is that each young person that can study at a higher education institute means a real and better life opportunity. Every young person who has the opportunity to be educated is progress for everyone.

Private universities have played a significant role in the growth of tertiary education. Figure 4.2 shows how countries such as Chile, Brazil, Paraguay, the Dominican Republic, Panama, Peru, and Costa Rica have more than 50% of all university undergraduates enrolled in the private sector.

The Khipu Institute, Peru. The development of private offerings in institutes and technical education has stagnated as a result of excessive state regulation, in contrast to the situation at the university level. Therefore, there are actually fewer students graduating from technical schools than from universities; the resulting imbalance is proving disadvantageous to the country, as the labor market needs more qualified technicians than tertiary education graduates.

The Khipu Education Corporation has its headquarters in Cuzco, Peru and is an educational institution comprised of an institute, a university, and both primary and secondary colleges. "We believe in development and emphasizing technological innovations," says Roberto Portugal, President of the Khipu Corporation. Portugal has contributed to both educational development and advances in information from this time.

The Khipu Institute bases its continuous adaptation of education on local needs and has designed teaching and learning processes around their practical applications in the field of work. The corporation has a research focus based on Andean cultural identity with an emphasis on values. This understanding of both the realities of the productive sectors and the search for synthesis with the Andean culture makes a difference among the students, who become truly empowered. The institute works on both technical skills and personal skills. The market knowledge and the development of work skills mean that graduates of the institute have a 100% possibility of employment, with most beginning work before completing their classes. Enhanced employment possibilities are enticing for students, who wish to receive training appropriate to local labor market requirements and access to immediate employment.

As an educational corporation, the focus of the Khipu Institute is on community development through adapting research in technologies significant to the region in which it operates. Portugal emphasizes that its differentiation comes from identifying and getting to know the Andean culture and reinforcing it by using it as a basis for learning, while also covering the educational learning gaps from school. "A 'Zero cycle' of three months allows us to identify gaps in the students' academic knowledge, and it is during this period that we work on standardizing the different academic levels of those who enter the Institute. During this time we work on skills such as reading comprehension, mathematics, and other skills which students need. The model includes the development of computer and study skills and methods to clarify the vocational aptitudes of the students and ensure that they begin at the right level, in addition to the development of entrepreneurship. A unique characteristic is that there is no admission exam, and it is in the first two study cycles where students decide for themselves the specialization for which they are most suited."

"The teachers are professionals with both a high practical and vocational level, although they are not trained pedagogues. However, this is not the reason that turnover is high, nor is it due to this salary, which is not the principal source of income. The salary is, in fact, greater than local market rates," says Portugal, in order to reinforce the idea that students in the institute look above all for practical training. The responsibility of the teacher is primarily to highlight for the students the realities of the chosen employment field.

"Our teaching and learning processes are more learner-centered. We believe the ability to learn is more important than the quality of the education imparted by the teacher who, in the Khipu system, is more a companion to the student and an e-learning facilitator. In the case of the Khipu Institute, the syllabus is prepared by the institution itself, with the teacher accompanying the student during their learning. In this way, the process becomes more academically and empirically robust, and the teachers have a complete understanding of the type of information the student is going to receive. This idea of being proactive about the design of the academic content is a characteristic of the institution," states Portugal.

The way that students finance their studies is simple: The more they achieve, the less they pay, reflecting the effort and motivation that they put in.

"The nighttime and afternoon sessions are cheaper, given that the students need to work during the day. We have academic scholarships as well as Scholarship 18. Of the 3,000 students at the Institute, 700 for example have Scholarship 18. In addition, as part of its social responsibility program, a business organization involved in mining is offering a full scholarship for outstanding students from this year onward," states Portugal.

The intention for the future is to continue diversifying into professional majors such as agriculture management and communication technologies. The Khipu Institute is certified by the Ministry of Labor and has been awarded an ISO 9001–9008 certification in quality management. Both the institute and the university have been accredited by the National System for the Accreditation of Educational Quality – SINEASE.

Continental University, Perú. The growth in the offerings of private university education in Peru is a result of new legislation by the Peruvian government that has facilitated returns on investment, a more significant factor in private education. In 2004, there were 232,632 undergraduates enrolled in private universities (from a total of 515,117 tertiary education students), but by 2012, this had increased to 642,203 from a total enrollment of 963,784. The increase in overall enrollment was significant and was driven by the higher enrollment in private colleges.[28] However, despite the increase in student enrollment, the number of graduates from private universities is very similar to the number of graduates from public universities, meaning that the dropout rate from private institutions is high. The problem is not only access to education but also quality of education.

The Continental Educational Corporation is comprised of a higher technological institute and a university. It began in 1983 with a computing and technical college. The aim of the corporation was to have an impact and generate development in the region. The Continental University was established more recently, in 1998, and by 2015 it had a presence in Huancayo, Lima, Arequipa, and Cuzco.

The first Continental University campus was set up in the city of Huancayo, one of the principal cities of the Peruvian highlands. However, achieving success has been a challenge; the university opened in 1998 with a temporary operating license and was supervised for eight years until the authorities were satisfied.

---

[28]   INEI 2015.

From that point on, both the university and the Continental Educational Corporation have expanded, mirroring the economic growth in the Junin geographical region in which it is located. Junin is the site of the La Oroya mine and the largest smelting center in the country and is one of the most important mining areas in Peru. It is also the site of the El Mantaro and Malpaso hydroelectric dams, which are situated on the Mantaro River. Both agriculture and animal husbandry are important in Junin, with the export of potatoes making up 46% of total regional agricultural exports, according to PromPerú.

The intention of the Continental Educational Corporation with respect to higher education in Peru is to offer a quality, affordable education in an environment where young people not only seek to be employees but also entrepreneurs. The founding president, Fernando Barrios, believes that one of the unique features of the institution, as well as one of the keys to its success, is that it has become increasingly entrepreneurial and has found a model that combines both the business and academic fields. Nevertheless, this is an educational and management design that requires a lot of commitment. "Our target market suffers not only economic difficulties but also from poor-quality education and psycho-emotional issues. The sector D student who aspires to the emerging C group is unlikely to have had the benefit of a good education. For young people (those between sixteen and seventeen) the socioemotional area is involved as they are unclear for example about what they want to study. They might have family issues, and come from marginalized and vulnerable communities," explained Barrios, when referring to the quality of education offered at their institutions.

This model of student success initially begins by motivating the students in the classrooms. When working toward a defined model, the objective is to make an early impact at the school and on the parents, to inform them of the offer and generate loyalty through lived experiences. This objective is the epicenter of various activities such as talent contests, leadership competitions, and scholarships in entrepreneurship and innovation offered to 9th-grade students (14–15 years old). The students identify their objectives and understand that they will need good grades to enter the university. "The formula is to actively seek out students who want to access all these resources," says Barrios.

The organization has also developed a model based on predictive analysis. The model is completely analytical and uses an information-based system: It consists of carrying out an economic, academic, and psycho-emotional study to identify and prevent student dropout. In this way, by having a personalized analysis of each student, an individualized study plan can be drawn up to be followed not only by the student him/herself but also by the teachers, professors, and tutors involved in their growth and development. The institution is committed to the success of the student, ensuring that those who enter the system learn, finish their studies within the time anticipated, and go on to subsequently enter the labor market.

In this way, such factors as motivation and predictive analysis, combined with the teaching method that concentrates on competencies and emphasizes learning achievements, mean that the methodology is unique and "embedded in society," according to Barrios.

By the year 2015, the university offered 25 different professional degrees and had 18,000 students, with 56% of the students studying engineering. The high proportion of students enrolled in engineering programs resulted from the school focusing on developing competitive courses linked to the production requirements of the region. The university has four international accreditations that have been awarded by the International Evaluators Network (RIEV) and the National Accreditation Council of the Republic of Colombia, and is the first university accredited in Peru by the European National Agency for Evaluation and Accreditation (ANECA).

Interamerican Development University (UNID), Mexico. From 2005 to 2012, the sector of the population 25–34 years old that completed secondary education had grown by 8 percentage points, from 38% to 46%. The OECD average however, is 83%, and although Mexico is widening enrollment to include those between the age of fifteen and nineteen, this measure is still not enough. The percentage of students as a proportion of the population in this age range grew from 48% to 54% between 2005 and 2013. Despite this, in 2013 Mexico was one of only two countries in the OECD where fewer than 60% of young people between fifteen and nineteen years old were enrolled in formal educational programs.[29] Such low enrollment has a direct effect on the chances young people have of obtaining employment.

From primary to tertiary level, spending on education in Mexico as a proportion of GDP rose from 4.4% in 2000 to 5.2% in 2012, which coincides with education spending in other OECD countries. In 2012, Mexico invested 3.9% of GDP in primary and secondary institutions and 1.3% of GDP in tertiary institutions, just below the OECD average of 1.5%. At the tertiary level, total spending by Mexico rose by 35% during the same period, slightly more than the increase in enrollment, which indicated a small increase in the spending per student. In this way, the spending per tertiary student in Mexico for all services – including R&D activities – was approximately three times greater than the spending per student at the primary level.

Currently, however, only one in five people between the ages of twenty-five and sixty-four has a university degree. The current expectation is that 38% of young people will be able to go to college, approximately 4% of young people in Mexico will obtain a Master's degree, and fewer than 1% will complete a Doctorate. In 2013, 44% of students graduated with social science degrees, while 22% graduated from engineering disciplines.[30]

The Interamerican Development University was the result of an innovative proposal for higher education in Mexico. The objective of the institution was to address the needs of the labor market in the country,[31] and the model that inspired the foundation of the university was a combination of those referred to as "non-traditional models" in Europe, the United States, and Canada. The proposed

[29]   OECD 2015a.   [30]   OECD 2015a.   [31]   UNID 2016.

model of higher education, rooted in these "non-traditional models," consisted of two years of intensive formation in the areas most associated with the requirements of the industry, and one additional year to obtain the degree. In the words of the UNID Director Carlos Güereca, UNID seeks to produce graduates with a strong grounding in three essential elements: leadership, values, and intensive use of technology.[32]

The aim of the UNID educational model is to offer a well-rounded education capable of responding to today's requirements for innovation and efficiency, which simultaneously reinforces the relationship between the education and production sectors. The intention is to contribute to the economic and social development of the country and ease the transition between the world of education and the world of work. The importance of values-driven education, which includes the teaching of corporate social responsibility, is, according to the rector, one of the unique aspects of UNID. The belief is that the educational experience needs to impact all aspects of the student's life, personal or professional, in addition to developing social responsibility, communication, and values. In the same way, the institution is notable for the constant entrepreneurial and interdisciplinary dialogue that takes place between students during their education. The organization promotes professional leadership, familiarizing students with the process of making decisions that reflect the fundamental values and requirements of society.

The study program features courses designed to improve skills in the areas of communication and humanities, and students also have the opportunity to participate in many social-action projects. A few of the associations and activities in which UNID students have participated are Telethon, Daydreaming A.C., Youth Missions, visits to orphanages and refuges, and donating to disaster funds, among others. In this way, students are sensitized to the needs of others and develop a commitment to their society as a whole and their

[32]   Zacateks 2013.

community in particular. As the rector states, education transforms the lives of the students not only because it permits them to have access to new opportunities derived from the skills and learning that allow their successful insertion into the labor market, but also because it "transforms families, transforms communities and will eventually change Mexico."

"The idea is to facilitate rapid integration into the labor market in two main ways: optimizing time so that the student can obtain their university title in two years and their degree in three. To this end, as part of the study plan, the student will undertake a work experience placement for one whole semester organized with the help of the work center."[33] According to information supplied by the rector, this professional experience is undertaken one year before graduation and is designed to facilitate a rapid incorporation of the student into the labor force. In this way, during the last year of their studies, 45% of the students combine studying with working in the business where they undertook their work experience, and 85% finish their education with a job already lined up.[34]

To respond quickly and easily to the needs of those mature students who work but also wish to continue their studies, UNID has created a sister organization, UNID Virtual, which offers twelve programs that are 100% online by way of a digital platform. UNID Virtual offers students the flexibility to administer and organize their time effectively according to their needs and responsibilities; they can learn at their own pace and are not limited by the obligation to use a physical space.

From the UNID President: "Mexico faces significant challenges regarding education. University education for various reasons is a possibility for only 30% of young people in Mexico, one of them being geographic accessibility. By 2021, seven million young people will unable to study due to lack of university places. But the biggest challenge facing education in Mexico is paying urgent attention to

[33]   Zepulveda 2010.   [34]   Pacheco 2016.

the human qualities. We need to define the base and the standard which will measure the human qualities of a professional and educate them in ethics and values so they can effectively respond to those timeless questions asked by people: Who am I? Where do I come from? Where am I going?"[35]

UNITEC University Corporation, Colombia. In Colombia, higher levels of education give access to better employment opportunities. Among employed adults in 2013, statistics showed that those with a tertiary education in Colombia made more than twice as much (134% more) than those who only had a secondary education, compared with 60% more on average in OECD countries.[36]

Education is therefore extremely important, with two-thirds (67%) of the young adults (those 25–34 years old) in Colombia having completed a secondary-level education by 2014. Colombia is more advanced in this regard when compared to other Latin American countries except Chile, Costa Rica, México, and Brazil, but the educational level of young people still continues to be a figure below the OECD average of 83%. Nevertheless, 28% of young adults in Colombia completed higher education in 2014, which is the highest value for all the countries in Latin America.[37]

The UNITEC University Corporation is a Colombian higher-education institution located in the city of Bogota.[38] In 1977, a group of professionals directed by the founder of the organization, Dr. Diógenes Parra Walters, began putting together a feasibility project with the aim of opening an educational institution offering innovative educational programs. The goal was to respond to the educational and training needs of the moment, and to incorporate the heretofore most marginalized young people into the higher education system. The courses offered consisted of majors in Computers and Systems, Hotel Administration, Textile Design, and Marketing. Subsequently, in 1979, courses in Airline and Travel

---

[35]   Zenit 2016.   [36]   OECD 2015b.   [37]   OECD 2015b.
[38]   UNITEC 2016.

Agency Administration and Visual Arts and Cinematographic Sciences were added.

The maintenance and consolidation of academic programs in the technical area offered by the institution during its first thirteen years of operation permitted it to narrow its focus and thereby strengthen its educational mission, ultimately positioning UNITEC at the forefront of the productive sector and the community in general. As a result, at the end of 1992 the Colombian Institute for the Promotion of Higher Education (ICFES) authorized the corporation to offer programs in the professional technical field. By the end of 1995, three new majors had been created, with the wider range of programs broadening the appeal of the university. Those programs were: Financial Administration and International Business, Commerce and Financial Administration, and Design and Graphic Production. The corporation subsequently registered two further programs in the technological area, Telecommunications and Publicity, along with two more in the professional area, Cinema and Television. In 2002, UNITEC received recognition as a university from the Colombian National Education Ministry.

The pedagogical concept behind the model draws on theories of the cognitive approach that emphasize the dynamic nature of the student. It stresses the importance of both individual and teamwork and recognizes autonomy, self-discipline, and research as well as the transformational role of students and pedagogues in the process of teaching and learning. This model fosters education and learning in which research plays an important role in both academic courses and practical training; and helps develop the ability to discover, investigate, and problem-solve issues integral to the discipline. Observation and reading about theoretical, personal, labor, and sociocultural issues are encouraged, as is the development of competencies that permit the student to form hypotheses and interpret and propose solutions to problems in context.

In its projection for 2020, the UNITEC University Corporation plans to be recognized as the institution making the most significant

contribution to the generation, transfer, and advancement of understanding, as well as for the quality of its processes and its groundbreaking educational methodology. UNITEC also pursues other goals,
such as the strength of its academic offerings at both the undergraduate and postgraduate levels, including in-person, distance, and virtual
learning options. Consolidation of the university campus is also
necessary, as is the broadening of participation in providing solutions
to real-world problems, commitment to continuous process-
improvement, interaction with the world of business, and permanent
and efficient links with international projects.

The UNITEC University Corporation operates on the principle
that education is public and has as its ultimate goal the development
of the individual potential of all those who participate in its social
programs. From this foundation, the final objective is to form leaders
and entrepreneurs with intelligence and critical thinking skills who
are able, from an independent, reflective, and ethical position, to
promote development and contribute to improving the social, economic, and cultural environment. With this in mind, the educational
project seeks to stimulate the intellectual, creative, and social capabilities of those in its educational community, helping them to
become recognized as important members of the international learning community.

In 2015, UNITEC offered twenty-five academic programs
approved by the Ministry of Education in the technical, professional,
and specialization fields, and had more than 3,500 students. This
educational project is geared toward producing well-rounded undergraduates through focusing on leadership and entrepreneurship. It
currently has nine campuses in the city of Bogota.

Maria Cano University Foundation, Colombia. The Maria
Cano University Foundation (FUMC) is a higher education institution
founded in 1987 in the town of Medellin. It was inspired by Maria de
Los Ángeles Cano Márquez, the first female leader of Colombia, and
set up by a group of academics and intellectuals with the objective of
offering educational programs of quality, relevance, and social impact.

The first program was Speech Therapy, followed by Occupational Therapy in 1988.

"The founders come from different sectors but are members of another institution, the Columbian Cooperative University, focusing on social solidarity and improvement. The two universities share these guiding values and have a very close relationship," according to the director of the Center for Business Research and Development at FUMC, Nelson Alberto Rúa Ceballos. "One of the studies that was carried out at the national level in Colombia was focused on examining the reasons behind the dropout rate in education. The national rate in the region is 50%, although the dropout rate in Medellin is only 28%; nevertheless, the FUMC has been able to improve on this figure and has a dropout rate of 13% or even less in some programs. That percentage is our current benchmark and the studies that we are currently undertaking will help us to improve even more. Educational dropout impacts students and their families because without education, it is not possible for people to achieve upward mobility in the labor market."

The first success that the organization had was in ensuring that the students who were enrolled completed their studies. During 2016, a study was run with the aim of getting to know the students and understanding the reasons why they might choose to abandon their education. It is anticipated that the information yielded by the study will help develop creative and innovative strategies that might have a stronger impact on dropout rates than those currently employed. To achieve this goal, FUMC will develop a program enabling the institution to work in close partnership with students, which it hopes will serve as an example to other institutions in Colombia.

A second factor behind the success of FUMC is the pedagogy employed, which is a German method for incentivizing students to develop competencies and motivation for learning. The goal is that the student will research and discover the information necessary to continue the learning process for themselves. The method helps to develop competencies in the student, with additional learning activities (classroom research, work experience, etc.) completing the process. In this regard, "a developmental process is designed based on the interests of the student, with an investigative focus that provides the opportunity for formational research. Our methodology provides a link with entrepreneurship, thus providing a unique focus," indicates Rúa Ceballos.

The third success factor is improved access to the programs. To achieve this, the university set up a broad range of affordable payment options to ensure that no student is unable to continue with the program due to economic difficulties. The competitive prices and the participation of organizations offering financial assistance, whether entirely free or through deferred payment, ensure the success of the program.

Regarding employment conditions at the university, professors enjoy both personal and salary benefits. In 2015, with the approval of the Teacher's Statute, further decisive advantages in the compensation package offered to teaching staff were added. According to Rúa Ceballos: "The institution provides a lot of support for different programs, for example for participation in seminars, conferences, etc. As an example, we accept 98%–99% of the proposals submitted by professors who wish to participate in these activities."

The university is also working on a study to determine the impact of the FUMC graduates on society, partly as a result of the Ministry of Education Observatory asking for the grading requirements for the programs. "It is important to know the final product; although the study began over a year ago and we still don't have the results, it does allow us to understand the wider environment and how the programs are responding to the needs of society. It makes it possible to have the information necessary to improve the academic programs," says Rúa Ceballos.

Presently, FUMC offers several programs in three faculties. The Faculty of Health Sciences offers Speech Therapy, Psychology, and Physiotherapy; the Faculty of Business Sciences specializes in Public Accounting, International Business, and Business Administration; and the Faculty of Engineering offers Systems Engineering, Software, and Robotic Automation. Additionally, the university has opened branches in the cities of Cali, Popayán, and Neiva, which offer the physiotherapy program and specializations by both distance and virtual learning.

With more than 4,500 current students and more than 12,000 graduates to date, the institution has a direct impact on its community, its city, and also the country as a whole. It also turns out outstanding professionals in the disciplines of physiotherapy and speech therapy, specialties not developed until the 1980s that are now the "standout" disciplines of the institution.

GUIDELINES FOR CREATING EDUCATION FOR EVERYONE

The growth of the middle class in Latin America goes hand-in-hand with the rise in the level of teaching. The increase in investment in education and the decrease in the dropout rate indicate an overall improvement but are not sufficient in themselves to guarantee continued improvement. These indicators reflect the demands of an increasingly competitive society and the new Latin American middle class. There is a desire for better education at each and every level, along with a requirement for increased graduate employability, well-paid employment, and opportunities for advancement.

Before the growth of the middle class in Latin America, public education could not keep pace with the needs of a more prosperous society. The reasons for the lack of sufficient higher education programs may vary, but among those worth mentioning are the low educational level and social status of education professionals, outdated educational systems, and limited state involvement.

These six cases show that it is possible to offer quality academic services to the population sector that is demanding them. They also demonstrate the strength of the innovation process, which has enabled the expansion and consolidation of the educational market in diverse countries. From these cases, we conclude that:

- The high student desertion rate in the lower levels of education (primary and secondary) as well as the low access to tertiary education (university and technical) are significant issues. This has an influence on the training of young people for acquiring their first job, increasing the number of "neets." For that reason, the challenge is how to ensure the incorporation of the most vulnerable young communities into work or student life.
- A high-quality secondary education should be guaranteed, one that subsequently provides access to tertiary education.
- Due to the absence of the State, each country lacks an education of homogeneous quality, generating different academic levels that are insufficient for obtaining access to a higher or post-secondary education.
- The state should recognize and qualify the different educational institutions, thus guaranteeing the monitoring and verification of processes so as to ensure a quality education for everyone.
- The state should participate in the formation of a quality teaching staff, with decent remuneration that provides teachers the status they require and thus attracts the best profiles.
- There is an increase in the demand for quality education and positive growth projections, reflected by the increase in enrollment by the MoP. This ensures a return on investment for those private institutions that want to offer an affordable and quality education.

Therefore, the following actions have been developed to design the new education models and management structures in the cases analyzed:

- The analysis of current needs and characteristics of the MoP in order to design the methodologies and the approach to the market aligned to these needs.
- Innovative teaching methodologies, with international education standards focused on obtaining identifiable results in the development of the child.
- Recognition of the need to select, train, motivate, and develop the teaching faculty, who are the ones responsible for "making it happen."
- The widespread availability of digital information and accessibility to information that can assist in the practical implementation of education programs or "learning by doing."

- The design of a pricing system consistent with the middle class. This system takes into account the ability to pay and is also backed up by a system of deferred payment and scholarships according to financial necessity.

- The analysis of current needs of the labor market and the adaptation of educational programs to these needs in order that current labor market demands can be met.

- A needs-analysis identifying the strengths and weaknesses of the student and offering a personalized study program that addresses both academic demands and family circumstances (night classes, family problems, etc.) and that offers financial backup if necessary.

Today in Latin America, access to higher education is imperative in order to address the need for skilled and specialized human resources capable of fulfilling human capital requirements and improving competitiveness as well as ensuring that social problems do not increase. The states should consider their important roles in terms of defining a long-term and medium-term plan of national educational development in each country. This national plan should incorporate the normalization and accreditation of the institutions as well as the professor's standards and the implementation of new technology appropriate to the community.

"The lack of access to education is guaranteed to provide continuing social inequality, generating exclusion and lower political participation and citizen interaction with existing institutions. The result is, logically, the continuation of the poverty cycle, an increase in labor and social conflicts and an ongoing problem of local unemployment and underemployment; all of which encourage crime and keep mortality and marginalization high."[39]

In sum, an education for everyone guarantees social, economic, and political progress in Latin America, resulting in a better quality of life for its inhabitants.

[39]   Aponte-Hernández 2008.

REFERENCES

Aponte-Hernández, E. 2008. Desigualdad, inclusión y equidad en la Educación Superior en América Latina y El Caribe: tendencias y escenario alternativo en el horizonte 2021. In A. L. Gazzola & A. Didriksson (eds.), *Tendencias de la Educación Superior en América Latina y el Caribe*: 114–154. Caracas: Instituto Internacional de la UNESCO para la Educación Superior en América Latina y el Caribe.

Banco Mundial. 2016. Datos: índice Gini. *Banco Mundial*. Accessed March 14, 2016. http://datos.bancomundial.org/indicador/SI.POV.GINI/countries?display= default

Bentaouet Kattan, R. & Székely, M. 2015. *Analyzing the Dynamics of School Dropout in Upper Secondary Education in Latin America: A Cohort Approach.* Washington, DC: World Bank.

Birdsall, N. M., Campos, J. E., Kim, C., Corden, W. M., MacDonald, L., Pack, H., Page, J., Sabor, R. & Stiglitz, J. E. 1993. The East Asian Miracle: Economic Growth and Public Policy. Main report. A World Bank policy research report. New York: Oxford University Press.

Brandt, Y. 2015. Education: The Most Powerful Investment in Our Future. *UNICEF*. Accessed February 22, 2017. https://blogs.unicef.org/blog/education-the-most-powerful-investment-in-our-future

CEPAL. 2012. Informe regional de población en América Latina y el Caribe 2011: invertir en juventud. *CEPAL*. Accessed December 13, 2015. www.cepal.org/es/publicaciones/3130-informe-regional-de-poblacion-en-america-latina-y-el-caribe-2011-invertir-en

CEPAL. 2014. CEPAL publica estimaciones de las paridades de poder adquisitivo de los países de la región. *CEPAL*. Accessed February 14, 2016. www.cepal.org/es/noticias/cepal-publica-estimaciones-de-las-paridades-de-poder-adquisitivo-de-los-paises-de-la-region

Didriksson, A. 2008. Contexto global y regional de la Educación Superior en América Latina y El Caribe. In A. L. Gazzola & A. Didriksson (eds.), *Tendencias de la Educación Superior en América Latina y el Caribe*: 21–54. Caracas: Instituto Internacional de la UNESCO para la Educación Superior en América Latina y el Caribe.

Ferreyra, M., Avitabile, C., Botero Álvarez, J., Haimovich F., & Urzúa, S. 2017. *At a Crossroads: Higher Education in Latin America and the Caribbean. Directions in Development – Human Development.* Washington, DC: World Bank.

Jabonero, M. 2014. Educación, crecimiento y desarrollo en América Latina. *El País*. Accessed May 29, 2016. http://internacional.elpais.com/internacional/2014/09/04/actualidad/1409864542_745677.html

INEI. 2015. Educación Universitaria. Instituto Nacional de Estadística e Informática. Accessed February 2, 2016. http://m.inei.gob.pe/estadisticas/indice-tematico/university-tuition

Lancho, R. 2016. 'El reto más grande de la educación en México es poner una atención urgente a la calidad humana'. *ZENIT*. Accessed May 19, 2016. https://es.zenit.org/articles/el-reto-mas-grande-de-la-educacion-en-mexico-es-poner-una-atencion-urgente-a-la-calidad-humana

OCDE. 2009. Programa para la Evaluación Internacional de los Alumnos OCDE. Informe Español. *MECD*. Accessed February 16, 2016. www.mecd.gob.es/dctm/ievaluacion/internacional/pisa-2009-con-escudo.pdf?documentId=0901e72b808ee4fd

OECD. 2014. Educación, competencias e innovación para una América Latina más dinámica e inclusiva. In OECD (eds.), *Perspectivas económicas de América Latina 2015: Educación, competencias e innovación para el desarrollo*. Paris: OECD Publishing: 17–28.

OECD. 2015a. Mexico. In OECD Indicators (eds.), *Education at a Glance 2015*. Paris: OECD Publishing.

OECD. 2015b. Colombia. In OECD Indicators (eds.), *Education at a Glance 2015*. Paris: OECD Publishing.

OEI. 2014a. Mirada sobre la educación en Iberoamérica: Avances en las metas educativas 2021. *OEI*. Accessed November 28, 2015. http://oei.es/xxivcie/Miradas2014Web.pdf

OEI. 2014b. Mirada sobre la educación en Iberoamérica: Avances en las metas educativas 2021. *OEI*. Accessed February 4, 2016. http://oei.es/xxivcie/Miradas2014Web.pdf

Pacheco, R. 2016. Entrevista con Rodrigo Pacheco – Grupo Imagen. *Grupo IMAGEN*. Accessed February 12, 2016. http://carlosguereca.com/entrevista-con-rodrigo-pacheco-grupo-imagen/?utm_content=bufferaf070&utm_medium=social&utm_source=twitter.com&utm_campaign=buffer

Penfold, M. & Trinkunas, H. 2015. Prospects for Latin America's Middle Class after the Commodity Boom. Brookings. Accessed August 10, 2017. www.oei.es/quipu/Informe_preal2006.pdf

Programa de Promoción de la Reforma Educativa en América Latina y el Caribe. 2005. 2006: Cantidad sin calidad: Un informe del progreso educativo en América Latina. *OEI*. Accessed March 10, 2016. www.oei.es/quipu/Informe_preal2006.pdf

Regalado-Pezúa, O. 2013. Brechas en la educación superior en turismo en el Perú. *Oikos* 33: 79–96.

Regeneración. 2017. Este año 131 mil 589 jóvenes rechazados de la UNAM. Accessed August 22, 2017. http://regeneracion.mx/este-ano-131-mil-589-jovenes-rechazados-de-la-unam

Reimers, F. 1999. Education and Poverty in Latin America Can Schools Make Any Difference? *DRCLAS*. Accessed February 22, 2017. http://revista.drclas.harvard .edu/files/revista/files/education_in_latin_america.pdf?m=1437076654

UNESCO. 2016. Education: Expenditure by Level of Education as % of Total Government Expenditure on Education. *UNESCO*. Accessed January 10th, 2016. http://data.uis.unesco.org/

UNID. 2016. *UNID*. Accessed March 22, 2016. http://unid.edu.mx

UNITEC. 2016. *UNITEC*. Accessed April 13, 2016. www.unitec.edu.co

Zacateks. 2013. Entrevista al Rector de la UNID Carlos Güereca. Youtube. Accessed March 11, 2016. www.youtube.com/watch?v=Uoedj0I5STM

ZENIT. 2016. Interview with Carlos Güereca, UNID. Accessed February 17, 2016. www.unitec.edu.co

Zepulveda, P. 2010. La incorporación de las tecnologías móviles en la formación profesional. *Educamericas*. www.educamericas.com/La-incorporacion-de-las-tec nologias-moviles-en-la-formacion-profesional

5 "My House, My Pride"
The Housing Problem in the Middle of the Pyramid

Lucía Rodríguez-Aceves, José Manuel
Saiz-Álvarez, Edgar Muñíz-Ávila,
and Mario Adrián Flores-Castro

INTRODUCTION

We used to live in a room of 4 by 4 square meters made of wood. When it rained, water leaked all over the beds. My two kids commonly got sick with respiratory infections due to humidity. It was really tough ... We had to choose between buying diapers, food or medicines ... Sometimes I could not sleep, and I wondered if our life was going to be always that way. After a few years, when we had saved some money, we bought a small piece of land, but it was too expensive for us to purchase the materials to build.

Francisca Garcia, a woman from San Cristobal in Mexico[1]

Traditional housing markets have largely ignored the Middle of the Pyramid (MoP), as formally built homes are too expensive, and mortgage financing is only available for the highest income segments of most countries' populations, mainly affecting the percentage of vulnerable people. In consequence, because of insufficient government resources to create solutions for the low-income housing needs, new approaches are needed to respond to the challenge, to think more broadly and creatively about ways to attend to all income groups and their changing needs. As a result, social entrepreneurs and companies such as housing developers, financial intermediaries, and suppliers of construction materials are working together with the families themselves to create innovative solutions for tailored products, services,

We sincerely wish to thank Henning Alts Shoutz, marketing CEO of *Patrimonio Hoy*, who kindly agreed to share his time and experience with us.
[1]   Testimonial from Francisca García, a beneficiary from the *Patrimonio Hoy* program in San Cristobal México.

119

and linkages to make improved housing affordable and accessible to low-income households. This situation is even worse for those at the Bottom of the Pyramid (BoP).

It is the purpose of this chapter to globally present the landscape of the poor housing challenge, with emphasis on middle-income countries located in Latin America and the Caribbean (LAC). After having introduced the situation via trends and statistics, three cases describe how the private sector can successfully address the housing challenge, based on innovative, inclusive, and social business models. The first case is the promising Viste tu Casa program, launched by Colcerámica in Colombia and sponsored by the Colombian multinational company Corona. Viste tu Casa is a pioneer program focusing on a step further in the housing value chain (aesthetics and hygiene). The second case is a well-known program, Patrimonio Hoy, encouraged by CEMEX Mexico and LATAM. Patrimonio Hoy leads the paradigm shift of companies providing housing for low-income families, instead of governments or not-for-profit organizations. The third case is a program launched in Mexico by Francesco Piazzesi and is called Échale a tu casa. This program adds value to rural housing by improving the quality of life through the use of ecologically friendly facilities, such as bio digesters and solar water heaters. Finally, based on a discussion of similarities and differences among these cases, six lessons are identified that inform solutions to solve the poor housing challenge: (1) solutions rooted in a deep understanding of market needs through systematic and soundly designed ethnographic methods; (2) innovations adapted to flexible and adjustable models applied in low-income markets; (3) programs including the commitment of the company; (4) confidence with adaptive learning to promote the company; (5) inclusive and social models in other industries to replicate them in other sectors, areas, and parts of the supply chain; and (6) these policies complement quadruple helix economic development schemes defined by the use of strategic alliances among firms, academic institutions, NGOs, and community leaders.

POOR HOUSING: CHALLENGES AND OPPORTUNITIES

Living conditions affect all aspects of human development. For example, inadequate housing conditions such as overcrowding, lack of electricity, poor wastewater treatment, indoor air pollution, and lack of sewage and sanitation facilities substantially increase the probabilities of contracting respiratory illnesses.[2] For most people in emerging economies, to have an adequate shelter is a challenging and painful process. Today, 1.6 billion people live in inadequate housing (one that harms their health, safety, prosperity, and opportunities) around the world, representing almost 20% of the population. In addition, more than 100 million people worldwide are homeless.

The macro trend of rapid urbanization, with millions of people migrating from rural areas to cities (looking for a better life), has created immense challenges for cities. A billion people – 32% of the global urban population – live in urban slums. In fact, based on current trends in urban migration and income growth, it is estimated that by 2025, about 440 million urban households around the world will occupy crowded, inadequate, and unsafe housing or will be financially stretched.[3] If no serious action is taken, the United Nations reports that the number of slum dwellers worldwide will increase over the next thirty years to nearly 2 billion. This housing problem is most intense in emerging countries, for example in India, where 15% of urban slums and 11% of rural housing lack water, latrine, and electricity within the home. According to the World Health Organization (WHO), worldwide, one in three people does not have access to safe drinking water, two in five do not have a basic facility for washing hands with soap and water, and more than 673 million people still defecate in the free air.[4] The Water and Sanitation Program (WSP) of the World Bank has tried to solve (or at least reduce) this problem by increasing the availability of

[2]   Bessarabova 2014.   [3]   Dobbs, Manyika, & Woetzel 2015.
[4]   United Nations SDG 2020.

functioning latrines, sanitation products, and latrine product attributes (e.g., perceptions of cleanliness and durability).[5]

Regarding the LAC countries, housing is the most extensive category of MoP household spending after food. The size of the region's MoP real estate market is estimated at USD 184 billion PPP,[6] and current investment is valued at approximately USD 60 billion annually. The region is the most urbanized in the developing world, with roughly 80% of its population currently living in cities.[7]

The lack of housing is one of the leading challenges in LAC, especially for vulnerable people, whose percentage is detailed and compared among countries in Table 5.1. However, poor quality construction is the most relevant. Almost 40% of families in the region live in a house beyond repair and have no land-title, water, sewerage, electricity, adequate space, or building materials.[8] In Table 5.2 we compare the percentage of households with access to improved sanitation facilities in LAC countries, with Paraguay, Guatemala, and El Salvador being the most affected.

Brazil has an 8 million home deficit that affects 28.5 million people, with the São Paulo State having the highest housing deficit (1.48 million houses), 50% of which is concentrated in small towns.[9] Colombia reports a total deficit affecting approximately 35% of all households (68% are considered to be MoP), while Peru and Nicaragua have rates of about 75%.

The lack of affordable housing is also a severe problem for low-income families in Mexico. Insufficient access to financing and materials, along with a lack of technical skills, preclude low-income families from living in safe and adequate conditions. In 2006, Mexico had one of the worst housing shortages in the world, with a need for 1.5 million new homes annually, and another 3.7 million existing units that are estimated to be inadequate. In 2015, the housing deficit was about 8.9 million homes. Moreover, 18% of the population live in a

---

[5]   O'Connell 2014.   [6]   Azevedo et al. 2015.   [7]   Bouillon 2012.
[8]   Stickney 2014.   [9]   BambooFinance 2014.

Table 5.1 *Percentage of vulnerable people*

	2010	2011	2012	2013	2014	2015	2016
Argentina	35.283	30.639	26.778	22.646	22.038	17.451	18.348
Bolivia	ND	40.118	37.374	38.02	38.644	38.417	38.36*
Brazil	ND	38.73	38.482	38.396	38.479	39.073	38.649*
Chile	ND	40.156	ND	36.12	ND	38.119	37.119*
Colombia	34.492	36.168	35.987	36.472	37.278	37.478	38.793
Costa Rica	39.333	35.446	35.941	37.07	34.821	36.631	35.721
Dominican Republic	38.355	39.602	41.616	40.778	41.036	41.892	40.54
Ecuador	38.176	39.627	40.687	41.585	43.567	42.341	43.548
Guatemala	22.011	24.068	28.957	31.346	30.072	31.956	31.5
Honduras	27.88	26.12	25.027	27.184	30.922	ND	ND
Jamaica	21.675	ND	20.619	ND	ND	ND	ND
Mexico	39.179	ND	39.33	ND	40.809	ND	ND
Nicaragua	31.275	33.331	36.668	ND	35.725	ND	ND
Panama	34.828	37.045	33.722	34.068	32.748	30.79	ND
Peru	38.405	41.497	41.298	41.81	42.221	43.814	41.679
Paraguay	38.482	36.833	38.209	38.282	38.023	38.647	38.317*
El Salvador	37.595	39.206	41.147	42.555	42.63	45.062	43.415*
Uruguay	34.522	30.842	29.454	28.197	26.429	25.806	26.028*
Venezuela	45.523	45.182	42.074	42.947	44.207	45.484	44.212*

Source: Own elaboration based on data from the Inter-American Development Bank

Notes. * estimated. ND "No data available"

Table 5.2 *Percentage of households with access to improved sanitation facilities*

	2010	2011	2012	2013	2014	2015	2016
Argentina	89.175	90.39	91.827	91.299	90.648	90.774	91.428
Bolivia	ND	57.677	59.938	61.2	58.719	56.313	58.744*
Brazil	ND	76.959	77.674	75.966	72.873	80.502	76.447*
Chile	ND	94.936	ND	95.552	ND	96.527	96.039*
Colombia	89.391	89.975	90.455	91.762	91.365	92.313	92.442
Costa Rica	96.707	96.729	97.277	97.275	98.211	97.865	97.842
Dominican Republic	68.156	68.962	69.641	70.791	73.077	75.115	76.225
Ecuador	82.308	82.249	84.998	85.332	88.521	89.534	89.437
Guatemala	48.99	52.657	53.678	54.173	56.96	56.047	57.395
Honduras	51.056	52.697	51.211	52.699	57.582	ND	ND
Mexico	88.717	ND	91.081	ND	92.359	ND	ND
Nicaragua	ND	ND	ND	ND	36.953	ND	ND
Panama	ND	ND	ND	ND	70.053	72.11	ND
Peru	77.026	77.02	77.423	77.833	77.749	77.633	78.688
Paraguay	42.501	43.044	47.347	49.812	55.75	55.075	53.545*
El Salvador	51.491	51.757	53.596	53.147	53.609	54.532	53.762*
Uruguay	91.797	92.801	94.079	94.428	94.742	95.453	95.856*
Venezuela	92.866	93.274	93.858	94.089	93.823	95.702	94.538*

Source: Own elaboration based on data from the Inter-American Development Bank
Notes: * estimated, ND "No data available"

house owned by a relative, 20% rent, 1% own their home but in an informal settlement, and only 3% are paying a mortgage. In LAC the average density, calculated by the number of members per room as a proxy for crowding (see Table 5.3), is one of the main housing problems existing on the continent, with Guatemala, El Salvador, Nicaragua, and Bolivia having the highest average density.

It is noteworthy that in the LAC region, self-builders – a traditional private-based initiative to solve the housing shortage – account for nearly 60% of the total housing construction market. Even though low-income families are estimated to spend 30% of their incomes on building or improving their homes, about 80% of the population does not have a formal contractual property title, and hardly any have the technical skills to properly design and estimate the cost of a project, select the right materials, and use them appropriately. Regardless of the aggregated power of the low-income population, individual transactions are small, and incomes are low.

The size of the challenge is immense. Globally, to replace today's substandard housing and build the additional units needed by 2025, it would require an investment of USD 9 trillion to USD 11 trillion for construction; with the addition of land, the total cost could be USD 16 trillion. In LAC, only an investment of at least USD 310 billion will close the region's current housing gap.[10] Such a challenge requires a serious commitment from public funding and public policies.

In fact, officials in charge of designing and implementing national housing policies are in a rush to innovate their traditional approaches for attending to affordable housing. Brazil is using pragmatic public–private partnerships involving three levels of government (federal, state, and local) to redevelop city land and create space for affordable accommodations in the center of São Paulo. Mexico succeeded in providing subsidies and is now re-calibrating its policies to promote better-located housing. Bolivia has managed

---

[10]   Stickney 2014.

Table 5.3 *Average density (number of members per room, proxy for crowding)*

	2010	2011	2012	2013	2014	2015	2016
Argentina	1.251	1.232	1.226	1.232	1.24	1.236	1.177
Bolivia	ND	1.882	1.808	1.713	1.88	1.797	1.796*
Brazil	ND	0.578	0.562	0.552	0.559	0.537	0.549*
Chile	ND	0.579	ND	0.61	ND	0.899	0.754*
Colombia	1.287	1.247	1.242	1.19	1.171	1.153	1.125
Costa Rica	0.782	0.769	0.749	0.745	0.728	0.736	0.731
Dominican Republic	1.197	1.155	1.158	1.152	1.081	1.096	1.063
Ecuador	1.402	1.322	1.255	1.349	1.387	1.344	1.319
Guatemala	2.876	3.007	2.68	2.678	2.474	2.41	2.518
Honduras	1.576	1.599	1.632	1.488	1.549	ND	ND
Mexico	1.212	ND	1.175	ND	1.156	ND	ND
Nicaragua	ND	ND	ND	ND	2.055	ND	ND
Panama	ND	ND	ND	ND	1.303	1.277	ND
Peru	1.497	1.457	1.417	1.399	1.376	1.385	1.372
Paraguay	1.611	1.489	1.549	1.497	1.452	1.436	1.461*
El Salvador	2.029	2.001	1.931	1.881	1.847	1.803	1.843*
Uruguay	0.898	0.888	0.908	0.902	0.881	0.88	0.882*
Venezuela	1.371	1.357	1.328	1.28	1.269	1.222	1.257*

Source: Own elaboration based on data from the Inter-American Development Bank

Notes: * estimated, ND "No data available"

to increase the supply of low-cost housing for the poor but is trying to leverage private sector support and keep prices reasonable. In Argentina, policymakers are eager to design and implement a modern housing policy right from the start. Peru is trying to figure out how to maximize the impact of significant investments in transportation infrastructure. Urbanization in Paraguay is dynamic, but still well below the regional average – giving authorities the opportunity to shape the future today.[11] As well as in the LAC countries, in emerging economies there is usually a correlation between outstanding mortgage to GDP and GDP per capita to explain why MoP is generally expulsed from the mortgage market, as MoP lack available housing, are expelled from financial instruments and institutions because of their low income, and are not inserted into mortgage market infrastructures.[12] As a result, it is difficult for MoP to find affordable housing.

Another issue affecting the poor housing challenge is the lack of access to financial resources. Low-income families do not necessarily receive regular paychecks or government subsidies or grants, nor do they have access to banks or credits. Instead, many of them rest on "ROSCAs," which is a global phenomenon occurring in rural and urban areas, also known as "tanda" in Mexico, "susu" in Ghana, and "chit funds" in India.[13] A ROSCA consists of a group of people who deposit a daily, weekly, or monthly fixed amount of money in a common pot that is allotted in part or whole to each participant in turn. The allocation of the fund is repeated on a set basis until all participants have received the kitty. In this way, the first receiver of the fund obtains a loan from all the other ROSCA participants, while the last receiver in the queue has been saving for the whole ROSCA cycle. Basically, and given the shortage of legal regulation,[14] the system works based on trust, reputation, and participation in the community while attracting investors when deposit and loan rates

[11]   Treviño 2016.   [12]   Khare 2016.   [13]   Smets 2000.
[14]   Wei & Lijuan 2011.

from formal banking systems are not favorable.[15] Participants who received the kitty in urban areas commonly used it for family emergencies or buying, constructing, or improving houses. It is noteworthy that ROSCAs operate in the informal financial sector, beyond official regulations and the control of the central bank.[16]

An example of a ROSCA is the case of Bahari Widows group, found in Kwanza Location in Kenya and established in 2004. It has fifteen members, all women, from thirty to ninety-seven years old. In the group, there are six officials: the chair, the vice chair, the treasurer, the vice-treasurer, the secretary, and the vice secretary. Mama Peres is the backbone and founder of the group, as she is the only person with a college education, and she is the main decision maker. The group is based in an agricultural community, and none of the members of this group are employed. They all depend on farming for their livelihoods. They contribute Kshs 60 (USD 0.7) every two weeks and utilize this money for farming and running a nursery school (Mbamaonyeukwu 2013).

Even though policymakers are doing their best, due to some needed resources the challenge can only be overcome with the involvement of the private sector to supply innovative and tailored solutions, as MoP have enough money to build, although generally low quality and small homes, while BoP cannot afford to build homes at all. In the next section, examples of a variety of solutions that have emerged are mentioned. In particular, three successful cases of companies committed to solving the poor housing challenge are described.

THE PRIVATE SECTOR AS SOURCE OF SOLUTIONS VIA INNOVATION

Despite the crowding-in effects generated as a result of state intervention through expansive fiscal policies linked to higher public

[15]   Ahn et al. 2016.
[16]   ROSCA has been mainly studied and applied in Africa, as in Ethiopia by Kedir & Ibrahim, 2011; in Cameroon by Etang, Fielding, & Knowles, 2011; in Uganda by Peterlechner, 2009; and in Egypt by El-Gamal, El-Komi, Karlan, & Osman, 2014.

spending, it is necessary for public–private collaboration schemes to foster housing growth for MoP. Factors driving the involvement of the private market into the home construction industry are economic stability, the increase of credit availability, lower interest rates, expanded financing terms and payback periods, and contracts to encourage partnerships between banks and construction companies. In some regions, such as LAC, these factors have improved in recent years. Therefore, large corporations traditionally focused on high-income populations have recently created innovative strategies for the social housing market. For example, some companies have created subsidiaries to target low-income customers, and new businesses specializing in that income niche have emerged. In fact, four broad types of the private sector and innovative blended (public–private) business models have appeared to serve the MoP housing segment.

The first business model based on innovation is a micromort-gage, which combines microfinance credit instruments with government subsidies for the purchase of houses built by the private sector. This model is characterized by selling mortgages directly at developer sites, applying a multifaceted credit scoring and upfront savings scheme to reduce risk in lending to clients without formal credit histories, and state-of-the-art information systems and payment services at convenient locations.[17]

Second, the core house model combines direct government subsidy programs with medium-term unsecured loans for building new housing on land already owned by customers. The houses built fulfill government standards for low-income housing, including access to basic services such as water and sanitation. Additionally, their design facilitates rapid, low-cost assembly as well as future room additions. Finally, given their steady income streams and access to direct payroll deductions, this approach currently targets public employees.[18]

---

[17] Stickney 2014.   [18] Stickney 2014.

Third, the rent-to-own model does not rely on government subsidies but instead enables customers to build a credit history and save for a down payment by initially renting homes. Critical to this model is the supply of low-cost housing built by developers at certified standards of quality, including the provision of basic services and infrastructure. Also essential is the relationship with mortgage lenders committed to issuing mortgages once clients have met the necessary obligations upon completion of their rental period.[19] This business model is exemplified by the case "Échale a tu casa," which is explained in detail subsequently.

Finally, the home improvement model provides short-term unsecured loans to MoP families to incrementally build or improve their homes. Technical assistance, building materials of guaranteed quality at discounted prices, and access to qualified labor often accompany the loans. These additional services and connections commonly involve building alliances between financial institutions and construction companies, suppliers of materials, and other private sector entities.[20] Two examples where this business model applies are Colcerámica and Patrimonio Hoy, which are described subsequently.

Along with the innovative business models that have traditionally emerged to solve these housing-related problems, different opportunities for the private sector appear along the housing value chain to introduce new private and disrupting solutions based on innovation.[21] These new solutions will involve the following stages: (1) Help to secure land and tenure; (2) Assistance to ensure or improve services (water, sanitation, electricity, etc.); (3) Aid to access finance, subsidy, and savings; (4) Support to obtain or produce quality construction materials; (5) Design advice and building services; (6) Construction and technical assistance; and (7) Post-construction quality assurance and sales (i.e., fittings).

[19] Stickney 2014.   [20] Stickney 2014.   [21] Bessarabova 2014.

As previously stated, in the next paragraphs we explain three particular cases with a substantial impact in the LAC countries. All of them are involved in different stages of the housing value chain and have implemented innovative solutions to respond to the poor housing challenge. The first case is linked to Colombia, as the Colombian housing market after the 1999 financial crisis is an example of applying macroprudential measures, such as the use of loan-to-value limits, that limit the vulnerabilities stemming from the housing market. In this respect, Colombia actually has two restrictions: the loan-to-value ratio for a loan targeted toward the financing of Social Interest Housing (defined as a house or apartment whose value is below 135 monthly minimum wages) is 80%, and all other mortgage loans have a loan-to-value limit of 70%. In Colombia, the loan-to-value ratio is at 53%, below the regulatory ceiling.[22] As a result, the mortgage growth has decelerated, which has impacted housing prices, which can benefit MoP.

Colcerámica "Viste Tu Casa" (Colombia)

Colcerámica, a business unit of the Colombian Multinational Organization Corona, launched Viste tu Casa (in English, Furnish Your Home), a profitable business model through which the company sells its products at affordable prices to low-income customers who want to improve their homes and living conditions. It is helpful to present an overview of the business that created the program to contextualize its source.

Organización Corona S.A. was founded in 1881 and is based in Bogota, Colombia, with operations in the United States, South America, and China.[23] It is a family-owned group of companies with more than 125 years of experience, made up of 6 companies engaged in the manufacturing and marketing of products for the home improvement and construction industries. Today, Organización Corona has more than 13,000 employees, of which 90% are

[22] Roch 2017. [23] *Bloomberg Business* 2016.

Colombians.[24] It manufactures and sells tiles, porcelain products, and plumbing fixtures and offers floor and wall tiles, ceramic electric insulators, tableware, faucets, and raw materials for the production of ceramics. Currently, the company exports its products to more than thirty-two markets worldwide and has nineteen manufacturing plants, a supplier office in China, and a merchandising facility in Mexico. Colcerámica, the company responsible for creating and developing the program Viste tu Casa, is a business unit of Organización Corona dedicated to manufacturing and commercializing products that provide integrated solutions for bathrooms, kitchens, and floor and wall tiles for homes, offices, shops, and institutions. The business unit operates eight manufacturing plants in Colombia (Cundinamarca and Antioquia), the United States, Central America, and Brazil. Nevertheless, it was in the local market where Colcerámica identified an opportunity to create and test innovative business models to offer integral solutions for housing improvement in the segment of low-income families.

In 2006, Colcerámica identified the low-income communities (defined by earnings less than four monthly minimum legal wages, or about USD 1200 as a family; their living conditions rank among the lowest according to the SISBEN13 classification) as a particular niche with the potential to buy products that could improve the aesthetics and hygiene of their homes. These low-income communities can receive subsidies granted in Colombia by four institutions: (a) the National Housing Fund (FONVIVIENDA), a government agency serving families of workers in the informal sector; (b) the Family Welfare Agencies, serving families of workers in the formal sector; (c) the Military Housing Promotion Agency; and (d) the Public Agricultural Bank (Banco Agrario), operating in rural areas.[25] Complementary to this public program, Colcerámica differed from the other programs focused on serving low-income sectors regarding housing improvement. They started with a research process to deeply understand the

[24]   EMIS 2016.   [25]   Arbeláez, Camacho, & Fajardo 2011.

needs of this particular market segment. The findings suggested that the market wanted to have friendly financing, quality of life, trust, and closeness with the products and service providers. It is noteworthy that for this particular segment, financing, quality, warranty, and advising are more important than price.

In consequence, the executives of Colcerámica created a strategy to offer this market segment the possibility to improve their quality of life through an accessible financing program allowing customers to obtain a durable and trustable product, warranty, and support, both in the service and the brand. Also, deliveries were on time and complete, and the after-sales service was available immediately. Above all, during the purchasing process decision, clients received helpful tips on how to choose the most suitable products to create harmonious environments at home, and company executives tested the model for several months in different regions.

In 2007, the project started operating in Bogota, Cali, Medellin, Cartagena, and Barranquilla. In the beginning, the program was fully subsidized by Colcerámica. In addition, managers determined that people from the local communities should form the sales force where the products were offered. The main reason was the importance of creating close and trusting relationships with the customer segment. Consequently, female-headed households were the first candidates to be hired for the job. These women, or VC program advisors, received training regarding environment decoration, color combinations, materials, and textures, all to build harmonious spaces at the customers' homes. A sales method was created for women advisors to visit neighborhoods, always in big groups, to pique the interest of the families in the niche and often to bring a mobile center where customers could interact with the products that the company offered.

In 2008, the program was a proven commercial success. Also, it had a valuable social impact on thousands of families that received the benefits of VC. From 2007 to 2008, sales increased almost fivefold. In 2009, sales dropped 50%, and a change in the program was needed and imminent. Therefore, a consolidation process began, especially with the creation of a strategy to modify the financing system. At the beginning of the program, Colcerámica financed 100% of the sales with their credit, and the change consisted of inviting financial allies to lend money. Consequently, in 2010, approximately 40% of the sales were with Colcerámica credit, 10% in cash, and 50% were credit with third parties. This change allowed more than ten financial allies to join the program in order to diminish risks and to facilitate the operations. These economic partners are now in all the regions where the program is operating, and this fact accelerates sales. Nevertheless, Colcerámica decided to maintain a credit balance to have the advantages of both types of credit systems. First, profitability when giving their own credit, and second, fewer risks when third parties support loans.

Today, the program has seven service centers in the Colombian cities of Bogota, Cali, Barranquilla, and Cartagena. All of them are places where customers buy products and receive financing with small payments depending on their expenditure capacities. The purpose is to increase clients' accessibility and the number of families that can improve their houses step-by-step, without crashing their economies.

In sum, the business model for VC is to sell products directly to communities through a network of more than 200 female heads of household who are trained as salespersons. The wall and flooring materials are sold in small quantities and at affordable prices, and financing, as well as technical assistance, is provided. The attributes that differentiate the program from the competitors are the advisors' visits to customers' homes, the responsive and tailored financing, the close relationship with the community, the positioning of the brand in the segment, and the portfolio of products based on quality and variety. Surprisingly, VC does not compete with price.

To reach out to distant communities and to build its sales force, Colcerámica works with local organizations, schools, and foundations such as Corporación Kayrós. Alliances with Colombia-based complementary models, such as Promigas's Brilla, Empresas Públicas de

Medellín, and Codensa, have also contributed to VC's successful financing scheme.[26]

As stated by Mateo Camacho, Channel Sales Manager at VC, the program has been in place for more than seven years, and it has been a process of constant learning and improvement: "We have been working with the program more than seven years now... It has been an ongoing process of learning through trial and error because this is a new business model that has not yet been tested in the industry where we are specialists."

This learning process has been possible thanks to the support of shareholders and top management leaders. They showed at all times their commitment and support to VC, even though the team members in charge of creating and launching the program were not experts in financing or supporting communities. As evidence, the program was not initially profitable, but top managers were patient and decided to maintain the program anyway.

Several challenges were present in the beginning of the program. One of the most important was to find the right strategy to make it sustainable. Another was to identify the key factors that could facilitate the entrance to the market, since the lack of trust from the communities was hindering the implementation of the program. Challenges also existed inside the company. Corona-Colcerámica was good at selling large quantities of products to wholesalers, and internal processes were designed to do that. VC pushed the company to develop new methods (e.g., logistics, training) to sell directly to small customers, and consequently, it created important changes in the organization.

Regarding the impact of the program, VC has benefited 80,000 families throughout Colombia. Each year, more than 24,000 deliveries of Colcerámica products are made in the regions where the program operates. In 2007, incomes were near USD 1 million. From 2013 until 2015, the program generated annual sales of more than USD 5 million.

[26]   Stickney 2014.

Regarding job creation, 219 regular jobs were created in 2015, mostly for female heads of household, who have a salary, social benefits, and sales commissions. On average, this number has been similar in the three previous years. In addition, through social programs in the communities where VC operates, more than USD 600 million was donated to improve community places, schools, and parks.

One additional benefit for the company is the number of awards received because of its impact in the communities. For example, the company received the Sharing Value Award 2015, which was created by the Chamber of Commerce in Bogotá and is given to the companies that, aside from having a profitable business model, have improved the social, economic, and environmental conditions of the communities.

In the future, the company is expected to expand the program to more cities in the country, since there are a lot of families that need to improve their homes. At the same time, the company is willing to keep training women advisors to increase their capabilities and competencies and, therefore, satisfy customers.

CEMEX Patrimonio Hoy (Mexico). Patrimonio Hoy (PH; Spanish for Patrimony Today) is a subsidiary of the multinational Mexican cement manufacturer CEMEX. PH's purpose is to provide low-income families (e.g., with an income of USD 3–5 per day) with access to financing, building materials, technical expertise, and related services, allowing them to build or expand their homes more quickly and efficiently. This inclusive business model focuses on low-income families in urban and semi-urban areas. To provide context about the origin of the program, the next paragraphs include a short description of the company's background.

Cementos Mexicanos S.A. (CEMEX)

Cementos Mexicanos S.A. (CEMEX) was founded in 1930 as a result of the merging of two companies, Cementos Hidalgo, founded in 1906, and Cementos Portland Monterrey, founded in 1920. CEMEX provides high-quality products and reliable services to customers and communities throughout the Americas, Europe, Africa, the Middle East, and Asia. The company produces, distributes, and sells cement, ready-mix concrete, aggregates, and related building materials in more than 50 countries, and maintains trade relationships with more than 100 nations. CEMEX serves two main customer segments: the formal segment, which consists of traditional large-scale clients and middle- and upper-income individuals; and the informal segment, which consists of the do-it-yourself home builders and low-income customers. In 1994, an economic crisis severely impacted the Mexican economy, and, as expected, the construction industry was remarkably affected. Sales in the formal segment dropped by as much as 50%, whereas sales in the informal/self-construction segment only dropped between 10% and 20%.[27] The company realized that the high-level dependency on the formal sector left it vulnerable to business cycle swings in Mexico. This was the origin of the initiative to expand sales to the informal sector.

In 1996, CEMEX issued a "Declaration of Ignorance" about the market segment characteristics. As a result, the company performed in-depth market research to gain a better understanding of the low-income market in Mexico. In particular, CEMEX integrated a multi-disciplinary team and sent it to Mesa Colorada in Guadalajara, Mexico, a slum of the metropolitan area, to understand how low-income families lived and built their houses. Guadalajara was chosen because it has been considered a traditional test market in Mexico. The team lived in the community and studied the situation of the families for one and a half years, and the insights from the exercise allowed the company to become more innovative and creative. The research findings showed that the informal segment consumers required financing and close ties with sellers to build trust, and they were convenience-driven in the sense that price was not as important as credit and delivery. Also, the market had a very high growth

[27]   Letelier, Flores, & Spinosa 2003.

potential, demand was more or less steady, and there was a small revenue per customer.

Additional aspects were also considered in the integration of the program. For example, low-income families in Mexico commonly use "tandas" for family emergencies, education, and housing. In addition, women are the key drivers of savings in families. Also, they are responsible for managing expenses with the limited "allowance" they receive from the men, and they are very creative in allocating the money for all the necessities. Finally, regarding housing, low-income people in the city live in settlements made of raw cinder blocks, and in the worst cases they live in structures made of cardboard and corrugated sheet metal. Most houses are overcrowded, causing social problems including friction within the family and children taking to the streets.

Developing the program strategy required the program designers to overcome such challenges as building trust and convincing the poor that they would indeed be able to build a house with CEMEX. They also had to convince people that credit was not a barrier for the poor as part of PH. Finally, the team had to change their own mindset regarding the inclusion of the social objectives of the program and not only sales. In consequence, the three key areas of improvement/ change for CEMEX before launching PH were: (1) To identify ways to provide access to credit for the poor before selling cement; (2) to increase the brand perception of CEMEX as a responsive social company to earn trust; and, (3) to improve distribution methods and construction practices to make it cost-effective for CEMEX, distributors, and low-income customers.

In 1998, PH was launched as an innovative experiment that enabled impoverished people to pay for services and building materials to upgrade their homes. The program pursued profit and social responsiveness at CEMEX, and mainly tried to overcome the four biggest obstacles for low-income families when building their houses: lack of financing, lack of technical knowledge, lack of planning in terms of timing and budget, and, finally, lack of adequate storage spaces to maintain the purchased construction materials, which is an issue related to logistics and transport. PH organizes and facilitates the self-construction process through an integrated offer, enabling clients to build and pay approximately USD 700 for a 9m2 room, with weekly payments of USD 10 in a 70-week plan schedule.

Some of the PH success factors were: (1) the program was created based on an in-depth knowledge and understanding of low-income families' challenges and necessities when they are building their houses; (2) the CEMEX distribution network was critical to scale the scope of the program, because it generated demand and local economic activity; (3) the network of local promoters, comprised of women from the communities that spoke the same language as the customers, understood their necessities, so trust was naturally built; (4) financial sustainability was achieved, as the model promoted and encouraged family savings, which are key to acquiring a credit history – the financing offered varied accordingly to the project, starting at USD 1,500 and going up to USD 5000 based on a saving-credit system, with weekly payments that started at USD 19 with a duration of 70 weeks; and (5) integrality, as the program offered technical support, credit-savings, quality materials, trusted and fast delivery, and accessibility. In sum, the customer had access to services for savings, financing, technical assistance, advice during the building process, a personalized project, and in some occasions, subsidies from the federal government through the Housing National Commission (CONAVI is the Spanish acronym). The customer received the needed construction materials on time and at the address defined, generating savings of about 50%.

From 1998 to 2006, the evolution of PH, and its closeness with the market, allowed the company to create additional inclusive and social business models for MoP sub-segments, especially those in extreme poverty;[28] for example, the Assisted Self-Construction Integrated Program (in Spanish, Programa Integral de Autoconstrucción

28   CEMEX 2020.

Asistida or PiAC) was designed to enhance low-income families' self-building capacities by offering the training, funding, and technical assistance needed to construct their own homes. The business model was based on a public–private partnership involving local governments, nonprofit organizations, and universities. Another program was the Self-Employment Production Centers (in Spanish, Centros Productivos de Autoempleo; SPCs) that comprise the core component of PiAC. At these centers, low-income families receive training and materials to manufacture brick blocks to be used to construct their own homes or to improve existing structures. SPCs can also be customized for building other materials, such as roofing, urban infrastructure, and even clean cooking stoves. Half of the blocks produced are provided to families for use in home construction, repair, or expansion as payment for their labor. The state or local government, NGOs, social entrepreneurs, and other actors buy the other half of the blocks for infrastructure development. The resulting proceeds are reinvested in the centers.[29] In 2014, PH introduced ConstruApoyo, a component of PiAC that allows the use of prepaid cards to purchase building materials in Colombia. CEMEX currently runs seventy-two SPCs in eleven states throughout Mexico, five in Colombia, and two in Guatemala. Finally, the ecological concrete cook stoves project was introduced, which employs an efficient technology that represents a solution to the problem of traditional cooking with open fires or rudimentary cook stoves, which cause the premature death of 4 million people annually in developing countries. This technology allows a reduction of up to 75% of the wood used as fuel.[30]

In 2013, PH evaluated the program and the environmental changes affecting the MoP segments. As a result, the executives of the program initiated important innovations in the model, such as more flexible offers regarding amounts and payments (e.g., weekly, biweekly, or monthly). In addition, multiple payment options (e.g., in

[29]   Schmidt 2014.   [30]   CEMEX 2015.

banks, convenience stores – OXXOs, CEMEX centers, or cell phone fees) were more accessible to the customer, as were advice and technical support in the client's address. Based on this, the program ensures the best offers for customers, because the payment options and the particular necessities are well known. Finally, a platform called CRECIMIENTOS (in English, Growing), allows more innovation, creation, and promotion of inclusive and social business models in partnership with strategic allies, such as governments, academic institutions, NGOs, and social entrepreneurs in countries where CEMEX is present.

In 2017, PH has more than 100 service centers in 5 countries in Latin America (Mexico, Dominican Republic, Nicaragua, Costa Rica, and Guatemala), with a presence in 31 states in Mexico. Under the umbrella of PH and other social and inclusive business models, CEMEX has contributed to increasing the quality of life for more than 2.6 million Mexicans. So far, more than USD 290 million in credits have been given to families, with an on-time payment return of 99%. The network of local promoters consists of 800 people, most of them women who sell and manage credits, who receive continuous and integral training and experience in addition to income. More than 3.7 million square meters of housing have been built, and every month 5,000 new families are benefited. In parallel, working with the housing sector in the MoP has allowed the company to gain experience and influence on other topics such as secure land tenure, education and capability development, employment, health, security, and social cohesion.

Regarding the challenges for the future of PH, the first is to be able to quickly adapt to changing environments. In response to this, the company is creating an efficient model capable of giving support to the MoP in Mexico, but also overseas without having a local presence. Also, PH has developed an integral offer, enriched with construction services that will support the expansion and scalability of the LAC countries. Finally, PH will increase efforts to keep working with the Mexican government, and governments of other countries, by executing joint programs to improve housing conditions. Regarding inclusive and social business models, the challenge is to reach more families in extreme poverty; to contribute to the strengthening of the do-it-yourself construction segment; to innovate and create more jobs that allow the MoP to become business owners; and to expand this model into the value chain of CEMEX.

Échale a Tu Casa (México)

¡Échale a tu casa! (EAC) (In English, Give Your House a Go) is a program that addresses the lack of decent housing for Mexicans at the middle of the pyramid. It is an auto-construction model focused on community-based financing and the construction of safe, ecologically friendly, and adequate homes to offer both dignity and (resale) value to low-income homeowners.[31]

The EAC is designed to bring community organization to the conventional practice of self-construction in rural areas, in which families usually fend for themselves rather than work together. It is based on four essential elements: social inclusion, financial training/education, technical training, and continuity, in the sense that once the knowledge is transferred, people have the opportunity to keep building houses and improving the quality of life in their communities. The program was born in 1997 as an NGO created by Francesco Piazzesi Tommasi.

Francesco comes from a family of Italian immigrants who moved to Mexico to escape the effects of the Second World War in Europe. In 1957, his father founded a family business called ITAL Mexicana, which specialized in the manufacturing and sale of construction machinery. Francesco began working for ITAL Mexicana when he was seventeen years old, and today he is still involved in guiding the business, along with his two brothers. Today, ITAL Mexicana sells an average of 300 machines a year via distributors in almost all the capital cities of Central and South America.[32]

---

[31]   ASHOKA 2016.   [32]   ITALMEXICANA 2015.

Since he was young, Francesco has been motivated to find housing solutions for the poorest families who lack decent homes. In the 1980s, he took the initiative to collaborate with CRATerre Institute at the architecture school in Grenoble, France, to design a machine that could use dirt as a raw material to be used for the self-construction of homes. In 1985, Francesco tested the first Adopress machine in a Chalcan community in the state of Estado de Mexico, and in 1987, he founded the nonprofit organization Adobe Home Aid to promote what he called social housing using the Adopress machine. Ten years later, Francesco founded Ecoblock International, a for-profit structure that served as a necessary financial intermediary to benefit communities doing self-construction through producing and selling Adoblock, so that they could be legally paid for their work.

In 2003, the initiative showed that scaling the idea would be impossible using philanthropic means alone. Therefore, Francesco decided to enroll in a doctoral program to focus on designing a more active program structure. In 2006, after publishing an award-winning thesis on sustainable housing microfinance, Échale a tu casa was established as the model that exists today under the umbrella of the preexisting Ecoblock International.

The core of the Échale a tu casa model is the organization of the traditional auto-construction process into a community-based effort that characterizes the entire building process. Once Échale a tu casa identifies a community that would most benefit from the program (with the help of state and local governments, and occasionally philanthropic organizations), Francesco and his team approach the community leaders with an explanation of how the project is structured. Échale a tu casa's architects always offer to build a model home to gain the community's trust. In the end, the community must decide on its own whether to implement the project or not. If residents choose to proceed, they elect a representative housing committee that becomes responsible for designing the homes, overseeing project finances, and managing the whole project. To participate in the program, all households must be able to prove land rights to the property on which they wish to build, and the land must not be located in a high-risk zone, such as a flood plain, a nature reserve, or a very low-income area.

Échale a tu casa provides the materials needed for construction and trains five community members per house as builders; these Social Housing Production Units (SHPUs) are paid directly by Échale a tu casa for the entire construction period. The community's participation as home builders not only provides employment but also strengthens households' incentives for repayment.[33] Échale a tu casa provides technical advice and support throughout the entire process, as well as the machinery necessary for producing building materials and payment for the time and effort that families contribute to building their own homes. Neighbors band together into work groups that jointly provide building materials and lay the foundations for every new home in the community, thus achieving economies of scale, while also strengthening social relationships between families. The efficiency of this collaborative self-construction reduces the average time for completing a home in these communities from several years to just two months.

In particular, the average credit for home improvement totals USD 1,000. Initial loans are provided for new houses, and repayments from home loans fund home improvements in the same communities. To be qualified for a loan from Échale a tu casa, each household must complete a socioeconomic profile, earn at least three minimum wage salaries per household (minimum wage is approximately USD 4.62 per day), and set up a savings account through Échale a tu casa and save at least 10% of the home value (this usually takes about six months).

Another key element of Échale a tu casa's approach is the financing model via a legal structure known as SOFINCO (Sociedad Financiera Comunitaria –Community Financial Partnership). Families who put their savings into SOFINCO funds are primarily buying owner's shares in that fund, allowing their savings to be

---

[33] Bessarabova 2015.

leveraged as a financial guarantee to obtain loans from the government or private banks. This strategy overcomes the biggest financial barrier that families in the middle of the pyramid face in Mexico: the inability to furnish a financial guarantee for credit. The SOFINCO funds, managed by the local community housing committee, can be combined with federal housing subsidies to finance an Échale a tu casa self-construction project in that particular community.

The final innovative component of the Échale a tu casa model is the use of adobe blocks as the primary building material. Using specialized equipment known as the Adopress machine, which is manufactured by ITAL Mexicana, both men and women of all ages, including youths and even children, get involved in this stage of the construction process, gathering dirt and mixing it with water and small amounts of additives such as lime or cement. In addition to being much more aesthetically pleasing than the materials traditionally used in self-construction, the resulting adobe blocks (known as Adoblock) are also light, resistant, and environmentally friendly. It is worth mentioning that this technology has also been exported to Belize, Egypt, Haiti, Nicaragua, and the United Arab Emirates.[34]

Regarding environmental impact, houses built through Échale a tu casa are environmentally sustainable, as they are constructed of earth blocks, and all are equipped to harvest rainwater, reducing the use of municipal water by 20%. Houses are further equipped with (1) Bio-digesters, which drastically reduce the leakage of septic tanks and latrines into underground water sources; (2) Wood-saving stoves to diminish the use of wood for cooking by 70%; (3) Solar water heaters, which provide hot water with zero gas consumption; and (4) Solar energy efficient lamps, which reduce the use of municipal energy by 10%.

The way in which the program is financed consists of three components: (1) Savings of 10% of the value of the project, either

---

34   Schmidt 2014.

home improvement or new construction; (2) A federal subsidy, when available, of 40% of the value of the project; and (3) The credit of 50%.

Also, during the construction process, each family member working on the project earns about USD 12 per day. Regarding the credit, at the beginning of the project it was about 80%, and in 2015 the rate decreased to 30%. Échale a tu casa is pushing to reduce the interest rate.

Three success factors of the program have been identified. First, selecting the right financial vehicle to provide credit and to encourage clients to save. The goal is to offer the highest possible interest rate for savings and the lowest rate for loans. Second, facilitating access to funding. Obtaining funding is still one of the greatest barriers to home ownership. Although finding interested funders is not difficult, the challenge is making them understand that exorbitant interest rates are not necessary, and that including clients as partners delivers value to all stakeholders. Third, selecting partners with well-guided intentions. In other words, paramount to this model's success is identifying partners and funders committed to social and financial gains.

In 2013, the program helped 6,000 projects. In 2014, Échale a tu casa built 30,000 houses and facilitated 150,000 home improvements. There are also significant social impacts in participating communities, including the creation of five temporary jobs for each house built. Échale a tu casa estimates that 200,000 people have gained temporary employment for the duration of the construction project.[35] According to the Mexican Nacional Bank and Value Commission (CNBV for their acronym in Spanish), in 2015 the SOFINCO fund served more than 23,000 savers and 36,000 creditors, and it had about USD 5 million in assets, USD 3.9 million in credits, and USD 3.8 million in deposits.

Recently, the program won an award given by the American Business Customs (ABC) Foundation, which is a group of businessmen that get together annually to promote social impact programs. In

---

[35] Bessarabova 2015.

2007, Échale a tu casa won the Mexican housing national award, and in 2011, Francesco Piazzesi received an award from the World Economic Forum for being an outstanding social entrepreneur.

In planning for the future, the program consistently reviews and updates its structure and procedures to make sure it is offering clients the lowest interest rate and creating the greatest social impact by helping families in building their homes. Also, the model is going to be replicated in the LAC countries and India, which are regions that also have difficulties rooted in poor housing conditions.

Another initiative, started by a social entrepreneur who later became an Ashoka-fellow, is "The Sun Shines for All" (TTSFA) project, developed in Brazil. TTSFA focuses on supporting the development of rural areas, and its approach aims to fill the gap in one particular stage of the housing value chain: assistance in securing or improving services (mainly water, sanitation, and electricity). In Box 1, the TSSFA program is described.[36]

Electric power helps to improve quality of life and offers opportunities for income generation, while also helping to reduce massive immigration to cities, so the TSSFA program has a substantial chance to be scaled within Brazil and in many other emerging countries. In the next section, we present a comparison of the three cases previously described, as well as some lessons learned during their compilation.

COMPARISON AND CONCLUSIONS

This section presents the main findings after comparing the three cases described, regarding their similarities, differences, and best practices. Also, some lessons and practical implications are summarized, to provide some valuable tools to decision makers working in the private sector.

Regarding the comparison, eight dimensions were analyzed – country, industry, size, scope, focus on the housing value chain,

---

[36] Mugica 2004.

segment approach, expected growth, and impact – as well as six types of innovation (see Table 5.4). In short, the three cases all offer an integral solution for housing needs, including access to financing, support in the development of design and construction skills, and, in the case of PH and EAC, affordable access to building materials.

Interesting differences are evident among the three cases regarding their focus on the housing value chain. VC dedicates its effort toward post-construction quality assurance and sales or, in other words, low-income families that already have a house and need to refine their environment. In contrast, PH and EAC serve customers needing to build their homes incrementally. Additionally, PH and EAC could be considered core house business models, as they combine government subsidies with unsecured loans for building new housing on land already owned by customers.

Regarding the segment approach, VC has a national scope in urban slums and rural areas. PH has an international reach, with a presence in five countries in the LAC region, and mainly focuses on urban slums. EAC has a presence overseas, and the segment of interest is in rural areas. The expected growth, in the case of VC, is national. In contrast, PH and EAC are expecting to scale their business models to additional countries in the LAC region and in other continents.

Finally, impacts vary according to the peculiarities of the programs, such as the year of creation, commercial channels to connect with people, companies' characteristics supporting these programs, and of course the country of origin. In general, impacts are related to the number of benefited families, the number of square meters built or improved, the number of jobs created, and positive externalities in the communities as part of parallel initiatives related to addressing other challenges such as education, health, and social issues, among many others.

Innovation is latent in the three cases. For example, EAC has a significant focus on providing a sustainable solution, regarding the additional characteristics implemented in the new houses built in

Table 5.4 *Cases comparison: Dimensions of the solutions created*

Dimensions	*Patrimonio hoy*	*Viste tu casa*	*Échale a tu casa*
Country	Mexico	Colombia	Mexico
Industry	Construction and building materials	Construction and remodeling	Construction and building materials
Size and scope	Large (5 countries)	Medium (4 regions within Colombia)	Medium (10 states within Mexico)
Focus on the housing value chain	1. Assistance to access finance, subsidy, savings 2. Assistance to obtain or produce quality construction materials 3. Design advice and building services 4. Construction and technical assistance	Post-construction quality assurance and sales (i.e., fittings)	1. Assistance to access finance, subsidy, savings 2. Aid to obtain or produce quality building materials 3. Design advice and building services 4. Construction and technical assistance 5. Ongoing support for community development
Segment approach	International/Urban slums	National /Urban slums and rural	International/Rural

149

Table 5.4 (cont.)

Dimensions	Patrimonio hoy	Viste tu casa	Échale a tu casa
Expected growth	More countries in Latin America	More regions in Colombia	More countries in Latin America and India
Impact	• 2.6 million people in Mexico • US $290 million in credits • 800 promoters • 3.7 million square meters	• 80,000 families in Colombia • 219 promoters • 600 Colombian pesos to improve the communities	• 200,000 jobs created during construction • US $3.8 million in assets • 30,000 houses and 150,000 home improvements in 2014
Innovation/ product and process	The first in implementing a line extension that added substantial value because of the identification of an unattended growing market. It led the paradigm shift of companies profitably providing housing for the MoP, instead of governments or not-for-profit organizations.	The first in attaining a new element in the housing value chain (aesthetics and hygiene).	1. Houses fully equipped with bio-digesters, wood-saving stoves, solar water heaters, and solar energy lamps. 2. The Adopress machine; participating families can create adobe blocks quickly and easily using locally sourced dirt. 3. The organization of the traditional auto-construction process into a community-based effort.

Innovation / financial aspects	CEMEX modified the existing *Tanda* system within the Mexican communities and called it *Patrimonio Hoy*. People now save and also obtain access to credit based on their savings.	Offers tailored and with agile financing.	The SOFINCO funds, which are managed by the local community housing committee.
Innovation / network	Promoters within the community (mainly women)	Promoters within the community (mainly women)	Rural community leaders
Innovation / Service	Implementing remote advice and technical assistance	Seven service centers that work as places where women-advisors can get together. The centers also work as exhibitors of the products.	*Échale a tu casa* brings the machines to the rural areas.

Source: Own elaboration based on cases comparison

rural communities (e.g., bio-digesters, wood-saving stoves, solar water heaters, and solar energy efficient lamps). VC saw an opportunity in the market and focuses on exploiting a step further in the housing value chain. PH has continuously innovated its ways to satisfy customers' needs, such as by implementing a savings payment using cell phones or by offering technical support at a distance. Table 5.4 presents a comparison of the dimensions that characterize the solutions created by the three companies analyzed.

Lessons Learned

Based on interviews with the principal actors involved in the three business models previously described, we identify seven lessons, outlined in the following paragraphs.

1. Deeply understand market needs through systematic and soundly designed ethnographic methods. The purpose is to know the customers' motivations, demographic characteristics, economic aspects, primary necessities and barriers, customs and traditions, and idiosyncrasies, among many other elements. Results are the basis for conceiving any comprehensive and social business model, because solutions must be integral (e.g., financing, technical support, channel), adaptable to each family's need, and should involve the community. This lesson is supported by comments from Francesco Piazzesi, Échale a tu casa founder: "Interestingly, the most complicated issue when we launched Échale a tu casa, was the difficulty to change the mindset of the low-income families. They used to think ... we are not worthy of having a better quality of life because we are poor, we have not any income, and we cannot do anything." Also, "They have all the capacities, they only lack the opportunities," said Israel Moreno, General Manager of Patrimonio Hoy. This situation can be reversed if managers identify social needs and satisfy them by applying innovative processes focused on reducing poverty gaps in housing from private initiatives, as previously seen.

2. To be innovative and to adopt flexible and adjustable models for the variety of needs found in the different segments of the low-income markets (e.g., MoP, BoP, extreme poverty). The purpose is to leverage the acquired knowledge and trust and to diversify the offering of products and services

to specific segments. For example, the programs launched by CEMEX derived from PH (e.g., PiAC, SPCs, and cook stoves, among others).

3. Programs must have the support and commitment of the whole company, including shareholders, executive managers, and other levels of the organization. Therefore, companies must have a sense of creating a positive impact on the communities and, consequently, should be patient even if the beginning of the model's deployment is not profitable. For example, in the cases of CEMEX and Colcerámica, with PH and VC, both programs required a considerable amount of time until they became profitable: "Company stakeholders, the president of the board and top executive managers, have always shown their compromise in generating value to the communities hosting us," said Mateo Camacho, Channel Sales Manager at VC.

4. Participants in the projects must feel confident with adaptive learning within the company to promote it. This means they should learn from the implementation and execution of the programs, adapt internal processes, and fulfill the necessary operations capable of responding to needed changes. In consequence, the company should be flexible and open to change. For example, changing the channels and volume of operations, as with MoP and BoP, has particular requirements (e.g., direct sales, small amounts in each deal, accompaniment during the purchase decision) that must always be fulfilled.

5. Firms should learn from successful implementations of inclusive and social models in other industries to replicate them in other sectors, areas, and parts of the supply chain. For example, by building from scratch, expanding the house, or improving home environments. Once the models are tested and are sufficiently robust, they must be scaled to be applied in new regions and countries with similar necessities, as is the case of Échale a tu casa and their plans to expand into India. "Now, the next objective is to come into the LAC countries and in the medium term to India. Both are perfect locations, because of the severe housing challenges they suffer... The trip has already started," said Francesco Piazzesi, Échale a tu casa founder.

6. Even if negotiations with governmental institutions are required to create or increase subsidies, or to change regulations when necessary, it is vital for success and to enhance the impact of the initiatives that companies should facilitate strategic alliances with academic institutions, NGOs, and community leaders.

7. Whenever possible, it is desirable that companies demonstrate their interest in the communities by funding social or environmental initiatives that, openly and without any retribution, benefit people. This strategic business policy increases trust-based relationships with the community and allows firms to identify, target, and meet social needs.

In sum, it is critical to scale up public–private partnerships for creating integrated solutions to offset the poor housing challenge. Addressing the lack of accommodation should be done through public measures rooted in expansive fiscal policy, and by designing programs to foster public–private partnerships reinforced with social programs to help disadvantaged populations by offering quality-based public services, especially in rural areas. Innovative solutions, such as combining the sale of construction materials, technical assistance with self-building, help with mortgage equity, financial education, and even renting services at affordable prices, are crucial. Additionally, citizen involvement, as in the cases of Francesco Piazzesi and Fabio Rosa, who later became social entrepreneurs and Ashoka-fellows, is one of the many paths to overcome the housing challenge in the LAC region.

REFERENCES

Ahn, D., Kahn, W., Kim, K.-K., & Shin, H. 2016. Analysis and Design of Microfinance Services: A Case of ROSCA. *Engineering Economist*, Vol. 62, No. 3, pp. 197–230.
Arbeláez, M. A., Camacho, C., & Fajardo, J. 2011. Low-Income Housing Finance in Colombia. IDB Working Paper Series, 256, Inter-American Development Bank.
ASHOKA. 2016. Francesco Piazzesi. Ashoka Fellows. Accessed September 10, 2016. www.ashoka.org/fellow/francesco-piazzesi#intro
Azevedo, V., Balgun, A., Bouillon, C., Duke, D., & Gallardo, M. 2015. Un mercado creciente de US$750 mil millones. Inter-American Development Bank (IDB). Accessed April 12, 2016. http://publications.iadb.org
BambooFinance. 2014. Bamboo Finance Impact Report. Progress in context. *BambooFinance*. Accessed November 12, 2016. www.bamboofinance.com/wp-content/uploads/bamboo-finance-impact-report-2014.pdf
Bessarabova, T. 2014. Housing at the Base of the Pyramid in Brazil. Challenges and Opportunities. Aspen Network of Development Entrepreneurs (ANDE) & Business Call to Action. Accessed April 27, 2016. www.businesscalltoaction.org/resources/publications

Bessarabova, T. 2015. ¡Échale! a Tu Casa: Providing Low-Income Families Opportunities for Home Ownership. Business Call to Action. Accessed June 5, 2016. www.businesscalltoaction.org/case-studies/2014/04/echale-a-tu-casa-pro viding-low-income-families-opportunities-for-home-ownership/

Bouillon, C. (ed.) 2012. Room for Development: Housing Markets in Latin America and the Caribbean. InterAmerican Development Bank. Accessed March 1, 2017. https://publications.iadb.org

Bloomberg Business. 2016. Building Products Company Overview of Organización Corona S. A. Bloomberg. Accessed November 8, 2016. www.bloomberg.com/ research/stocks/private/snapshot.asp?privcapId=9156569

CEMEX. 2015. Building a Better Future. Annual report. CEMEX. Accessed July 13, 2016. www.cemex.com/CEMEX_AR2015/index.html

CEMEX. 2020. Responsible Business. Inclusive Business Models. CEMEX. Accessed June 24, 2016. www.cemex.com/sustainability/responsible-business/ inclusive-business-models

Dobbs, R., Manyika, J., & Woetzel, J. 2015. The Four Global Forces Are Breaking All the Trends. McKinsey & Company. Accessed July 24, 2016. https://assets .documentcloud.org/documents/2069315/the-four-global-forces-breaking-all-the- trends.pdf

El-Gamal, N., El-Komi, N., Karlan, D., & Osman, A. 2014. Bank-Insured ROSCA for Microfinance: Experimental Evidence in Poor Egyptian Villages. *Journal of Economic Behavior and Organization* 103: S56–S73.

EMIS. 2016. Colombia Company Profiles. Euromoney Institutional Investor Company (EMIS). Accessed September 22, 2016. www.emis.com/php/company- profile/CO/

Etang, A., Fielding, D., & Knowles, S. 2011. Trust and ROSCA Membership in Rural Cameroon. *Journal of International Development* 23(4): 461–475.

ITALMEXICANA. 2015. Acerca de Ital Mexicana. Ital Mexicana. Accessed July 15, 2015. www.italmexicanamty.com/acerca.htm

Kedir, A. M. & Ibrahim, G., 2011. ROSCAs in Urban Ethiopia: Are the Characteristics of the Institutions More Important Than Those of Members? *Journal of Development Studies* 47(7): 998–1016.

Khare, H. S. 2016. Barriers Constraining the Low and Middle-Income Housing Finance Market in Bangladesh. International Finance Corporation – The World Bank Group. Accessed October 28, 2017. www.ifc.org/wps/wcm/connect/ca4a1326-a425-464b- aa13-33fc44659498/Barriers-Constraining-the-Low-and-Middle-Income-Housing- Finance-Market-in-Bangladesh.pdf?MOD=AJPERES

Letelier, M. F., Flores, F., & Spinosa, C. 2003. Developing Productive Customers in Emerging Markets. *California Management Review* 45(4): 77–103.

Mbamaonyeukwu, V. S. (2013). ROSCAs: An Instrument for the Sustainable Development of the Solidarity Economy. A Paper Submitted to the Asian Solidarity Economy Council, on the Occasion of the 5th RIPESS International Meeting of SSE. Manila, Philippines, October 15–18, 2013.

Mugica, Y. 2004. Fabio Rosa and Social Entrepreneurship. The Kenan-Flagler Business School University of North Carolina. Accessed June 15, 2016. www .ideaas.org/admin/editor/imagensUpload/File/DistributedSolarEnergy_3.pdf

O'Connell, K. 2014. What Influences Open Defecation and Latrine Ownership in Rural Households? Findings from a Global Review. The World Bank Group. Accessed October 29, 2017. www.wsp.org/sites/wsp.org/files/publications/ WSP-What-Influences-Open-Defecation-Global-Sanitation-Review.pdf

Peterlechner, L. 2009. ROSCAs in Uganda – Beyond Economic Rationality. *Savings and Development* 109–140.

Roch, F. 2017. Housing Finance and Real Estate Markets in Colombia. IMF Working Paper, 17/190, International Monetary Fund. Accessed October 29, 2017. www.imf.org/en/Publications/WP/Issues/2017/08/18/Housing-Finance-and-Real-Estate-Markets-in-Colombia-45176

Schmidt, J. 2014. CEMEX Patrimonio Hoy: Providing Integral Housing Solutions for Low-Income Families. Business Call to Action. Accessed July 15, 2016. www.businesscalltoaction.org/case-studies/2014/11/cemex-patrimonio-hoy-pro viding-integral-housing-solutions-for-low-income-families/

Smets, P. 2000. ROSCAs as a Source of Housing Finance for the Urban Poor: An Analysis of Self-Help Practices from Hyderabad, India. *Community Development Journal* 35: 16–30.

Stickney, C. 2014. Many Paths to a Home: Emerging Business Models for Latin America and the Caribbean's Base of the Pyramid. Inter-American Development Bank (IDB). Accessed June 10, 2016. https://publications.iadb.org/en/publication/ 16840/many-paths-home-emerging-business-models-latin-america-and-caribbeans-base

Treviño, L. 2016. How Latin America's Housing Policies are Changing the Lives of Urban Families. November 4, 2016. The World Bank. Accessed March 6, 2017. http://blogs.worldbank.org/sustainablecities/how-latin-america-s-housing-policies-are-changing-lives-urban-families

United Nations SDG. 2020. Sustainable development goals. Water and sanitation. Accessed June 24, 2020. www.un.org/sustainabledevelopment/water-and-sanitation

Wei, W. & Lijuan, Z. 2011. Discussion on Legal Regulation Problem of ROSCA. Proceedings of the 2011 International Conference on Future Computer Science and Education, ICFCSE 2011, 506–508.

6 Banking the Unbanked

Innovative Business Models Championing the Financial Inclusion of Latin America's MoP

Eileen Daspro and Jasenko Ljubica

I finally know what distinguishes man from the other beasts: financial worries.

Jules Renard

AN OVERVIEW

Numerous studies by the International Monetary Fund,[1] The World Bank,[2] and/or action-oriented think tanks such as the Center for Financial Inclusion (CFI)[3] have unveiled the plethora of opportunities that financial inclusion presents. According to the World Bank,[4] as of 2017, 2 billion people worldwide lacked access to formal financial services – an important tool for reducing poverty and improving global prosperity. Despite some modest improvements in the past decade, financial inclusion is still a major obstacle to development in Latin America, where only 47% of households have access to formal financial institutions, in comparison with 60% of households in emerging markets in Asia. Financial inclusion provides opportunities that include the ability to boost job creation and development, increase investments in education and directly help middle-income people manage risk, absorb financial shocks, and improve the quality of their lives through the ability to purchase products that they could only dream about before.[5] Being able to save, make noncash payments, send

The authors would like to offer a sincere thank you to the editors for their guidance and to all of those who helped us with the construction of this chapter. We trust they will recognize themselves.

[1]   IMF 2015.   [2]   The World Bank 2015.   [3]   The World Bank 2015.
[4]   The World Bank 2015.   [5]   *The Economist* 2013.

or receive remittances, obtain credit, or purchase insurance can be instrumental in raising living standards and helping businesses prosper.

However, being "unbanked," or financially excluded, means these people do not have bank accounts and cannot access related financial services[6] such as consumer and business loans as well as other types of financial products that would help improve their businesses and lives. Middle-income families and micro-entrepreneurs, thus, struggle to meet financial requirements to invest in their businesses, rendering them unable to pay basic operating expenses, purchase inventory,[7] and buy essential household products and services such as home appliances and internet that would upgrade their quality of life. The LAC's unbanked lack formal credit histories and loan guarantees, which limits their access to financing. Similarly, their income streams are more difficult to verify since they tend to fluctuate and are, therefore, less compatible with long-term financing obligations. Consequently, LAC's middle-income market segment's financial demands, needs, and preferences have been unattended either by large mainstream banks (focused on larger loans to borrowers with formal credit histories and traditional forms of collateral) or by other microfinance institutions.[8] This is exacerbated by the MoP member's notorious lack of financial literacy, which, combined with the lack of access, relegates them to positions outside the formal financial system.[9]

By failing to understand and take into account these overwhelming challenges, a number of companies and entrepreneurs failed by rendering their business models without sound scalability. A "one size fits all" approach, such as the French food company Danone used in Brazil,[10] is one example. Duplicating their existing

---

[6]   Adrian & Shih 2011.   [7]   Arping, Loranth, & Morrison 2010.

[8]   Terrier, Valdés, Tovar, Chan-Lau, Fernández-Valdovinos, García Escribano, Medeiros, Tang, Vera Martin, & Walker 2011.

[9]   For additional information on financial concentration in LAC, see Srinivas, Whitehouse, & Yermo (2000) and Impavido, Lasagabaster, & Garcia-Huitron (2010).

[10]   Seghal, Lauster, Mayr, & Panneer 2010.

business model focused on bulk selling and monthly credit card payments without awareness that LAC MoPs micro-entrepreneurs do not possess such financial instruments and, hence, cannot pay and do not buy in those quantities, is one example. Failures such as these and, unfortunately, many others, however, made companies and entrepreneurs understand that sheer replication and/or slight modification of business models are insufficient for success in LAC. Slowly but surely they started to comprehend that understanding the business environment and culture of the market is critical and success requires longterm local investments and a deep understanding of local business ecosystems and consumer preferences.[11]

Accordingly, innovative business thinkers have recently turned to the wider community in order to spawn collaborations with members of the local business ecosystems, forming innovative "inclusive business models" (IB models). These models reflect the private sector's approach to providing goods, services, and livelihoods to people at the middle of the pyramid that are both commercially viable and scalable by making them a part of the value chain of companies' core business as suppliers, distributors, retailers, or customers. These innovative business models do not seek trade-offs between financial and social returns but rather continuously seek solutions through which both can be optimized simultaneously. Inclusive businesses achieve direct development impacts through the provision of essential goods, services, and decent jobs. They also unlock new forms of innovation and entrepreneurial activity critical to accelerating inclusive growth.

In this chapter, we present business opportunities emerging from the problems faced by the large number of the unbanked in the middle-income population of LAC. We continue by elaborating the challenges facing companies tackling these opportunities, and we provide a series of case studies presenting innovative solutions used by successful companies as solutions to these challenges.

[11] Seghal, Lauster, Mayr, & Panneer 2010.

We complete the chapter by providing constructive conclusions and recommendations for practitioners, with emphasis on the opportunity in attending to the unbanked, who lack access to credit to make the purchases they aspire to and need but don't have the means.

SPOTTING THE OPPORTUNITY

Financial inclusion, according to the Global Findex,[12] implies having an account that allows for provision of loans, savings, and payment of goods and services, but financial inclusion can also include access to credit, where the population can use cards or loans for their needs. For the underserved and unbanked populations, financial inclusion is critical to ending global poverty and plays a significant role in providing sustainable livelihoods to disadvantaged groups all over the world.[13] As the World Bank notes, banking is the first step toward financial inclusion. Despite its critical importance, there exist wide regional differences in the number of adults with access to financial services, as indicated in Table 6.1. Nearly 50% of the population in Latin America and the Caribbean are still missing the benefits that financial inclusion provides.

Nonetheless, since 2011, the number of unbanked people worldwide has decreased 20%, from 2.5 billion to 2 billion.[14] Accounting for population growth, this means that approximately 700 million people opened an account during that period – which is a 20 percent drop in the number of unbanked.[15] This is a continuation of the trend driven by a 13% rise in account ownership in developing countries. East Asia and the Pacific region increased account ownership by 25% and made significant progress expanding account ownership among the poor. Adult account ownership rose from 55% to 69% within three years. Europe and Central Asia are home to seven of the ten developing economies with the highest share of adults who paid a bill or made a payment through the Internet. Account ownership among adults

[12]   The World Bank 2015.   [13]   Karnani 2007; Prahalad & Hart 2004.
[14]   The World Bank 2015.   [15]   *The Economist* 2013.

Table 6.1 *Percentage of adults age 15+ with a financial account*

Region	Percent %
Latin American Caribbean	51.4
High OECD countries	94
East Asia Pacific	69
South East Asia	46
Middle East	14
Sub Saharan Africa	34

Source: World Bank, 2014

increased from 43% in 2011 to 51% in 2014. The percentage of unbanked adults on the lower 40% of the income ladder decreased by 10%. The Middle East region increased account ownership of adults from 11% in 2011 to 14%. Men are twice as likely to have an account as women are, and 7% of adults in the poorest 40% of households now have an account compared to 19% in the richest 60%. However, more than 85 million adults in the region remain unbanked. South Asia has added 185 million adults with new accounts since 2011, but there are clear opportunities to boost usage of accounts. Forty-six percent of adults in 2015 own an account, up from 32% in 2012. In India, 43% of adults with an account made no deposits or withdrawals in the past year, and 230 million with an account pay their obligations in cash. In Sub-Saharan Africa, 34% of adults in 2015 had an account, an increase from 24% in 2011. Twelve percent of adults in the region have a mobile money account compared to just 2% globally.

Latin America and the Caribbean (LAC) made impressive progress in bringing the poor into the financial system as well. In 2011, 39% of the population was banked but by just 2014, that number had risen to 51%. Nevertheless, 201 million people across the region remain unbanked. Data from the World Bank suggest that shifting payments of remittances and government transfers from cash to account transfers could provide important further gains in banking the financially excluded across the region. For example, in Brazil, 88% of government transfer recipients do so into an account. In Argentina, account ownership among the poorest 40% of households doubled to 44% from 2011 to 2014. Across LAC, 28% of adults make payments directly from their account using a debit and/or credit card, as compared to 14% in developing countries. However, large opportunities remain to increase the use of those and similar financial tools. There are 135 million adults who have an account but still make every-day transactions in cash. Peru and Colombia remain at the top of the LAC financial inclusion country rankings. Starting from 2015, Bolivia, Colombia, Ecuador, and Uruguay have all begun to implement previously adopted legislation and strategies specifically designed to increase access to financial services. Congruently, Bolivia has made financial inclusion a priority since its current constitution is in force since 2009 and continues to move toward greater inclusion. Colombia's financial inclusion strategy is also in full implementation process. Ecuador is implementing its strategy by initiating payment systems, electronic money, and credit facilities. In addition, Argentina and Nicaragua have adopted legislation that encourages various aspects of financial inclusion, although without comprehensive national strategies.

The size of the middle-income segment in the LAC region is at a historic high. The World Bank[16] defines middle-income consumers as those who earn between USD 10–50 per day. From 2000 to 2009, 73 million inhabitants across the region overcame poverty and joined the middle-income segment for the first time.[17] This middle-income segment now represents 30% of the total population across the LAC region, according to World Bank,[18] and projections will reach 50% of the total population by 2020. As incomes rise across the region, a large new MoP market in need of a variety of financial services is making a "financial inclusion boom" ready to happen. Indeed, the magnitude of

---

[16]   Ferreira et al. 2013.   [17]   Ferreira et al. 2013.   [18]   Ferreira et al. 2013.

needs of the rising MoP segment is overwhelming. As the new members enter MoP they bring with them all the needs, desires, and preferences they lacked while at the BoP. New middle-income Latin Americans want to modernize their homes with air conditioners, plasma television sets with cable or satellite installations, microwave ovens, and computers with internet connections. They also prefer flexible payment options and acquiring financial savings instruments that allow them to prepare for their and their children's future. Above all, the LAC MoP members need to start building trust and credit history with providers of these services, as some of our interviewees stated: "Finally, I can afford to buy my son a laptop computer. Not only am I happy to see his dream fulfilled but I am more peaceful as I know it is going to help him through school." And, "I don't like cards nor banks. It's like spending money that does not exist or giving it to someone you never met for safekeeping. I handle my own cash and If I can't see it, for me it just doesn't exist."

On the other hand, MoP entrepreneurs and micro-entrepreneurs have similar needs. They require capital for the improvement of their stores, as well as operational capital. In order to upgrade their businesses, they need technology to accommodate the new financial tools such as credit and debit cards, now in the hands of their customers. At the same time, the providers of these products and services must find an innovative solution that enables them to satisfy the rising needs of the MoP customers and entrepreneurs while keeping their business models feasible and scalable. The following statements of our interviewees clearly reflect this: "If all of that what you (– the interviewer) said is true and I can safely use it, I could start calling myself an entrepreneur. This way I am only a *tiendita* (small store) owner trying to survive another day." And, "All business people know that the iconic economic ratio is profit. If I can't make it, I have a boss too who won't care for my needs not even when he fires me."

Evidently, demographic changes, economic growth, and advances in technology are at the same time generating a gap between this growing market segment and their unattended needs but are also

Table 6.2 *Opportunities, challenges, and innovations for the microfinancing in LAC's MoP*

Company	BCI Bank (alliance with Rabie & Transtel)	Casas Bahia	Elektra
Opportunity	The size of the "unbanked" MoP segment (micro-entrepreneurs and customers) Opportunity to achieve CSR objectives Opportunity to achieve leading position in the Chilean banking industry	Governmental interventions, economic growth and socio-cultural changes improving the financial power of the middle segment The (rising) size of the "unbanked" MoP segment MoP segment's needs for financial inclusion High interest rates charged to the MoP population by the "Financieras"	The (rising) size of the "unbanked" MoP segment Lack of providers of financial services and/or products interest/able to aid MoP customers to afford consumer goods through innovative financing schemes
Challenge	Low profit margin when operating with MoP segments Lack of customer trust and the socio-culturally embedded fear toward banks Lack of knowledge of the middle-income market	Lack of business and financial literacy of the MoP segment MoP's low and erratic income flows Lack of products adapted to MoP's unique needs	Lack of business and financial literacy of the MoP segment MoP's low and erratic income flows Lack of financial responsibility of the MoP segment

Innovation	Alliances with partners in possession of established distribution networks and experience with MoP Partnership with IT and internet companies to provide mobile banking solutions installed on Rabie truck reaching remote customers Business training for MoP customers (entrepreneurs) Number of custom microfinancing products for MoP retailers	Customer-centric business model providing microfinancing solutions for the MoP for purchases of home appliances and everyday necessities through a personal-relationship-based audit Lower interest rate for customers due to self-financing policy of the Casas Bahia Technological tools (centralized system of customer information) speeding up the procedures and serving as a fraud detection and prevention	On-site rate and payback time determination system Home-visit audit system Interests charged on full amount borrowed
Effect	Alliance partners achieve cost reduction, knowledge and trust acquisition among MoP customers Alliance partners increase sales, improve relations and trust	The lowest interest rates, prices and default rates in the industry The largest number of buyers and monthly issued bills Constant business expansion (own factory)	Low default rates Customer-tailored micro-loans and payback terms Opportunity to afford services and goods not affordable before Increase in the quality of life

Table 6.2 (cont.)

Company	BCI Bank (alliance with Rabie & Transtel)	Casas Bahia	Elektra
	with MoP customers and manage less cash, therein improving security	Customer-tailored micro-loans and payback terms	
	Customers have wider product range, lower prices, and more flexible payment options	Opportunity to afford services and goods not affordable before	
	MoP micro-entrepreneurs develop their business skills through training received	Increase in the quality of life	

Source: Authors

making the fulfillment of such needs, in terms of financial inclusion, more possible than ever before. On one hand, access to affordable, diverse financial services is expanding and deepening in many parts of the world.[19] On the other hand, despite the availability and growing awareness of multi-level benefits of financial inclusion, approximately 2 billion people worldwide still either lack access to financial services or do not use them. For providers, new disruptive technologies (e.g., cloud technology) coupled with progressive public policies offer exciting cost-effective opportunities to expand access at a scale unimaginable a few years ago. Such a triad of elements entailing the rise in banked and the large number of the unbanked, along with technological and policy interventions, reflect a unique business opportunity. However, such solutions must address head-on the myriad of problems emerging from this void.

THE CHALLENGE

Companies wishing to address these opportunities face a number of barriers. Such barriers include the lack of financial literacy of the target socioeconomic segment and MoP's low and erratic income flows, as well as a lack of products adapted to their unique needs. Geographic distances and high transaction costs for financial institutions operating in remote locations as well as high transport and opportunity costs for people banking with formal financial institutions further extend challenges that companies must overcome. Many requirements for obtaining financial products, such as complicated paperwork and physical collateral, assume erroneously that all clients can easily produce identification documents and proof of stable income.

Research by Colombian Central Bank's Center for Latin American Monetary Studies[20] further shows that poor financial literacy represents a significant barrier to accessing and properly using formal financial services in most LAC countries. According to this

---

[19]   The World Bank 2015.   [20]   Garcia et al. 2013.

study, financial isolation often results in lack of financial understanding, which in turn makes people further distance themselves from formal financial institutions. Even though some banks offer products that are, to a certain extent, suitable for the needs of middle-income people, the same people had either no knowledge or an incorrect understanding of those products and/or were reluctant to use them. In addition, an OECD study[21] revealed that poor financial literacy limits people's awareness of the opportunities that financial products provide as well as affects the quality of their financial decisions aiming to improve their overall well-being.

Financial inclusion is particularly low in rural and remote areas and among less educated people. Low population density, difficult geography, and lack of accessible banking infrastructure significantly raise costs for financial institutions to reach rural areas. The overall supply of digital-banking services is relatively good, but its use is limited in these areas for several reasons. On one hand, in 2012, LAC had an internet penetration level at 40%[22] and fixed and mobile broadband penetration below 20%,[23] which is far below the developed world average. On the other hand, fear and lack of knowledge and, thus, trust in technology deter the use of sophisticated technology for financial transactions. As an interviewee remarked: "I do not have a TV but we have a cantina (Spanish: a traditional bar) in the town with one. Every time I watch it, I see someone's life destroyed or turned into living hell because of banks. The crisis (global financial crisis) everyone is talking about only proves it. So much jobs lost people in despair. Frankly, I can't see one reason to ever have anything to do with them (banks)."

A further challenge is high levels of violence and criminal activity in the majority of the LAC countries, which affects both the supply and demand, among other areas, of financial services. Eighty percent of countries lack cybersecurity strategies or critical infrastructure

[21]   Roa et al. 2014.   [22]   Jordan, Galperin, & Peres 2013.
[23]   Jordan et al. 2013.

while just starting to work on citizen education in this regard, which is the reason why LAC faces a cost from cybercrime equivalent to USD 90 billion per year;[24] this, again, is a significant deterrent for companies in this sector. In general, cumulative crime costs the region about 3.5% of its GDP, imposing a range of costs to the affected countries, including the loss of productive life years, the deterrence of investment, capital flight, and a general loss of confidence in the rule of law.[25] As a direct result, financial institutions either withdraw from or avoid certain countries and/or areas of the region. For most banks, the cost of serving low-income people is very high, as they must maintain a high number of accounts with a low volume of financial transactions. This generally makes having an outlet in poorer areas unprofitable. The majority of financial institutions, especially the international banks, which are viewed as the rich people's banks, focus on servicing high(er) income segments. For the middle-income customers, banking is relatively expensive as they discover bank charges and fees almost on par with their transactions. In addition, given the distance of the community from the bank, travelling expenses increase the overall transaction cost.

THE SOLUTIONS

Tackling the aforementioned opportunities in LAC's MoP, successful companies using innovative business models are reaching middle consumer segments by offering financing mechanisms through existing retail outlets. Existing traditional retail outlets, which are mostly owned by MoP members themselves, not only have the advantage of geographical proximity to the target consumer – they also maintain enduring relationships with local customers, which include the offering of informal, trust-based loans still preferred by their middle-income customers. To reach small-scale retailers in harder-to-reach areas, including distant, rural areas and crowded, urban settings, successful companies have employed independent, specialized

---

[24]   Lewis 2017.   [25]   Leggett, Jitman, & Guerra 2017.

distributors who, within their operating life, build and develop a large distribution network and enjoy a strong reputation and trust among middle segments. As MoP, micro-entrepreneurs have little working capital and limited or no access to financial services; these innovative solutions often rely on extended payment terms, allowing retailers to purchase inventory on credit. Traditional stores are often small, with little space for extra inventory, run by a staff with little or no formal business training and scarce working capital. They require small, frequent deliveries and thus the ability to buy on credit or pay-per-use services that match their consumers' limited, sporadic cash flows. Vendors of goods and services that lack distribution infrastructure and adequate payment mechanisms to conduct transactions with the customers share these challenges. Successful business models, thus, include financing for suppliers, retailers, and consumers who lack the savings for large, up-front purchases whether they be for basic household expenses or the purchase of working capital needed to run and modernize a business.

Innovative companies are beginning to address the "last mile" (complex logistics involved in reaching the MoP customers) challenges through electronic transaction platforms, providing customers with the benefits of convenience, efficiency, security, market access, and integration into the formal financial system. Inclusive business models use technology to provide unbanked and under-banked customers with the means to use money in electronic form, a convenient, low-cost, secure, and transparent alternative to cash. With electronic transactions, customers save time and money. They are also less vulnerable to robbery and corruption. As these technologies require certain understanding for their proper use, successful companies have trained their customers and their customer's customers in the actual service offered as well as in basic business and finance principles.

Inclusive business models, which offer consumer finance to the MoP, generate revenue in the form of interest income by lending to customers the company knows are creditworthy based on their experience doing business with them in the past, rather than through formal credit histories. Companies outside the financial sector generally employ these models, although some may operate their own consumer finance divisions. Some companies focus on their direct customers while others lend to their customers' customers as well, based on the experience their customers have had with the MoP members in the past. In the process, companies develop valuable knowledge of customers' purchasing and payment habits, particularly if they allow customers to buy on credit. Through inclusive business models, companies leverage existing customer knowledge to offer credit for other uses to those with a history of timely payments.

In the following, we present a number of case studies depicting the aforementioned models through which companies are helping to turn underserved populations into dynamic consumer markets. A summary of the three cases analyzed is found in Table 6.2.

Case Study 1: BCI-Rabie (Chile) – The Partnership for Everyone's Success

Banco de Crédito e Inversiones (BCI) is a Chilean bank, headquartered in the Chilean capital, Santiago, specializing in savings & deposits, securities brokerage, asset management, and insurance. Juan Yarur Lolas and a group of entrepreneurs, to support small and medium enterprises in Chile, founded the bank in 1937. Currently, BCI is the third largest private bank for loans and the fourth bank in number of customers in Chile. In 2014, BCI had more than 300 branch offices in the country with more than 10,500 employees along with overseas offices in the United States, Japan, Brazil, Mexico, and elsewhere.[26] In 2014, it received ranking among the fifty most successful emerging market companies and won the Chilean Banking Award. The Bank specializes in retail banking, which includes small and micro enterprises ("Banca Empresarios-Nova"), as well as low-income individuals and informal micro-entrepreneurs ("Banca Emergente"), both of which are divisions within BCI.

Several factors contributed to the BCI decision to target the middle-income business and consumer segments in Chile. One of these factors is the sheer size of the opportunity: 64% of Chile's one million micro-enterprises are

[26] The World Bank 2015.

currently unbanked.[27] This vast, unbanked market provided BCI with an opportunity to expand its market share in Chile's banking industry. The second factor is that serving the middle-income segments gives BCI the opportunity to fulfill its corporate social responsibility objectives. In doing so, BCI has had a profound impact on the improved living conditions of the middle-income population.[28] Another important factor that may have driven BCI to target the middle-income group is that this segment provides BCI with the opportunity to fulfill its vision of being a market leader in the Chilean banking industry. Since banking services connote a risky product, many banks are unwilling to venture into the low- and /or middle-income target segments. The strategic decision of BCI to venture into this new territory enables it with an important first-mover advantage and the eventual opportunity to be a market leader in Chile by reaching out to underserved, growing segments.

With such a vision, BCI Nova developed an inclusive business model gradually. Together with the Banco Interamericano de Desarrollo (BID), BCI launched the model "Microcréditos a la Puerta de tu Almacén" (small loans at your grocer's door). The project focused on increasing access to credit to unbanked and underbanked low-income portions of the Chilean economy through its new USD 20 million Banca Emergente Unit. Banca Emergente's mission is to "do well and do it well" (hacer bien, y hacerlo bien), by extending access to financial services to underserved micro-entrepreneurs and individuals in Chile through access to credit, which could support business growth. The following statement issued by BCI reaffirms this commitment: "To be truly successful, companies need to have a corporate mission that is bigger than making a profit. It should always be remembered that the customers are the basis of the Institution's success and commercial relations with them should therefore be maintained with a long-term perspective."[29]

Potential Banca Emergente borrowers are identified in two ways: (i) through the existing network of BCI Nova branches and credit analysis ("ejecutivo" model); and (ii) through Banca Emergente's strategic alliances with corporate, nonprofit, and public partners ("alliance" model). The alliance model is an inclusive business model created in response to BCI earlier difficulties, primarily low profit margin, upon attempting to penetrate the lower and middle market segments. The challenge of low profit margins was a problem not only for BCI but also for other companies targeting these customers.[30] Ultimately, BCI was able to overcome this barrier through the alliance

---

[27]   BCI 2011.   [28]   BCI 2011.   [29]   BCI 2014.
[30]   Department on Economic and Social Affairs 2010.

model by reducing costs through reliance on existing distribution channels of its partners rather than creating their own.

Another barrier was customer trust, especially considering the sensitivity of the banking product and the socio-culturally embedded fear middle-income customers have had toward banks. BCI had to overcome this by making those customers aware of the importance of banking services and creating a level of trust in them. BCI also faced the problem of lack of knowledge of the middle-income market. Accordingly, BCI created alliances with established organizations that possessed large existing distribution networks serving the lower and middle-income markets and, hence, trust among the customer base. Under this model, potential customers can be:[31] (a) owners of small shops that commercialize an alliance partner's products; (b) informal micro-entrepreneurs; (c) low- /middle-income individuals; or (d) individuals participating as clients in Banca Emergente alliance partners, such as utilities companies or business training centers. The use of microloans is limited to the purchase of goods provided by the alliance partner as working capital or for purchase of fixed assets for micro-entrepreneurial activities, a format known as "Experience-Based Customer Credit." It is another form of hybrid inclusive business model, generating additional revenue in the form of interest income through lending to customers that the Bank's alliance partners know are creditworthy through experience of doing business with them in the past.[32] BCI lends to its customers' customers as well, based on the experience its customers have had with those people in the past. This successful inclusive business model presumes financing for retailers who lack either the savings for large, up-front purchases (store renovation) or the working capital for recurring or even day-to-day expenses (purchasing inventory). BCI, through its alliance partners, provides the option to purchase on credit, access third party financing, and even, in some cases, cash loans.

Alliances are consolidated through the coordinated work between small grocery store owners, large and medium-sized suppliers, and BCI. The capital involved reached USD 2 million, spent in conjunction between BCI Nova and the BID's Multilateral Investment Fund, or FOMIN (Fondo Multilateral de Inversiones).[33] The model considers three main factors:[34] (1) satisfy the needs of the micro-business owner; (2) do business in conjunction with the alliance company; and (3) transfer the technological development that BCI currently possesses to the beneficiaries. In turn, the small grocers

[31]   BCI 2012.   [32]   Jenkins et al. 2012.   [33]   IADB 2013.
[34]   BCI 2014.

have access to continuous and direct financing with each of its suppliers; they receive commercial and financial training; and they have exclusive benefits with each of their suppliers without having to commute to reach them. The alliance partners increase their sales, improve relations and trust with their customers, and, lastly, manage less cash in their distribution channels, and therein improve security. This is a virtuous model since by growing the grocer's business, necessarily the supplier's sales grow, and in the same manner the volume and value of financial services provided by BCI will increase among these segments. Customers, as another vital part of the value chain of this inclusive model, select among a wide product range and benefit from lower prices and more flexible payment options.

The first step of the Alliance model is the identification and selection of BCI and alliances among companies. This selection is based on several key criteria:[35]

I. Innovation, either in terms of business models or methodologies used;
II. Impact on the target group (MoP entrepreneurs and customers) measured as the number of individuals to be added to the value chain or improvement of living standards the business opportunity represents;
III. Potential for replication or expansion within the company and BCI;
IV. Equal opportunities in terms of gender and ethnicity;
V. Environmental and socially sustainable enterprises and alliances that have no negative environmental or social impact; and
VI. Micro- or small businesses or individuals with income per capita less than USD 3200 a year as beneficiaries of the alliances.

The model itself has four components:[36]

I. Training or capacity building in appropriate credit analysis methodologies for the micro-enterprise segment;
II. Technical assistance to project beneficiaries to promote increased financial literacy and responsible credit management;
III. Creation of new and innovative strategic alliances with BCI corporate clients with large distribution networks and micro-entrepreneurial client bases to provide increased access to financial services in currently unbanked and underserved populations; and
IV. Development of lessons learned for public communication to enhance the replication capability. This model leverages the alliance partners' distribution channels and platforms to increase the scalability of the project by:[37]
   a. Making use of a customized and innovative risk-sharing financial instrument unavailable in local financial markets;

[35]   BCI 2014. [36]   BCI 2014. [37]   Jenkins et al. 2012.

b. Providing financial education and business skills training for low-income segments to promote responsible indebtedness;

c. Developing new credit and risk management methodologies to facilitate loan underwriting in the informal low-income sector.

One of the main objectives of this model is to generate financial awareness through training in order to empower the underserved, bankable population so that they understand the service offered to them and are able to compare and evaluate alternatives and make responsible financial decisions. Therefore, the model usually includes some form of capacity building for storeowners and staff, who have typically had little to no business training. Such capacity building can take different forms, including classroom or virtual training as well as one-on-one coaching. Often, Alliance partner's employees who received training prior to providing it do the training or the capacity building for the retailers. The capacity building includes the following activities:[38]

I. Developing customized financial education courses for each partner company;

II. Developing and promoting general financial education courses;

III. Planning financial education events in collaboration with other entities (such as NGOs).

In order to reach the lower income communities at a lower cost, BCI at the end of 2010 signed alliances with several large corporations such as Coca Cola – Embonor, Rabie, and Arcor, which allowed it to deliver financial support to more than 1,700 grocers. The project considered a 36-month execution period and expected to generate alliances with the main companies of Chile and reach at least 10,000 micro-business owners. One of the most innovative alliances is the one that BCI made with Rabie, the largest Chilean distribution company, to grant small shopkeepers throughout the country a complete financing plan. The system allows small businesses to boost their prospects by providing access to a line of credit without interest rates, repaid via credit card payments. This offers multiple benefits. Any retailer supplied by Rabie or who joins Rabie may obtain a line of credit with a fixed cost, allowing them to stock their store. One of the benefits provided by the new surcharge is greater security for the grocer and the supplier as it works through a bank credit card that activates the electronic transfer of funds, reducing the use of cash. Rabie's clients purchase with that card and pay their bill later. This "Integral Financial Plan" is part of the innovation

---

[38]   Jenkins et al. 2012.

programs BCI is developing in order to offer a memorable service experience to customers, especially grocers, and as such represents a cutting-edge innovation in the Chilean banking system.

There are a number of benefits for small retailers, formulated under the "Club of Benefits Rabie" slogan. In addition to financing and training, merchants have the opportunity to offer special promotions in cooperation with the BCI and Rabie. The store owners receive training in a variety of business skills. In turn, BCI and Rabie develop valuable knowledge of customers' purchasing and payment habits, particularly through enabling the customers to buy on credit. Thus, BCI and Rabie leverage existing customer knowledge to offer credit and products for various uses to those with a history of paying on time. As Sergio Vázquez, credit collection manager at Rabie, stated, "In addition to financing, the smaller stores receive valuable training and special offers. We work with them on marketing, product displays and financial education and so that they can distinguish between working capital, investment and credit for consumption."[39] This service is beneficial to Rabie as well, which, according to internal figures, handles 10,500 invoices daily.

The company Transtel, who added to its operation a bankcard category that opens new business prospects, has provided the technological support that enables the operation of this project-based alliance. An automated payment system is introduced in the form of mobile POS machines installed in Rabie distribution trucks. Rabie trucks, thus, transformed into "bank branches on wheels," and banking is now possible without closing the family store to go to the bank. Redelpro, the network provider for the payment system, made the implementation of mobile solutions technology possible. This allowed retailers to supply their businesses by accessing different financing schemes according to the purchases of their stores, obtaining discounts and benefits. These electronic transaction platforms create new opportunities for consumer and small business finance to middle-income consumers and businesses that are both convenient and secure while integrating both simultaneously into the formal financial system.[40] Electronic or e-money technology includes point-of-sale terminals used to access stores of e-money, as well as back-end switching and processing infrastructure that moves e-money and keeps records. With electronic transactions, individual customers save time (previously spent traveling great distances or waiting in long lines) and money (in the form of travel costs and forgone wages). They are also less vulnerable to

---

[39]   Banking News 2010.   [40]   Gradl & Jenkin 2011.

robbery and corruption. E-transaction platforms such as those used in this alliance reduce the cost of serving customers because shared technology platforms, distribution channels, and even brands offer economies of scale. The "e-Transaction Platforms model" is high-volume, low-margin and requires a critical mass of customers. As a result, the model involves a number of solutions for getting to critical mass quickly and cost-effectively. One such solution is leveraging established retail networks (such as Rabie's) to develop large footprints of agents – people or businesses contracted to sign up customers and facilitate their transactions. During the shift from cash to e-money, alliance–partner capacity building is essential since they are the face of the e-transaction service to the customer, fulfilling the vital roles of customer education, enrollment, transaction support, and exchange between cash and e-money. The Alliance model, therefore, relies on training the Rabie's employees in the actual service being offered, in customer acquisition and in business and finance – which is critical to maintaining the liquidity necessary to help customers exchange cash for electronic value and vice versa.

Case Study 2: Casas Bahia (Brazil) – Making Dreams Come True

> When my father arrived in Brazil, he realized the average population was not wealthy. Thousands of people were migrating from the northeast region to work in São Paulo. That is why our name is Casas Bahia (Bahia is the largest state in the northeast region). This population needed all kinds of basic goods, such as linens, towels, and sheets. My father's vision was to fulfill the needs of these people. However, how could they pay for it? The answer was simple: financing.
>
> Michael Klein[41]

Casas Bahia is a Brazilian retailer that began operating in 1952 when its owner, a Nazi concentration camp survivor named Samuel Klein, immigrated to Brazil after World War II. He started as a door-to-door salesperson selling electronics, appliances, and furniture. Today, more than half a century later, he has built one of Brazil's largest retail companies, serving more than 10 million customers, with 330 stores across the country, 22,000 employees, and annual revenues exceeding USD 1 billion and a leading 20% market share. The company has operations in three Brazilian regions and eight states. The best-selling product category for Bahia is furniture, with a 31% sales share,

---

[41] Foguel & Wilson 2003.

followed by television sets, which hold 14%, and audio products, which hold 10%. The principal reason for Casas Bahia's success is its innovative business model, unchanged from the day the company was founded: offer top quality brands to the people at the middle of the economic pyramid who have no formal or regular income and whose average monthly income is about two minimum wages (BRL 400 / about USD 116). Many of these MoP consumers work as domestic servants, street vendors, and construction workers and could otherwise not afford a television set or a refrigerator given their lack of stable income or formal credit history. Casas Bahia, therefore, set out to fulfill their dreams through a business model reflecting an innovative mix of financing and technology that provided its customers with an easy, simple, and safe way to purchase items they could have otherwise not been able to buy.

Since most Brazilian MoP members are usually unbanked and have no formal financial histories, banks were unwilling or highly reluctant to service this segment of the population. Traditionally, the so-called Financieras, consumer credit companies that operate solely to serve the MoP while charging high interest rates (up to 14% monthly), have been meeting the financing needs of the MoP to a certain extent, which leads many MoP to avoid them when possible.

Accordingly, Casas Bahia emerged to serve this untapped market by creating a unique financing model with a motto: "Total dedication to you." Samuel Klein remarked in this regard: "A good merchant always looks ahead. He understands that others (customers) need to live too. He wants to earn money but also lets others do it too. The sun rises for everyone."[42] With this mentality, they seek to create a balance between profit and social responsibility. Casas Bahia attends to the underserved and provides financing in a way that both the customer and the company win, creating a bond of loyalty between them.

The financing model has several key points. Casas Bahia uses a "passbook" or "carnet," which serves two purposes. It allows the MoP customers to purchase goods from Casas Bahia in small monthly installments for up to fifteen months by either saving money for, for example, six months and buying the appliance later, or buying now and repaying the loan later within the same period. The passbook is only payable in Bahia's store, which allows the store to maintain a close relationship with its customers since they must

---

[42]   Lam 2014.

visit the store monthly to pay their bills. This mode of payment accounts for 90% of Bahia's sales, with the rest being credit card (4%) and cash (6%) payments.

Casas Bahia begins the financing process by conducting a credit check of the prospective customer through Servicio de Protecao ao Credito (SPC). If the customer has a negative SPC score, Casas Bahia cannot offer them the option to finance their purchase on credit until they resolve the issue. On the other hand, if the customer has a positive SPC score, two solutions are available. First, if the merchandise price is less than BRL 600 (about USD 175), no proof of income or any additional financial-related documentation is required and the purchase is possible based solely on the customer's provision of proof of a valid home address. Second, if the price of the merchandise exceeds BRL 600, Casas Bahia's innovative proprietary system for evaluating a customer's creditworthiness comes into play. The first step in this system is determination of a credit limit based on a customer's formal and informal income sources, occupation, and projected expenses. If the Bahia's system approves the credit, which takes just one minute, the sales personnel can authorize the sale. If the system rejects the customer, the credit analyst takes him/her.

The credit analysts are central figures in Casas Bahia's business model. Highly trained credit analysts approve or reject a customer by asking a series of targeted questions in order to determine creditworthiness, which takes about ten minutes. These questions help determine the customer's honesty, "sizing them up" and monitoring body language and physical signs, such as wrinkles around the eyes (if a customer, for example, works as a construction worker under the sun). Such interaction serves dual purposes of detecting potential fraud and building relationships, since relationships are very important at Casas Bahia.

In order to detect fraud, credit analysts receive classroom and informal training where they learn personal "grooming" skills, the value and effectiveness of a positive attitude, and the crucial importance of building a long-term relationship with a customer, with an end goal to "transform a customer who enters the store as a client, into a friend when s/he leaves the store." In his biography, Samuel Klein confirmed this by stating: "Our motto is trust. Trust of our employees, suppliers and above all the trust of our customers. Regardless of whether our customers are janitors or masons, if they are trustworthy, we will help them fulfill their dreams."[43] This creates a virtuous

---

43   Lam 2014.

cycle as credits are largely approved based on relationships and the trust that underlie it. That way, when the customer's financial situation improves, s/he will continue to buy at Casas Bahia and will not switch to a competitor, thus building loyalty. Such loyalty also provides the company with a very positive word-of-mouth effect, which is, according to the company's experience, a very valuable commercial tool.

After completing the classroom training, future credit analysts accompany an experienced colleague for two weeks in the store, with a principal focus on implementation of classroom skills into practice with a special emphasis placed on cross selling. Cross selling is very important for Bahia, as 77% of the customers make repeat purchases, which is a testimony of the importance of trust and relationship building at Casas Bahia, for itself. In the same vein, one unique aspect of credit analyst training also involves "the art of saying no to a customer." This means that a positive attitude is necessary toward all customers even if s/he is unable to receive credit (which is the case for 16% of Bahia's customers). The approach to customers is respectful for his/her potential as a future customer. For example, if the customer's dream is to purchase a refrigerator with an icemaker that is out of his/her price range, credit analysts will try to explain to the customer that a better purchase would be a standard refrigerator. This way, Casas Bahia is keeping the customer's dream alive by providing a product of his/her desire in the acceptable price range and at the same time protecting the customers from their own cravings.

The main reasons for credit denial are threefold: negative SPC rating, credit limit, and third-party financing. As mentioned, in the case of negative SPC credit history, Casas Bahia cannot do anything; they apologize and assure the customer that, when the problem is resolved, Casas Bahia will be ready to serve them. In the case of an insufficient credit limit, Casas Bahia usually suggests similar products of different brands and/or models not to turn the customer away emptyhanded. In the case of third party payment, Casas Bahia realized that this method usually leads to default. The main reasons for that is the fact that the third person, the one who should pay the bill instead of the customer, does not have genuine motivation to do so, as well as any additional motive the customer may have for not paying the bill. Third party payment as well as unemployment and overspending are the principal reasons for default at Casas Bahia.

Due to their innovative, customer-centric business model, Casas Bahia's default rates are far below the same rates of that of their competitors. Bahia's general default rates average 8. 5% of their loan portfolio while their main competitor has an average of 15%. Michael Klein, son of the owner,

Samuel Klein, claims that the reason for such an advantage is the fact that Casas Bahia self-finances its loans, unlike the competitors who collaborate with banks and other financial institutions to provide financing.[44] This makes their interest rates significantly higher while simultaneously eliminating the critical relationship-building component between the company and the customer. Other retailers are not motivated to understand the customer and their default risk as the retailer does not include credit; they only sell the product. This is also one of the principal reasons for Casas Bahia's policy of minimizing its dependence on credit from commercial banks. The only portion of external financial providers in Bahia's model is the one used for financing of the interest rates, which, according to law, is not an option for retailers to do on their own in Brazil.

Technology also plays a critical role in the Casas Bahia business model by spurring the rapid growth the company has experienced. Firstly, it speeds up the credit approval process, which used to take an average of thirty minutes and required an average of thirty credit analysts per store. Due to automation, stores now require only up to five credit analysts per store while reducing the average time for credit approval to up to ten minutes. Technological improvements also have facilitated procedures with the customer. Previously, they printed the passbook directly from the computer and sent the bill directly to customers' homes, which resulted in problems with fraud due to lies about receiving the bills or simply forgetting to pay the bill because of the passbook being too large to fit in their pockets. Casas Bahia now prints pocket-sized passbooks that constantly reminds them of their obligations, and the paperwork can be done in stores, requiring only a mandatory signature of the customer to confirm the bill's receipt. Technology also aided in fraud detection as Casas Bahia now has a centralized system of customer information available in real time in all stores. In cooperation with companies such as Cisco and Telefonica, Bahia installed an IP network that connects all stores, warehouses, and docking facilities and helps manage work in those work units. Technological solutions also entail financial analysis of total unit sales, total revenues, total financed value, average down payment, average interest paid, average payment period, and so on, thus increasing productivity, efficiency, and effectiveness. Further, Casas Bahia developed a system able to perform multi-level analysis of the data that produces reports regarding individual stores and groups stores by city and/or region, product, and similar

---

[44]   Foguel & Wilson 2003.

variables. Such a system allows tracking and analyzing the 6 million customers that enter Casas Bahia stores every day, generating more than 900,000 new sales monthly, equal to BRL 31 million (about USD 9 million). Through gradual evolution of their business model over decades and by maintaining the same culture and customer-centric approach, Casas Bahia has become a leading Brazilian retailer with what may certainly be one of the most innovative consumer finance models in the emerging markets. The customer focus, as they say in Casas Bahia, is what made them successful: "It is all about fulfilling the customer dream. My sales agent has to be very well dressed, shaved and always smiling. If he has a personal problem, he cannot come to work. I will never allow him to transmit to my customer anything but perfection."[45]

The same model enabled the company to achieve the average financing term of six months, with an average interest rate of 4.13% – a far cry from any competitor – with an average bill value of BRL 440 (about USD 128) with an average default rate of 8.5%. The secrets to their success are multiple. First, Casas Bahia installs the merchandise in customers' homes, which makes collections easier to execute. Second, Casas Bahia has a very strict internal audit regime. Audit teams visit the stores without prior notice and check money in the cash registers, the inventory, cleanliness, quality of the in-store advertising, and so on, making sure everything is always in order. Third, Casas Bahia evaluates the locations in which they will set up their stores by checking the number of inquiries to the SPC in order to examine the commercial activity of the area, as every new store, according to the company politics, must have a minimum of at least 100,000 new buyers. Fourth, due to its size, Casas Bahia is able to purchase goods for significantly lower prices than its competitors and thus offer significant discounts to its customers.

Moreover, the success of Casas Bahia's business model has also resulted in approximately USD 1.4 billion of company revenues on annual basis produced by approximately 10 million buyers who make payments on approximately 800,000 bills monthly. Casas Bahia's future business plans are focusing on expansion of business opportunities, especially in the furniture market. Such orientation resulted in the installation of Bahia's own factory, called Bartira. It is also here that Bahia's motto, "Total dedication to you" manifests itself as the company applies a reverse engineering process by firstly

---

[45]   Foguel & Wilson 2003.

determining what the customers can afford to pay and then designing and producing the furniture accordingly.

Bahia will be facing certain threats as well, such as the expansion of credit card use throughout Brazil, which may not require store visits and may hinder a crucial component for the Bahia's relationship and trust-based business model. It will be interesting to see innovations in their business model trickling up to the higher segments of the market, considering their success at the base and the middle of the pyramid.

Case Study 3: Elektra (Mexico)

Grupo Elektra is a Mexican company that started out as a radio manufacturer in 1950 when founded by Hugo Salinas Rocha. Today, it is Latin America's leading specialty retailer and consumer finance, banking, and financial services company. Its unique business model enables emerging middle-class consumers in Mexico and the Americas to afford consumer goods through innovative financing schemes. This is possible through an extensive network of distribution, modern technology, solid management practice, and aggressive promotion of their brand through TV Azteca, a sister company in the Salinas business group. In addition, the Salinas Group includes Banco Azteca and Advance America. These companies provide financial services in Mexico and the United States. The same Group owns B-Store, a movie and video rental club; Afores Azteca and Seguros Azteca, a pension and an insurance company; Total Play, a telephone, television, and internet Service Company; and Enlace TPE, a telecommunications company. As of 2015, Grupo Elektra had 70,000 employees working in more than 8,096 points of sale across Mexico, Guatemala, Honduras, Peru, Panama, El Salvador, and the United States, of which 4,392 were in Mexico, 2,364 in Advance America stores in the United States, and the rest in Grupo Elektra stores and Banco Azteca banks throughout Latin America.

Elektra's products and services target 67% of Latin American MoP families, or 37% of this total represented by consumers in the C- and D+ socioeconomic classes with limited monthly incomes ranging from MXN 7800 to MXN 13499 (about USD 417–USD 722) per month. Grupo Elektra includes three divisions: the commercial division, the services division, and the financial division. In the commercial division, Elektra sells electronics, white goods, furniture, appliances, cell phones, and computers. In the services division, Elektra provides money wire services such as Western Union and offers for sale extended product warranties, the purchase of cell phone air time, the delivery of remittances though a national money wire service called Dinero Express, and the sale of airplane and bus tickets. In the financial division, customers may obtain consumer and personal loans, savings accounts, and debit and credit cards, as well as a retirement pension plan. In 2014–2015 Grupo Elektra`s revenue grew by 7%, despite store closures in Brazil, and as such is poised for continued growth in the years to come.

Approximately 65% of all the store sales are credit based, enabling aspiring middle-class LAC consumers, who lack the cash to pay for consumer goods up front and are mostly ineligible for credit through banking institutions, to finance their purchases on credit. Elektra even produces and sells through the store its own line of motorbikes, called Italika. Italika sales represent 50% of the total domestic market motorbike sales, thanks both to the solid product reputation and, more importantly, the accessible payment options through its sister company, Banco Azteca, which makes it a more affordable and attractive transport option for large segments of Mexican MoP consumers.

Elektra`s consumer financing model enjoys an astonishingly low default rate of less than 3%. Details of its innovative business model reveal the secret behind the company's success. First, there are no legal limits on interest levels charged in Mexico and much of Latin America, and there is limited government oversight. According to Mario Gordillo, Elektra's former Financial Service head, "Our customers are not concerned about the interest rates they are paying. All they want to know is the amount of the weekly installment and if they can afford it." Moreover, Elektra does not require its sales agents to divulge the annual percentage rate of 50%–120% or the total annual loan costs over the weekly installment plan, and thus, generally they do not. Instead, representatives emphasize weekly payment amounts over total interest rates in the long term. For the most part, Elektra management affirms, consumers just want to know what they have to pay each week and are less concerned with the actual high interest rates.

For example, a sound system may carry a price tag of 691 pesos, but in larger, bold print, a ticket reads 16 pesos, the weekly installment price for the consumer if he were to finance the purchase. Elektra charges interest on the full amount borrowed for the life of the loan, not on the declining balance. Elektra`s clerks earn commissions on top of a modest weekly salary of approximately USD 120 by selling additional services such as warranties or service agreements or by persuading a customer to spread out the pay period over the longest possible period: 104 weeks. Elektra will finance multiple purchases for customers, as long as the risk of default is not too excessive.

The next seemingly daunting task is assessing the credit worthiness of the Elektra consumers, who generally do not enjoy regular formal sector jobs. Mexico has no rating system of individual consumers' credit worthiness. As such, Elektra developed a system to evaluate and approve financing for consumers and, to do so, required detailed information about each consumer. This process starts in the store with a customer inquiry about financing, with entry of personal information into Elektra's proprietary software. An interest rate is fixed at the time of purchase and a weekly repayment schedule is agreed upon. Elektra will require a guarantor, and within twenty-four hours the customer will receive a visit from an Elektra credit and collections officer known as a portfolio manager (PM) to evaluate the potential customer's credit worthiness.

PMs seek out the prospective clients on motorbikes in their homes to interview them personally and their neighbors about the candidate's creditworthiness as well as confirm exactly where the customer lives and map the location. The portfolio manager's job is to ascertain the income sources of the household – the quantitative part of the assessment. However, the portfolio manager also provides a qualitative evaluation of customers based on the prospective client's home cleanliness, ownership of appliances, etc. The PM will even go so far as to interview employees in neighborhood stores to obtain more customer information. According to Gordillo, "This subjective assessment is what really makes the difference." The PM will even knock on doors and talk to neighbors to get information on the prospective customer. Generally, the manager may authorize up to USD 1150 in loans, as long as the weekly monthly payment does not exceed 20% of the customer's household income. Elektra approves approximately 50% of credit requests. Not surprisingly, the credit approval process is complex, costly, and time consuming and explains in part the higher costs Elektra faces when providing consumer financing to the emerging middle class. This cost is reflected in the high APR rates Elektra customers pay.

Default rates are very low, in part because the PM is responsible for both credit authorization as well as collections. Their salaries are also 90% variable, based on collections, and PMs may have their number of total accounts decreased if in fact more than 250 of their 650 accounts become past due. Middle-income Mexicans tend to be anxious about maintaining their reputation and thus generally pay back what they owe, regardless of the hardship faced. In addition, those who slip behind receive frequent visits from the PMs, who remind them of their overdue bills. Given the impact on their own salary, PMs are careful only to authorize credit on strictly defined criteria with a focal point placed on the candidate's potential for repayment.

CONCLUSIONS

As of 2014, 400 million individuals in LAC were unbanked, being the middle of the pyramid – a growing sector lacking access to financing due to insufficient firms and innovations oriented toward their needs. The countries and cases presented in this chapter exemplify this phenomenon; significant numbers of consumers across Chile (36.7%), Mexico (60.9%), and Brazil (36.9%) are still financially excluded. This is due to low or unstable income levels, lack of formal credit histories, geographical isolation, and high-risk credit profiles. Similarly, unbanked LAC consumers at the MoP can ill afford to make consumer goods and services purchases that emerging middle-class consumers worldwide dream of. For unbanked micro-enterprises, financial exclusion precludes the purchase of physical assets or investment in the working capital needed to grow their businesses through increased inventory, store modernization, or new equipment. Attending these underserved, growing MoP segments in Latin America will be of increasingly strategic importance to the survival of any company operating in the region's emerging market. The companies presented in this chapter identified the segments, quantified their size and importance, developed innovative solutions that overcame common obstacles, and enlisted the assistance of valuable local partners whose local presence and trusted reputation helped the companies gain access to these untapped segments.

The inclusive business models described in this chapter share a number of characteristics in common. First, they all stem from an emerging middle-class consumer or company need or desire that could be ameliorated through access to financing. Specifically, in the case of BCI, middle income consumers needed access to credit to make purchases and small retail micro-enterprises needed access to financing to modernize their stores and expand their inventories. In the Casas Bahia case, middle-income Brazilian consumers hoped to finance consumer purchases, and in the case of Elektra, emerging middle-class consumers aspired to purchase appliances, electronics, and furniture on credit they would have otherwise not been eligible for. In all three cases, financing was provided through existing distribution channels in the target communities, thereby circumventing the obstacle of geographic inaccessibility. In the case of Casas Bahia and Elektra, the retailers themselves offered consumer financial services and developed unique systems to assess creditworthiness of consumers with irregular incomes or nonexistent formal credit histories. The success of all three models was built in great part upon the trust-based relationships created and developed among the MoP debtors on the one hand and their creditors on the other hand, to whom the responsibility of collections was vested in trained, financially literate, trusted locals. For example, BCI empowered small retail channel partners to provide credit to local consumers whose payment history, albeit informal, they already knew. In the Casas Bahia case, locals in the targeted communities were hired as employees and credit analysts of the retailers' products with whom relationships were formed. Similarly, in the Elektra case, local program managers played an essential role not only in granting credit but also ensuring collections, since their incomes depended upon it. Credit worthiness, collections, and the entire customer relationship management was empowered by robust technological platforms in all three cases, which provided real time information to creditors when making potentially risky financing decisions and has proven crucial in keeping consumer default rates low.

A third attribute in two of the cases presented is the key role played by alliance partners. In BCI, alliances with Rabie allowed BCI immediate access to small retailers nationwide, even in the remotest of locations. This was essential for them to overcome the potential obstacle and cost of access. Moreover, financing through the Inter-American Development Bank reduced the risk premium initially faced by BCI when undertaking the micro-finance project. Elektra, on the other hand, has relied less on external alliances; it benefits significantly from the services provided by companies within its same business group, Grupo Salinas, which include advertising of its products and services through TV Azteca and consumer financial services through Banco Azteca.

The cases of BCI, Casas Bahia, and Elektra together reveal how the financial inclusion of emerging middle-class consumers and businesses in Latin America creates a virtuous cycle for all those involved. Consumers and businesses gain access to products, services, and capital they need or want, and, as seen in the case of BCI, they also are provided valuable financial, business, and technical training to improve the likelihood that the resources provided are used wisely. The companies that target them, BCI, Casas Bahia, and Elektra, in turn, grow their sales to a growing segment of consumers whom otherwise would be too hard to reach or too risky to bank. Finally, emerging middle-class communities grow and prosper, as community members are enlisted in the inclusive business models as retailers, employees, or promoters, therein enhancing not only the projects' credibility but also the livelihoods of those directly involved.

From the analysis of the cases, the lessons that can be drawn are the following. Firstly, innovations in the MoP are oriented toward the fulfillment of unmet necessities and aspirations. The new middle classes are growing and are doing some purchases for the first time, but they lack the access to some of them or the knowledge to analyze what is best for them. The cases here presented exemplify how identifying and tending to specific needs of the segment can help create a successful business. Second, in order to create innovations that are accepted and meaningful for the middle of the pyramid, it is vital to understand the demographic. As previously stated, they often lack knowledge about what is best for them, but their new aspirations sometimes prevent them from admitting said lack of knowledge. Therefore, firms need to earn the customers' trust and loyalty in order to thrive, both the companies and the clients. Creating trust or using the already-built trust relationships with other people or with certain distribution channels will help the innovations be accepted by the MoP. If the customers feel that they are being heard and that they won't get tricked, they are more likely to start using a product or service, and eventually revisit the firm due to the earned loyalty. Lastly, the treatment of the customers and their aspirations is critical for their acceptance and trust. The new middle classes are growing and escalating, but they still have certain limitations the top of the pyramid does not. What firms need to do is craft their innovations in a way that is appealing to the MoP but also present them in a way that is understandable for them and that highlights the benefits they would be getting from the purchase. Additionally, in case their desires cannot be met due to different reasons that can include credit limit, it is important that the employees do not make them feel ignored or mistreated. Instead, the customers need to receive validation of their wishes but also be oriented toward what is best for them, or within their current possibilities. With this, the clients will feel well-treated and are more likely to return once they have the means to fulfill their original desire, and not be left empty-handed.

REFERENCES

Adrian, T. & Shin, H. 2011. Financial Intermediaries and Monetary Economics. In B. M. Friedman & M. Woodford (eds.), *Handbook of Monetary Economics* 3: 601–646. San Diego, CA: Elsevier.

Arping, S., Loranth, G., & Morrison, A. 2010. Public Initiatives to Support Entrepreneurs: Credit Guarantees versus Co-Funding. *Journal of Financial Stability* 6: 26–35.

Banking News. 2010. BCI Nova y Rabie realizan alianza para facilitar el financiamiento de los almaceneros. Accessed August 16, 2017. www.ebankingnews.com/noticias/bci-nova-y-rabie-realizan-alianza-para-facilitar-el-financiamiento-de-los-almaceneros-003089

BCI. 2011. Informe Sustentabilidad 2011. *BCI*. Accessed August 15, 2017. www.bci.cl/medios/2012/investor/dectos/rse/BCIInformeSustentabilidad2011.pdf

BCI. 2012. Informe Sustentabilidad 2012. *BCI*. Accessed August 15. 2017. www.bci.cl/medios/2012/investor/bci-sustentabilidad/descargas/informe.pdf

BCI. 2014. 2014 Annual report. *BCI*. Accessed August 15, 2017. https://bci.modyocdn.com/uploads/2f13b10f-9c52-4ac8-9180-587a3bfe7529/original/AnnualReport14.pdf

Dabla-Norris, E., Deng, Y., Ivanova, A., Karpowicz, I., Unsal, F., VanLeemput, E., Wong, J. 2015. Financial Inclusion: Zeroing In on Latin America. Working Paper

15/206, International Monetary Fund. Washington, DC. Accessed August 13, 2017. www.imf.org/en/Publications/WP/Issues/2016/12/31/Financial-Inclusion-Zooming-in-on-Latin-America-43312

De La Torre, A., Ize, A., Schmukler, S. L. 2012. Financial Development in Latin America and the Caribbean: The Road Ahead. The World Bank. Washington, DC. Accessed August 13, 2017. http://siteresources.worldbank .org/LACINSPANISHEXT/Resources/FLAGSHIP_eng.pdf

Department on Economic and Social Affairs. 2010. Rethinking Poverty: Report on the World Social Situation. United Nations. Accessed August 15, 2017. www.un .org/esa/socdev/rwss/docs/2010/fullreport.pdf

Ferreira, F., Messina, J., Rigolini, J., López, L. F., Lugo, M.A., & Vakis, R. 2013. Economic Mobility and the Rise of the Latin American Middle Class. World Bank. Accessed February 25, 2017. https://openknowledge.worldbank.org/bit stream/handle/10986/11858/9780821396346.pdf?sequence=5

Foguel, S. & Wilson, A. 2003. *Casas Bahia: Fulfilling the Dream*. Ann Arbor, MI: The University of Michigan Business School.

García, N., Grifoni, A., Lopez, J. C., and Mejía, D. 2013. "Financial Education in Latin America and the Caribbean: Rationale, Overview, and Way Forward," OECD Working Papers on Finance, Insurance and Private Pensions, No. 33, OECD Publishing.

Gardeva, A. & Rhyne, E. 2011. Opportunities and Obstacles to Financial Inclusion: Survey Report. Publication 12. Center for Financial Inclusion – Accion International. Accessed August 15, 2017. https://centerforfinancialinclusionblog .files.wordpress.com/2011/07/opportunities-and-obstacles-to-financial-inclusion_ 110708_final.pdf

Gradl, C. & Jenkin, B. 2011. *Tackling Barriers to Scale: From Inclusive Business Models to Inclusive Business Ecosystems*. Cambridge, MA: The CSR Initiative at the Harvard Kennedy School.

IADB. 2013. The Year In Review. IADB. Accessed August 12, 2017. https:// publications.iadb.org/bitstream/handle/11319/6422/IDB%20Annual%20Report %202013.%20%20The%20Year%20in%20Review.pdf?sequence=1

IMF. 2015. Annual Report 2015 – Tackling Challenges Together. Accessed October 15, 2017. www.imf.org/external/pubs/ft/ar/2015/eng/pdf/ar15_eng.pdf

Impavido, G., Lasagabaster, E., & García-Huitrón, M. 2010. New Policies for Mandatory Defined Contribution Pensions: Industrial Organization Models and Investment Products. Latin American Development Forum Series, World Bank, Washington, DC. Accessed August 1, 2017. https://digitallibrary.un.org/record/ 698679?ln=en

Jenkins, B., Ishikawa, E., Geaneotes, A., & Paul, J. 2012. Inclusive Business Solutions: Expanding Opportunity and Access at the Base of the Pyramid. The World Bank. Accessed August 12, 2017. http://documents.worldbank.org/curated/en/2012/10/17101976/inclusive-business-solutions-expanding-opportunity-access-base-pyramid

Jordan, V., Galperin, H., & Peres, W. 2013. Broadband in Latin America: Beyond Connectivity. Economic Commission for Latin America and the Caribbean (ECLAC). Accessed August 12, 2017. http://repositorio.cepal.org/bitstream/handle/11362/37524/LCL3588_en.pdf;jsessionid=B223C960946CB7FE78BB8814754FD45E?sequence=1

Karnani, A. 2007. The Mirage of Marketing to the Bottom of the Pyramid: How the Private Sector Can Help Alleviate Poverty. *California Management Review* 49/4: 90–111.

Lam, C. 2014. 15 frases marcantes de Samuel Klein fundador da casas bahía. Exame. Accessed February 2, 2017. http://exame.abril.com.br/negocios/15-frases-marcantes-de-samuel-klein-fundador-da-casas-bahia/

Leggett, T., Jaitman, L., Guerra, J. A. 2017. Homicide and Organized Crime in Latin America and the Caribbean. In L. Jitman (ed.), *The Costs of Crime and Violence: New Evidence and Insights in Latin America and the Caribbean*. Inter-American Development Bank. Washington, DC. Accessed August 15, 2017. https://publications.iadb.org/bitstream/handle/11319/8133/The-Costs-of-Crime-and-Violence-New-Evidence-and-Insights-in-Latin-America-and-the-Caribbean.pdf

Lewis, J. A. 2017. The Costs of Cybercrime: Is the Region Prepared? In L. Jitman (ed.), *The Costs of Crime and Violence: New Evidence and Insights in Latin America and the Caribbean*. Inter-American Development Bank. Washington, DC. Accessed August 15, 2017. https://publications.iadb.org/bitstream/handle/11319/8139/The-Costs-of-Crime-and-Violence-New-Evidence-and-Insights-in-Latin-America-and-the-Caribbean-Executive-Summary.pdf

Prahalad, C. & Hart, S. 2004. *The Fortune at the Bottom of the Pyramid*. Berkeley, CA: University of California Berkeley.

Roa, M. J., Másmela, G. A., Bohórquez, N., Pinilla, D. A. 2014. Financial Education and Inclusion in Latin American and the Caribbean Programs of Central Banks and Financial Superintendencies. Center For Latin American Monetary Studies. Banco De La República, Colombia. Accessed August 15, 2017. www.cemla.org/PDF/otros/2014-10-Financial-Education-Inclusion-LAC.pdf

Roa García, M. J., Másmela, G. A. A., Bohórquez, N. G., & Pinilla, D. A. R. 2011. Financial Education and Inclusion in Latin America and the Caribbean: Programs of Central Banks and Financial Superintendencies. Books. Centro de Estudios Monetarios Latinoamericanos, CEMLA.

Seghal, V., Lauster, S., Mayr, E., & Panneer, G. 2010. Roasted or Fried: How to Succeed with Emerging Market Consumers. Booz & Co. Accessed August 13, 2017. www.strategyand.pwc.com/reports/roasted-fried-succeed-with-emerging

Srinivas, P. S., Whitehouse, E., & Yermo, J. 2000. Regulating Private Pension Funds' Structure, Performance, and Investments: Cross-Country Evidence. Social Protection Unit, Human Development Network, The World Bank. Accessed August 1, 2017. https://mpra.ub.uni-muenchen.de/14753

Terrier, G., Valdés, R., Tovar, C. E., Chan-Lau, J., Fernández-Valdovinos, C., García Escribano, M., Medeiros , C., Tang, M. K., Vera Martin, M., & Walker, C. 2011. "Policy Instruments to Lean against the Wind in Latin America." IMF Working Paper 11/159, International Monetary Fund, Washington, DC. Accessed August 13, 2017. http://citeseerx.ist.psu.edu/viewdoc/download?doi=10.1.1.228.6856&rep=rep1&type=pdf

The Economist. 2013. Mammon's New Monarchs: The Emerging-World Consumer is King. *The Economist.* Accessed August 12, 2017. www.economist.com/news/business/21569016-emerging-world-consumer-king-mammons-new-monarchs

The World Bank. 2015. Global Financial Inclusion. The World Bank. Accessed: August 12, 2017. www.worldbank.org/globalfindex

7 Great Products for the MoP Consumption Practices

Jorge L. Alcaraz and Miguel A. Lopez-Lomelí

INTRODUCTION

Middle class population accounts for about 48% of the whole world, which in expenditures represents 53% regarding the global GDP. The middle of the socioeconomic pyramid from developing economies is also an important market. In Latin America, this sector of the population grew 50% in just the past decade.[1] This trend is reflected in the growth of consumption and demand of different products, both essential and discretionary. As the market has been changing, the tastes and preferences of the middle-income sector from middle-income countries have been changing as well. Having more disposable income than the base of the pyramid, but not as much as the top of the pyramid, the MoP looks for new products that fulfill their aspirations but are not too expensive for them to afford. Firms have to innovate and develop new products that tend to this segment of the population, in a way that the products offered not only remove features from products aimed for the upper classes but are more than adaptations of those aimed toward the lower classes. In order to understand this phenomenon, we analyze here different firms from different industries in Latin America.

These are the cases of Grupo Fabricas Selectas (Mexico) with toy balls; Sanchez y Martin (Mexico) manufacturing bar soaps and detergents; and Tricot (Peru), Topitop (Chile), and Permoda (Colombia) performing in the garment sector. From these firms we can derive lessons regarding how they have successfully achieved the preference of the consumers of the middle of the pyramid. Among the most important lessons is the following: These firms are strongly focused

[1] Fidelity 2013; Long & Shapiro 2018.

on R&D in order to create products with a strong value that consumers of the middle of the pyramid really appreciate, and thus
consumer preference is gained. Even though all innovations need
focus on R&D, the MoP represents a different challenge since often-
times the innovations aimed at the middle class are only downgraded
versions of products for the top of the pyramid or improved versions of
those for the lower classes, instead of new products actually tailored
for the MoP. In addition, some firms have created commercial networks and alliances to meet middle-of-the-pyramid consumers' wants
and needs.

IMPORTANCE OF EMERGING MARKETS AND MIDDLE-OF-THE-PYRAMID CONSUMERS IN CONSUMER GOODS

In the context of the global market, emerging markets (EMs) are
considered an important business opportunity. EMs comprise about
85% of the world's population; represent almost 75% of the global
GDP growth; have a large, mostly productive population segment age
25–59; and have 90% of the world's proven oil reserves.

EMs sales to consumers represent an estimated market potential that could exceed USD 20 trillion annually by the end of 2020.
Companies doing business in emerging markets focus on fulfilling the
needs of fast-growing emerging middle-class[2] consumers who belong
to the Middle of the socioeconomic Pyramid (MoP); 48% of the world
population belongs to the middle-of-the-pyramid consumers who
globally expend USD 15.365689 million, representing 53% of the
global GDP.[3] In Latin America the middle class represents 30%, as
the result of 50% growth in the past decade.[4]

Additionally, in 2014 world population surpassed 7 billion, and
the segment below age thirty accounted for 46.5% in EMs, which
accounts for 90% of the global population aged under thirty[5]; EMs
represent a strategic source of growth for consumer-packaged goods

[2]   Atsmon et al. 2012.   [3]   Euromonitor 2017.   [4]   Fidelity 2013.
[5]   Euromonitor 2015a.

(CPG) companies. For instance, by 2020 Unilever expects to get 70% of its total sales from EMs; Procter & Gamble (P&G) intends to add 1 billion new customers and take contribution from emerging markets of approximately 40% in 2016.[6]

In Latin America, expenses by population in the middle socio-economic sector have been increasing from 2011 to 2016; these are the cases of Argentina, Bolivia, Brazil, Chile, Colombia, Costa Rica, Ecuador, Guatemala, Mexico, Peru, and Uruguay per available information from Passport database. Mexico, for instance, regarding the share of consumers' expenditures as a percentage of GDP, passed from 23.4% in 2011 to 25% in 2016; Colombia moved from 23.6% to 24.3%; and Peru from 24% to 24.8%, just to name a few.

The increases of middle-class households and available income have allowed the growth of consumption and the demand of optional products, not only essential products. Among these items are those related to personal care and clothing. These trends are in line with the increase of consumption products in Latin America. Specifically regarding the apparel industry, sales in Colombia, Chile, and Mexico have increased between 2011 and 2016 (17.4%, 18.1%, 27.2%, respectively); the situation is different in Brazil, where sales have decreased. Similar behavior remains for beauty and personal care; here Brazil increased as well. Regarding products related to the traditional toys and games category, even when there is a decreasing trend for non-electronic toys in Latin American countries, in terms of demography the situation changes and trends for children under age six and between seven and twelve concentrates the largest market share, with growing trends between 2011 and 2016.

In order to understand the current context, former statistics from Latin America are useful. One of the most important industries in the world, valued at approximately USD 8 trillion,[7] is the consumer-packaged goods (food and beverages, clothing, tobacco,

[6]   Kapoor 2015.   [7]   Hirose et al. 2015.

and household products).[8] Regarding home care, its global value is estimated to be USD 155 billion in 2014. In Latin America it was estimated to be USD 26 billion in 2014, up by 15% and accounting for 16% of global sales. Brazil and Mexico remain the major economies and consumption markets in Latin America.[9] Laundry is the largest category within home care in Mexico, with sales valued at MXN 62646 million (USD 4.253 million).[10]

In the case of the garment industry, according to the Inter-American Development Bank, in 2010 the expenses of the people from the middle and the bottom of the pyramid on clothing represented 5.5% (USD 42 million) of the total. In order to get an idea of how important these expenses are, we have made a comparison with other sectors during the same year. What people spend on clothing is similar to food services, food not at home, (5.8%, USD 44 million), power (5%, USD 38 million) and health (4%, USD 31 million). Furthermore, and more important, is that expenses in basic consumption goods, including clothing, have grown during the last decade; additionally, the number of poor people decreased and the middle class increased.[11]

The average trends in terms of expenditures on clothing in Latin America are a good indicator. Nevertheless, these trends are not the same for all the countries in the region, which intrinsically have considerations to assess. For instance, in Brazil the clothing sector grew from USD 92 million in 2000 to $125 million in 2010, representing 36% growth. The same sector in Chile fell 26%, going from USD 195 million to USD 144 million. In Mexico, growth of just 5% during the same period, going from USD 96 million to USD 101 million. And for Peru, a growth of 56%, from USD 68 million to USD 106 million.

Most firms, both multinational companies (MNCs) and local businesses, have the challenge to address the needs and desires of the MoP consumers by developing products, services, and

[8]   INVESTOPEDIA 2015.   [9]   *Euromonitor* 2015a.
[10]   *Euromonitor* 2015b.   [11]   Azevedo et al. 2015.

commercialization models to serve this important segment.[12] BoP and MoP consumers face the main key challenges in their purchasing process of products and services: availability (where the products can be found), affordability (fair or low pricing), and acceptability (customer perception), which need to be addressed by the firms trying to win over these consumers.[13]

CASES IN THE CONSUMER GOODS SECTOR

In the following section, we present some specific cases of firms and their particular challenges in addressing the middle class consumer segment. We also analyze how they adapted their products, processes, and business model in order to fulfill the needs, tastes, and preferences of consumers from the MoP.

First, we present the case of Grupo Fabricas Selectas (GFS) and one of its products, Pelotas Payaso. This Mexican firm has been for many years leading the toy ball market in that country with plastic toy ball products focusing on both the consumers from BoP and those from the Top of the Pyramid (ToP). Due to the dynamic changes in this industry and the business environment, a new opportunity appeared when Grupo Fabricas Selectas realized that there was a commercial gap. To fill this gap, the firm had to focus on the development of a toy ball product targeting the MoP consumers, who did not like the cheap line designed for the BoP consumers and were not willing to pay the price of the ToP consumers' line.

The second case refers to another Mexican firm, Sanchez y Martin, who manufactures bar soap and detergent. We analyze how this firm has successfully faced the threats that global company entries, such as Colgate Palmolive and Procter & Gamble, represent to this local firm. Specifically, we will focus on three of its products (Lirio, Util, and Ruth) developed to fulfill the middle- and low-income consumer needs.

---

[12] Jaiswal 2008. [13] Andreson & Billou 2006.

Finally, we will present three different firms from different countries: Tricot from Chile, Topitop from Peru, and Permoda from Colombia. The study of these three cases will be useful to illustrate how these firms have changed, adapting their productive as well as managerial activities to the new tastes and preferences of the middle-income sector regarding the apparel industry. These firms have adopted and implemented the fast fashion model in order to fulfill the new needs in the MoP.

Grupo Fabricas Selectas: Toy Balls

Consumption in Mexico is a big, growing market, accounting for a percentage of the GDP that increased from 23.4% in 2011 to 25% in 2016. Grupo Fabricas Selectas was founded more than sixty years ago by the Garcin family. It is a key manufacturer of Toy Balls in Mexico and also distributes and commercializes them. Additionally, GFS manufactures, distributes, and commercializes a wide brand portfolio competing in a diversity of important product categories such as sponge balls, marbles, party disposable products, fluffy and teddy toys, balloons, molton sport balls, stockings and women's and girl's underwear, and imported candies. GFS contributes to the Mexican economy with more than 1,500 collaborators, with 5,000 products and a worldwide presence through exports to 42 countries.[14]

Their toy division represents 80% of their business, and toy balls count for 20% of this. During 2015 sales of toy balls represented 30 million units, which were commercialized 54% through the traditional channel via wholesalers, distributors, and low-priced toy stores and 46% through modern retail (supermarket chains).

In the last few decades, the commercial environment in the Mexican toy industry has experienced major changes due to several reasons, such as the NAFTA implementation, the country's economic recovery, and growth of the socioeconomic middle-class segment, which represents more than one-third of Mexican households.[15] The

---

[14]   Grupo Fabricas Selectas 2020.   [15]   CONAPO 2015.

new competitive environment in this emerging country, translated into the pursuit of new strategic business models along with innovation processes that overcome the traditional approaches of managing the Mexican firms' businesses, are aiming for maintaining or increasing their competitive positions in their respective industries.

Under this scenario, Grupo Fabricas Selectas developed a new product with the aim of serving this important segment of the Mexican population. Initially, it was thought to be commercialized via wholesalers and traditional low-priced toy stores. However, an opportunity arose to commercialize it through Walmart group (modern retail) as part of the program of this retailer in Mexico to address the middle of the pyramid consumers within their "Prichos" format.

Once the new product was developed, meeting the right pricing with a higher quality versus the low-priced line, and with the right value equation, its introduction represented an instant success in consumers' acceptance and sales volume, becoming one of the best initiatives for consumers in the MoP for both GFS and Walmart in Mexico.

The traditional channel sells a low-priced toy ball at approximately MXN 6.00 (about USD 0.41); this is the bottom of the pyramid (BoP) version (not purchased in modern retail). The top-of-the-pyramid version, sold in modern retail, is priced at MXN 40 (about USD 2.72); this is a high-quality ball that additionally is decorated with licensed characters (from Disney, Nickelodeon, Mattel, etc.) printed on both sides. The attraction of a toy ball with printed licensed characters is that they have a role of "substituting toy products" vs the expensive figurines or other type of licensed executions of toys that consumers cannot afford. Children feel that they are playing with the character printed on the toy ball, and parents are willing to pay the price for it.

In 2012, aiming to increase sales and market share, the commercial area of the company realized that through the years they had been focused on commercializing two versions of toy balls, the low-priced for the bottom of the pyramid consumers and the high-priced one focused on the top-of-the-pyramid consumers. Given the importance of the middle-of-the-pyramid consumers segment, they decided to look for a solution that would better meet their customers' expectations, who, as mentioned previously, did not like the cheap line aimed at them but were not willing to pay the price of the ToP consumers' line.

A new toy ball was developed based on a combination of innovation in manufacturing processes and optimization of costs in combination with a new approach to use the licensed themes and characters. The new ball had a target price of MXN 14.00 (USD 0.95) and initially was to be commercialized via wholesalers and traditional low-priced toy stores to implement a new quality and price tier for the MoP consumers. However, the sales department of GFS realized that this new toy ball would have a better chance to succeed if introduced as part of their strategies via modern retail, specifically through the Walmart's Prichos program.

Prichos is a well differentiated section. It is a "store within a store," aimed to satisfy the needs of the MoP consumers, based on the concept of "one price for every item sold." Initially, the price was MXN 13.90 (about USD 0.94), selling a mix of innovative, opportune and seasonal products within the categories of gifts, home, decoration, toys, haberdashery, stationery, health and beauty, cleaning, hardware, cars, and pets. The seasonal products have shown a growing participation, which became a differentiator of the format.[16]

As part of the joint commercialization efforts, the idea of this new toy ball was presented to the Walmart Group, which immediately accepted it for Prichos. The Walmart's Prichos toy ball was launched in 2013 at the target price of MXN 14.90 (USD 1.01) at an approximately 60% discount versus the top-of-the-pyramid ball version, and sold in modern retail (supermarkets) at more than 200% the price of the BoP version. This new Stock Keeping Unit (SKU) had an

---

[16]   Walmart 2009.

excellent overall quality and was printed on one side only, with important and attractive licensed characters such as Angry Bird, Frozen, Minions, Princesses, etc. This toy ball was merchandised at points of sale with spectacular in-store visibility linked to new movie (with licensed characters) launches.

Once the new product was introduced into the market with this new proper value, it represented an instant success in consumers' acceptance. Yearly sales went from 712,400 units to 1.4 million in 2014, a 99% increase, and kept on growing. This represented one of the best initiatives for consumers in the MoP for both Grupo Fabricas Selectas and Walmart in Mexico. GFS continued to sell to the BoP and ToP on top of this SKU with minimum cannibalization since the product is oriented to a specific segment of consumers and is only sold through Walmart's Prichos.

The strategy of GFS was to innovate their manufacturing processes to be able to meet a specific target brand value, which is the price (premium) a consumer is willing to pay for a specific brand above a baseline.[17] Thanks to the capacity of GFS in achieving innovation in their manufacturing processes, GFS was able to produce a new high-quality product at a new price tier satisfying the MoP consumers' expectations. The success of this solution is based on three pillars: research and development, innovation in manufacturing processes, and MKT and Commercialization in a specific store format for MoP.

The R&D efforts were aimed toward developing a toy ball with the characteristics, wants, and needs the MoP had, but at fair target pricing. In order to do that, there was the need to innovate in the manufacturing process to produce high quality products with good cost-optimization strategies. After manufacture, it was necessary to have correct distribution channels and marketing strategies. In this regard, Walmart's Prichos model became a key ally for visibility and accessibility, using licensed characters attractive for the customers and presented in special assorted cases.

[17] AMA 2014.

Grupo Fabricas Selectas, along with its key national retailers, has focused on the strategy of creating outstanding in-store visibility/merchandising by placing gigantic toy ball product displays in strategically located positions close to the toys shelves area of the point of sale. This retail visibility strategy allows for superior consumer product awareness and fosters impulse purchases. In addition, in the Walmart stores the toy ball version for middle-of-the-pyramid consumers is specially located and only sold at the Prichos area.

Sánchez y Martin: Bar Soap & Detergent

The laundry market is significant in the home care industry, with sales of MXN 62646 million (USD 4.253 million) in Mexico. Sanchez y Martin was founded in 1929 and has been one of the leading Mexican soap and packaged detergent companies for more than eighty-seven years, manufacturing and commercializing many successful local brands.[18] This company has successfully faced the entry of global companies such as Colgate Palmolive in the 1920s[19] and Procter & Gamble in 1948[20] by developing detergent and soap brands such as Lirio, Util, and Ruth that through the years have consolidated their position in the Mexican market.

The need to be competitive against global brand entries made the company focus on developing products for the middle- and low-income consumer segments. Lirio is one of the leading pure bar soaps; it is dermatologically oriented and has a strong presence in Mexico. The challenges of the heavily competitive market and business environment led Sanchez y Martin to realize the need and opportunity to develop a competitive advantage against global brands by developing products that would better meet the needs of the MoP and BoP consumers.

This competitive advantage was achieved through a deep understanding of these consumer segments and the dynamics of the market and an emphasis on innovation in the development of new products in

---

[18]   Sanchez-y-Martin 2016.   [19]   Colgate-Palmolive 2016.
[20]   Colgate-Palmolive 2016.

the manufacturing process, along with the implementation of advanced technology for their manufacturing facilities.[21] This can be observed in the development of new lines of products aimed toward specific customers within the middle of the pyramid, fulfilling the specific needs and desires they have in terms of practicality, affordability, accessibility, and tradition.

The commercial management of Sanchez y Martin has been very clear that in Mexico, with regard to these types of consumer products and their target consumers' segments, the role of the women is critical as housewife and shopper for the family. They classify the female shoppers for these types of products in Mexico in four categories: The Traditional, The Spoiler, The Equilibrated, and the Aspirational woman. Their focus, due to the MoP and BoP consumer segments, is on the "Traditional housewife." The other three may be inclined to buy brands that are more expensive.

So, what Sanchez y Martin did was the following. In the case of the Lirio bar soap a new product line was developed on top of their basic generic Lirio Neutro, which can be considered the Mexican equivalent of Ivory Soap in the United States.[22] Thus, Lirio Bar soap developed a product line with additional line extensions – Lirio Dermatologico, Lirio Antibacterial, and Lirio Natura – launched to meet this important segment of the Mexican population. In the case of Util detergent, it is a product developed for multiuse cleaning of clothes, dishes, floors, diverse surfaces, and many more.

This allows the MoP consumers to buy only one product with multiple applications and benefits. To make it multiuse, critical was to develop a softer scent that would be acceptable for washing clothes as well as dishes and floors. This was a real breakthrough, coming up with one detergent to clean everything in the home.

In the case of each brand, there are three axes that in combination made possible the innovation and development of successful products with great value for MoP and BoP consumers.

[21]   Sanchez-y-Martin 2016.   [22]   P&G 2016.

The key axes of success for each of these brands from Sanchez y Martin are MoP consumer understanding; tradition/intergenerational recommendation, which translates in a strong brand familiarity; manufacturing cost efficiency; specialization in the commercialization in traditional stores; and positioning of Lirio as a multiuse cleaning product (not as an archetypal detergent).

In the case of Lirio bar soap the axes are the following. First, there is a deep understanding of the Mexican consumer insights, especially of the MoP and BoP segments and their wants, needs, and attachment to local culture. The consumer target is the Mexican woman, belonging to the SEL's C and D+, whose main concern is how other people see her family members, in terms of personal care and hygiene. This traditional Mexican woman does not appreciate the "Aspirational woman" used in advertising by the bar soap global brands to represent women who belong to SEL's A and B.

Second, they capitalize on the local culture and tradition by emphasizing their product's pureness, years in the market, and preference by the previous consumer generations – grandparents and parents of current consumers. This also extends to a strong focus and specialization in the commercialization on the Traditional Stores (Mama & Papa's or High Frequency stores) channel, which is the store format mainly used by MoP and BoP consumers (versus the focus of global brands in modern retail), even though their products are sold in all retail channels.

Third, they aim toward cost efficiency in production by constantly optimizing the production processes and updating their plant with new production technology that allows for very competitive, affordable prices for these consumer segments. As an indication, one of their bestselling SKU's is sold in modern retail at MXN 8.00 (USD 0.54) (18% below the category leader). This is also supported by management decisions on when to rationalize the product lines and SKU's that are not commercially or financially attractive, with a constant emphasis on canceling those SKU's or line versions, optimizing production, distribution logistics and allocation costs in shelves, and efficiencies in both the company and in points of sale.

In the case of detergent Util the axes are the following. First, they have a deep understanding of Mexican consumer insights, especially of the MoP and BoP segments – their wants, needs, and attachment to local culture. The consumer target is the Mexican woman, belonging to the SEL's C- and D, whose main concern is to optimize the family economy through purchasing high value products.

Second, there is an emphasis on performance: providing one detergent for all – a multiuse product – and developing a detergent scent that is milder versus competition and is effective for cleaning clothes as well as dishes and floors and other surfaces. This was a critical move since in the home care category the cleaning of clothes, dishes, and floors typically require different products, one specialized in each, thus making consumers buy three products for their home cleaning. This product development provided economization to the MoP and BoP consumers by allowing them to buy only one product that performs very well in all types of cleaning. As in Lirio bar soap, the commercialization of Util detergent also has strong focus and specialization in the commercialization in traditional stores, becoming the leader in this channel since in addition to the traditional sizes they produce a 10kg size that allows traditional store owners to sell by smaller quantities at more affordable and competitive prices (versus the focus of global brands in modern retail).

Lastly, cost efficiency in production is critical, constantly optimizing the production processes and updating the plant with new production technology that achieves very competitive, affordable prices for these consumer segments. For a modern perspective, the 1.1 kg size is sold in modern retail (supermarkets) at MXN 19.20 (about USD 1.30) (1.1 kg) (28% less than the category leader and 20% less than another key competitor), with an additional 10% more product in the package. As in the case of Lirio Bar soap, Util commercialization is also supported by management decisions on when to rationalize the product lines and SKU's that are not commercially or financially attractive – with a constant emphasis on canceling those SKU's or line versions, optimizing production, distribution logistics, allocation costs on shelves, and efficiencies in both the company and points of sale.

Tricot, Topitop, and Permoda: Fast Fashion

Patterns of behavior regarding the spending and consumption of clothing vary from one country to another (see Importance of Emerging Markets section). These differences in behavior regarding expenditures are due to the different priorities of people from Latin American countries,[23] in this case for clothing. For instance, in Mexico the preferred use of informal savings is for clothes and shoes, but in the case of Peru it does not even show among the top five uses of informal savings.[24] Nevertheless, Peru is one of the countries with the biggest growth of expenditures and Mexico is on the other end of the spectrum. This is probably because in Mexico people perceive clothes more as an aspirational good.

As a matter of fact, the consumption trends and expenditure priorities are changing in the middle class segment, and personal spending, considering apparel in this topic, is becoming one of the priorities for these consumers.[25] The clothing industry in 2010 reached USD 125 million in Brazil, USD 101 million in Mexico, and USD 106 million in Peru, but decreased to USD 144 million in Chile (a decrease of 26% compared to 2000). Actually, there are countries, such as Mexico, where an important size of the middle class population (about 40%) prefer branded goods to cheaper options.[26] Clothing is no longer seen as just a basic consumption good; low income people want better and more attractive products, including apparel, because they want a better appearance. As Mr. Aquilino Flores, Topitop's owner, states, "Working people are interested in looking good just as much as rich people are."[27]

---

[23]   Boumphrey 2015.   [24]   IADB 2015.   [25]   *Euromonitor* 2015c.
[26]   *Euromonitor* 2015c.   [27]   Moffett 2011.

So, it is clear that the tastes and preferences of the middle-income sector in middle-income countries have been changing in recent decades. In Latin American countries, the trend has been the same regarding the apparel industry. People want to get better and more attractive clothes because they want to look better. But more important, they want to feel better and are willing to pay affordable prices in order to fulfill their new "needs."

Enterprises in the apparel industry have adapted to these changes by implementing the fast fashion model. This is the case for Tricot, Topitop, and Permoda, among other companies in Latin America. They have successfully copied this model, developing shopping experiences through continuous innovation all along the value chain, from the raw material suppliers to the retail store, including the integration of different financial services with the aim of building long-term relationships with customers.

In this sense, given the global exposure of the clothing sector and its dynamic and continuously changing trends, there is potential for enterprises to adapt and provide the products that people are demanding. The challenge here is to figure out how enterprises can shape and conduct their activities along and across the value chain in order to meet the needs of this special, attractive, and buoyant market. In other words, how can firms from this sector manufacture a product sufficiently standardized and at the same time properly personalized to ensure better benefits for both the firm and customer satisfaction?

This general behavior shows that enterprises in the apparel sector should be aware of new trends in order to effectively meet the demand. And this is not only in terms of production but satisfaction as well. Firms from this sector must make its customers feel like they really belong to a higher social stratum. However, for this aim, and as stated, firms need to have in mind that different markets could have different behaviors, thus enterprises must develop special strategies for each market since "one size fits all" probably won't produce the best results. It is important to develop an in-depth knowledge of each market not only in terms of economics and demographic features but also habits and lifestyles,[28] which will be useful in order to accurately adapt and shape the business model to particular conditions such as local cultures.[29]

Thus, firms must create value in their products to supply the customers' needs. In order to do so, enterprises have to innovate their own business activities in several areas. However, the challenge goes further since customer needs must be met at affordable prices. The innovations must be efficient in the product, the process, the supply chain, the distribution channels, and so forth. Next, we are going to present the cases of Tricot, Topitop, and Permoda. Other interesting examples are presented in Table 7.1: Milano and Marisa (information has been mainly gathered directly from the firms' web sites, reports, and news).

Tricot. Tricot is a Chilean clothing retail store that offers fashion products for all the family (men, women, girls, and boys), but with a special focus on women. The firm has been in the market for more than sixty years. During this time, the market conditions have been changing and Tricot has had to adapt its offerings to these different conditions. Opportunites have allowed the firm to increase its presence and now it has more than sixty stores in the country. The target market of this firm has been the lower-middle-income sector and the lower-income sector.

Tricot is an enterprise whose main aim is to offer fashion clothing at the best prices also of quality. The continuous awareness Tricot has for textiles and mainly garments has made them a fashion specialist firm and has earned them the nickname the "Chilean Zara." Tricot has invested in the modernization and standardization of the stores, resulting in more attractive facilities, both inside and outside; they are modern stores in terms of fashion, physical conditions, and technology alike.

[28]   Boumphrey 2014.   [29]   Ey 2014.

Table 7.1 *Milano and Marisa S. A.*

Milano	Marisa S. A.
This is a clothing retail store founded in 1934. Nowadays, Milano has more than 250 stores spread across Mexico, reaching people in urban and rural areas. The target of this clothing store chain is the Mexican lower-income class. Originally, Milano offered only clothes for men; however, it has expanded its offer of products to clothes for women, young boys, teen girls, children, and babies. Milano has passed through several changes that have allowed them to remain in the market for all this time. Among these changes are the acquisition of the clothing retail store by other firms. In 2006 it was acquired by Advent, a US investment fund, and in 2012 Milano was acquired by a Mexican firm, Kaltex, with 100% of the ownership. Since Kaltex manufactures synthetic fibers, thread, fabrics, and clothing among others and it is the supplier for Milano's clothing, it can be seen as an integrated company. This fact has let Milano offer affordable prices that linked with a strategy addressed to the design of fashion garments allowing the renewal of the stores' inventory every single	This is a Brazilian clothing store founded in 1948. At its very beginning the target market was women; in 1999 they expanded their product offerings to men and children and also sold house textiles such as bedsheets, table linen, shower towels, and others. The social sector that Marisa is focused on is the middle-lower-income population. The firm has been growing and nowadays it is integrated with more than 400 stores in the country. The main competence is small retail enterprises. Since Marisa was founded, it has been changing and adapting to different conditions, investing in the modernization of its own "look," creating innovative and more attractive environments. In the same regard, the designs of the products are continuously changing as well, following national and international fashion trends. Marisa's innovations have also included financial services such as credit cards, credit lines, flexibility on payments, insurance products, and personal loans. With these financial products, Marisa is looking for the development of long-term relationships with its customers.

Table 7.1 (cont.)

Milano	Marisa S. A.
month, which is fundamental for the business model. Another relevant strategy is the flexibility of payment methods with credit card that Milano offers to its customers; they can also get special benefits as Milano's cardholders.	

Source: Self-developed based on secondary data, retrieved from the firms' web sites, reports and news.

The business model that Tricot is following, the "fast fashion," requires a highly renewable process of inventory. New and fashionable designs change in short order, requiring the renewal of the stock of products every two weeks. It is also important and necessary to adapt the products to a more specific taste, quickly reacting to any indication of change. With this, every time people visit the stores, they are going to find different products, and this has a direct impact on the growth of visitors in quantity and in frequency as well.

To maintain this pace of work, it is really important to have efficient logistics management in order to make sure that fashion clothes will arrive at the right time in the stores; otherwise, the clothes won't be in fashion anymore, losing the value for the customer. Tricot has suppliers in India and China that enable it to meet these conditions. Furthermore, it has a sourcing office in China that assures on the one hand a proper logistics process and on the other the quality standards of the clothes.

This tight control is essential but so is the improving, modernization, and constant update of the distribution centers. The information technologies are also a fundamental part in order to avoid excessive time for the gathering of data and its respective analysis, which has a direct relationship with the decision-making process. Tricot is aware of this and has implemented actions for both cases, first investing in its distribution centers and second the execution of business intelligence programs.

Related to technology, Tricot implemented a new security system that gives more safety to its customers when using its Tricot credit card (biometric id security control), the "Tricard." Actually, Tricot has incorporated financial services into its business model since 1997, establishing the firm Tricard S.A. With this independent enterprise, Tricot is managing the financial area, offering credit cards and also loans for its customers. In 2013 Tricard launched its VISA Tricard, which the cardholders can use not only for Tricot purchases but also from other businesses. About 40% of Tricot's customers make their purchases using the credit card, a number the company wants to make grow.

All these changes and new strategies are an attempt to expand the target market to different sectors beyond the lower-middle-income population. This way, Tricot states that its core business is fashion clothes at affordable prices, and it does not exclude any particular socioeconomic sector. Related with this, Tricot's expansion has been in all of the country, including places where the earnings of the population are much higher than others, and they have established stores in public thoroughfares and also shopping centers, reaching with this strategy the middle-income sector. Another helpful way to achieve that goal (trickle up) is with social networks and an online store.

Topitop. This Peruvian company started activities in the 1970s with a modest sewing workshop making men's polo shirts. Nowadays, Topitop is a vertical integrated firm and one of the biggest clothing retail stores in Peru, with more than seventy subsidiaries. It has also expanded its available of products, including a wide variety of clothing for men, women, teens, and kids. Due to its growing strategy, it has been known as the "Andean Zara." The target market of Topitop is the lower-middle-income sector, which is very attractive given the growing consumption trends.

Topitop has had to make several changes in order to adapt to the new market requirements, changes and strategies that have meant the success of the firm. In 2007 Topitop transformed the corporative identity and the commercial brand (and design) into a more attractive one: It went from "Topy Top" to "Topitop." The stores were remodeled with new and better furniture, illumination, disposition of products, etc. More recently, the company has also worked on the implementation of music, in-store image consulting, and intelligent fitting rooms. With this, Topitop is trying to develop a complete shopping experience for customers, aiming to promote a strong attachment to the brand.

This concept has been standardized with the idea that customers experience the same feelings in any store of the firm. But even when it is a standardized concept, people are not necessarily going to find the same products in all the same places. Actually, the strategy of Topitop is focused on understanding what people want and producing it for them. In this sense, the flexible structure that Topitop has allows it to have a new collection in a short period of time, just forty-five days from the design to the shelves. This capability also enables Topitop to continuously change and renew the inventory. Since the firm is keenly oriented to provide lifestyle and fashion garments (actually the clothes are designed with new fashion trends) for its customers, and trends in this sector are rapidly changing, this is a fundamental ability.

What Topitop has also been attending to in order to offer fashionable clothes with quality at affordable prices is permanent investment programs on machinery and technology. Recently, Topitop has been integrating different software that enables the firm to manage more efficiently the inventory system and also to track online every single stage of the value chain. Another important action that Topitop has undertaken is related to a digital strategy, with the incorporation of social networks such as Facebook, Instagram, Pinterest, and Twitter to its business model; also the web site is an important platform in this regard, although it does not have an online store.

Related to financial services, it only has a co-branded credit card (see Table 7.1). These last two areas could be interesting opportunities to explore in the near future considering the trends that have been showing in the middle-income sector.

Basically, Topitop has integrated the fast fashion business model to its own productive process with great success. One of the key points in the rise of this firm was that it ventured to non-traditional areas. That is to say, it set up stores near poor neighborhoods that had been disregarded many times before, and it also got into several regions in the country (and abroad), not only the capital city.

Topitop has followed a regional internationalization strategy, entering nearby countries such as Ecuador and Venezuela. However, its range is even larger since an important percentage of its annual production (more than half) is exported to several countries such as the United States and other countries in Europe. Given its inherent quality advantages stemming from the raw materials, specifically cotton, and the quality of the textile process, Topitop manufactures for different well-known labels and this is how exports from this brand enter other countries. Furthermore, the named advantages also have been helpful for Topitop to trickle up to the target sector through the famous brand Hugo Boss.

Permoda. It is one of the most well-known retail clothing stores in Colombia. The firm has been in the market for more than thirty years. It started with a wholesale concept and with products only for the male sector. Nowadays, it has changed its business model; it has expanded the variety of clothes for young men and women and for teens. The wholesale concept changed as well to retail, and now it holds about 150 stores, not only in the country but abroad (Ecuador, Costa Rica, Venezuela, Peru, and Mexico) as well. Following the principles of fast fashion, this Colombian firm offers to its customers fashion clothes at fair prices. The target sector of Permoda is the middle-income population.

In order to achieve success in this new venture, Permoda has been conducting several activities along and across the firm. The stores are spacious facilities where the firm has positioned its four different brands. The designs are created in New York and Milan; the clothes are manufactured in Bangladesh, China, India, Mexico, Peru, and Colombia; there is a logistic hub located in Panama; and the headquarters are in Bogota, where decisions are made.

With this arrangement, Permoda can react quickly to any change in particular preferences in the fashion market, adapting its activities and its products to new and different markets. This entails continuous renewal of the stock, maintaining the garment collection in just short periods of time. In this sense, a close relationship with the customers is highly relevant. The information that can be gathered for them is fundamental for success. But the analysis of all this data is as relevant because it tracks the impact that any decision has and evaluates the outcomes that could impact the customers.

In terms of online activities, Permoda has an active presence on several social networks, creating new content constantly. Facebook, Instagram, YouTube, and Twitter are the main virtual platforms for communication with its customers, generating priceless sources of information. The online store is another way that Permoda has expanded the scope of the firm. What still has yet to explode, in comparison to other similar enterprises, is the integration of financial services, which, as has been seen, are useful tools for the attraction of more customers and the creation of long-term relationships with them. This takes on more relevance given the current trends in the middle-income sector in terms of expenditure, revenues, and particular interests for fashion.

LESSONS

These firms have developed and applied actions specifically addressed to solve the needs and tastes of the MoP. In order to satisfy these needs and tastes, firms must be aware of different situations related to market trends, customers, and products, as well as internal changes. In this section, we are going to identify and discuss some lessons learned from the firms under study. These lessons, by the way, represent successful strategies positively impacting the competitiveness and performance of the firms.

In the case of Grupo Fabricas Selectas, it has shown deep consumer and market knowledge and a strong management vision as well as a combination of R&D, innovation in manufacturing processes, a marketing strategy, and a commercialization creating a specific store format. Arising from this, we want to highlight two actions developed and implemented by GFS, which became a solution that successfully met MoP consumers' expectations. Its pillars are the customer relationship management strategy between GFS and Walmart-Mexico and a proactive approach by GFS's management and commercial organization in analyzing the dynamics of their market. Grupo Fabricas Selectas demonstrates that it has been performing under the marketing concept, a business philosophy oriented to satisfying the market, with a customer-focused organization and coordination between different functions of the firm.[30]

In the case of Sanchez y Martin, the firm has maintained a continued and responsive research and product development to add innovations that have made their products competitive in this highly dynamic market. Through building on target consumers' knowledge, cost efficiency, and product multi-performance, it has managed to succeed by providing the MoP and BoP with local brands that are strongly linked to local consumer culture, capitalizing on tradition and generational recommendation and with a commercialization focused on traditional stores via the most important wholesalers. Competitive pricing focused on MoP is reached via constant optimization and efficiency of production and supply chain (product line optimization), additionally by supplying a special SKU (10 kg) for the commercialization of Util detergent, to be sold by smaller dosages at traditional stores, meeting very well this channel in selling to MoP and BoP consumers. The strategic axes they follow with their lines of products are examples of a market-oriented organization that

[30]   Kohli & Jaworski 1990.

understands its customers' needs. This type of organization is based on a strong role of innovation and technology, which are vital in order to develop better solutions to address new business opportunities among the MoP consumer segment.

In the case of the firms performing in the apparel business, it is important to have in mind that people from the middle- and lower-income sectors want to look better and demand clothes that meet the newest and trendy characteristics of the market but at affordable prices. However, lower prices should not be the main topic to focus on since people from this sector are particularly interested in characteristics that make them feel socially included; indeed, they are willing to spend more for differentiated services and products.[31] The enterprises analyzed here have been dealing with these issues and have had to adapt their former business models to the new conditions.

All of these firms have been changing by adopting the fast fashion model, and innovation for these companies is mandatory. As seen, the core point is to develop real and priceless shopping experiences. As such, modern facilities with good illumination, disposition of products, continuous rotation of stock, and new collections, international as well as national, along with regional adaption of fashion trends, music, fragrances, and customer services, etc., are important features that are going to allow the firms to meet the customers' needs, tangible and intangible (social, psychological, emotional). Implementation of new technology in all the activities and a tight control of the whole supply chain are also essential along with speed and efficiency in communication[32] among different processes, areas, and stores.

Among the enterprises reviewed here, we can find two different structures. On the one hand, Topitop is an integrated enterprise (Milano could be considered an integrated firm as well), and on the other hand, Tricot and Permoda have suppliers from different countries. It is clear that both models are working well (other examples of

[31]   Barki & Parente 2010.   [32]   Rabino 2015.

this same model are Zara and H&M); the key point lies in the control processes that the enterprises have along the supply chain and the system and programs that allow them to take decisions at the right moment. No matter the model or structure the firms have, suppliers play a strategic role in their success.[33] Other similar and relevant innovations in the growing process of these firms is that they are establishing their stores in underserved areas, even shantytowns. At the same time, they consider shopping centers a different market target. Accordingly, when going abroad they prefer shopping centers.

Two more aspects to have in mind are the following. The first includes the integration and intensive use of new technologies such as social networks as a channel of communication with customers, the creation and management of content, and the online shopping. But it also comprises tangible technologies such as radio frequency identification in fast fashion retailing, which could improve the relationship with the clients.[34] And second, the integration of financial services into the business model – going beyond just a points reward card or traditional credit card – could be an important tool to obtain more customers and build long-term relationships.

CONCLUSIONS

Given the economic development of the countries and the dynamics of the industries where these companies operate, the MoP consumers segment represents a new, important commercial opportunity. The companies analyzed in this chapter have in common several factors that are relevant and enabled them to take advantage of important opportunities in the lower consumption business in different industries. In this final section, we describe these factors and the main lessons that could be useful for other firms.

These companies used a combination of different resources such as research and development, innovation in manufacturing processes, cost efficiency, deep knowledge of target consumers, and

---

[33] Bandinelli et al. 2013.   [34]   Madhani 2015.

marketing strategies developed for the MoP consumers, combined with a commercialization strategy through specific store formats that are oriented to the MoP consumers' expectations. Additionally, in some cases some of these firms have capitalized on the local brands' ties with local consumers that are strongly linked to the local consumer culture, using them as a competitive advantage vs international brands.

Networking and alliances are fundamental innovation tools for success. The firms analyzed here, in one way or another and to different extents, have built links with other organizations. For GFS, the networking established with Walmart has, literally, resulted in a fundamental part of its success, not only related to the toy balls strategy but also in terms of the whole firm. These links, relationships, and alliances are useful to meet the target market (MoP) but also could help to trickle up the market, which is what Topitop is doing with Hugo Boss.

Related as well, but in this case innovating within their own firm's organizational structure, is the relationship between the different departments. GFS is developing strategies between joined departments, e.g., the sales and marketing departments. Sanchez y Martin is also working in the same way, and firms in the fast fashion industry are no different. In this last case, Tricot, Topitop, and Permoda have to perform with a pretty close relationship throughout the process. As a matter of fact, it has been a requirement for the success of these firms.

Also, for all these firms, the analysis of the dynamics of the market has been essential. Because of this, GFS could identify a gap to fill in the MoP with play balls, Sanchez y Martin developed a multiuse product, and Tricot, Topitop, and Permoda adapted their former business model to the fast fashion model. Nevertheless, in order to really bridge the identified gap, a profound understanding of the importance of research and development has been required. With this, and based on innovation, new products have identified and then developed. As a result, the firms' competitiveness increased due to the added value – the intrinsic value that the products have for the customers.

Related to the value that the products have for the customers, the firms studied here are market oriented. In this regard, these firms are continuously innovating to accurately identify the tastes and preferences of the customers, even as they change. They use customer relationship management strategies for this aim and are perenially generating useful information for the decision making process. They really understand what their customers are demanding, in both tangible and intangible terms. In this sense, even when this could be a price sensitive sector, price shouldn't be the main topic because the customers, when acquiring the products, want to meet needs and deeper desires as well.

As discussed, this is happening with the toy balls, bar soaps, and detergents, and similarly in the garment sector. While the firms are truly understanding the market, they are also contributing to the development of a strong attachment to the customers regarding the brand. That is to say, they are building solid and lasting relationships over time.

All these changes imply and embrace a high level of adaptation (international, national, and regional) as well as integration and the use of new technologies. At the same time, this is also related to the process of innovation, which allows the development and offering of products and services demanded by the customers. In brief, this is a virtuous cycle such that when firms enter into it, one action leads to the other, creating benefits not only for the enterprises but the customers as well.

In sum, what can be learned throughout the different areas of the consumption industry is that the middle of the pyramid has specific characteristics, and any innovations must be undertaken in response to those characteristics. Firstly, it is important to understand the mindset of the population, which can be evaluated in terms of accessibility, affordability, and identification. All the firms presented here exemplify how innovations have to be presented in a format and a distribution channel the customers are likely to use, which can be within a shopping center, a supermarket, or a store inside a supermarket.

Affordability is key, as low or fair pricing is an attractive feature for the middle of the pyramid, since they have more disposable income but still have the need to analyze their budget. In this sense, products have to offer an attractive alternative, both in terms of appeal and practicality, but one that is not too expensive for them, maintaining a balance in terms of cost–benefit. Lastly, identification with the brand or product can drive the sales of a new product. Using an approach appealing to the traditional practices of the group or based on identifying the mindset of the target market allows the firm to create a bond with the customers, which drives sales through loyalty and trust.

REFERENCES

AMA. 2014. Brand value definition. AMA. Accessed March 7, 2016. www .marketing-dictionary.org/ama

AMA. 2014. NSE/AMAI. AMAI. Accessed October 14, 2015. http://nse.amai.org/ nseamai2

Andreson, J. & Billou, N. 2006. Serving the World's Poor: Innovation at the Base of the Economic Pyramid. *Cite Seer X.* Accessed March 12 , 2017. http://citeseerx .ist.psu.edu/viewdoc/download?doi=10.1.1.582.3819&rep=rep1&type=pdf

Atsmon, Y., Kloss, M., Smit, S., & Matson, E. 2012. Parsing the Growth Advantage of Emerging-Market Companies. *Mckinsey Quarterly* 3(1): 10–14.

Azevedo, V., Baigun, A., Bouillon, C., Duke, D., & Gallardo, M. 2015. Un mercado creciente de US$750 mil millones: Descubriendo oportunidades en la base de la pirámide en América Latina y el Caribe. *IADB.* Accessed July 4, 2015. https:// publications.iadb.org/bitstream/handle/11319/6992/A_Rising_US$750_Billion_ Market.pdf?sequence=1

Bandinelli, R., Rinaldi, R., Rossi, M., & Terzi, S. 2013. New Product Development in the Fashion Industry: An Empirical Investigation of Italian Firms. *International Journal of Engineering Business Management* 1(31): 1–9.

Barki, E. & Parente, J. 2010. Consumer Behavior of the Base of the Pyramid Market in Brazil. *Greener Management International* 56: 11–23.

Boumphrey, S. 2014. De la base de la pirámide hasta las clases medias emergentes: consumidores en Latinoamérica. *Euromonitor.* Accessed July 2, 2015. http://go .euromonitor.com/base-piramide-hasta-clases-medias-emergentes-consumidores-latinoamerica.html

Boumphrey, S. 2015. Mexico: It's All about the Middle Class. *Euromonitor.* Accessed Jul 2, 2015. http://blog.euromonitor.com/2015/10/mexico-its-all-about-the-middle-class.html

Cachon, G. P. & Swinney, R. 2011. The Value of Fast Fashion: Quick Response, Enhanced Design, and Strategic Consumer Behavior. *Management Science* 57(4): 778–795.

Colgate-Palmolive. 2016. History. Colgate. Accessed February 2, 2016. www .colgate.com.mx/app/Colgate/MX/Corp/History/1806.cvsp

CONAPO. 2015. Número, tamaño y composición de los hogares en México. *CONAPO.* Accessed July 9, 2015. www.violenciaenlafamilia.conapo.gob.mx/ en/Violencia_Familiar/Tamao_de_la_poblacin_y_hogares_en_Mxico

Euromonitor. 2015a. Home Care 2014 Geographic Review: Developing World. *Euromonitor.* Accessed Jul 20, 2015. www.euromonitor.com

Euromonitor. 2015b. Home Care in Mexico. *Euromonitor.* Accessed July 1, 2015. www.euromonitor.com

Euromonitor. 2015c. The Middle Class at Home: Extract of the Executive Summary of Survey Results. America Economia. Accessed July 1, 2015. http://mba .americaeconomia.com/sites/files/the_middle_class_at_home_survey_extract .pdf

Euromonitor. 2017. Market Sizes | Historical/Forecast. *Euromonitor.* Accessed March 12, 2017. www.euromonitor.com

Ey. 2014. Rapid-Growth Markets Forecast. *EY.* Accessed July 10, 2015. www.ey .com/GL/en/Issues/Driving-growth/EY-rapid-growth-markets-forecast-february-2014

Fidelity. 2013. Emerging Markets Insight. *Fidelity Worldwide Investment.* Accessed July 12, 2015. www.fidelityworldwideinvestment.com/turkey/news-insight/emerging-markets-insight/default.page

Gardetti, M. & Muthu, S. 2015. Sustainable Apparel? Is the Innovation in the Business Model? - The Case of IOU Project. *Textiles and Clothing Sustainability* 1(1): 1–9.

Grupo Fabricas Selectas. 2020. #80

Hirose, R., Maia, R., Martinez, A., & Thiel, A. 2015. Three Myths about Growth in Consumer-Packaged Goods. McKinsey. Accessed July 8, 2015. www.mckinsey .com/insights/consumer_and_retail/three_myths_about_growth_in_consumer_packaged_goods

IADB. 2015. Un mercado creciente: Descubriendo oportunidades en la Base de la Pirámide en Perú. IADB. Accessed July 1, 2015. https://publications.iadb.org/ bitstream/handle/11319/7325/Un_mercado_creciente_Descubriendo_oportuni dades_en_la_base_de_la_piramide_en_Peru.pdf?sequence=1

INVESTOPEDIA. 2015. Consumer Packaged Goods – CPG. INVESTOPEDIA. Accessed October 11, 2015. www.investopedia.com/terms/c/cpg.asp

Jaiswal, A. 2008. The Fortune at the Bottom or the Middle of the Pyramid? *Innovations* 3(1): 85–100.

Joy, A., Sherry, J., Venkatesh, A., Wang, J., & Chan, R. 2012. Fast Fashion, Sustainability, and the Ethical Appeal of Luxury Brands. *Fashion Theory* 16(3): 273–295.

Kapoor, R. 2015. Unlocking Growth Potential in Emerging Markets: Diversification Success in Consumer Products. *Performance* 7(1): 12–23.

Khanna, T. & Palepu, K. 2013. *Winning in Emerging Markets: A Road Map for Strategy and Execution.* Boston: *Harvard Business Review Press.*

Kohli, A. K. & Jaworski, B. J. 1990. Market Orientation: The Construct, Research Propositions and Managerial Implications. *Journal of Marketing* 54 (April), 1–18.

Kozlowski, A., Bardecki, M., & Searcy, C. 2012. Environmental Impacts in the Fashion Industry. *Journal of Corporate Citizenship* 2012(45): 17–36.

Long, H. & Shapiro, L. 2018. Does $60,000 Make You Middle-Class or Wealthy on Planet Earth? Accessed November 11, 2019. www.washingtonpost.com/business/2018/08/20/does-make-you-middle-class-or-wealthy-planet-earth

Lundblad, L. & Davies, I. A. 2015. The Values and Motivations behind Sustainable Fashion Consumption. *Journal of Consumer Behavior* 15(2): 149–162.

Madhani, P. M. 2015. Enhancing Customer Lifetime Value in Fast Fashion Retailing with RFID Initiatives. *International Journal of Business and Globalization* 15(2): 205–237.

Moffett, M. 2011. A Rags-to-Riches Career Highlights Latin Resurgence. New York, Millenium Itesm. Accessed July 2, 2015. http://0-search.proquest.com.millenium.itesm.mx/docview/903826899?accountid=41938

P&G. 2016. P&G Ivory. P&G. Accessed July 2, 2015. www.pgshop.com/pgshop-brand-ivory/

Park, H. & Kim, Y. 2016. Proactive versus Reactive Apparel Brands in Sustainability: Influences on Brand Loyalty. *Journal of Retailing and Consumer Services* 29: 114–122.

Rabino, S. 2015. The Bottom of the Pyramid: An Integrative Approach. *International Journal of Emerging Markets* 10(1): 2–15.

Sanchez-y-Martin. 2016. Historia. SYM. Accessed Jan 18, 2016. www.sym.com.mx/historia.html

Walmart. 2009. Wal-Mart de México inaugura su tienda Prichos número 200 en Chetumal. Walmart Mexico. Accessed July 6, 2015. www.walmartmexicoycam.com.mx/sala_de_prensa/operadoras/walmartca/2009/mayo/walmart-mexico-inaugura-tiendas-prichos.html#sthash.MYhXQk9t.dpuf

Watson, M. Z. & Yan, R. N. 2013. An Exploratory Study of the Decision Processes of Fast versus Slow Fashion Consumers. *Journal of Fashion Marketing and Management: An International Journal* 17(2): 141–159.

8   It Is Show Time!

Otto Regalado-Pezúa and Ana Belén Perdigones

Otto Regalado-Pezúa and Ana Belén Perdigones

INTRODUCTION

The middle of the pyramid has been increasing in number and in purchasing power throughout the emerging markets. This increase creates, by extension, new opportunities for businesses to pursue. The new access to disposable income enables the new middle classes to make purchases they couldn't before, or at least not as frequently. Among the sectors the middle of the pyramid is starting to shift its gaze to are leisure and entertainment. New acquisitive power creates opportunities, and, in so doing, the new middle classes want to show their social escalation and enjoy entertainment they couldn't before. Following this train of thought, this chapter focuses on explaining innovations created with this middle-income population in mind and how innovations can provide them with new entertainment experiences that fit their new status and economic position.

Leisure and Entertainment

The economic growth of Latin America is having a favorable impact on the development of the region's middle class. Said growth translates into a continuous increase in the household income level. At the same time, this increased level of income and economic security results in families – with a greater propensity and availability for spending – now proposing the satisfaction of needs that were previously inaccessible, or if they did satisfy them, they sought to do so with activities that did not represent increased spending. With their increased income, they have more funds to invest in new products and services, but still face some economic restrictions. Because of this, new innovations are needed to create entertainment that is both appealing and affordable, a challenge that requires different considerations in emerging markets than in advanced economies. "Is the MoP a market with fewer options in comparative terms? I would say no, it is a market with many more options generated in different ways," stated Percy Vigil, CEO of MegaPlaza Norte. The CEO of the shopping center highlights the diverse opportunities in this thriving industry.

On a global level, the entertainment industry itself has been under-studied, since different sectors combine to form the whole of this industry; this heterogeneity makes it difficult to carry out general studies that encompass all entertainment.

The entertainment industry per se generates millions of dollars in revenue, so much so that in a country as large as Mexico, it contributes 6.7% of GDP, while the fishing industry contributes 4.8% and the construction sector contributes 4.3%.

This industry is very heterogeneous, perhaps because of its very nature. To define and outline what is understood by entertainment, there are various definitions proposed by different authors with varied academic backgrounds, and what they agree on is determining that entertainment is "that which the people find entertaining," while leisure is about the actions that involve freedom and enjoyment.[1]

"Entertainment is an activity, in terms of recreational, social or sports, which allows the consumer in general to disconnect from what is work and studies. Here you can find outdoor entertainment, at home, retail, restaurants and general entertainment that can be events," explains the entertainment expert and CEO of Papaya Fast in Peru (belonging to Papaya Holding), Tito Aguilar.

In this sense, given that entertainment can include a large number of activities and actions of various kinds based on the preference of the individual, the entertainment industry presents various features, and at the same time, it is composed of different categories, very heterogeneous among themselves, although in some ways compatible.

---

[1]   Bates & Ferri 2010.

As indicated by Tito Aguilar, "The comprehensive behavior of the entire entertainment category has not been evaluated, it has only been assessed in parts, such as restaurants, cinemas, and so on, but not the comprehensive offer."

The report by PWC regarding GEMO 2012–2016,[2] which is one of the sources of reference in the business, includes the following categories within the entertainment and media industry: cable or free-to-air television, internet, press, magazines, publishing market, cinema, music, and video games.

On a global level, according to the report on GEMO 2012–2016, a growth of 5.6% is projected between 2012 and 2016 – the volume has grown from USD 1.6 trillion in 2012 to USD 2.2 trillion in 2016. On a Latin American level, it was expected to increase from USD 84 billion in 2012 to USD 134 billion in 2016, with an annual growth rate of 9.7% (compared to 2012), making Latin America the region with the highest projected growth.

On the other hand, the expected growth analysis by categories of the industry was carried out. In Table 8.1, the evolution is visualized by industries on a global level from the year 2007 to 2011, with the projection of the different sectors from the year 2012 to 2016.[3]

Therefore, and considering the consumption behavior of the MoP, Andrich, Arroyo, and Canturini[4] identified the characteristics and values applied by the MoP when selecting its entertainment activities. These authors took as a reference the hierarchy of needs of Maslow, which states that as the most basic needs are satisfied, human beings develop higher needs and desires. Based on this hierarchy, we can transfer the different personal needs to the needs during leisure and free time. First, we cover the physiological needs, then the security requirements (personal, financial, health), followed by those of a sense of belonging (friendship, family), subsequently those of

---

[2] The consultancy firm PricewaterhouseCoopers (PwC) prepares, every four years, a report on the entertainment industry in which they project the global and regional trends: the "Global Entertainment and Media Outlook: 2012–2016" (PWC n.d.).

[3] PWC n.d.   [4]   Andrich, Arroyo, & Canturini 2009.

Table 8.1 *Evolution of the world media, leisure, and entertainment sector, in millions of USD*

	2007	2008	2009	2010	2011	2012	2013	2014	2015	2016	2012–2016 CAGR
Corporate publications	215,607	212,411	191,572	190,125	191,125	194,462	199,739	207,159	216,130	226,324	3.4
Consumer and education books publishing	114,329	114,944	113,599	113,530	112,066	112,173	112,706	113,623	114,634	115,719	0.6
Magazine publishing	87,094	85,550	75,948	75,855	75,221	75,337	75,687	76,651	78,211	80,184	1.3
Movie industry	82,258	82,019	83,359	84,897	85,433	87,877	90,724	93,651	96,714	99,657	3.1
Internet access	203,818	228,750	250,530	275,472	316,972	351,006	386,855	413,838	456,109	493,390	9.3
Online advertising	52,119	61,661	63,901	75,594	89,766	105,411	123,511	143,285	164,908	188,069	15.9
Newspaper publishing	195,917	187,998	168,328	169,091	167,968	168,553	170,553	173,264	176,906	181,224	1.5
External advertising	32,598	33,220	28,910	30,406	31,940	33,809	35,452	37,188	38,941	40,830	5
Radio	49,544	48,497	44,311	46,542	47,255	49,601	51,284	52,911	54,558	56,244	3.5
Discographic industry	56,793	54,221	53,154	49,270	49,886	51,124	52,771	54,810	57,141	59,741	3.7
TV advertising	171,271	173,158	160,561	179,479	185,005	196,507	203,833	224,710	231,555	254,745	6.6
Paid TV	167,529	179,555	190,565	201,016	215,536	229,092	243,368	258,148	274,151	290,596	6.2
Video games	44,449	54,022	55,201	57,459	58,723	62,349	66,206	71,243	76,878	82,976	7.2

Source: Recording Industry Association of America, Russian Association of Communication Agencies, State Administration for Industry and Commerce, Interactive Advertising Bureau Canada, Interactive Advertising Bureau, Interactive Advertising Bureau Norway, Interactive Advertising Bureau Spain, Interactive Advertising Bureau UK, Universal McCann, PricewaterhouseCoopers LLP, Wilkofsky Gruen Associates, PricewaterhouseCoopers LLP.

self-esteem (recognition), and finally those of self-fulfillment.[5] At the time of choosing the entertainment provider, it is also sought to satisfy these mentioned needs.

Moreover, the place should provide sufficient security measures, not only to avoid personal injury but also related to theft. Unfortunately, in Latin American countries, insecurity is an underlying problem, and the social group seeks a place that provides it with greater peace of mind; this originates from a crisis of lack of public spaces, especially among the middle and lower classes, since the top of the pyramid has access to private facilities such as country clubs.[6]

On the other hand, Bofarull states that since families currently seek active, enterprising, and creative leisure, they investigate the different alternatives offered by the entertainment industry.[7]

In this sense, for the families belonging to socioeconomic level C and D, there are several entertainment options available. The activities that can be enjoyed outside of the home are restaurants, cinema, indoor parks, parks, zoos or similar places, amusement parks, museums, shopping centers, sporting events, swimming pools, beaches, and country restaurants, among others.[8]

The Middle of the Pyramid: The Way They Move!

The entertainment industry is a significant market in Latin America, generating USD 2.05 billion in 2016 and it is expected to reach USD 2.09 billion by 2021. The sectors of the industry with the most market value are: Internet access (USD 27.651 million), Pay TV (USD 16.093 million), and TV advertising (USD 9.967 million).[9] Also, the food service industry in Latin America is flourishing, with a market value of USD 238 billion in 2016 and an expected increase to USD 270 billion by 2021.[10] It is evident that the entertainment industry is growing, but there are specific trends happening in each sector and in

---

[5] Gardner 1985.   [6]   López 2000; Andrich et al. 2009.   [7]   Bofarull 2005.
[8] Andrich et al. 2009.   [9]   Statista Research Department 2019.
[10] Rios Montanez 2019.

different countries in the area. Therefore, some cases are presented to exemplify how to innovate in different sectors.

THE MEAL BRINGS THE FAMILY TOGETHER AT THE RESTAURANT

The restaurant category is one of those preferred by the MoP since it involves leaving the house while accompanied by family or friends and enjoying time over a meal.

According to the study carried out by Passport, "A New Era of Growth and Competition in Global Consumer Foodservice in 2015 and beyond," Latin America will continue to offer various opportunities to develop the restaurant category. In the year 2014, there were new entries of international chains in the region.

Higher income and the reduction in poverty in countries such as Peru, Colombia, and Brazil have generated a growing demand and a diverse offering. In this sense, we can notice that the number of consumers that can afford the expense of eating outside of the home has expanded by millions throughout the last decade.

Figure 8.1 shows the absolute growth of the restaurant market in the most relevant countries in the Latin American region, as well as the projected growth expected for the year 2019. In this case, Chile, Peru, and Colombia, in that order, are the countries with the highest growth projection.

Moving on to identifying the peculiarities of each country, the *Euromonitor* report,[11] in analyzing full-service restaurants, observed that in Chile the segment of full-service restaurants reached USD 2.47 billion by 2014. In this country, restaurants that offer regional food led growth with 12%, while independent restaurants led sales in 2014 with a share value of 93%. The Mamut chain is the leader with a 15% market share.

On the other hand, Peru had a growth of 7% and spending of USD 2.3 billion. Additionally, Peru obtained the World Travel Award

[11]   *Euromonitor* 2015.

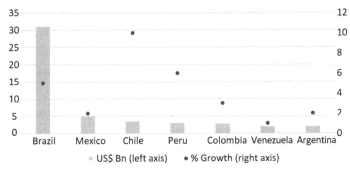

FIGURE 8.1 Food service value growth by market
Source: Passport Euromonitor, 2016

with the title "World's Leading Culinary Destination" for the third year in a row. The full-service pizza chains had growth of 42% in 2014, displacing the North American full-service restaurants, led by the Delosi franchise chain with a 43% market share.

In Colombia, full-service restaurants reached USD 7.42 billion in the year 2014. The incorporation of women into the labor world and the growth of the major cities led to an increase in the automotive population, which caused a change in the behavior of the consumer in this segment. The economy in Colombia grew 4.6% in the year 2014, exceeding the average in Latin America; this caused the average consumer to have more spending availability.

The case of Argentina is different. Independent businesses that operated pizzerias or grill restaurants in the year 2014 led consumption. After four years of double-digit inflation, spending in food service consumption went from expensive full-service restaurants to medium- and low-priced options. Regarding the latter, the independent businesses have adapted, offering economic menus and employing fast-food techniques so that food is more affordable for the MoP.

In Brazil, full-service restaurants achieved a growth of 12% in the year 2014, reaching USD 28.3 billion, mainly driven by the entry of international chains, with the North American chains presenting growth of 36%. On the other hand, we can notice a growth in the purchase of online food, which negatively affected the restaurants.

Lower-income consumers changed toward this type of service with the idea of not spending a lot of money, since they save the expenses related to parking, waiter service (a 10% tax on the final bill), and musical attractions that are very common, especially in independent restaurants. The other alternative for this segment is the "rodizio," which consists of a system whereby people pay a fixed amount, and they can eat all they want or can.

The Triumph of the Roast Chicken: Rokys, Peru

An example of innovation is the case of the Peruvian roast chicken restaurants: Rokys. In Peru, roast chicken is considered a typical and affordable dish for all types of families, as well as having a very pleasant taste for the Peruvian palate, having become the favorite food of the Peruvian family. In the year 2004, the National Institute of Culture of Peru declared said dish a Peruvian Culinary Specialty. In the year 2010, the Peruvian Government declared the third Sunday of the month of July Roast Chicken Day. With these two acts, roast chicken consolidated as a Peruvian symbol and tradition.

On the other hand, it is interesting to highlight the consumption level of this product in Peru. According to data of the year 2013, the Peruvian Gastronomy Association (APEGA, Spanish acronym) confirmed that roast chicken is the second dish most preferred by Peruvians, and the first option of food outside the home. In Peru, about 35 chickens are consumed per person per year, and in metropolitan Lima 70 kg of chicken per person per year. This positions Peru as the third highest chicken-consuming country in the region, after Brazil and Panama.[12]

Additionally, the insight of the Peruvian consumer is that he "celebrates over roast chicken"; it is the food of the Peruvian family. The majority of the restaurants that offer this dish are exclusively "pollerías" (chicken restaurants) since it is the only dish they offer, in addition to entrees, side orders (salads, French fries), and sodas. The

---

[12]   *El Comercio* 2015.

prices on the menu are very affordable; they vary between USD 13.50 and USD 19.50 for a family of four to five people.

Rokys and Norkys, another "pollería," started together. This happened because thirty years ago two colleagues who had worked for the same company took separate paths, from then on identifying one another as competitor and source of reference.

When Rokys began their operations, the roast chicken did not enjoy the mass consumption image that it has now, and it was the expansion of this chain that helped its development. Juan Miguel Galeas, the former marketing manager, said, "In the 1980's and 1990's this distinctive brand image was developed, and Rokys began to build a superior category to what they were selling, putting aside attributes that have always been considered aspirational. The restaurant is for a different public, but at affordable prices; in other words, the design of the restaurant is very similar to that of meat and grill restaurants, but only selling roasted chicken, which is a lower priced product."

"Each restaurant is adapted to the needs of the area, cutting across all marketing strategy. For example, the external aesthetics follows a standard branding base, but once inside the restaurant everything, from the supply of dishes to the price structure, is adapted to the area where the restaurant operates," highlights Galeas. A personalized internal and external aesthetic is designed for each facility: gold trims, luminous signs, the floors, the use of wood in the decoration, and ample space give the perception of elegant restaurants; therefore, the popular segment uses these restaurants for special occasions, for example weddings, anniversaries, and other ceremonies. In its growing process, restaurants expanded to the most modern districts of Lima, and with this development it has currently positioned itself as a restaurant for the middle class, which is an aspirational attitude for the MoP.

The innovation in processes arises from the growth of the company, and it is presented as an internal development completely adapted to each restaurant. This differential in operation generates complexity in strategic efficiency; for example, all the kitchens are different in space, proportions, furnishing, utensils, etc., which creates greater costs than a standardized restaurant chain. Profitability is not due to efficiency in costs or operation, but rather to economies of scale. By growing massively, the sales volume produced greater profitability and allowed for this diversity of structures.

The integrating proposal of entertainment services and elements is covering the MoP needs. For example, Galeas points out, "By using large spaces, it is possible to hold celebrations, birthdays and business parties around roast chicken, as well as the karaoke services while they enjoy their food. Here is innovation on the side of entertainment: bring together things that exist, and they become something new or combined in a different manner. Also, it is highly related to the concept of family: it is a place where you can go just as you got out of bed since it is an extension of your home. You do not need to get dressed specially to go there. The restaurant is not standardized; it has the chaos typical of the MoP's culture. The very structure of the restaurant makes people feel at home."

The intuition of each restaurant administrator identifies the needs of the consumer; they can perceive what promotions best fit in with the reality of their environment or how the waiter must treat the customer so that they feel good. The distinctive feature is that the treatment depends on each restaurant; sometimes it may seem exaggerated – for example, when the waiter takes a bow. In the same manner, the MoP customers expect a larger amount of food and for the server to treat them well since the price is higher than the market average. In this sense, it can be appreciated that they follow a different path than most firms. Standardization is the common route, since it gives more control over the operation, but Rokys identified that their customers vary widely throughout the branches. Therefore, they give relative autonomy to each location in order to provide the best service to each customer. Likewise, it is important to focus on the children, since they are a great influencer when selecting the restaurant in which to eat roast chicken. The kid's zone is made up of games for kids, activities on the weekends (painted faces in the most visited restaurants), the offer of a special children's menu, and special packages for birthday celebrations.

In this manner, the lunch or dinner of the MoP becomes a time of experiences for the entire family.

THE SHOPPING CENTER AS AN INTEGRATING PROPOSAL

The International Council of Shopping Centers (ICSC) is the largest association of commercial real estate on a global level.[13] For the Spanish Association of Shopping Centers (AECC, Spanish acronym), a shopping center is defined as "a group of independent and planned commercial establishments developed by one or various entities, with a unified criterion. The concept includes size, commercial mix, regular services and complementary activities that are related to its environment, and that permanently have a unified image and management."[14]

In Latin America, the retail sales had a market of USD 1028.39 billion for the year 2015, with projected sales of USD 1044.76 billion in 2016 and USD 1146.75 billion in 2020. This evolution can be seen in Table 8.2, where Brazil is the first in projected sales, followed by Mexico, Argentina, Venezuela, Colombia, Peru, and Ecuador.

The protagonists in these retail sales are the large areas, which integrate a broad supply of consumer products and services. The most relevant consumption areas in the region are Walmart Supercenter (from the USA), Carrefour (from France), OXXO (from Mexico), Soriana (from Mexico), Grupo Falabella (from Chile, with the brands: Sodimac, Tottus, and Falabella), and Cencosud (from Chile, with the brands: Easy, Jumbo, Wong, and Metro), and Ripley (from Chile).[15]

The ICSC has defined eight types of shopping centers with the objective of providing guidelines and understanding the differences

[13] *Equipar* 2016. [14] AECC n.d. [15] *Euromonitor* 2016.

Table 8.2 *Projection of retail sales by country, in millions of USD*

Region/Country	2015	2016	2017	2018	2019	2020
Latin America	1,028,397.70	1,044,760.10	1,066,331.40	1,091,259.70	1,117,820.70	1,146,754.00
Brazil	292,434.20	294,471.80	298,415.60	303,399.20	309,221.50	315,684.50
Mexico	203,020.30	207,368.80	211,943.50	216,777.60	221,718.80	226,961.50
Argentina	129,359.70	131,844.50	135,207.60	138,972.20	143,088.50	147,628.00
Venezuela	101,043.20	101,284.50	103,296.90	106,512.30	110,360.10	115,031.30
Chile	53,087.00	54,009.40	54,789.80	55,454.90	55,996.50	56,383.50
Peru	31,092.10	32,589.60	34,018.30	35,392.50	36,728.70	38,003.70
Ecuador	22,623.00	23,224.10	23,811.00	24,463.00	25,154.40	25,857.50
Costa Rica	13,542.80	14,050.00	14,473.90	14,966.00	15,346.20	15,757.40
Guatemala	11,215.10	11,776.60	12,409.20	12,988.40	13,621.50	14,251.00
Uruguay	12,343.30	12,671.00	12,971.40	13,455.20	13,739.30	14,049.60

Source: Passport Euromonitor (2016)

between them. Entertainment shopping centers combine retail stores with cinemas and theme restaurants.[16]

Lifestyle centers are the shopping centers that attract the MoP since the concept of the shopping center is related to family enjoyment more than the purely commercial transaction. The element that distinguishes the lifestyle shopping center is the role that it plays as a destination for various leisure activities, including restaurants, places of entertainment, and an architectonic design environment, and offering amenities such as fountains and street furniture, which are favorable for "browsing" in a casual manner.[17]

Colombia is one of the countries that leads the development of shopping centers in Latin America. The consumption in this country has increased in the central cities, not only Bogotá. Cali and Medellin were with projects of building centers from 2014 to 2016, and it has to be taken into account that Colombia had 7.15 square meters per inhabitant in comparison to the mean of 8.22 square meters per person in the region, giving it more than enought room for growing to the sector. By 2014, the 22% of visitants buy something, and the mean of expenditure is USD 988 monthly per family, making middle class a key factor with 42% of the population and 60% of the expenditure. According to the experts, shopping centers in Colombia have adequate access, sufficient numbers of people, and a commercial product mix. These are the main reasons why prestigious brands and international investors seek to position themselves in the Colombian market.[18]

According to León,[19] after interviewing Carlos Betancourt, executive director of the Shopping Center Association of Colombia (Acecolombia), 18 shopping centers were inaugurated in the year 2016, joining the 146 that existed. Colombia is growing in shopping center openings by between 280,000 and 400,000 square meters per year, and 500,000 square meters were opened in 2016. This growth

[16]   Regalado et al. 2009.   [17]   Regalado et al. 2009.
[18]   American Retail 2014.   [19]   León 2016.

comes from 2015, a year in which various projects were postponed. Despite that, the year 2015 closed with a two-digit growth in this sector.

In the year 2009, in Chile, the leading operators of shopping centers consisted of the groups Mall Plaza, Cencosud, and Parque Arauco, which accounted for a total of 87% of market share. In this country, the square meters per inhabitant were 14.9 while in the United States the figure was 194 square metres by the year 2014. Shopping centers had 25% of retail penetration while in developed countries this number rose to 50%.[20]

In the case of Brazil, 50% of the population belongs to the socioeconomic level C or lower-middle class. Brazilian shopping center traffic increased by 12.2%.[21]

In Peru, the sector suffered stagnation in the 1990s, but in the year 2000, the category began to take off. It has gone from having 8 shopping centers on a national level in 2004 to 78 shopping centers in 2015.[22]

On the other hand, Mexico is considered one of the most important markets in Latin America, leading the region together with Brazil. While Colombia and Peru have been developing in recent years, Chile and Uruguay present important growth perspectives.[23] Mexico has great potential for expansion in the shopping center industry. According to figures from the real estate services firm Colliers International, 850 shopping centers will be built in the region, of which 300 have already been constructed. In the case of Mexico, fifty-four new shopping centers have already been built, with 2 million profitable cubic meters. Javier Lomelín, director of the firm, stated that the growth expectation in the sector would remain at 10% from now until 2025.[24]

We can evaluate the success of a shopping center from different aspects, and one of them is the influx of patrons. With a greater

---

[20]   American Retail 2014.   [21]   Olguín 2015.   [22]   Arellano 2016.
[23]   Olguín 2015.   [24]   *Equipar* 2016.

number of visitors, there will be more probability of sales and, therefore, higher income. For a shopping center to be chosen as a place to buy or visit, a group of advertising and marketing strategies must be developed that can adequately communicate the messages that seek to capture the greatest attention of the public. What the shopping center offers to the public is a buying experience – a place where the goods and services required are provided, and where they can do leisure activities.[25] Shopping centers used to be only for the top of the pyramid due to the lack of disposable income of the middle class, but the rising of the new middle classes has allowed them to spend more time in leisure. With this shift, they are also willing to pay for more expensive products due to the associated prestige, but still with some restrictions in terms of affordability, requiring innovations that can provide a viable and attractive alternative.

Mega Plaza Norte, Peru: The Contagious Spark

At the beginning of the 1980s, the Camino Real shopping center opened (in the district of San Isidro), and the format was a success. For a long time, it attracted the attention of consumers from high socioeconomic levels. However, in the mid-1980s terrorist attacks became frequent, which countered the viability of this shopping center along with the fact that each store was individually owned, making it difficult when making decisions to reach agreement among all the owners.

Then, the Jockey Plaza Shopping Center, a mall aimed at the upper classes that promised to be the alternative to traveling to Miami, began operations in 1996. The initial good reception of the shopping center envisioned a new era, with Jockey Plaza based on a centralized management system in which tenants do not own their premises.

But then a series of negative precedents were generated in the financial system concerning shopping centers, since both the Jockey

---

[25]   Regalado et al. 2009.

and Larcomar (an entertainment center directed to the upper classes) frequently faced financial problems, appearing before investors and bankers as a business that could not be subject to credit. In this context, the idea arose of creating a shopping center in the northern cone of Lima. Although there was some fear, the market research indicated that the people demanded a higher-class establishment, although with certain peculiarities.

That was when MegaPlaza Norte opened its doors in 2002, after an investment of USD 25 million. It received in its establishment more than 300,000 people per month. People crammed the corridors of the shopping center; sales grew to surpass, in 2006, USD 200 million. In this way, the shopping centers ceased to be the privilege of the upper classes; the "northern cone" – northern area of the city, ceased to be called that name, instead to be called North Lima. MegaPlaza Norte was a turning point in the shopping center industry and showed that there were important segments of the population able to consume the recent offers that a mall provides. The CEO of MegaPlaza Norte, Percy Vigil, highlights its beginning: "We were the first to carry out brand activations in Peru; we made the retail industry and entertainment industry for the people for them to have a good time."

With the economic development of Peru and the growth of the middle class and its propensity for spending on consumption, the shopping center became an experience for the consumer. "It is important to define the tenant mix: once the target audience is well defined, it is necessary to comply with everything for everyone. Offer a secure surrounding, parking, and keep in mind the fact that with very few resources the greatest possible time can be spent outside of the home, for example, eat a chicken between four people, walk around to see free shows and end the afternoon with an ice cream or a dessert. You can spend a whole day outside of your home. There is nothing more economical, nothing safer, and nothing more relaxing than making this decision," highlights Vigil, describing the benefits provided by a shopping center.

In that sense, MegaPlaza Norte has a branded environment. A branded environment extends the experience of an organization or company's brand into the design of interior or exterior settings.[26] The benefits of a branded environment include better customer recognition, improved brand position, and higher employee satisfaction and retention, which translate into loyal customers and a higher share of their expenditure.[27] In reviewing several research studies on point of sale experience, important aspects come to mind for building a branded environment: symbols and colors, shopping environment, and physical structure and organization of space.

MegaPlaza Norte improves a branded environment by knowing the consumer and adapting the marketing techniques to the segment. That is to say, the MegaPlaza Norte itself has had to adapt to the demand of its visitors and their idiosyncrasies, moving away from the American parameters. MegaPlaza Norte is not a closed box with air conditioning, like the malls in other countries. It is an open and natural ventilation establishment; in addition, the ambient music is danceable and its food court resembles a village square, with a stage in the center.[28] "It is important to create iconic elements within the Shopping Center. For example, giant fishbowls have been built. It has been a great investment but it is a meeting point for families: Everyone is standing there. They are iconic elements within such a large surface," said Vigil in reference to the constant innovation related to the architecture and organization of the space.

In addition, knowing the characteristics of the MoP segment helps to create a consumer journey appropriate to each visitor profile. The men and young people of socioeconomic levels A and B (upper- and upper-middle class) visit the malls on the weekends. Women of socioeconomic status A visit shopping centers in the morning or at night to shop. The time spent by people in a shopping center is three to four hours. Besides, in the C+ level, the permanence is six hours. Men in socioeconomic levels A and B stay in the mall for one to two

[26] Alawadhi 2009. [27] Floor 2006. [28] Regalado et al. 2009.

hours because they already know what they are going to buy. The men and women of the C+ socioeconomic level visit the malls on weekends in search of entertainment.

The MoP may have less disposable income, but their massive influx makes it profitable. This is the reason why it is important to make the duration of stay longer since consumption is slow and thoroughly deliberated. The family arrives at mid-morning at the shopping center to buy something, but the idea is, they may stay as long as possible. This behavior is studied and defined regarding what will be the consumption routes and the needs of the family as the day advances. They can find a little music, entertainment, and children's activities. The family can spend a happy day at no cost. The tranquility that comes from a safe environment allows them to enjoy it. One thing that the CEO of MegaPlaza Norte has made clear is that "we must try to make the mall alive and for the client to feel that it is the best alternative. If there is a crisis tomorrow, we are the ones who are going to present the best alternative; it must be the first option as the place in which you consider spending more time."

"Based on our experience, there are two very important factors; the first is the arrival and acceptance of the brands. The consumer knows that these brands have been exposed in other markets, such as the A/B markets, so the consumer has already identified and makes them the desired brands. Therefore, when brands arrive, they want to obtain them and generate a great capacity of consumption," highlights Vigil.

Indeed, two important factors stand out: The first is the brands and the story behind the brand. The second factor is the capacity of the brands to offer massive scale. Again, there are differences in the ticket price, but the volume makes the difference.

"Brands are noticing that they have a relevant market and are also starting to turn towards this type of segment. It happens in 90% of the brands when trying to enter a market, and therefore there will be no story to tell. Except for the cases in which it is a very particular product, such as food fairs and products, it is very different from a standard offer of a food court or standard restaurants of a market like a shopping center," highlights Vigil.

For example, many of the brands that offer their products at various points of sale of Lima actually have the higher level of sales in the stores located at this shopping center. This situation shows that the average ticket may be at similar levels or even less than in other stores, but the revenue from global sales is much greater. This applies to all the brands and franchises; one of the most famous Starbucks in Peru is the one located in MegaPlaza Norte, and there is also a Kentucky Fried Chicken (KFC).

"We can achieve this result by offering the consumer a product with an experience above his expectations; with high standards, the market response will occur anyway. Where price will no longer be the barrier, on the contrary, the price justifies the benefit. It is surprising to see how they react. For this consumer, it is harder to pay, but he has the will to pay; he pays for a service that he perceives, feels, and values," highlights Vigil. One of the success factors of MegaPlaza Norte has always been not stigmatizing segments C and D, either for the level of spending that they generate or for the product/service they want to receive. The middle of the pyramid looks for goods that are affordable for them, but that separate them from being bottom of the pyramid, and in doing so, they are willing to spend more time and money for better products, even if they are not the same as those for the upper class.

Regarding the behavior of the Peruvian and Latin American consumer in a shopping center, many similarities can be found, especially the main behavioral guidelines. "The aggressiveness of some things, being so recurrent, is inherent in some markets. Although in general, it is very similar with Chile, for example, the arrival of brands for the middle class and the response of this target are more or less the same. The great impulse given to activations, they have become accustomed to large flows of public in Peru, and not noticed outside," reaffirms Vigil.

Currently, the MegaPlaza Norte shopping center has grown enormously, and it continues to be a point of reference for all the professionals of the retail industry in Peru. Among the shopping centers that brought about a change in the sector in the country where they operate is MegaPlaza Norte. It has been selected for the sixth year in a row as the preferred shopping center of Metropolitan Lima, according to Arellano Marketing.

"The size of the current industry makes it massive in general, even segment A–B. We are receiving approximately 3 million people per month, with an increase of between 20% and 30% in the months of July and December. A specialized company registers and manages the statistics and defines the flow of people that we have in the shopping center in a regular manner," concludes Vigil.

EXPERIENCE WINS! BEATING PIRACY AND FREE PLATFORMS

The cinema is the third entertainment activity demanded by the MoP. It is one of the categories presented around an experience. "This is because, like concerts, the need to see a movie or listen to music can be easily satisfied and in a very accessible manner through other platforms, such as cable TV or the Internet. Therefore, when the consumer goes to the cinema, he is not only covering the need to see the movie but also living the experience provided by visiting the movie theater itself," states Tito Aguilar.

The cinema may appear to be an endangered industry due to the different alternative channels that may be, on occasion, more economical or even free.

The price of cinema entrance varies from country to country. A study by BBC World precisely defined and compared movie prices in different countries. Excluding Chile and Cuba, which are, in comparison, the most expensive and cheapest, respectively, the countries with the most expensive movie tickets include Argentina (USD 8.45), Belize (USD 7.50), and Brazil (USD 7.00). The cheapest include El Salvador (USD 2.50), Costa Rica (USD 2.94), and Mexico (USD 3.30).[29]

---

[29]   Llorente 2016.

The same study by BBC World shows the relationship between movie ticket price and GDP per capita in different Latin American nations. In spite of GDP differences, the admission price in Chile is the most expensive of all the region (USD 9.20); it is also one of the countries with the highest income per capita (USD 14528). Accordingly, the value of a cinema ticket only represents 0.06% of the average annual income of a Chilean citizen. Very close is Guatemala, which has an average income of USD 3676 and a movie ticket costs USD 4.00. Thus, a national from that country needs to spend 0.5% of his salary to go to the cinema. In the rest of the countries, most of the citizens must pay an average of 0.06% of their wages to go to the cinema.[30]

At present, the multi-cinema format is positioned as a success factor within the entertainment market, since they can make various movie options available in a single place, and the experience is significant: airplane type seats, surround sound, and 3D options, among others.[31] Also, Percy Vigil validates this format as an option for access to the cinema to satisfy all tastes, enhanced by the ability to attend with family or friends. This is the reason multi-theaters have been growing hand in hand with shopping centers, since they complement the different services available. Cinema is an attractive industry, having a market value of USD 2.284 million in 2016, according to a report by Statista Research Department.

In this case, MegaPlaza Norte is betting on the massive nature of the products and services that appear to belong to "the very few." It currently has the largest cinema in Peru with the greatest number of seats, which gives it the movie theater with the highest flow of patrons on a national level – when just fifteen years ago it was assumed that piracy (of films) would displace the cinema market. "The more you offer, the people pay; For example, we have 4D rooms where the ticket is visibly higher. They perceive the benefit," said

---

[30]   Llorente 2016.   [31]   Andrich et al. 2009.

Vigil. He highlights the idea that they pay for the experience rather than the product.

On the other hand, the movie theater presents price strategies addressed at the MoP. For example, they have Spectator's Day, in which normally on Tuesdays and Wednesdays tickets are sold at half-price. Other strategies focus on the differentiation of movies; for example, premieres are more expensive than a film that has already been showing for some time. On Cinephile Day the entrance price is half, or even less. About this, Tito Aguilar states, "The MoP consumer likes to have options. For example, if he does not have much money one month, he only goes to the cinema once, on Spectator's Day. If that person has a little more money the following month, for example, he goes to the movies twice."

THEME PARKS IN LATIN AMERICA

Theme parks are the fourth option of preference for the Latin American middle class. The amusement characteristics and the diverse offerings for the entire family and all tastes result in this type of entertainment enjoying high acceptance among Latin Americans.

Niels Segersbol, former manager of HappyLand in Peru, and an expert in the theme park sector, states that for the middle class, going to a theme park is an aspirational factor.

"Leisure activities are carried out to forget the stress of the large city. One of the primary drivers of the Latin American middle class is family, that is why it is important to have the family consensus at all times. The main factors sought by this segment when selecting their entertainment activity are the possibility of carrying it out in big groups and the security that it can offer," adds Segersbol.

Initially, the Latin American family that has a reduced budget goes to zonal parks, which are public spaces located in the residential districts of the large majorities that offer a series of services and activities for outdoor leisure. These zonal parks are the preference of the district municipalities and have low average standards, for example in the security provided in their open spaces. "It is for security that families prefer to spend a little more and have better-quality services when going out to spend time together with the family," comments Segersbol. Therefore, when the family nucleus has a larger budget available for this type of entertainment, theme parks present a better alternative compared to zonal parks, since they provide group activities with the characteristics sought: convenience and security.

Theme parks are outdoor parks and indoor parks, the latter with facilities assembled. Thus shopping centers have become the ideal place for this type of entertainment.

The outdoor theme park industry consolidated well. Ulloa points out that they originated from parks where games, fireworks, and live entertainment were carried out.[32] In 1583, the first game park was founded in Copenhagen, Denmark, and it is now the oldest park in the world. The theme park concept was pioneered in 1955 by Walt Disney, has enjoyed constant innovation, and has become a reference in the region and the world; for example, in the United States there are currently more than 700 amusement parks.

The theme park industry moves by economic cycles; in 2011, for example, this industry experienced a greater growth after recovery from the global financial crisis. According to Global Entertainment and Media Outlook 2007–2011, a report by the consultancy firm PwC, "The global tourist spending in theme parks had an annual growth of 4.6% between 2007 and 2011."

The last review of theme park attendance[33] indicates that the growth of the industry continued at 5% from 2014 to 2015 (the industry had already a 4% increase from 2013 to 2014), reviewing the performance of the Top 25 of the parks on a global level. The statistucs are distinguished between amusement parks and aquatic parks, with amusement parks enjoying an attendance growth of 4.1% among the Top 25 parks on a global level from 2013 to 2014 and an attendance growth of 5.4% from 2014 to 2015. This can be seen in Table 8.3,

[32]   Ulloa 2012.   [33]   PWC n.d.

Table 8.3 *Ranking of the 10 leading parks on a world level, in USD*

Rank	Park and Location	2013	2014	2015
1	Magic Kingdom At Walt Disney World, Lake Buena Vista, FL	18,588,000	19,332,000	20,492,000
2	Disneyland, Anaheim, CA	16,202,000	16,769,000	18,278,000
3	Tokyo Disneyland, Tokyo, Japan	17,214,000	17,300,000	16,600,000
4	Universal Studios Japan, Osaka, Japan	10,100,000	11,800,000	13,900,000
5	Tokyo Disney Sea, Tokyo, Japan	10,100,000	11,800,000	13,600,000
6	Epcot At Walt Disney World, Lake Buena Vista, FL	11,229,000	11,454,000	11,798,000
7	Disney's Animal Kingdom At Walt Disney World, Lake Buena Vista, FL	10,198,000	10,402,000	10,922,000
8	Disney's Hollywood Studios At Walt Disney World, Lake Buena Vista, FL	10,110,000	10,312,000	10,828,000
9	Disneyland Park At Disneyland Paris, Marne-La-Valle, France	10,430,000	9,940,000	10,360,000
10	Universal Studios At Universal Orlando, FL	7,062,000	8,263,000	9,585,000
	Total	**121,233,000**	**127,372,000**	**136,363,000**

Source: Themed Entertainment Association (TEA) and the Economics practice at AECOM

where the North American parks are the reference and Asia a market with potential. Aquatic Parks show an attendance growth of 2.8% among the Top 20 on a global level in the 2013–2014 period, and 3.7% in the 2014–2015 period, as shown in Table 8.4.

Latin American parks have experienced growth of 5% in 2014 and 1% in 2015, according to Table 8.5. The investments made in the park Beto Carrero, World (Brazil), related to the new area of the park under the intellectual property theme of Madagascar, translated into 150,000 additional visits in 2014, and by the year 2015 the attendance increased by 10%. The Parque Mundo Aventura (Colombia) increased by 300,000 visits in the year of the Soccer World Cup (2014) but in 2015 posted an attendance decline of about 5%. On the other hand, in Guatemala, Mundo Petaha had a growth of 8%, adding approximately 80,000–90,000 visits, supporting the growth of its economy. On the other hand, the Soccer World Cup held in Brazil had an adverse impact on the attendance at various parks, as in the case of El Salitre Mágico (Colombia) in 2014.

For the aquatic park industry, the Latin American region, due to its growth and stability, has become a lower risk investment. As shown in Table 8.5, three of the Latin American parks appear in the Top 20 on a global level. This fact suggests that this type of park is becoming an option for success. If it is also considered that bathing in a swimming pool is one of the preferences of the middle class, then the aquatic park is presented as a symbiosis between the swimming pool and theme park, which is attractive for the MoP. Besides that, in 2015 the performance was basically flat. The region's economic and political volatility are apparent in the varying performance of the parks.[34]

A success story in outdoor theme parks due to the level of adaptation to the needs of the MoP in Latin America is Play Land Park, in El Salvador. The itinerant theme park Play Land Park started in San Salvador sixty years ago. It includes in its offering the option of

[34]   PWC n.d.

Table 8.4 *Top 20 global aquatic parks, in USD*

Rank Park and Location	2013	2014	2015
1 Chimelong Waterpark, Guangzhou, China	2,172,000	2,259,000	2,352,000
2 Typhoon Lagoon At Disney World, Orlando, FL	2,142,000	2,185,000	2,294,000
3 Blizzard Beach At Disney World, Orlando, FL	1,968,000	2,007,000	2,107,000
4 Bahamas Adventure Waterpark, Paradise Island (Nassau, New Providence), Bahamas	no data	1,850,000	1,868,000
5 Thermas Dos Laranjais, Olimpia, Brazil	1,650,000	1,939,000	1,761,000
6 Aquatica, Orlando, Fl	1,553,000	1,569,000	1,600,000
7 Ocean World, Gangwon-Do, South Korea	1,700,200	1,604,000	1,509,000
8 Caribbean Bay, Gyeonggi-Do, South Korea	1,623,000	1,493,000	1,434,000
9 Aquaventure Waterpark, Dubai, U.A.E	1,200,000	1,400,000	1,400,000
10 Wet'n Wild, Orlando, Fl	1,259,000	1,284,000	1,310,000
11 Hot Park Rio Quente, Caldas Novas, Brazil	1,284,000	1,288,000	1,288,000
12 Therme Erding, Erding, Germany	1,000,000	1,000,000	1,235,000
13 Wet'n Wild Gold Coast, Gold Coast, Australia	1,250,000	1,200,000	1,200,000
14 Shenyang Royal Ocean Park-Water World, Fushun, China	1,100,000	1,172,000	1,150,000
15 Tropical Islands, Krausnick, Germany	no data	1,000,000	1,100,000
16 Sunway Lagoon, Kuala Lumpur, Malaysia	1,100,000	1,100,000	1,077,000
17 Schlitterbahn, New Braunfels, TX	1,027,000	1,037,000	1,037,000
18 Aquapalace, Prague, Czech Republic	1,035,000	1,018,000	997,000
19 Atlantis Water Adventure, Jakara, Indonesia	980,000	960,000	970,000
20 Beach Park, Aquiraz, Brazil	964,000	949,000	970,000
21 Piscilago, Girardo (Bogotá), Colombia	1,035,000	1,018,000	970,000
Total	26,042,200	29,332,000	29,629,000

Source: Themed Entertainment Association (TEA) and the Economics practice at AECOM

Table 8.5 *Top 20 theme/aquatic parks in Latin America, in USD*

Rank	Park and Location	Type Park	2013	2014	2015
1	Six Flags Mexico, Mexico City, Mexico	Amusements/Theme Park	2,345,000	2,368,000	2,368,000
2	Beto Carrero World, Santa Catarina, Brazil	Amusements/Theme Park	1,530,000	1,818,000	2,000,000
3	Bahamas Adventure Waterpark, Paradise Island (Nassau, New Providence), Bahamas	Aquatic Park	no data	1,850,000	1,868,000
4	Thermas Dos Laranjais, Olimpia, Brazil	Aquatic Park	1,650,000	1,939,000	1,761,000
5	Hopi Hari, Sao Paulo, Brazil	Amusements/Theme Park	1,537,000	1,668,000	1,668,000
6	La Feria De Chapultepec, Mexico City, Mexico	Amusements/Theme Park	1,152,000	1,552,000	1,584,000
7	Parque Mundo Aventura, Bogotá, Colombia	Amusements/Theme Park	1,209,000	1,423,000	1,389,000
8	Hot Park Rio Quente, Caldas Novas, Brazil	Aquatic Park	1,284,000	1,288,000	1,288,000
9	Parque Xcaret, Cancún, Mexico	Amusements/Theme Park	1,200,000	1,212,000	1,287,000
10	Plaza De Sésamo, Monterrey, Mexico	Amusements/Theme Park	1,086,000	1,221,000	1,221,000
11	Mundo Petapa, Guatemala City, Guatemala	Amusements/Theme Park	1,054,000	1,138,000	1,199,000
12	Fantasialandia, Santiago, Chile	Amusements/Theme Park	14,047,000	1,111,000	1,003,000
13	Piscilago, Girardo (Bogotá), Colombia	Aquatic Park	1,035,000	1,018,000	970,000
	Beach Park, Aquiraz, Brazil	Aquatic Park	964,000	949,000	970,000
15	Parque De La Costa, Tigre, Argentina	Amusements/Theme Park	no data	1,020,000	956,000
16	Parque Acuatico Xocomil, San Martin Zapotitlán, Retalhuleu, Guatemala	Aquatic Park	786,000	767,000	940,000
17	Parque Actuatico El Rollo, Morelos, México	Aquatic Park	300,000	470,000	510,000
18	Wet'N Wild Sao Paulo, Sao Paulo, Brazil	Aquatic Park	395,000	496,000	496,000
19	Rio Water Planet, Rio Janeiro, Brazil	Aquatic Park	350,000	400,000	400,000
20	Wet'N Wild, Cancún, Mexico	Aquatic Park	250,000	255,000	259,000
	Total			23,963,000	24,139,015

Source: Themed Entertainment Association (TEA) and the Economics practice at AEC

"itinerancy," being able to move and get closer to the area where the middle-class segment locates, taking advantage of the high value that the segment attributes to proximity to be able to enjoy its leisure time. To date, it has visited more than twenty-two countries, and it is one of the most sophisticated amusement parks, having become the largest conglomerate of mechanical games in all of Latin America. The manner in which it travels in each country is organized strategically depending on the climate and on the different holidays of each country, to take advantage of the calendar dates where the MoP have a greater likelihood of leisure and free time, such as school vacations or national holidays. For example, in Guatemala, at the end of every year, they install themselves in the Campo de Marte, where it is already a tradition to visit this theme park. The entry ticket is USD 0.70, and the games vary between USD 2.00 and USD 2.70. Another example is the case of Peru, where Play Land Park receives 1 million visits at the different temporary fairs. The stay of the visitors, of different ages, varies between three and five hours and has an average ticket price for rides in Lima and provinces of USD 18.00.

Weather Out: Happyland, Chile

Considering indoor theme parks, a success story in the region is HappyLand, a company of Chilean origin that has operations in Chile, Colombia, and Peru.

The primary success factor has been to exploit the growth of the new channel in these countries. This method combats the climatic and seasonal effect very well, besides utilizing the influx of people attracted by the physical space itself and the variety of services where they are located, such as shopping centers. Also, the growth and expansion into the provinces of shopping centers originated by economic development have facilitated the penetration of said indoor theme parks. This fact has allowed the company to consolidate itself in the market, becoming a reference for similar offerings in the sector.

The second success factor is the variety of the offering; in other words, the mix of products and services they offer, going hand in hand with the demand of their area of influence, apart from security and cleanliness. Niels Segersbol highlights a particular characteristic of the segment: "They want to concentrate everything on a single site." In other words, going out with the entire family involves engaging in activities where everyone enjoys themselves, while managing the logistics involved in transferring the entire family. For these reasons, they value highly the fact that all the services that they seek are in the same place.

The third success factor is innovation. It is indispensable in the theme park industry, along with the experience of the organization and the knowledge of the segment, enabling theme parks to adapt the variety of their services to the needs of their direct and regular customers. Furthermore, and as a result of these constant innovations, being associated with the International Association of Amusement Parks and Attractions (IAAPA) accredits them with the end user and drives them to innovate continuously.

These indoor theme parks become a convenient option for consumers since they take advantage of the services of the shopping centers. These include free parking and accessibility with public transport along with other complementary amenities – such as restaurants, stores, cinemas – to attract the influx of people. There is an additional important benefit: guaranteed security inside the facilities.

Another example of the indoor theme park is Divercity, a Colombian company present in Bogota, Barranquilla, Lima, Guatemala, and Panama. Divercity has presented Divermarketing, a platform that seeks to practice responsible marketing among minors, reproducing in its facilities a city that has an infrastructure created for children, with banks, a fire station, veterinary service, and a hospital, among others. The idea is that each of the establishments or most of them have a real brand that sponsors it, in this manner putting the original brands in contact with the children. It has currently been in the Latin American market for more than ten years, focusing its offer exclusively on children. For example, in Peru, the company works with more than thirty brands of different sectors, with which it seeks to spread a sense of social responsibility toward the community, to promote education, and, mainly, to foster a connection between children and companies in a non-invasive manner.[35]

TIME VERSUS PRICE: VIVA AEROBUS, MEXICO

Transportation is an important factor that impacts not only entertainment options such as tourism but also business opportunities; but, what are the needs of the passenger? The main reasons reported for traveling in Mexico are: leisure with 35%, visiting friends and relatives with 35%, and businesses with 30%. As can be seen, the motivation for travel is equitable among the main reasons for traveling in this country.

In the case of Viva Aerobus Mexico, an opportunity was identified in 2006 to enter into passenger air transport. This company started operating at Monterrey airport in 2006 as the first low-cost company in Latin America. Its investors are the Irelandia Aviation group and the RyanMex group, which also belongs to the bus company IAMSA. Furthermore, Irelandia Aviation has VivaColombia (launched 2012) and Viva Air Perú (founded in 2016 and launched 2017) as low-cost airline companies in Latin America.

At the time of its launching, it faced very price-sensitive passengers, who had previously only traveled by bus, and a sector focused on few travelers: only 4% of the population took a plane and the rest traveled by bus.

The CEO of Viva Aerobus, Juan Zuazua, points out, "The middle class is always seeking to raise resource options. It tries to solve a need for transportation from one place to another, where time and safety are important factors. At same cost and security, if time is equal or less, the formula is perfect. No one is against saving their time."

The target customer is the passenger whose travel needs are met by taking a bus in order to visit family or for tourism or business. Therefore, the strategy focused on practical options for the segment.

---

[35]   Taipe 2016.

"We have a passenger who has never flown," stresses Zuazua. "Therefore, as a company, we should innovate on how to reach the segment, not so much on the business model side of a small cost, as this model has already been developed in Europe and the United States of America."

The first step is to focus on the user experience; the goal is to make the travel experience as easy as possible. "It is important to give them confidence by approaching the product to the consumer, speaking their language, and directing the promotions towards them," highlights Zuazua.

For example, Viva Aerobus has worked each of the five touch points: purchase, documentation, boarding, flight, and baggage delivery. In addition, there are videos on the website educating those who have not flown before, and there is a frequently-asked-questions section to resolve pre-trip questions. Another example is that when they receive their reservation, they receive the "10 steps to access the flight" information so that they can enjoy the trip. In all communications, clear messages are sent that are designed to prepare the passenger.

Similarly, Viva Aerobus has studied the itineraries and the schedule of the routes. "The passenger is accustomed to travel at night, and to make him arrive by plane at the same time as if it were by bus can be an important factor when evaluating the alternatives," points out Zuazua.

"He is a smart traveler since he is very sensitive to the price, but not so much to the time. He likes to buy directly and without intermediaries," said Zuazua. On the other hand, alternatives and are generated close to these segments. For example, the sale of plane tickets is offered within the bus terminals for those who do not have internet access or a credit card. Another alternative is to book the ticket online and pay at a convenience store. They could also pay with the credit card online at the time they make the reservation.

Likewise, the virtual model is an advantage since everyone has a cell phone and there are more and more smartphones. "This acts in favor of Viva Aerobus, since it is in the internet where more tickets are sold and it is an advantage to reach this passenger. This MoP segment has gone from the television to the cellphone, skipping the computer, since they do not have a computer at home, but they are connected directly through the cellular," concludes Zuazua.

Through the study of consumer behavior and preferences, Viva Aerobus simplifies the model and improves the customer experience, always being the most economical. "There have been more airlines, but our share of mind is related to that we are actually the lowest, substantially," Zuazua specifies.

"Every day you learn from the consumer and through innovation and continuous improvement as you simplify your business model. You always have to see how to satisfy your basic needs: from the time you buy the ticket, pay it, when you arrive at the airport, take the flight and when they get off the plane," completes Zuazua.

Viva Aerobus competes in a market of 37 million passengers, while the bus company of the same group, IAMSA, reaches the passenger who is traveling by bus rather than by airplane (a market of 270 million passengers). It is only a matter of time before the airlines capture much of the market and, in parallel, that the consumer migrates to the Internet, especially with the growth of the smartphone.

Latin America closes 2015 with a tourism market of USD 16.13 billion and it is expected to reach USD 19.15 billion by 2019 according to the Passport Euromonitor platform.

CONCLUSIONS

The entertainment industry presents itself in an understated manner but with sustained growth in recent years, with growth projections for the coming years accompanied by the economic development of the region and the acquisitive power of its inhabitants.

Changes are occurring in the preferences of the MoP consumer of the region since there are needs that have not yet been satisfied or have been partially satisfied. The higher income received by the segment and the access to credit facilitate the satisfaction of the entertainment needs through a varied offering. This situation makes the MoP entertainment consumer a more demanding customer who expects to receive what he deserves in exchange for the payment made. Let us remember that he is going from enjoying free entertainment options to paid entertainment options.

Analyzing the situation and the competitive advantages that we have dealt with in the five cases examined in each one of the categories, we can highlight various characteristic points, which could constitute the transversal elements of the leading entertainment groups of the MoP:

- Analyze the segment characteristics: It is important to consider the needs and motivations of all members of the family when designing the consumer journey. The family is seeking activities that can be carried out altogether, at least at the same place. The shopping centers or restaurants with key differentiators for the MoP become successful.

- Socializing with family and friends: It is crucial for the segment to cover its free time needs with activities that involve family and friends. Furthermore, the entertainment activity should enable the possibility of carrying out the activity with many people, in terms of infrastructure. This habit is due to the inherent need for the sector given the value assigned to the family in its scale of priorities, as well as wanting to share these moments of enjoyment and reward (higher income also entails a greater effort to achieve it) with loved ones. That is why it is important to consider the design of the shopping experience. For example, one of Rokys success factors is to provide an enjoyable meal for everyone. The same happens in the other cases reviewed in this chapter, where MegaPlaza Norte adapts the scheduled journey to the needs of all components of a family.

- Physical access: The MoP prefers entertainment alternatives that are accessible; that is, close to home and in proximity of car parks, bus stops, etc.

- Access to credit and increasing income: There are currently more and better financing mechanisms available for this emerging middle class in addition to the increase in income for this segment. This translates to a greater availability of money and an increased spending trend, significant for all the analyzed categories. Recurring and non-sporadic spending can be put toward brands that were aspirational, and now accessible. It is also possible for other types of events such as concerts to command higher ticket prices because they are unique or specialized events.

- To have a backstory: Not only having a recognized brand, but having an experience with the brand that generates a differentiation in the segment. An aspirational brand must treat the MoP as they expect to be treated, in other words, being a brand that understands them and adapts to their needs and motivations.

- Constant innovation: This is characteristic of the entertainment industry; nevertheless, the middle class continually seeks to be surprised. Additionally, since it is a novelty, the MoP values highly being able to differentiate themselves in their entertainment activities. Therefore, participating in new or innovative activities constitutes an important driver when selecting leisure activities. For example, MoP pays more in 4D at the cinema because the novelty of new activities at the HappyLand is appealing and draws the families back to the park.

- Digital trends: The use of technology maintains exponential growth, given the penetration trend of the smartphone and internet access. The different companies exploit this to generate differentiation in the services offered and the experience received by clients or users. Also, the MoP will be increasingly accessible and more comfortable using digital elements, which will help generate a greater differentiation among companies in the future and also create new communication channels. For example, buying cinema tickets online, so they can skip over the queue.

- Inherent MoP characteristics: They are comfortable at crowded places featuring open and natural ventilation, and enjoy establishments similar to village places, with danceable music, elements that recall the places where their parents or grandparents were born. In addition, the MoP values security, access, convenience, and the possibility to satisfy the whole family.

The MoP segment is similar to others regarding innovation of the entertainment offering: They need to be always surprised. The fact that they are just starting to request these services does not imply that they will always be happy with the same thing, and can be expected to be more demanding as they continue to request what best suits their lifestyle.

The entertainment business entails a critical component of constant innovation in all the categories: eating out, visiting shopping centers, going to the cinema or theme parks. The offering must always be changing or adapting or offering limited editions to keep the client "hooked" on the satisfaction of these needs.

Although we may think that the entertainment categories would be the first to be affected in the event of stagnation or recession of the economy of a country, we should consider that spending would always take place in the entertainment sector, since there are substitute products and services with a lower price. In this sense, the budget destined for these activities could be reduced, but it will not disappear, especially if we consider the importance for the MoP of sharing with family and friends.

Finally, it is necessary to point out that the MoP has always tried to satisfy, one way or another, its entertainment needs but that now it has greater possibilities for doing so. Leisure time, weekends, public holidays, and vacations are allies of the entertainment industry.

REFERENCES

AECC. nd. Asociación Española de Parques y Centros Comerciales – AECC. Nuestra razón de ser. Accessed September 1, 2016. www.aedecc.com/es/quienes-somos

American Retail. 2013. Los cambios del mercado tras 30 años en Chile. Accessed July 11, 2020. www.america-retail.com/weekly/los-cambio-del-mercado-tras-30-anos-de-centros-comerciales-en-chile

American Retail. 2014. La evolución de los centros comerciales en Colombia. Accessed July 11, 2020. www.america-retail.com/industria-y-mercado/la-evolucion-de-los-centros-comerciales-en-colombia

Alawadhi, A. M. 2009. *Retail Branding through Sensory Experience: Local Case-Study at Chocolaterie Stam*. Ames, IA: Iowa State University.

Anderson, C. 2006. *The Long Tail: Why the Future of Business Is Selling Less of More*. New York: Hyperion Books.

Andrich, J., Arroyo, C., & Canturini, F. 2009. *Análisis de las opciones de entretenimiento familiar, fuera de casa, en los niveles socioeconómicos C y D en Lima Sur: plan de negocios de un parque de atracciones.* Lima: Universidad ESAN.

Arellano, R. 2013. Cómo clasificar la clase media en América Latina. *América Economía.* Accessed September 1, 2016. www.americaeconomia.com/analisis-opinion/como-clasificar-la-clase-media-en-america-latina

Arellano. 2016. Conference: Annual Meeting of Sociedad Peruana de Marketing 2016.

Bates, S. & Ferri, A. J. 2010. Studies in Popular Culture. Popular Culture Association in the South.

Bofarull, I. 2005. Ocio y tiempo libre, un reto para la familia.

El Comercio. 2015. Pollo a la brasa: el favorito de los peruanos. *El Comercio.* Accessed September 1, 2016. http://elcomercio.pe/gastronomia/noticias/pollo-brasa-favorito-peruanos-noticia-1826726

Equipar. 2016. RECON Latin America 2016. *Equipar.* Accessed December 1, 2016. www.revistaequipar.com/noticias/recon-latin-america-2016

Euromonitor. 2015. *A New Era of Growth and Competition: Global Consumer Service in 2015 and Beyond.* London: Euromonitor.

Floor, K. 2006. *Branding a Store: How to Build Successful Retail Brands in a Changing Marketplace.* London: Kogan Page Publishers.

Gardner, M. P. (1985). Mood States and Consumer Behavior: A Critical Review. *Journal of Consumer Research* 12(3): 281–300.

Llorente, A. 2016. ¿En qué países de América Latina es más barato y más caro ir al cine? *BBC.* Accessed September 1, 2016. www.bbc.com/mundo/noticias/2016/01/160121_cine_precios_america_latina_entrada_all

León, M. Y. 2016. En lo que resta del año se abrirán 18 centros comerciales. Accessed September 1, 2016. www.portafolio.co/negocios/empresas/resta-ano-abriran-18-centros-comerciales-496741

López, R. 2000. El espacio público en la ciudad europea: entre la crisis y la iniciativa de recuperación. *Insumos.* Accessed November 2016. www.insumisos.com/lecturasinsumisas/El%20espacio_publico%20en%20ciudades%20europeas.pdf

Olguín, C. 2015. México lidera centros comerciales en América Latina: ICSC. Real Estate Market & Life Style. Accessed June 1, 2016. www.realestatemarket.com.mx/articulos/capital-markets/11466-mexico-lidera-centros-comerciales-en-america-latina-icsc

PWC. n.d. Global Entertainment and Media Outlook (GEMO) 2012–2016. Medios y entretenimiento, 13ª edición. Accessed December 1, 2016. www.pwc.es/es/publicaciones/entretenimiento-y-medios/assets/global-entertainment-and-media-outlook-2012-2016.pdf

Regalado, O., Fuentes, C., Aguirre, G., García, N., Miu, R., & Vallejo, R. 2009. *Factores críticos de éxito en los centros comerciales de Lima Metropolitana y el Callao*. Lima: ESAN Ediciones.

Rios Montanez, A. M. 2019. Latin America: Foodservice Sales Revenue 2016–2021. *Statista*. Accessed April 1, 2019. www.statista.com/statistics/870923/foodservice-sales-value-latin-america

Rogers, E. 1995. *Diffusion of Innovations*. (4th ed.). New York: Free Press.

Romainville, M. 2016. Marketing Infantil: ¿por qué se apuesta por las experiencias? *El Comercio*. Accessed November 1, 2020. http://elcomercio.pe/economia/personal/marketing-infantil-que-se-apuesta-experiencias-noticia-1886575

Statista Research Department. 2019. Latin America: Media & Entertainment Market Value 2016–2021, by sector. Accessed April 1, 2019. www.statista.com/statistics/257388/media-entertainment-spending-in-latin-america-by-sector

Taipe, A. 2016. Divercity prevé captar 6 nuevas marcas en su parque temático. *El Comercio*. Accessed September 1, 2016. https://elcomercio.pe/economia/negocios/divercity-preve-captar-6-nuevas-marcas-parque-tematico-265465-noticia

Trinidad, M. 2016. En lo que resta del año se abrirán 18 centros comerciales. *Portafolio*. Accessed November 1, 2016. www.portafolio.co/negocios/empresas/resta-ano-abriran-18-centros-comerciales-496741

Ulloa, E. 2012. *Plan de marketing para la creación de un parque temático de entretenimiento y diversión para niños de 6 meses a 8 años y sus padres en la ciudad de Guayaquil, 2012*. Quito: Pontificia Universidad Católica del Ecuador.

9 Money, Money, Money
Innovating Access to Credit

Mauricio Cervantes and Jose F. Moreno

INTRODUCTION

A major problem in the world nowadays is the lack of access to financing for the lower classes; in developing countries, this issue also affects a big part of the middle class.[1]

The financial system does not want to give credit to people who do not have steady employment, collateral, or a verifiable credit history. These people are referred to as the "unbankable." Even when money is available, their lack of information hinders credit access for this large segment of the population. In the 1970s in Bangladesh, people started working on group credit schemes that attenuated these problems, and the group models have since been replicated around the world with relative success.[2] The availability of the Internet and the growing interest in social problems have promoted the concept of "internet social lending," causing a revolution in the area of extending credit to favored sectors.[3]

Access to formal credit is one of the most unsatisfied needs in Latin America, not only for low-income or bottom-of-the-pyramid (BoP) people, but also for a great part of the middle of the pyramid's (MoP) consumers and entrepreneurs. Based on the World Bank's Financial Inclusion data,[4] in 2014 only 53% of the poorest 40% of the world (ages 15+) had an account at a financial institution, and only 9% of this population had borrowed from a financial institution (Table 9.1).

In this chapter, we will analyze innovations that have been implemented in Latin America to help solve the problem of lack of

---

[1]   Khavul 2010.   [2]   Zaman 2004.   [3]   Solarz 2011.
[4]   http://datatopics.worldbank.org/financialinclusion

financing for the population of scarce resources. Banco Compartamos (México), Fondo Esperanza (Chile), ProMujer (Argentina), CrediAmigo/AgroAmigo (Brazil), Cumplo (Chile), and Regalii (USA) are the companies that we analyze in this chapter. They were innovative in their business model, their group lending work, their social commitment, and their integral way of attacking the problem with education and other elements. Banco Compartamos was innovative as the first bank in the stock market to use the group microcredit scheme. Fondo Esperanza innovated through offering entrepreneur training and networking opportunities. ProMujer is more of a solidarity group mainly focused on loans to build or improve housing. CrediAmigo/AgroAmigo is the largest microcredit program mainly oriented to agricultural production in South America. Additionally, technology has played an important role in the innovation of microfinance institutions for the MoP in particular. For instance, Cumplo is an innovative crowdfunding peer-to-peer (P2P) platform: Most of the activities in the exchange process are done online, and borrowers define their own conditions for time, amount, and rate. By disintermediating and establishing new forms of trust, Cumplo provides personal loans at affordable rates, and investors have received an average return of 10.3%. Another great example of how innovation has arrived in the financial industry is the case of Regalii. It focuses on improving the lives of hardworking MoP immigrants and their families by revolutionizing the way to send money abroad (i.e., remittances). This novel process makes money transfers instantaneous, safe, and completely transparent, allowing customers to track their family finances and make payments to more than 500 utility companies in 10 different countries.

Through new business models, new funding sources, international alliances, training, networking, financial and health programs, technology platforms, the Internet, mobile phones, and more, these companies are able to give small amounts of credit in a fast and economic way to MoP customers and some BoP customers.

INNOVATION IN FINANCIAL INCLUSION

Financial inclusion means that individuals and businesses have access to useful and affordable financial products and services that meet their needs – transactions, payments, savings, credit, and insurance – delivered in a responsible and sustainable way. Access to a transaction account is a first step toward broader financial inclusion, since it allows people to store money and to send and receive payments. A transaction account can also serve as a gateway to other financial services, which is why ensuring that people worldwide have access to a transaction account is the focus of the World Bank Group's Universal Financial Access 2020 initiative.[5]

Financial access facilitates day-to-day living and helps families and businesses plan for everything from long-term goals to unexpected emergencies. As bank account holders, people are more likely to use other financial services, such as credit and insurance, to start and expand businesses, invest in education or health, manage risk, and weather financial shocks, which can improve the overall quality of their lives.[6]

Financial inclusion or inclusive financing is the delivery of financial services at affordable costs to disadvantaged and low-income segments of society, in contrast to financial exclusion, where those services are not available or affordable.[7] In other words, by not having access to formal credit, the low-income population – and in Latin America, part of the middle-income population – has limited options to borrow money, and those few options are very expensive and risky.

On the other hand, by having access to proper financial services, the poor and the middle class could invest in physical assets and education that would help them to reduce income inequality and make them contributors to economic growth in the long term.[8]

[5]   www.worldbank.org/en/topic/financialinclusion/brief/achieving-universal-financial-access-by-2020
[6]   www.worldbank.org/en/topic/financialinclusion/overview   [7]   www.cgap.org
[8]   Mehrotra & Yetman 2015.

Based on this argument, the World Bank and other international financial institutions have been focusing their resources and efforts on improving the rate of financial inclusion around the globe.

International funders of the financial inclusion proposal had already committed at least USD 31 billion to the project in 2013.[9] However, while these numbers have continued to increase year after year in all other developing regions of the world, Latin America and the Caribbean have seen these funds decreasing in recent years.

Still, there is a profound need for access to better and less expensive financial services among the low-income population in this region. For-profit organizations have identified this great market opportunity and have been looking for innovative ways to bring together low-income populations and formal financial services.

An example of the most inaccessible financial markets is in the BoP, and in Latin America countries even part of the MoP is included. The majority of the people in this market segment are considered unbankable. Additionally, if loans are given, they are for small amounts and thus administration costs are very high, so commercial banks tend to avoid working with them based on the principle of revenue and cost. In Table 9.1, we compare some financial inclusion data from Argentina, Bolivia, Mexico, Colombia, Chile, Brazil, Venezuela, and Peru, and for comparative purposes we also include the average of these countries, the world average, and data from the United States. Of the poorest 40% of the United States, 87% have an account at a financial institution, while in Bolivia, Mexico, and Colombia that figure is about 20%. The world average is 53%.

In all of the concepts, the average for Latin American countries is not only below the world average but also below the averages for European and Central Asian developing countries (except for credit and debit card usage, which are similar). Even compared to Bangladesh, Latin America is the worst in the concepts of "Borrowed any money in the past year" and "Borrowed from financial

9   https://openknowledge.worldbank.org/handle/10986/23499

Table 9.1 *Global financial inclusion, country statistics*

Concept/Year 2014	Argentina	Bolivia	Mexico	Colombia	Chile	Brazil	Venezuela	Peru	Average Latin America	World	Bangladesh	Europe and Central Asia (developing Only)
Account (% age 15+)	49	54	37	46	74	70	73	43	54	69	50	65
Account at a financial institution, income, poorest 40% (% ages 15+)	38	43	26	35	67	57	60	27	42	61	40	56
Used the Internet to pay bills or buy things (% age 15+)	4	7	3	5	20	5	17	2	5	17	14	17
Borrowed any money in the past year (% age 15+)	37	45	32	41	45	40	44	36	38	47	37	44

Borrowed from a financial institution, income, poorest 40% (% ages 15+)	5	13	4	9	12	7	6	7	7	9	10	11
Credit card (% age 15+)	24	7	10	14	30	27	29	12	18	18	0	21
Debit card (% age 15+)	41	28	25	26	60	59	66	28	41	48	6	51

Source: Author with data from http://databank.worldbank.org/data/reports.aspx?source=1228#

265

institutions, income 40% poorest." This table shows the deep lag in financial inclusion suffered by Latin America. However, this is also a big opportunity: Banco Compartamos in Mexico has a program that after only a few years is serving 2.8 million customers with a net margin of 19.4%. Governments, nongovernmental organizations (NGOs), and financial institutions should innovate in creative ways to solve the problems of low financial inclusion.

Financial innovation is present everywhere: in our wallets (e.g., credit cards), in the streets (e.g., ATMs), and in our offices and homes (e.g., internet trading companies). Continuous innovation is part of the engine that drives the constant growth of the financial industry. The primary function of the financial system is to facilitate the allocation and deployment of economic resources. This function of the financial system demands a constant innovation process that includes new products, services, and market adaptations to new regulations, technologies, economies, or market changes. The impact of financial innovation on society has been controversial, with some arguing that it has a negative effect, as evidenced by increasing market volatility and tax avoidance. However, innovation in terms of financial inclusion has not come from the large financial institutions. It has been developed mainly by NGOs or microfinance institutions (MFIs), and it is thanks to their innovation that the financial system has increased its scope to attend to the MoP and part of the BoP.

One of the main problems that banks encounter when lending to the MoP is the risk that the clients have not entered into the contract in good faith; have provided misleading information about their assets, liabilities, or credit capacity; or have an incentive to take unusual risks in a desperate attempt to earn a profit before the contract settles. In the finance literature, this problem is known as "moral hazard."[10] A moral hazard occurs when one party in a transaction has the opportunity to assume additional risks that negatively affect the other party. The decision is based not on what is considered

[10]   www.investopedia.com/terms/m/moralhazard.asp

right, but on what provides the highest level of benefit, hence the reference to morality. This can apply to activities in the financial industry, such as the contract between a borrower or lender, as well as those in the insurance industry. Another of the problems that banks face when lending to MoP clients is the "adverse selection" problem. Adverse selection occurs when one party in a negotiation has relevant information that the other party lacks. The asymmetry of information often leads to making bad decisions, such as doing more business with less profitable or riskier market segments.[11] In the case of insurance, adverse selection can be seen in the tendency of those in dangerous jobs or high-risk lifestyles to get life insurance.

The first wave of innovation in the financial industry began in the 1970s with group lending, using peer monitoring for reducing adverse selection and moral hazard problems. The second wave of innovation began in the 1990s and has been based on technology change. New lending schemes require a high degree of reliable and secure technology. Information and communication technologies infrastructure promotes advancements in the microfinance industry, including the increasing use of mobile technology to provide borrowers with cheaper access to bank transactions. Furthermore, internet platforms have facilitated lending, investing, and multiple transactions online. As information technology infrastructure improves in developing countries, it creates a better foundation for new internet-based lending models to appear, adapt, evolve, and spread. Cumplo and Regalii are two good examples of microfinance institutions that have innovated in this field.

Group Microcredits Solution

Among the different types of financial innovations, one of the most remarkable in the last few decades was the group lending model, or Grameen model, with the Nobel Committee awarding

---

[11]   www.investopedia.com/terms/a/adverseselection.asp#ixzz4ecWCTDYU

the 2006 Nobel Peace Prize to Muhammad Yunus for this outstanding innovation.

The idea of alleviating poverty through microcredits began to be implemented in the late 1970s, predominantly in Bangladesh where various models were amalgamated to form what is known today as the "Grameen model." The challenge was to provide credit to families considered unbankable by the financial system. Professor Yunus and some of his colleagues at Chittangong University began experimenting with different methodologies with poor families in a few villages. They formed "peer groups" of borrowers who were jointly responsible for the group microcredit repayment. Several of these small groups (typically five people) were organized into a large unit that met weekly. In the beginning, groups were formed by occupation and irrespective of gender, but later they began to form groups by gender and village. The success of the experiment resulted in the government establishing the Grameen Bank under a special ordinance in 1983. After several years of experimentation, a "franchising approach" was taken toward the Grameen model, which generated a rapid expansion of the project in the 1990s.[12] Feedback from the field, as well as academic research and international experience, contributed further to this rapid expansion. Because of the success of the model, microfinance institutions (MFIs) in more than forty countries have used it and have done so not only in the BoP but also in the MoP in Latin America. As seen in Table 9.1, MoP customers in Latin America have financial inclusion problems, and thanks to the group lending innovation they have begun to receive microcredits. Although much of the MoP population in Latin America remains unbankable since many of them work in the informal sector and do not have real estate or assets to guarantee the loans, they live mainly in cities and have the best financial education. These factors facilitate the group lending model's spread.

[12]   Zaman 2004.

In studying the applicability of the innovative Grameen model in other countries, we are especially interested in exploring its use in emerging countries where the innovative financial model could play a relevant role for the MoP. Therefore, we have focused our study in the context of Latin America.

Banco Compartamos (Mexico)

In Mexico, the most important regulated microfinance vehicles are the "For-profit Financial Partnerships (Sociedades Financieras Populares, SOFIPOS) and the "Non-profit Savings and Microcredit Co-operatives" (Sociedades Cooperativas de Ahorro y Crédito, SOCAPS). There were 43 of the former institutions, attending to 3.5 million clients with financial assets of USD 1.79 billion in 2016[13] and 147 of the latter institutions in 2016.[14] Both SOFIPOS and SOCAPS are allowed to take deposits. There is also a large volume of non-regulated MFI's known as Multi-Purpose Financial Companies (Sociedades Financieras de Objeto Múltiple, SOFOME-ENRs), of which there were 1,657 institutions with outstanding loans of USD 25.9 billion[15] in 2016, as well as NGOs that offer microfinance, some of which may choose eventually to formalize into any of the afore-mentioned legal categories. There are two credit bureaus, which serve a large share of the adult population. However, many MFIs are reluctant to report information about their clients, and such reporting is not legally required, although second-tier funders make such information a condition for granting the loan. Two laws that seek to expand financial inclusion have recently been enacted within a short period of time. The Law of Correspondent Banks regulates banking services through agents and points-of-service, while the Mobile Bank Law, one of the first of its kind in Latin America, established a

---

[13]   Exchange rate mx/usd 17.5 (August 2017). Mexican Association of SOFIP, www .amsofipo.mx/indicadores2016.html

[14]   www.gob.mx/cms/uploads/attachment/file/229019/anuario-estadistico-2016.pdf

[15]   Exchange rate mx/usd 17.5 (August 2017). www.gob.mx/cms/uploads/attachment/ file/229019/anuario-estadistico-2016.pdf

framework for mobile banking. Adoption of this framework has been slow, however, and it is believed that the larger commercial banks, rather than MFIs, will be some of the biggest beneficiaries. As such, both laws are likely to be made more flexible in the near-to-medium term. In addition, there has been an expansion of the banking arms of major retailers, such as "Banco Azteca," "BanCoppel," and "Banco Wal-Mart," into small-scale consumer lending over the past decade.

The country's leading microfinance bank, "Compartamos" (Latin America's largest MFI), originally started as an NGO and is now a formal bank listed on the Mexican stock exchange. At the beginning of the 1990s, "Banco Compartamos" sent representatives to Bangladesh to learn the Yunus (or Grameen) model, and as a result the majority of MFIs in Mexico have followed their example. Initially Banco Compartamos, as the Yunus model proposes, was focused only on services for women, providing them with opportunities for development. Toward the year 2000, a great transformation happened when the company took on the name "Financiera Compartamos." In 2002, it issued investment certificates, becoming the first microfinance institution to make this type of offer to the investing public. In 2006, it was authorized to operate as a Multiple Banking Institution, giving rise to Banco Compartamos. In 2007, it carried out an Initial Public Offering of Shares and initiated its listing on the BMV. The sale was oversubscribed by thirteen times, and Compartamos was soon worth USD 1.6 billion. In 2007, Yunus declared that he was shocked by the news about the Banco Compartamos IPO and considered it a retrograde step for microfinance.[16] In 2008, the bank reached the figure of 1 million customers served and 314 Service Offices. In 2010, it got first place in the list of the best companies to work for in Mexico, according to the Great Places to Work survey. As a further demonstration of the Bank's ability to access various sources of funding, on September 6, 2013, the Bank carried out the successful placement of stock with an

---

[16]   Yunus 2007.

overshoot of 2.58 times. In October 2013, the issuer received Standard & Poor's "BBB / A2" global rating, which according to the rating agency reflects a good business position, very strong capital and profitability, moderate risk, below-average financing, and adequate liquidity based on terms defined by its criteria.

In 2013, Banco Compartamos was recognized as the "Best Microfinance Bank 2013" by *LatinFinance* magazine. Mix Market recognized the company for its transparency and social performance and awarded it the certificate Mix S.T.A.R. 2013. At the end of 2013, the installation of the SAP technology platform began; in 2014, progress was made with this approval, and at the end of the year, all Compartamos Service Offices operated credit products under this technology. During 2015, a very important step was taken in the promotion of savings accounts: The "Comprehensive Savings Program" was launched. Also in 2015, the debit cards were changed from Carnet to Visa, which made it possible to extend the acceptance of the card in thousands of shops and ATMs. Additionally, the bank made important efforts to strengthen its technology platform, a situation that made it possible to significantly boost the development of the funding product. In social responsibility, during 2015, Banco Compartamos benefited 273,750 people with an investment of USD 3.75 million in items such as formal education, financial education, entrepreneurial culture, volunteering and sharing days with the community, and solidarity aid in contingencies. Banco Compartamos had an active participation in these areas, positively affecting the lives of the communities.

In Table 9.2, we can see the products (credits) offered by Compartamos (as of April 2017); the amounts range from USD 230 to USD 1188 with periods between four and twelve months. The most striking thing is the interest rates charged to customers (APR) from 70.8% to 120%. Banco Compartamos justifies these amounts because its services are very individualized and generate annual administrative costs of 58.7%. However, its net margin in 2015 was 19.4% (USD 158 million); these numbers provoke the envy

Table 9.2 *Banco Compartamos loan characteristics*

Product	Amount USD*	Term	Annual Percentage Rate (%)
Women Credit	$290	16 weeks	77.30
Additional Credit	$400	5 months	83.90
Individual Credit	$1,188	12 months	70.80
Trade Credit	$410	10 biweeklies	90.00
Growth and Improve Credit	$570	12 months	82.00
Growth and Improve Credit CCR	$570	12 tetra weeks	90.00
Additional Credit CCR	$316	4 months	88.00
Growth and Improve Credit for CI	$570	6 months	85.00
Compartamos alliance credit	$286	6 months	120.00
Furnish you home credit	$230	12 tetra weeks	78.40

* Exchange rate mx/usd 17.5 (August 2017)
Source: At April 17, 2017, www.compartamos.com.mx/wps/wcm/con
nect/8eacb90d-9cf6-4933-8031-de34e7559ddd/CAT+y+Comisiones+1er
+semestre+2017.pdf?MOD=AJPERES&CACHEID=8eacb90d-9cf6-4933-
8031-de34e7559ddd

of commercial banks that lend to AAA firms and are particularly outstanding considering the economic situation of the customer base.

As of December 2015, Banco Compartamos had a presence in 32 states of the Mexican Republic, serving a total of 2,861,721 customers with 233,685 active accounts. Compartamos offers loans ranging from USD 86 to USD 5714[17] to microentrepreneurs in segments of the population between C and D (as defined by The Mexican Association of Market Research Agencies, AMAI). The majority of the customers are women (88.2%) who have very basic productive

---

[17]   Compartamos data is in Mexican pesos; we convert to dollars using exchange rate of mx/usd 17.5 (August 2017).

activities. The total loan amount was USD 1.31776 billion.[18] The average balance per customer as of December 31, 2015, was USD 460; this capital is mainly used by customers to buy inventory or raw materials for their microenterprises. Annual interest rates charged to the customers range from 70% to 120% (see attached Table 9.2). In addition, the Bank has been offering other benefits to its clients, including life insurance.

Banco Compartamos has been able to serve millions of customers. Of these, the majority are women entrepreneurs who before becoming clients did not have access to loans for working capital. Its clients use the loaned funds to invest in machinery and raw materials, growing their businesses and thus improving their quality of life and that of their family. The investment of the bank's loans in productive activities generates a virtuous cycle for its clients and cash flows for the repayment of credit, as well as business growth and better living standards, a sign of the success of the issuer's business model. During 2015, 84% of its clients renewed their credits. The Bank's business model is highly intensive in human capital and is based on credit officers who serve their clients in a personalized way, following the group lending model of Yunus.

At present, the Bank offers credit products (women's credit, growth and improvement credit, individual credit, trade credit, furnish and repair home credit), savings accounts, and insurance products (women's insurance and individual insurance). Its main product is women's credit, with a weight of 62% of its portfolio (Table 9.2).

Fondo Esperanza (Chile)

Serving the whole Chilean territory, Fondo Esperanza (FE) is an innovative institution of social development that supports entrepreneurs from low-income households by offering services of microcredit using the Yunus group lending methodology. They also offer entrepreneur training and networking opportunities.

[18] www.themix.org/mixmarket/profiles/compartamos-banco

In 2015, FE supported more than 102,000 entrepreneurs with their 52 offices in Chile.[19] The total outstanding loan amount was USD 50.93 million, with an individual loan average of USD 499.[20] In the same year, Jorge Camus explained that less than a quarter (23%) of the Chilean population had access to the basic services of credit, based on results from the Casen survey. In the same context, he explained that loan sizes had been increasing, while the number of debtors had been decreasing from 2013 to 2015, signaling that only the highest income segment of the population had access to formal credit.[21]

Fondo Esperanza is trying to solve the problem of lack of access to credit that Chile suffers, like many other countries in Latin America. More specifically, Fondo Esperanza focuses on giving loan opportunities to the most vulnerable 20% of the Chilean population. This population is, most of the time, excluded from the formal banking system, leaving them with access only to informal credit, which is very expensive.

Fondo Esperanza began with microlending for development projects in 2002. At the beginning, they only offered individual microcredits. After a study of their clients' experiences and a demographic analysis, FE decided to develop their own methodology for group lending, giving them great results. This innovative method allowed FE to increase their clientele from 5,259 members to almost 39,000 between 2005 and 2009. [22]

The innovative FE group lending format is based on a progressive credit program, whereby a group of borrowers (twenty-one to twenty-five entrepreneurs) who live in the same region join voluntarily to get a loan. Every member of the group has the same responsibility to pay back that loan, but they can develop businesses independently. In addition to interest payments, FE credit receivers

[19]   www.fondoesperanza.cl
[20]   www.themix.org/mixmarket/profiles/fondo-esperanza
[21]   www.df.cl/noticias/opinion/columnistas/acceso-al-credito-en-la-realidad-actual-de-chile/2015-06-11/172926.html
[22]   Franceschi & Patricia 2011.

commit to attending meetings and trainings to improve their businesses. This type of credit has a cost of 36% annual interest rate, in addition to the administration fees, which depend on the size of the line of credit.[23]

FE communal banks are based on five fundamental principles: solidarity, responsibility, trust, honesty, and respect.[24] Each group has a weekly or bi-weekly meeting for members to track repayments, monitor the evolution of group members' businesses, and receive an education. The advisor of the communal bank coordinates these meetings. These advisors are part of the personnel of Fondo Esperanza.

Although microcredits and group lending are concepts used before in other countries, it is important to mention that at the time that FE began to implement group lending and their other attached services, there were not many institutions attempting group lending. Even nowadays, there are not many institutions that offer this option, and Fondo Esperanza is one of the very few that has implemented it successfully. The combination of group lending, entrepreneurship education, and social networking opportunities makes Fondo Esperanza unique and a leader in microfinance services in Chile.

In addition to the innovations in their group lending methodology, some of Fondo Esperanza's other successful innovations include: (1) the creation of an entrepreneurship school in 2007, where members can receive training in different formats; (2) the launch of a networking program called "Redes"; and (3) the creation of an electronic magazine named Mercadito FE, where members can promote their products.

However, the success of Fondo Esperanza is based not only on its pioneering services but also on the efficient way it gathers and manages contributions from its founders and innumerable partners. The Ford Foundation, Anglo American, Kiva,[25] and Fundacion

---

[23]   This credit cost is based on information from 2016.   [24]   www.kiva.org
[25]   Supported Fondo Esperanza from 2008 to 2014 with USD 2.4 million in paid loans that affected nearly 10,000 borrowers.

Microfinanzas BBVA are probably the most significant partners and supporters of FE.[26] The Ford Foundation has supported several pilot projects since the beginning of FE in 2002. Fundacion Microfinanzas BBVA and Fondo Esperanza joined efforts in 2011 and created Fondo Esperanza SpA.[27] This new institution allows poor people in Chile to have access to products and financial services they couldn't afford before. With this joint project, clients of FE got access to life insurance (such as microseguro "mi familia") and loan insurance, in addition to the original credit services. Fundacion Microfinanzas BBVA represents the nonprofit side of the Spanish institution Banco Bilbao Vizcaya Argentaria (BBVA),[28] which in 2007 began to create partnerships with several already successful microfinance institutions around Latin America. Currently, Fundacion MF BBVA has a presence in Colombia, Peru, the Dominican Republic, Argentina, Panama, Puerto Rico, and Chile. The main goal of this foundation is to promote economic development, social sustainability, and financial inclusion for low-income populations. Fundacion MF BBVA is the owner of 51% of Fondo Esperanza SpA's resources.

Fondo Esperanza is currently the most recognized microfinance institution in Chile. It has received awards and recognition from Fundacion Prohumana, MicrofinanzaRating consulting, and Mix Market. The latter is a nonprofit organization headquartered in Washington, DC, that shares institutional data from MFIs to broaden transparency and market insight. Mix Market classifies FE with five diamonds based on its transparency and information quality.

Fondo Esperanza is also a member of the largest network group of microfinance institutions in Chile (Red para el Desarrollo de las Microfinanzas en Chile, A.G.). This membership allows FE to

---

[26]   It is important to mention that Fondo Esperanza is also associated with the organization Hogar de Cristo, but they work independently.

[27]   Fundacion Microfinanzas BBVA holds 51% of the shareholder capital of Fondo Esperanza SpA, with Fondo Esperanza holding the remaining 49%.

[28]   It is important to mention that Fundacion MF BBVA has total autonomy from the financial group. They are legally independent in management and governance.

improve its indicators of transparency and also to gather information from other Chilean MFIs. FE has projected a continuous growth for the upcoming years.

ProMujer (Argentina)

Innovative group lending is not as popular in Argentina as in other countries of Latin America, based on data from Mix Market and Argentina Network of Microcredit Institutions RADIM (Red Argentina de Instituciones de Microcredito).[29] Group lending in Argentina can be categorized into two types: Communal Bank or Solidarity Group.

Table 9.3 helps us to understand the composition of the micro-finance institutions in Argentina. Individual credits represent the main component of this industry, while those institutions specialized to support the development of the MoP and the BoP represent only 7% of this sector.

The format of Solidarity Group in Argentina is mainly focused on loans to build or improve housing. Successful MFIs in this area are Foundation Social ProVivienda, "Fundacion ProVivienda Social" (FPVS); Holy Family Foundation, "Fundacion Sagrada Familia"; and Roof, "Techo." However, if we focus on group lending in its format of Communal Banks in Argentina, it is crucial to talk about the case of ProMujer-Argentina. ProMujer has not only successfully delivered loans for a third of the amount that the big microcredit institutions in Argentina (focused on consumer loans)[30] have delivered, but it has also supported and changed the lives of more borrowers than any other MFI in Argentina, and the foundation of this success is in its process innovation.

ProMujer is focused on improving the lives of Argentina's women by offering economic support, training, and health insurance.

---

[29] www.reddemicrocredito.org
[30] FIE Gran Poder and Cordial Microfinanzas are good examples of microcredit insti-tutions in Argentina that are mainly focused on consumer loans for the low-income population.

Table 9.3 *Microfinance institutions in Argentina*

General Indicators	Type of Institution			
	Individual Credit	Solidarity Group	Communal Banks	Total
Number of institutions	29	20	2	51
Number of employees	783	177	69	1,029
Number of credit counselors	334	71	32	437
Size indicators				
Number of active borrowers	56487	7.206	11.082	74.775
Number of active loans	60737	6.67	11.948	79.355
Total in loans (usd*)	95,713,451	2,301,075	4,974,990	102,989,515

1 ARS = 0,05736 USD, November 14, 2017

Source: Author with information from www.reddemicrocredito.org/images/Publicaciones/Mapeo_Semestre1_2017.pdf

Last Update: June 2017

In addition, ProMujer is an international MFI that offers its services in Argentina, Mexico, Nicaragua, Peru, and Bolivia. ProMujer delivers a unique integrated package of financial, training, and health care services via communal banks. These "banks," following the Yunus group lending model, are actually lending groups of twenty to thirty women who band together to receive small loans to start or invest in their businesses. In the event that one woman cannot make a payment, the other women of the group step in and support her.[31] These groups meet every two weeks not only to make a payment on their loan but also to receive business and empowerment training and preventive health education.

[31] http://promujer.org/how-we-do-it

ProMujer strongly believes that delivering multiple services to clients under one roof minimizes the critical time they spend away from their families and businesses while allowing the institution to be cost-effective and efficient. In addition, ProMujer has proved that these novel communal banks are a good way to support the development of low-income communities. "The shared responsibility and camaraderie fostered by communal banks, combined with the supportive learning process of our programs, creates a powerful support system. Clients can then bring what they've learned into their homes and communities" (ProMujer).

ProMujer started its services in Argentina in November 2005. However, ProMujer has been serving women since 1990. The venture was founded by two visionary leaders, Lynne Patterson and Carmen Velasco, who believed that given the right opportunities, women could become powerful agents of change. They began in Bolivia and have been expanding offices around Latin America, specifically in Mexico, Brazil, Nicaragua, and Argentina.

The first Argentinian office was opened in the city of Salta, a northern province near the Bolivian border. In 2006, ProMujer expanded to the Northern Province of Jujuy, and in 2008 to the province of Tucuman. The Inter-American Development Bank, the JP Morgan Chase Foundation, and the Weberg Family Trust provided the seed funding required to open the Argentinian chapter. It is important to mention that ProMujer's headquarters are located in New York City. For that reason, a lot of its funding comes from grants and donations from North American foundations.

As of December 2015, ProMujer-Argentina had 8,875 clients with an average loan balance of USD 336, 561 communal banks, and 4 neighborhood centers.[32] In addition, the outstanding loan amount was USD 2.99 million and the average client repayment rate was above 96%. Nevertheless, the most interesting aspect of ProMujer's

32 https://promujer.org/content/uploads/2016/10/2015_Audit.pdf

statistics (in all five countries where it serves) is the way that its success is measured. In addition to financial information, ProMujer uses Health Indicators (such as health services provided) as a way to measure its progress. Indicators such as the number of cancer examinations, diabetes tests, medical consultations, and dental services completed are some of the statistics that ProMujer is always concerned with improving. This focus makes ProMujer different from other MFIs.

CrediAmigo and Agro Amigo (Brazil)

Due to the overall influence of the government in Brazil, and its very centralized institutions, it is almost impossible to conceive a successful microfinance institution (or program) that is not supported and managed by the Federal Government. Sanchez (2002) explains that until 1997, the development of microfinance services in Brazil lagged substantially in comparison to the rest of Latin America. The reason for this was, in part, the restrictions on the ability of NGOs to serve as financial intermediaries and mobilize externally financing, and a strict usury law limiting interest rates charged by NGOs to unsustainably low levels.

The two largest microcredit programs of Brazil are CrediAmigo and AgroAmigo. These institutions aim to solve the problem of access to credit for entrepreneurs and farmers in certain regions of Brazil. CrediAmigo is part of the National Microcredit Program of the Federal Government in Brazil. More specifically, CrediAmigo is managed and supported by the state institution Banco Do Nordeste, which also manages AgroAmigo, the second largest microcredit program. With these two programs, Banco do Nordeste works on one of the national strategies of the "Brazil Without Poverty Plan" to stimulate the productive inclusion of the extremely poor.

CrediAmigo is the largest production-oriented microcredit program in South America. In 2015, CrediAmigo facilitated access to credit for 2,030,820 entrepreneurs belonging to the informal and formal sectors of the economy in Brazil, with a total loan portfolio of USD 762.2 million and an average loan amount of USD 375.[33]

CrediAmigo grants credits to solidarity groups or individuals. As in other countries, their original methodology of solidarity groups consists of the voluntary union of people interested in getting credit who take joint responsibility for the payment of benefits. This methodology of group lending has helped to consolidate CrediAmigo as the country's largest microcredit program, providing access to credit to more than 2 million Brazilian entrepreneurs who previously had no access to the financial system.

In addition to loans, CrediAmigo offers a unique service to entrepreneurs of monitoring and guidance for a successful implementation of the business plan (and strategies) that helps borrowers to integrate their projects competitively into the productive market. In addition, Banco do Nordeste opens checking accounts for its customers without charging an opening fee or account maintenance fee, in order to facilitate the receipt and handling of payments.

The second largest microfinance program in Brazil is AgroAmigo. This novel program represents the Rural Microfinance Program of Banco do Nordeste, operated in partnership with the Northeast Institute Citizenship (INEC) and the Ministry of Agrarian Development (MDA). After ten years of operation, it has become the largest rural microfinance program in Brazil and Latin America, serving more than a million borrowers.

The AgroAmigo program aims to improve the social and economic profile of the farmer families in the Northeast and North of Minas Gerais and Espirito Santo. With its particular methodology, this program encourages the development of productive activities, both agricultural and non-agricultural.

The success and innovation of AgroAmigo has been recognized internationally. In 2009, it received the prize of ALIDE in recognition of best practices in financial institutions and development as an

33   www.themix.org/mixmarket/profiles/crediamigo

innovative credit product. In 2010, AgroAmigo ran for the ENAP Prize for innovative practices in federal public administration and was awarded second place. In 2012, AgroAmigo received the Excellence Award in the category of Best Financial Inclusion initiative for its products and services. In 2016, AgroAmigo's loan portfolio was USD 1.0419 billion, with 1,037,550 borrowers and a loan average of USD 1004.[34] Table 9.4 presents a summary of the main characteristics of these institutions.

TECHNOLOGICAL SOLUTION

It is impossible to conceive of any economic activity without two of the greatest innovations of our current time: the Internet and the mobile phone. These two technological innovations have not only changed the way people communicate around the world but also the way business is done in every productivity sector.

The financial sector is no exception in trying to integrate these technological innovations into the credit business framework. More specifically, some microfinance institutions have been pioneers in the integration of the Internet, the mobile phone, and financial services, allowing people from low- and middle-income segments to get access to financial services in a faster and easier way. However, in many countries it is difficult for technological innovation based on platforms such as the Internet, mobile apps, etc., to reach the BoP; for instance, in Bangladesh only 0.4% use the Internet to pay bills or buy things (see Table 9.1), and the average in Latin America is only 7%. The high-income classes use traditional banking systems to solve their financial needs, so it is the MoP population that has been receiving the benefits of technological innovations.

In the following pages, this chapter will mention some of the most recent and innovative strategies that microfinancial organizations dedicated mainly to the MoP population have created to

---

[34]   www.themix.org/mixmarket/profiles/agroamigo

Table 9.4 *Main characteristics of the institutions analyzed*

Institution	Banco Compartamos[1] (Mexico)	Fondo Esperanza[2] (Chile)	ProMujer[3] (Argentina)	CrediAmigo[4] (Brazil)	AgroAmigo[5, 6] (Brazil)
Problem that it is trying to solve	Lack of access to financial services for micro-entrepreneurs	Lack of access to credit for the most vulnerable population	Lack of access to financial services and business training for women	Lack of access to credit for entrepreneurs	Lack of access to credit for farmers
Customers served (thousands)	3,196.67	123.83	250	2,065	1,282
Loans granted (thousands)	8,802.68	315.24	n/a	4,243.18	505.28
Main Innovation	It is the first MFI to become public bank in the Mexican Stock Market.	It combines group lending methodology with business training.	It mixes financial services with education and health goals.	It combines loan services with business plan training and implementation.	Improve the social and economic profile of the farmer families

Sources:

[1] www.themix.org/mixmarket/profiles/compartamos-banco
[2] www.themix.org/mixmarket/profiles/fondo-esperanza
[3] https://promujer.org/content/uploads/2016/10/2015_Audit.pdf
[4] www.themix.org/mixmarket/profiles/crediamigo
[5] www.themix.org/mixmarket/profiles/agroamigo
[6] Information at 2016

increase access to their services and, therefore, to improve the financial inclusion of this segment of the population.

One main source of innovation has been the Internet, and one specific aspect of social lending is the so-called unknown-to-unknown for-profit or nonprofit lending, a subset of Peer-to-Peer lending (P2P). The Internet and social networks such as Facebook established a foundation to empower the resurgence of social lending in this new context.

In this new model, members register on the website and can act either as a lender or a borrower. Typically, borrowers ask for a loan by explaining what they are going to do with the money and the maximum interest rate they are willing to pay. On the other side, lenders bid on pieces of the loan. Usually, the interest rate is fixed, and the amount is bigger and the maturity is longer than for typical MFI loans. Collateral is not required and there are no prepayment penalties.

To overcome the adverse selection problem, internet companies first perform a deep credit check on the MoP borrowers. Borrowers are classified into credit rating categories using different systems, ranking borrowers into similar risk categories while reducing uncertainty to lenders. Consequently, interest rates vary according to the borrower's perceived creditworthiness. Additionally, after each loan that is paid on time, borrowers receive stars or points that reduce their risk perception.

One of the pioneers in internet lending was PlaNet Finance in 1998.[35] Prosper, and its British sibling Zopa, are online marketplaces for social lending. The Zopa website describes social lending as people lending and borrowing money with each other, sidestepping the banks. While social lending has been going on in families and social groups for hundreds of years, the Internet has opened it up for everybody.

Prosper has sought to bring this financial technology to bear in small loans. Technically, it is not microfinance but combines some

---

[35]   Coleman 2007.

functions of consumer finance, social investing, and microfinance with an online marketplace. Prosper allows individual borrowers to post their request for a loan with a proposed interest rate. Lenders, in turn, can shop on Prosper and bid to fund loans. As with a loan syndication, lenders may spread their risk by buying small parts of multiple small loans, such that a dozen or more lenders may fund a single loan.

Kiva is a nonprofit organization that connects socially motivated lenders with developing world micro-entrepreneurs through the Internet. Kiva works with MFIs in developing countries to build internet profiles of borrowers. Rather than waiting for individual loans to be financed, Kiva's MFI partners first approve and disburse the loan, which is then refinanced by several internet lenders.

In October 2007, eBay launched Microplace to help link individual investors to purchase a part of institutional investors' microfinance securities. Rather than disintermediation, Microplace is pursuing democratization of investing as an online registered broker–dealer that sells participation in wholesale loans and securities issued by social investors to MFIs.[36] All of these innovations have reached a large number of small entrepreneurs in the MoP.

Cumplo (Chile)

Technology, credit, and innovation are very difficult to separate in the unique formula of the Chilean startup, Cumplo. Cumplo is an innovative crowdfunding (P2P) platform that allows Chilean borrowers and lenders to meet.[37] Most of the activities of the exchange process are done online, which makes this business already unique. However, an important component of this incomparable business model is that borrowers define their own conditions in time, amount, and rate. This new and original vision of how the financial system should work makes Cumplo one of the most groundbreaking startups in Latin America.

[36] Bruett 2007.   [37] www.cumplo.cl

While P2P is not new, it has a huge potential when applied to finance in Latin America, a region where debt is extremely expensive for borrowers (especially when the loan comes from a retailer rather than from a bank). By disintermediating the sector and establishing new forms of trust, Cumplo brings personal loans to the next level – at affordable rates.

Since 2011, Cumplo has already helped 1,600 new and small business owners to get loans at an average rate of 13%, while the average rate for general credits (in small amounts) in Chile nowadays is about 29%. However, the benefit is not only on the borrower's side but also on the lender's side. Investors that use Cumplo to give credit to small businesses have received an average return of 10.3%.

Cumplo is also an example of how the financial systems in Latin America are not clearly prepared for innovation, and instead of supporting new ideas, they diminish them. In 2012 (a few days after starting), Cumplo received a complaint filed by the regulatory commission for banks in Chile ("Superintendencia de Bancos"). The reason for this complaint was mainly that Chilean regulations for banks say that only licensed banks can receive cash deposits. Cumplo's cofounders, Nicolas Shea and Jean Boudeguer, had some meetings with the regulatory commission in order to explain their model and specifically to clarify that they are a credit exchange platform and not a bank.[38]

Anna Heim from the Next Web wrote about this complaint, saying that "when the news emerged that Cumplo would go under investigation, a group of high-profile personalities including a former minister sent an open letter to the Chilean Newspaper El Mercurio, denouncing a 'persecution of *entrepreneurship*.' This reflects the high-level connections that Shea and Boudeguer have built during their careers, but also the democratizing power that Cumplo can have."[39]

[38]   www.lasegunda.com/Noticias/Economia/2012/06/753429/cumplocl-y-denuncia-de-la-sbif-es-una-de-las-mayores-trabas-al-emprendimiento

[39]   http://thenextweb.com/la/2012/11/17/8-companies-that-hope-to-democratize-finance-in-latin-america/#gref

Regalii (United States)

Another great example of how innovation has arrived in the financial industry, not only in Latin America but in the whole world, is the case of Regalii. Founded in 2012 in the Bronx neighborhood of New York City by a group of Latin American entrepreneurs,[40] Regalii is an application program interface (API) that financial institutions use to let consumers manage all of their family's bills anywhere in the world.

Regalii found his vision on trying to improve the lives of MoP immigrants that send money (remittances) to their families abroad. Its business model is based on an innovative process of instantaneous and completely transparent money transfers that allow its customers to track their family finances and make payments directly to utility companies based in their home countries.[41]

Regalii's three main clients are banks and card issuers, remittance companies, and mobile wallets. For that reason, Regalii's solutions are focused on serving people in the MoP, who have relatively easy access to credit and mobile technology.

Edrizio De la Cruz, cofounder of Regalii, explains that the main goal of his firm is to unlock millions of dollars in support of families in Latin America by replacing traditional remittances with gift cards, via SMS, for the same supermarkets and stores where families already shop. In this way, the people who send money to their families in their country of origin can facilitate the "picking up" process and yet maintain some control over how the money is spent.

According to the Inter-American Development Bank (IADB), Latin American migrants sent about USD 65.38 billion in remittances to their home countries in 2014, setting a new record high after being stagnant since 2008 due to the US recession. A considerable share of these remittances is lost in the fees charged by traditional money transfer companies, such as Western Union or Money Gram, that

---

[40]   www.pbs.org/newshour/bb/startup-helps-families-send-money-back-home-country
[41]   www.regalii.com

charge about 8% commission on average. This fact is part of Regalii's motivation to take an innovative approach and help migrants directly buy goods that their families back home really need, and save some money.

The remittance economy represents more than half a trillion dollars today and is expected to reach a trillion by 2020, according to the World Bank. More specifically, in Latin America and the Caribbean countries, remittances are still an important source of income for many families. Regalii processes thousands of payments daily, in more than 8 countries (including Mexico, which is the largest receiver of remittances in the world), with more than 37,000 partners. Regalii has a shiny future with its innovative vision of this trillion dollar market.

COMPARISON AND CONCLUSIONS

The problem of financial inclusion concerns most governments and financial institutions in developing countries, especially Latin America, where not only the BoP but also the MoP have financial access problems. The problem is far from being solved, but many institutions have shown that major improvements can be made with innovation. Latin American MFI has shown us that successful international business models, such as the Yunus group lending model in Bangladesh, can be successfully imported and adapted to another culture.

Governments have been able to support success stories such as CrediAmigo and AgroAmigo in Brazil. Both are under the supervision of Banco do Nordestes (Brazil development bank); offer microcredit through the group lending model; and have programs that encourage the development of productive activities, monitoring entrepreneurs and guiding their successful implementation of a business plan. Both assist more than 3 million people, forming the largest MFI in Latin America.

Other microfinance institutions have innovated in very different ways. For example, Banco Compartamos evolved from an ONG to a bank on the Mexican stock exchange, showing that it is possible through securitization to assist a large number of people with good profitability for the shareholder. Thanks to its access to funds through the stock exchange, it has benefited more than 2.8 million people, very close to CrediAmigo and AgroAmigo but without any government support. These 2.8 million people are mainly women from the BoP, but more and more MoP clients that are not served by commercial banks require Banco Compartamos loans.

In addition to these innovations, others have emerged. Fondo Esperanza bases its success on combining the group lending model, entrepreneurship education, and social networking opportunities. FE founded an entrepreneurship school, launched a networking program, and created an electronic magazine. This holistic approach makes FE the leader in microfinance services in Chile.

In a similar way, ProMujer focuses on improving the lives of Argentina's women. In addition to working with the group lending model to offer economic support, the company includes business education and a strong program in health care services, including health care insurance.

However, the great challenge of group-lending-based support schemes with a holistic approach to education, supervision, training, and health support is their high cost of operation and long horizon to achieve results. However, technological advances have brought new approaches to address the problem of financial inclusion with very low operating costs and the possibility of including a large proportion of the MoP population in its services.

The new information and communications technologies, internet platforms, social networks, big data, etc., are revolutionizing the microfinance industry. Additionally, the so-called social lending platforms, for-profit or not for-profit, which are considered a subset of the Peer-to-Peer (P2P) loans, are spreading throughout the world, and Latin America has not been an exception.

However, the road is full of problems and challenges. Cumplo's innovative crowdfunding platform (P2P), which allows Chilean borrowers and lenders to meet online, generated so much stir in the Chilean financial system that the banking system has declared war and is trying to block its operations.

Technology fosters innovation in almost any field. Regalii's use of technology helps financial inclusion from a different angle. Regalii's application program interface allows consumers to manage all their family bills anywhere in the world, which is a major problem for immigrants from developing countries who need to provide financial support to their families.

This chapter presents great lessons for entrepreneurs of any area. To succeed in a challenging environment such as financial inclusion, firms have to tap all available tools:

a) Firms can finance with governments funds, NGOs, or through the stock exchange or social lending. Banco Compartamos's IPO allowed it to reach 2.8 million in 2015, the biggest in Latin America.

b) Firms can integrate into international networks to increase knowledge and scope. For instance, FE has alliances with The Ford Foundation, Anglo American, Kiva, and Fundacion Microfinanzas BBVA. Another excellent example is ProMujer, an international MFI that offers its services in Argentina, Mexico, Nicaragua, Peru, and Bolivia, with headquarters located in New York City. Additionally, the Inter-American Development Bank, the JP Morgan Chase Foundation, and the Weberg Family Trust provided the seed funding required to open the Argentinian chapter and a lot of its funding comes from grants and donations of North American foundations.

c) Firms can adopt business models that have proven successful in other regions and adapt them to regional needs. Compartamos, FE, and ProMujer have implemented and innovated the Yunus model from Bangladesh.

d) Firms can (and must) use all available technology to reduce costs and offer services previously unthinkable. This is the case with Cumplo, which adapted technological platforms developed by PlaNet Finance and Kiva, among others – and Regalii, which developed its own API.

e) Firms should include support services such as training, networking, health insurance, housing, and the publication of magazines. Excellent examples of this are FE and ProMujer.

f) Firms can include other services, such as insurance, credit or debit cards, accounts, and international transfers. Regalii created a great innovation in the sector with its international transfers.

Finally, firms must develop a holistic model, which benefits shareholders but also the entire society as a whole, and in a sustainable way. Social groups, education, training, health, and the social awareness of investors, combined with the technological support that reduces costs and increases speed and control, all together help reduce the problem of financial inclusion at a rapid pace.

REFERENCES

Bruett, T., 2007. Cows, Kiva, and Prosper.com: How Disintermediation and the Internet Are Changing Microfinance. *Community Development Investment Review* 3(2): 44–50.

Camus, J. 2015. Acceso al credito en la realidad actual de Chile. Accessed October 1, 2017. Diario Financiero, from www.df.cl/noticias/opinion/columnistas/acceso-al-credito-en-la-realidad-actual-de-chile/2015-06-11/172926.html

CGAP. 2017. About CGPA. Accessed August 1, 2017. www.cgap.org

Coleman, R. W. 2007. Is the Future of the Microfinance Movement to Be Found on the Internet? In International Trade and Finance Association Conference Papers (p. 1). Bepress.

Cumplo. 2017. Que es Cumplo. Accessed June 2017. www.cumplo.cl

Fondo Esperanza. 2017. Quienes Somos. Accessed March 1, 2017. www.fondoesperanza.cl/somos

Franceschi, O. & Patricia, C. 2011. *Innovación en el plan financiero de microcréditos en Fondo Esperanza*. Santiago de Chile: Universidad de Chile.

Heim, A. 2012. 8 companies that hope to democratize finance in Latin America. Accessed March 1, 2017. http://thenextweb.com/la/2012/11/17/8-companies-that-hope-to-democratize-finance-in-l atin-america/#gref

Investopedia Staff. 2017. Adverse Selection. Accessed March 1, 2017. www.investopedia.com/terms/a/adverseselection.asp#ixzz4ecWCTDYU

Investopedia Staff. 2017. Moral Hazard. Accessed March 1, 2017. www.investopedia.com/terms/m/moralhazard.asp

Khavul, S. 2010. Microfinance: Creating Opportunities for the Poor? *The Academy of Management Perspectives* 24(3): 58–72.

Kiva. 2017. How Kiva Works. Accessed March 1, 2017. www.kiva.org

Mehrotra, A. & Yetman, J. 2015. Financial Inclusion – Issues for Central Banks. *BIS Quarterly Review*. Accessed March 1, 2017. www.bis.org/publ/qtrpdf/r_qt1503h.htm

Muñoz, C. 2012. Cumplo.cl y denuncia de la SBIF: "Es una de las mayores trabas al emprendimiento." Accessed March 1, 2017. www.lasegunda.com/Noticias/Economia/2012/06/753429/cumplocl-y-denuncia-de-la-sbif-es-una-de-las-mayores-trabas-al-emprendimiento

PBS Newshour. 2015. Startup Helps Families Send Money Back to Their Home. Accessed June 1, 2017. www.pbs.org/newshour/bb/startup-helps-families-send-money-back-home-country

Pro Mujer. 2016. Get to Know Us. Accessed August 1, 2017. https://promujer.org/who-we-serve

Red Argentina De Instituciones De Microcrédito. 2016. Inicio. Accessed June 1, 2017. www.reddemicrocredito.org

Regalii. 2017. About Us. Accessed August 1, 2017. www.regalii.com

Sanchez, S. et al. 2002. Bringing Microfinance Services to the Poor: Cediamigo in Brazil. World Bank: En Breve. Vol. 7. Washington, DC.

Solarz, M. 2011. The Role of Social Lending in Financial Inclusion. In Financial Sciences, E. Research Papers of Wroclaw University of Economics:184.

The Economist Intelligence Unit. 2011. Global Microscope on the Microfinance Business Environment 2011: An Index and Study by The Economist Intelligence Unit. *The Economist*: 36–51.

The World Bank Group. 2014. Financial Inclusion Data. Accessed June 1, 2017. http://datatopics.worldbank.org/financialinclusion

Yunus, M. 2007. Remarks by Muhammad Yunus, Managing Director, Grameen Bank. *Microcredit Summit E-News* 5(1).

Zaman, H. 2004. *The Scaling-up of Microfinance in Bangladesh: Determinants, Impacts, and Lessons. World Bank Policy Research Working Paper No. 3398.* Washington DC: World Bank.

10 Inclusive Hedging
The Microinsurance Catalyst

L. Arturo Bernal, Isaí Guízar,
and Xiomara Vázquez

INTRODUCTION

Lack of insurance may have a huge impact on the wealth and welfare of low and middle-income people, in some cases making poverty cyclical. Around the world, low-income households' average insurance expenditure represents a low proportion of total expenses from their budget. Latin American insurance culture is no exception; further, this region presents a very low participation in health insurance, with respect to other regions.[1] There is some evidence that the latter is due to missing insurance markets, as well as a lack of insurance culture.

On the other hand, an important challenge faced by insurers of low-income and middle-class people is to maintain a balance between a low-price premium and provision of attractive insurance coverage features, while at the same time maintaining a profitable insurance business segment. Besides, given the fact that most of the population of prospective low-income microinsurance policyholders are settled in non-urban communities, operating cost derived from meeting insurance demand with supply is significant. That is, there is a challenge for insurance in the way it is distributed. Regarding premiums paid, the challenge is to make it attractive but with a sufficient coverage/claim ratio. Finally, there is a need for a better understanding of the insurance products in order for customers to evaluate and distinguish information on existing products; that is, there is a need for an insurance consumer education.

---

[1] A study by Microinsurance Network indicates that in 2016 only 8.1% of the Latin American population was covered by at least one microinsurance policy.

Other chapters of this book have analyzed some microcredit cases. In this chapter, we discuss some cases of microinsurance. While microcredit provides people with their present financial needs, microinsurance, in comparison, will provide their unexpected and future financial requirements. One of the main differences between traditional insurance and microinsurance is that policies associated with microinsurance are written in a simple and clear way. Also, premiums paid for microinsurance are lower.

However, in Latin America, as in any other region, there are still some challenges in the microinsurance sector, and even more when attending a segment like the MoP, who have more aspirations but lack opportunities, income, and an insurance culture. The challenges addressed here are the following: (i) high operating cost, derived from difficulties joining demand and supply in non-urban communities; (ii) high commissions and premiums, relative to the benefit derived from adverse selection and moral hazard problems; and (iii) lack of educated customers, due to lack of insurance culture.

The purpose of this chapter is to describe the way that some Latin-American companies have been creating innovative products to solve these challenges, while at the same time making substantial profits. As cases, we include Bradesco Seguros in Brazil. This company fulfills the distribution channel, using some mobile devices and branches such as pharmacies, bakeries, beauty salons, and other places that people visit daily. We also analyze the case of Aseguradora Rural, in Guatemala, which also solves the distribution channel challenge in addition to using information from other financial business segments to create a microinsurance product, solving the adverse selection and moral hazard problem. In Mexico, we analyze the GNP-OXXO case, which is a particular case where an alliance between an insurance company and the biggest chain store in Mexico created microinsurance products. Finally, there is the case of PROFIN, in Bolivia, which is a case of innovation in the education of the need of insurance. In sum, the different cases exemplify the importance of identifying the needs of the population segment. In particular, it became clear that looking for proper distribution channels is of vital importance. Customers from the base and the middle of the pyramid lack insurance services, and they would not be likely to receive them due to lack of accessibility and affordability. The firms here presented showed that providing fair pricing and distribution channels that are already familiar to customers, such as convenience stores and some banks, helps shorten the distance for the end-client. Additionally, educating the customers creates a relationship between the product and the firm. As mentioned before, there is a lack of insurance culture, but giving information and guiding the customers allows them to feel integrated and heard, driving more sales while creating awareness among the population.

WEALTH SHOCKS, LACK OF INSURANCE, AND DISTRIBUTION CHANNELS: A CHALLENGE TO SOLVE

Diseases, deaths, fire, floods, droughts, and unemployment are just a few examples of the numerous adverse shocks that population worldwide is prone to suffer. Lack of effective mechanisms to manage these risks can have catastrophic consequences. In the world of the poor, vulnerability is omnipresent in their daily lives and the occurrence of shocks can have devastating short- and long-term welfare impacts. For example, to afford the medical treatment of a family member, the poor household may be strained and rapidly deplete its bulk of wealth, perhaps built over a long period, condemning the household to live in persistent poverty and further exposing it to future perils. Consider the effects of weather shocks (such as floods or droughts) as another example. The occurrence of such events not only lowers current income and consumption of a household that depends on agriculture but also conditions its production choices for subsequent periods, often leaving the household trapped in low-risk, but low-yield production.

Employing insurance products seems to be a straightforward solution to ameliorate risk exposure, yet low-income households rarely insure. The Global Financial Inclusion Database published by the World Bank reports that only 2.23% of adults (older than 15 years) pay for health insurance in low-income economies, a remarkably low proportion when compared to upper-middle income nations, where this ratio is of 32.88%. The survey also reveals that lack of health insurance may not just be inherent to the very poor, but also prevalent in lower-middle income economies, as this proportion is found to be just 5.15%.[2] In the countries subject to this chapter, the uptake rates of health insurance are at the shallow end. In Bolivia and Guatemala, classified as lower-middle-income countries, the ratios barely reach 4%. Brazil and Mexico are categorized as upper-middle-income economies, yet not even the richest in these countries purchase health insurance. In Brazil, just 10.6% of the wealthiest 60%, while in Mexico, only 8.59% (see Table 10.1). The statistics of gross direct insurance premiums reported by the Organisation for Economic Cooperation and Development (OECD) paints a broader but similar picture of the state of the insurance markets in these countries. The indicator is defined as gross insurance premiums for direct insurance divided by the population, representing a proxy for the relative relevance of the insurance market in the country. In 2018, the average spending was below USD 261, as the insurance markets in Bolivia and Guatemala were almost absent. Although Brazil and Mexico's expenses are more significant, with values of USD 276 and USD 223, respectively, they portray significantly undeveloped insurance markets (see Table 10.2).

Though highly informative, the previous figures do not fully reflect the fact that actual participation (and expenditure) in insurance markets results from both a demand for the service (where some individuals may self-exclude from the market) and the limitations of the supply of the service (where some insurers may self-exclude from the market). While understanding the demand side has proved to be a

---

[2]   Low-income economies are those in which 2010 GNI per capita was USD 1005 or less. Lower-middle-income economies are those in which 2010 GNI per capita was between USD 1006 and USD 3975. Upper-middle-income economies are those in which 2010 GNI per capita was between USD 3976 and USD 12275 (World Bank 2011).

Table 10.1 *Employment of health or medical insurance in low and middle-income economies, Bolivia, Brazil, Guatemala, Haiti, and Mexico (percentage)*

Category	Low <USD 1005	Lower middle USD 1006–3975	Upper middle USD 3976–12275	Bolivia	Brazil	Guatemala	Mexico
Total adults	2.23	5.15	32.86	3.73	7.62	1.67	8.48
Male	2.82	5.53	33.87	6.07	7.40	2.78	10.79
Female	1.63	4.77	31.86	1.53	7.82	0.68	6.29
Income, poorest 40%	0.97	2.95	33.97	1.96	3.27	0.77	8.31
Income, richest 60%	3.11	6.64	32.12	4.93	10.60	2.27	8.59
Young adults (% ages 15–24)	1.30	3.71	24.97	1.12	3.12	1.73	6.65
Older adults (% ages 25+)	2.71	5.70	34.47	3.73	9.04	1.64	9.14
Primary education or less	1.19	4.23	37.45	2.93	5.64	0.00	5.45
Secondary education or more	3.14	7.00	25.36	4.07	9.43	3.79	10.77
Rural	1.82	4.56	38.01	2.29	6.43	1.07	7.07

Note: (1) The figures represent the percentage of people greater than 15 years old who personally paid for insurance. (2) Income classification is based on 2010 GNI per capita

Source: Global Financial Inclusion Database. The World Bank 2011. Accessed December 8, 2017.

Table 10.2 *Insurance spending per capita for the Group of Seven and selected Latin American countries, in USD*

	2014	2015	2016	2017	2018
The Group of Seven (G7)					
Canada	2,168	1,930	1,919	2,011	2,086
France	4,110	3,554	4,108	4,248	4,569
Germany	3,131	2,597	2,602	2,838	3,049
Italy	3,125	2,678	2,445	2,437	2,645
Japan	2,580	2,370	3,201	2,893	3,010
United Kingdom	5,098	4,598	3,950	5,113	5,643
United States	5,970	6,305	6,500	6,717	7,082
Latin America					
Argentina	405	418	422	393	427
Bolivia	n.a.	n.a.	43	43	47
Brazil	346	273	287	321	276
Chile	613	630	675	694	748
Colombia	199	163	162	179	185
Costa Rica	241	216	246	265	265
Guatemala	46	48	50	55	54
Mexico	224	203	194	211	223
Peru	116	118	106	109	122

Source: OECD Insurance Statistics 2015. OECD. Accessed March 13, 2017. www.oecd-ilibrary.org/finance-and-investment/oecd-insurance-stat istics_2307843x

complex task and would require a separate discussion,[3] there is consensus among academicians and practitioners that the low use of insurance among the poor is, to a large extent, due to lack of coverage. These types of markets are conventionally known as *microinsurance* because the insurance products are designed to service the segment of low-income people.

Dozens of research studies have aimed to understand the functioning and effectiveness of various strategies that low-income people

---

[3]   See Eling, Pradhan, & Schmit 2014 for an extensive review of the literature on determinants of microinsurance demand.

utilize to face risks in the absence of formal microinsurance markets. These strategies are conventionally classified into risk-management and risk-coping strategies.[4] The former are also known as ex-ante strategies because they include those that individuals implement before the realization of adverse shocks, such as migration of some household members, as well as income diversification. Risk coping strategies, also called ex-post strategies, refer to the actions taken by individuals after the realization of the shock and when the ex-ante mechanisms have not fully avoided the adverse effects of the shock. These mainly comprise the use of risk-sharing networks and either formal or informal financial mechanisms such as purchases and sales of assets, borrowing, and savings.

Informal strategies can be effective for managing some types of risks, but are not optimal. Returning to our initial examples, one can see how depletion of savings to afford medical treatment could help to cope with the shock but also compromise the households' ability to cope with future perils. In the second example, the choice of low-risk production could decrease the volatility of cash flows to future weather shocks, but it also eliminated the opportunity to generate greater incomes. Informal strategies will fail to offer adequate protection, especially in these circumstances where the shocks affect entire regions or groups of individuals. For instance, when members of community risk-sharing networks are equally affected, the locally based lender would be unable to collect the loan payments and supply credit when it is needed most, and households' assets would have lost full or partial value.

Provision of insurance products again emerges as a direct answer to problems associated with risk exposure. There are three major barriers microinsurance suppliers must overcome. First, obstacles associated with information asymmetry. These arise when in an economic transaction one party has more or better information

---

[4] A risk-coping strategy is designed to relieve the impact of the risk once it has occurred (Holzmann & Jorgenson 2001).

than the other. In an insurance transaction, the policy holder may unilaterally influence the likelihood of the risky event to occur by changing his behavior toward risky situations once insured. For example, a farmer could lower the application of pesticides once she purchased crop insurance. This is called *moral hazard*. If the insurer is unable to limit or control this behavior, moral hazard might lead to bankruptcies, since insurance claims can rapidly escalate. Other types of information asymmetry arise from the difficulties in distinguishing high- from low-risk clients.

The latter is known as *adverse selection*. The insurer finds it difficult to set the appropriate coverage premiums to maintain a balanced pool of policyholders. Whereas relatively low premiums would attract high-risk individuals in higher numbers than desired, higher premiums may drive low-risk policy holders out of purchasing insurance.

In this regard, in LAC's, commissions paid to intermediaries range from 2% to 35%, with a regional weighted average of 25%. The median commission rates across distribution channels range from 8% to 35%. Also, the gross written premiums per covered life were about USD 17, while in Asia and Africa are USD 4.9 and USD 12.3, respectively. With a weighted average claims ratio (claim/premium) of 79%, Asian insurers are paying out a higher relative proportion to clients than in Africa, or 30%, and in LAC's only, 29%. Both of these indicators could reflect a "wealthier" potential of microinsurance market in LAC's.[5]

These issues can be overcome with a proper insurance technology that helps the insurer to determine the risk profile of the individual user. In this regard, technology is becoming an important channel to improve the cost–benefit ratio of microinsurance business. In particular, insurers in LAC's have focused on call centers to solve

---

[5]   "Microinsurance Network 2011; Microinsurance Network 2018a; Microinsurance Network 2018b.

microinsurance distribution, compared to African insurers, who have focused more on mobile technology.

In the case of microinsurance, the challenges for risk profiling are tough because traditional actuarial analytical tools might no longer be usable. The insurer should not be surprised to find that low-income individuals are highly heterogeneous and often lack the most basic information such as valid documents of identity, medical records, or credit histories.

On the other hand, large operating costs associated with the provision of the financial service represent another barrier. For example, the costs associated with the initial contact with potential policy holders and those incurred in settling insurance claims. A major component of these costs is distance, not only geographic, but also the distance that arises from intangible differences such as ethnicity, language, culture, and social class.[6] Furthermore, functioning insurance products may require a minimum level of literacy from the client; unfortunately, low levels of education predominate among the poor (see Table 10.2). In general, distance hinders the channels of communication and raises the costs to prohibitive levels, thus creating barriers for the demand and supply of insurance to meet. The microinsurers must then be prepared to deal with deficiencies of the transportation and communications infrastructure.

In regard to distribution channels, one of the biggest challenges of microinsurers is dealing with the preference of agents and brokers to sell other insurance rather than microinsurance because the commissions they could get in microinsurance are low compared with traditional insurance, which suggests that agents are not the proper channel for microinsurance. In addition, the lack of distribution infrastructure, such as roads and payment platforms, has been a major barrier. This is due to the significant amount of time, effort, and

[6] See Gonzalez-Vega 2003 for an excellent characterization of origins and consequences of operating and transaction costs associated with the emergence of formal financial markets.

money required to collect and transfer information and administer products manually. In the microinsurance sector, distribution channels are an important issue, because with low margins in premiums, insurers need to find low-cost channels that can reach clients in large numbers.[7]

LOW-COST DISTRIBUTION CHANNELS, TECHNOLOGY, AND INSURANCE CULTURE: INNOVATIONS FOR MICROINSURANCE CHALLENGES

Bradesco – Brazil

Since the 1970's, the Brazilian bank Bradesco has been working on innovative products for low-income people, mainly in savings accounts and microcredits.[8] With the experience in covering low-income people, in 2010 the bank launched the first microinsurance project in Brazil: an insurance product called Primeira Proteção Bradesco (Bradesco First Protection), an accidental death and funeral insurance. In 2020, the products have monthly premiums of Rs.5.5 (USD 1.03); the insurance is valid for five years. With an accidental death benefit of Rs. 20,000 (USD 3731). This project had the purpose of showing that the low-income microinsurance could be profitable.[9] The project was very successful, selling almost USD 3.7 million of insurance.[10] Another example of a microinsurance product is Bradesco's residential insurance, named Bilhete Residencial – "Estou Seguro!" (Bradesco Home Insurance – "I'm Safe!"). In 2020, This product has a yearly premium of Rs.19.90 (USD 3.71), and it offers insurance against residential fire, explosion, or lightning, with coverage of up to Rs. 10,000 (USD 1865).

It is important to mention that Grupo Bradesco (Bradesco Group) is a leading financial services conglomerate in Latin America. The group is divided between its banking arm (Banco Bradesco) and its

---

7   Merry, Prashad, & Hoffarth 2014.   8   Bradesco 2014 Annual Report.
9   Berende 2013.
10   Bradesco Seguros 2015. Principles for sustainable insurance. 2014–2015 Report.

insurance arm (Bradesco Seguros). There are four types of players in the low and middle-income market in Brazil: banks, large independent insurers, small insurers, and informal funeral parlors and cemeteries. The four largest insurance providers in Brazil are Bradesco, Itaú, Brazil Prev, and Porto Seguro, with bank-led groups such as Bradesco and Itau Unibanco dominating the market.

Notwithstanding the foregoing, and given the experience in the financial inclusion sector, the innovation of the bank in the microinsurance sector came in 2012, when the bank got a grant from Microinsurance Innovation Facility to improve penetration in the microinsurance market, using mobile technology and bank branches. In this way, the bank started with market research. The study showed that one of the main risks facing low and middle-income clients in major Brazilian cities was violence. As a result, the subsidiary of the bank, Bradesco Seguros, launched the Expresso Premiável. This is a life, accident, and disability insurance with a personal accident and telemedicine component.[11]

At the same time, and as a part of the pilot program, Bradesco Seguros tested two kinds of technology to enable the provision of popular insurance: point of sale (POS) and mobile devices. POS has the advantage of capturing and transmitting a sale and client information in a quick and convenient way. It also provides a statement of the transaction and policy information that clients can view. Clients can also check the information about their policy on a custom website.[12] By 2019, the bank had USD 2.9 million in microinsurance contracts.[13]

With regard to solving the distribution channel challenge, and in accordance with their business strategy, Bradesco Seguros believes that the best way to reach people is through their daily activities. That is, to deliver equipment that allows easy and low-cost processing of insurance sales at pharmacies, bakeries, beauty salons, and other

[11]   Leach, Menon, & Sandisiwe 2014.   [12]   Siqueira, Solana, & Merry 2013.
[13]   Bradesco 2019.

places that people visit daily.[14] In this way, one of the innovations of Bradesco was Bradesco Expresso. This is Banco Bradesco's arm for its network of banking correspondents, set up by Banco Bradesco in 2012 to sell and distribute various financial services and products, including microinsurance, and comprised of small independent retailers, supermarkets, pharmacies, department stores, and retail chains. By 2019, Bradesco Expresso had a network of over 39,100 banking correspondents.[15]

Another innovation in the creation of Bradesco Expresso was to provide services and support to the bank correspondent network through representatives referred to as "multipliers." The multipliers also serve as insurance brokers on behalf of the Bradesco Group's insurance arm, Bradesco Seguros. In Brazil, insurance regulation only permits registered intermediaries (brokers) to sell insurance, requiring each multiplier to qualify and apply for a broker license. As registered intermediaries, the multipliers are responsible for training the banking correspondents, providing ongoing support, and monitoring performance. As an insurance administrator supporting sales and administration, Bradesco Group has the company Orizon. Orizon's primary responsibility is supporting the administration of the policies sold within the partnership. Bradeso Expresso works with POS solution providers, called value-added networks (VAN), to provide payment and connectivity services to Bradesco Expresso.

Finally, in order to rise to the insurance education challenge, Bradesco trained the broker to convey information and assistance while selling the product. The broker is trained to explain the benefits and to ensure understanding of the coverage, claims, and the monthly prize draw, which is an added feature of the product.

Aseguradora Rural – Guatemala

In Guatemala, gynecological cancer is one of the main causes of death among women. Liquidity constraints and inadequate and costly

---

[14] Munich Re Foundation 2013.   [15] Bradesco 2019.

public health facilities are the main causes.[16] Having this in mind, and as a part of a program of the International Labor Organization named Impact Insurance Facility, the insurance company Aseguradora Rural (Rural Insurance) created a microinsurance product, which is described further. The origin of this product was in 2011 when Aseguradora Rural (AS) got a grant from Impact Insurance Facility to implement a market study for low-income women. The study's purpose was to analyze the low-income women's health needs, before issuing a general microinsurance product. At that time, AS was associated with Empresa Promotora de Servicios de Salud EPSS (Health Promotion Company), a Guatemalan company whose main feature is to provide low-price health services and that has about 72 hospitals and 217 diagnostic centers and labs around the country.

The study incorporated two different regions in Guatemala, Momonstenango, and Rosa. In order to get more reliable data without incurring high survey costs, the company had the idea to offer free two-day medical tests. With these tests, they obtained a sample of 268 women. The study showed a high frequency of gynecological infections, as well as cancer concerns, and also revealed a high demand for low-cost health coverage, even in children. The study also showed that for children, Guatemalan people have access to free public programs.[17] In particular, the survey showed that the main concerns were associated with cancer (71% of women surveyed), diabetes (48%), heart problems (35%), hypertension (15%), HIV/AIDS (10%), and stress (9%). The activity had also the purpose of identifying the staff training needs and customers' concerns that EPSS could address.

Taking into account the survey results, in April 2012 Aseguradora Rural launched their first health microinsurance product in Guatemala, "Vivo Segura."[18] In the first 2 months after the

---

[16]   Budzyna, Chandani, & Magnoni 2013.   [17]   Aseguradora Rural 2020.
[18]   Before the launch of "Vivo Segura," Aseguradora Rural already had thirteen years in operation, in life and non-life insurance markets.

national launch it sold 8,000 policies. The product "Vivo Segura" is a collective life and a women cancer insurance, whose main objective is to prevent and to provide a treatment for this disease. The insured person has the right to the following: (i) two annual visits to the gynecologist, (ii) preventive tests related to cancer disease; (iii) when needed, cancer treatments; (iv) discounts on medicines and examinations in the supplier network; and (v) compensation in cancer diagnosis of 23,000 Quetzals (USD 2976). Payment is made to the beneficiary in the case of the client's death, regardless of the cause, in the amount of of 6,000 Quetzals (USD 776). The premium for the "Vivo Segura" is 30 Quetzals (USD 3.88) monthly or 321.45 Quetzals (USD 41.6) annually (all quotes at 2020 prices).

It is important to mention that Aseguradora Rural is part of a financial group in Guatemala named Grupo Financiero Banrural (Banrural Financial group). Another institution that is part of the same financial group is Banco de Desarrollo Rural (Rural Development Bank); the latter offers multibank services focused on small business, farmers, and artisans, with branches throughout the country of Guatemala, evidently mainly in rural communities. Thus, this bank already had experience in providing services to rural, low-income people. Having this in mind, the distribution channel for the new microinsurance product had to be through this already consolidated rural bank. Therefore, Aseguradora Rural launched the product "Vivo Segura," having Banco de Desarrollo Rural as the distribution channel. As with any other business, from time to time Aseguradora Rural upgraded their product, taking advantage of the information technology of Banco de Desarrollo Rural. In this way they adapted the system to collect the socioeconomic data of the "Vivo Segura" program.[19]

The target market of the product was non-urban micro-entrepreneurs already using Banrural microcredit and health services provided by EPSS and female clients of Banrual saving accounts. Each group had a potential of 200,000 policyholders.

---

[19]   Solana, Gontijo, Gonçalves, & Merry 2013.

Even when the bank had the market study, the channel distribution and the product had to be adapted to the demand. In this regard, in the microinsurance sector one of the big challenges is the insurance culture. That is, products of the traditional insurance market are not easy to understand, with concepts such as insurance fees, coinsurances, deductibles, etc. So, when people consider insurance, maybe the product is not totally understood – even for people who offer the insurance. In this case, Aseguradora Rural developed promotion activities, mainly through providing more information about "Vivo Segura" to doctors, so they could transmit it to their clients. As an example, the current online promotional slogan of this product is: "With only one daily Quetzal (USD 0.14) you can prevent the cancer disease."

In order to reduce the cost of insurance claims, Aseguradora Rural made an agreement with a pharmacy network to get a 50% discount on medicines related to insurance claims. Guatemala's insurance market is relatively small, with ten insurers being the main life and non-life insurers that drive the markets. According to Axco Insurance Information Service, on average this insurance company's reported gross written premiums were USD 68 million in 2014. Of these ten companies, Aseguradora Rural took fifth place.

One of the lessons learned from this case is that it was not just a matter of launching a generic microinsurance product such as life or health insurance in order to cover any disease; instead, the features of this insurance product must be informed by a survey, in this case taking advantage of the branches of the bank group to offer a free test and at the same time collect information for the design of the product. Also, the innovation came from the fact that it is not just an insurance product that covers medical services in case of one disease (in this case cancer); in order to offer low-price premiums, the product is linked to preventive services linked to that disease. In this way, the chances that insured people would have to claim the insurance were significantly reduced. Finally, another important lesson is to take advantage of the branches that already exist in an institution, not only because the product can be promoted and sold in those branches, but because the current customer information, including socioeconomic information, could be harnessed to calibrate the customers' needs and payment capacity in order to design the microinsurance product, which can minimize the adverse selection and moral hazard problem.

GNP-OXXO México

This case has to do with an insurance company that has taken advantage of the large national retail chains to boost their presence. The starting point was at the beginning of January 2014, when the convenience store OXXO, owned by the Mexican company FEMSA, together with the Mexican subsidiary of Citibank, Banamex, introduced a product designed for middle- and low-income people, "Saldazo." This is a debit card with a cost of USD 2 that allows clients to make deposits and withdraw money at the convenience store OXXO, which in many cases is open 24/7, but also at the bank. This had the purpose of achieving a bigger financial inclusion in Mexico.[20]

A few months later, in October 2014, with the purpose to increase the insurance penetration in Mexico, the insurance company GNP made an alliance with the same convenience store OXXO and offered an insurance product, "Segutarjetas."[21]

The description of the kind of insurance that OXXO offers is explained subsequently. It is clear that the convenience store took the previous experience of the alliance with the subsidiary of Citibank to create this new business segment. In particular, the main innovation in the insurance segment is to take advantage of the distribution chain. In this regard, OXXO is a chain of convenience stores in Mexico, owned by the Mexican company FEMSA. At the time we are writing this chapter, the company has 17,400 stores in Mexico, 80 in Colombia, and 79 in Chile. Also, it serves 13 million customers daily. On the other hand, GNP is an insurance company with more

[20]   *El Economista* 2014.   [21]   Gutiérrez 2014.

than 110 years experience in the insurance market in Mexico. This company is part of one of the largest Mexican business conglomerates: Grupo Bal (Bal Group), which includes such important institutions as the mining multinationals "Industrias Penoles" and Fresnillo, and also GNP seguros (GNP insurance), among other companies. It is important to mention that the president of the board of Grupo Bal, Mr. Alberto Bailleres, is also a member of the Board of FEMSA, and also one of the richest men in Mexico. That is, there is a great chance that the alliance among FEMSA and GNP was due to the intervention of Bailleres.

In this regard, the sub-director of business and affinity of GNP, Rafael Rodriguez, mentioned the following: "It is important that more companies help to preserve the health and well-being of the Mexican people, having the outreach of the OXXO stores, this alliance contributes to the rapprochement to more people." On the side of OXXO, the manager of telephony and services of FEMSA, Asensio Carrión, said: "The strategic alliance with GNP allows us to expand our financial products and services with innovative options that satisfy the needs of our clients, who today do not have this essential protection or who may wish to complement their protection and medical services."[22] According to the latter statement, of the 70.8 million adult people in Mexico, only 22% have insurance, life insurance being the most used.[23]

As we mentioned before, these two companies created the microinsurance product "Segutarjetas" (insurance cards). The product consists of four specialized micro health, life, and accident insurance policies and is sold in all OXXO stores in Mexico. The "Segutarjetas" include two for the health segment: protection for cervical, exclusively for women and breast cancer; and for men, one covering the first heart attack. The other two microinsurances offer protection for accidental death and personal injury protection: (i) insurance for breast and cervical cancer, for women of 18 to 50 years, with a premium of 149 pesos

---

[22]   Expansión 2014.   [23]   FEMSA 2014.

(USD 7.1) and coverage of 17,000 pesos (USD 810) per card; (ii) insurance for first heart attack, designed for men of 18–50 years, with a premium $ 8 pesos and coverage of $ 1,405 (USD 74) pesos per card; and (iii) insurance for personal medical accidents 149 pesos (USD 7.1) and coverage of $ 26,000 (USD 1238) pesos per card. For any of the "Segutarjetas," no special studies are required to recruit.

Once acquiring the "Segutarjeta," the customer can activate it through a phone call to the GNP line. The customer should provide personal data such as name, date of birth, address, phone code, and card code. After that, the customer will receive by email the contract and general conditions of the insurance.

PROFIN – Bolivia

Fundación PROFIN, founded and supported by Swiss Agency for Development (SDC) and in cooperation with the Danish International Development Agency (DANIDA), offers comprehensive financial services, especially microinsurance, in areas of rural Bolivia. PROFIN's mission is to offer comprehensive, adequate, and fair financial services to the productive sector in order to improve production, income, and life conditions through diversification and financial innovation.

PROFIN - Programa de Apoyo al Sector Financiero (Financial Sector Support Program, 1997–2005), was created to help small enterprises by offering diversified financial services that contribute to sustainable national economic growth. The objective of the program was to promote financial innovation processes and adjustments to the regulations and to facilitate access to diversified financial services for the productive sector. In 2005, SDC and DANIDA joined efforts to support and strengthen the development of rural financial services in Bolivia with the component of the "Sector Privado Agropecuario del Programa de Apoyo Programático a la Agricultura" (Private Agricultural Sector Programmatic Agriculture Program).

PROFIN Foundation, SDC, and DANIDA created "Programa de Mandatos de Intermediación Financiera e Innovaciones

Complementarias" (Financial Intermediation Mandates and Complementary Innovations Program, 2008–2012) in collaboration with the International Monetary Fund (IMF) and the Inter-American Development Bank (IDB) in order to increase financial services access in rural and peri-urban populations in Bolivia. This program aimed to expand coverage and diversify financial services by using technological and financial innovation.

In 2011, PROFIN Foundation, through a strategic alliance with National Life Insurance and America Insurance Companies, presented and granted the project "Vida Agrícola" (Farm Life, 2011–2013) to the International Labour Organization (ILO), represented by the Microinsurance Innovation Facility. "Vida Agricola" offers protection for agriculture, life, and property, combined or single, and is linked with technical assistance for non-financial risk management. PROFIN has worked on the basis of trust in the company and in private insurance so they can increase the number of customers and diversify risk on different types of crops and risk zones. On the other hand, the company works hard on the farmer awareness programs and the training of its own employees in order to have a better understanding and provide better explanations about the needs, importance, and benefits of the insurance. Profin works very hard on the awareness campaigns.

"Programa Apoyo al Sector Agropecuario y de Producción" (Agricultural Sector Support Program and Production, 2011–2013) was created in collaboration with DANIDA to improve access to innovative financial services for women farmers and indigenous men in rural and urban areas. This program paid special attention to gender and indigenous issues in order to ensure access to innovative financial services.

The next program created by Profin was PROSEDER (2011–2014) "Proyecto Desarrollo Económico Rural" (Rural Economic Development Project) in collaboration with SDC. This program aimed to improve the performance of local economic activities of poor and low-income producers in the rural areas of

Chuquisaca, Cochabamba, La Paz, Oruro, Potosi, Tarija, and the Chaco.

PRRD "Programa de Reducción del Riesgo de Desastres" (Disaster Risk Reduction Program, 2011–2014) was created and cofounded by the Swizz Helvetas Intercooperation to reduce the vulnerability and disadvantage of agricultural producers against climate variability and climate change through local technical assistance and transfer of financial risks. The PRRD worked with local governance risk and adaptation to climate change in management of public decentralization; risk diagnosis and municipal planning; climate risk reduction in agricultural production; and management communal agricultural risk and implementation of the Agricultural Risk Mitigation Fund. This contributed to the development of agricultural insurance nationwide in Bolivia.

The most recent project was "Proyecto de Microfinanzas Rurales" (Microinsurance Rural Project, 2012–2015), focused on vulnerability reduction and improving food assurance through agricultural insurance and the promotion and operation of microinsurance in rural areas as a consequence of climate change through mechanisms of risk transfer. It aims to cover physical integrity, heritage, and productive sources of small farmers.

One of PROFIN's main innovations is consumer education for those with little or no access to financial services, no collateral, and no historic credit. So, the first step is getting to know the process of the particular productive sector, the population's culture, and then developing the insurance product with considering for information, timing, and personal and business needs. A close customer relation is very important not only because of planning, monitoring, and evaluation but most importantly in terms of trust. Finally, PROFIN has demonstrated it is not only possible but compulsory to be a profitable organization in terms of number of customers, competitive and attractive interest rates, and hedge and repayment volume.

The financial education campaigns are oriented to the particular product, so the customer has a better understanding of the process, benefits, and effectiveness of the insurance. In the beginning, the campaigns used printed media as well as radio and TV broadcasting, but they were not very efficient. Once again, trust is a key issue in this sector, so PROFIN switched to promoters perceived as trustworthy in the target market. Using customers known by the community, personal relationships leveraged insurance. On the other hand, PROFIN has trained staff, insurance agents, and distribution channels in terms of this new market. And also, Profin worked on the reduction of operating cost of the agricultural insurance, in order to reduce the final cost for the customer.

The financial innovation is oriented to simplify documents such as insurance policies, so the customer can understand the terms easily; the insurance payments are small amounts and consider the income and expense flows and personal factors such as age, health, and specific risk; the hedge period could be reduced and is subject to the production cycle and seasonality; the distribution channel that includes sales, collection, and insurance payments is very close to the customer, and they use platforms and other technologies to simplify, facilitate, and increase the financial access and scalability of this innovative model. Finally, it should be said that this microinsurance must be sustainable; this is not financial help, subsidy, or an instrument to ameliorate poverty. On the contrary, this is a mechanism to promote welfare by managing risk.

COMPARISON AND CONCLUSIONS

Microinsurance is part of financial inclusion for low- and middle-income families and business. These segments of the population have been underserved throughout the years, creating an opportunity for innovation that can address the major challenges of the market. In this sector, we detected three main challenges to meet: (i) high operating cost, (ii) high commissions and premiums, and (iii) lack of insurance culture of customers. The purpose of this chapter is to expose some cases in LAC's that deal with these challenges in an innovative way.

In the case of Bradesco, in Brazil, the incursion in the microinsurance sector started because they already had experience in the financial sector for low- and middle-income people. They started with a study that showed that violence was a main risk in low income zones in some important cities in Brazil. After that, and given the success of this new segment, the bank sought to expand their microcredit segment. Even when this bank had many branches, it detected that in order to reach the low- and middle-income customers, and at the same time offer competitive microinsurance premiums, it was necessary to use, as distribution channels, small independent retailers, supermarkets, pharmacies, department stores, and retail chains. Also, the bank innovated in this segment by using technology point-of-sale terminals and mobile devices for insurance contracting as well as by training the sales staff through representatives referred to as "multipliers."

With regard of the distribution channel, a similar case is the Mexican alliance between the insurance company GNP and the biggest chain store in Mexico, OXXO. The alliance had its origin in a previous alliance of OXXO Citibank that launched a financial inclusion product, a debit product. Given the success of the previous experience, OXXO started the alliance with GNP in order to take advantage of the presence of OXXO around the country, with almost 17,000 stores in Mexico. These two companies could offer four kinds of microinsurance, resolving the distribution and high cost premiums challenges. The lesson to be extracted here is how a diversified and accessible alternative drives sales. Having a distribution channel already linked to the MoP is a great start, but alliances are also key for getting into the segment. Having locations of easy access, plus available options for the middle-income population, helps to grow economies of scale.

In order to meet the professional training staff, education, and high premiums challenges, Aseguradora Rural, in Guatemala, launched a microinsurance product called "Vivo Segura," with life and health components. One of the innovations of this case is that

Table 10.3 *Comparison of cases*

Company		Bradesco	Aseguradora Rural	OXXO - GNP	PROFIN
Industry		Microinsurance	Microinsurance	Microinsurance	Microinsurance
Country		Brazil	Guatemala	México	Bolivia
Size					
Challenge		Distribution channel	Distribution channel and high premiums	Distribution channel	Lack of insurance culture of customers
Innovation in	Product	Expresso Premiável. A product that is sold using mobile devices and is distributed at pharmacies, bakeries, beauty salons and other places that people visit daily	Viva segura. A product that is linked to cover cancer disease but also provides for preventive treatment	Segu tarjetas. A product that is sold in almost 14,000 stores, only requires a phone call to activate it	Vida Agrícola. Agriculture, life, and property, combined or single, and is linked with technical assistance for non-financial risk management
	Process	Reduced operating cost by using branches that people are used to visit	Practical way to activate the insurance, just a phone call	Subcontracted production to firm abroad	Simplified documents such as insurance policies

Table 10.3 (cont.)

Company		Bradesco	Aseguradora Rural	OXXO - GNP	PROFIN
	Distribution	Bank branches and distributed pharmacies, bakeries, beauty salons. Also uses cheap technology such as POS terminals and mobile devices for contracting the insurance	Bank branches	Distributed in a convenience store with a deep penetration, 14,000 stores and 9 million customers in the country	

Source: Authors

this product encourages the use of the gynecological consultations and tests included in the health service package. The strategy had the purpose of reducing the risk of claims for the main coverage, mainly on cancer and death, which made premiums lower. Also, the bank took advantage of their already established branches, not only to promote the microinsurance products but to gather socio-economic information to improve their products. Finally, the case of PROFIN, in Bolivia, which is an innovative case of education, oriented to simplify documents such as insurance policies so the customers can understand the terms easily. Since there is a lack of insurance culture, educating the customers helps them in the short term with decision making, as well as longer term due to the newly formed relationship. In Table 10.3, we present a comparison of cases.

REFERENCES

Aseguradora Rural. 2020. Seguro Colectivo de Vida y Cáncer de la Mujer. *Vivo Segura.* Accessed July 2, 2020. www.aseguradorarural.com.gt/aseguradoradnn/NuestrosSeguros/SegurosdeVida/ProductosBancaseguros/VivoSegura.aspx

Berende, M. 2013. *Distribution and Technology: Experiences and Lessons Learnt from Microinsurance Providers in India and Brazil.* Appleton, WI: The MicroInsurance Centre.

Bradesco. 2014. Annual Report. Bradesco. Accessed June 2, 2016. www.bradescori.com.br

Bradesco. 2019. Integrated Report 2019. Accessed July 2, 2020. www.bradescori.com.br/siteBradescoRI/uploads/file/2019/FINAL_2019_ING.pdf

Bradesco Seguros. 2015. Principles for Sustainable Insurance 2014–2015 Report. Accessed May 15, 2016. www.unepfi.org

Budzyna, L., Chandani, T., & Magnoni, B. 2013. *MILK Brief #24: "Doing the Math" – Health Insurance and Chronic Disease in Nigeria.* Appleton, WI: The MicroInsurance Centre.

El Economista. 2014. Saldazo, tarjeta de débito que puede adquirirse en Oxxo. *El Economista.* Accessed March 14, 2017. http://eleconomista.com.mx/sistema-financiero/2014/02/10/saldazo-tarjeta-debito-que-puede-adquirirse-oxxo

Eling, M., Pradhan, S., & Schmit, J. 2014. The Determinants of Microinsurance Demand. *The Geneva Papers on Risk and Insurance.* 39(2): 224–263.

Expansion. 2014. Ya Podrás Comprar Seguros En Las Tiendas Oxxo. Expansion. Accessed August 25, 2018. http://expansion.mx/mi-dinero/2014/10/21/ya-podras-compras-seguros-en-las-tiendas-oxxo

FEMSA. 2014. Acerca OXXO los Seguros GNP a los mexicanos. *FEMSA.* Accessed March 9, 2017. www.femsa.com/es/medios/acerca-oxxo-los-seguros-gnp-los-mexicanos

Holzmann, R. & Jorgensen, S. 2001. A New Conceptual Framework for Social Protection and Beyond 8(4): 529–560.

Gonzalez-Vega, C. 2003. *Deepening Rural Finance Markets: Macroeconomic, Policy and Political Dimensions.* Washington, DC: Rural Finance & Investment.

Gutiérrez, F. 2014. Protección al cliente, prioridad de regulación fintech: BID. *El Economista.* Accessed March 13, 2017. http://eleconomista.com.mx/sistema-financiero/2014/10/21/oxxo-incorpora-seguros-sus-estantes

Leach, J., Menon, A., & Sandisiwe, S. 2014. *Achieving Scale and Efficiency in Microinsurance through Retail and Banking.* Appleton, WI: The MicroInsurance Centre.

Magnoni, B., Poulton, D. & Zimmerman, E. 2011. *MILK Discussion Note #2: Are Existing Health Financing Mechanisms Sufficient for Poor Women in Guatemala?* Appleton, WI: The MicroInsurance Centre.

MaCord, M. & Biese, K. 2014. The Landscape of Microinsurance in Latin America and the Caribbean – 2014. Microinsurance Network and Munich Re Foundation.

Merry, A., Prashad, P., Hoffarth, J. 2014. *Microinsurance Distribution Channels: Insights for Insurers.* Geneva: ILO.

Microinsurance Network. 2011. Learning Journey. Aseguradora Rural S.A. Health and Life Microinsurance Products to Banrural Clients in Guatemala.

Microinsurance Network. 2018a. The Landscape of Microinsurance in Latin America and the Caribbean 2017. Accessed July 1, 2020. https://microinsurancenetwork.org/sites/default/files/MI%20Landscape%20Study%202017%20Final%20Report_EN_vf.pdf

Microinsurance Network. 2018b. Landscape of Microinsurance in Africa 2018: focus on selected countries. Accessed July 1, 2020. https://microinsurancenetwork.org/sites/default/files/MI%20Landscape%20Study%202017%20Final%20Report_EN_vf.pdf

Munich Re Foundation. 2013. *Sesiones de aprendizaje en microseguros: América Latina y el Caribe 2013.* Guadalajara: Forito del XIII Foro Interamericano de la Microempresa – Foromic. Accessed July 2, 2020. https://microinsurancenetwork.org/groups/landscape-microinsurance-africa-2018-focus-selected-countries

OECD. 2016. OECD Insurance Statistics 2015. *OECD.* Accessed March 13, 2017. www.oecd-ilibrary.org/finance-and-investment/oecd-insurance-statistics_2307843x

Siqueira, G., Solana M., & Merry, A. 2013. Learning Journey Bradesco Seguros. Microinsurance Innovation Facility.

Solana, M., Gontijo, L., Gonçalves, F., & Merry, M. 2013. Case Brief: Aseguradora Rural. Microinsurance Innovation Facility.

The World Bank. 2011. DataBank: Global Index (Global Financial Inclusion Database). The World Bank. Accessed March 14, 2017. http://databank .worldbank.org/data/home.aspx

From Mission Impossible to Mission Accomplished!
Innovative Business Models Strengthening Poor Distribution Channels

Jasenko Ljubica and Eileen Daspro

I remember, as a kid, I always admired a Coca (Coca-Cola) poster on Jaime's store wall and wondered how it tastes like. He would always try to fake he doesn't see me doing it. Once I was saving money to buy my first can for an entire month. Only after I finally had it did Jaime told me: the money is not the problem, I would give it to you free if I ever had it, but never did. When I asked why he told me: there's no one to bring it here.

Mexican Tiendita Customer[1]

A few years ago, delivery to my store was such that if my customers bought a chocolate, it would be white because it was so old. They wouldn't even think about returning it, because that was the norm. Not anymore. Now, when I make an order, I have the goods in a few days. Chocolates are brown and not white. I actually have to explain to some of my customers this is the real chocolate.

Mexican Tiendita Owner

INTRODUCTION

"Mom-and-pop shops" or "tienditas" largely owned by the lower-middle-income population, serving consumers from a similar socio-economic segment, have traditionally dominated distribution in the Latin America (LAC) area. Today, they represent roughly half the total

The authors would like to issue a sincere thank you to the editors for their guidance and to all of those who helped us with the writing of this chapter. We trust they will recognize themselves. A Special thank you goes to the Virtual Market S.A. employees and the CEO, Mr. Andres Gonzales Cuevas, whose enthusiasm and vigilance truly helped us to realize the realities of the subject we were dealing with. For all specifics, please refer to the tables and appendixes.
[1] Anonymous by choice.

retail sales to consumers living at the middle of the pyramid (MoP) in LAC.[2] There are both economic and cultural variables that explain their dominance in LAC retail. First, they are traditionally located in the neighborhood of the MoP consumers, enabling them to save time and money traveling to distant retail stores to purchase everyday necessities. Moreover, traditional distribution channels cultivate an important sense of trust-based social connectedness for both customers and vendors, unstained by racial, gender, and economic discrimination or other cultural challenges that may have plagued the MoP customers' relations with large producers and distributors. Given their size, economic power, and cultural relevance, tienditas represent a highly valuable distribution channel for any company aiming to serve LAC middle-income markets.[3]

However, in terms of effective distribution, LAC companies face unique challenges in their respective markets. They must understand and overcome barriers such as varying socio-cultural, economic, and educational disparities among MoP populations; harsh geography of territories; lack of access to rural communities; security concerns; and poor transportation infrastructure.[4] Moreover, companies have to understand mindsets, needs, preferences, and desires of their middle-income customers in order to determine the optimal way to serve them, placing special attention to costs, products, distribution channels, and far-flung community outreach.

Despite numerous challenges, innovative companies and entrepreneurs are increasingly serving the region's MoP through innovative business models that apply sustainable distribution strategies to bring an optimal range of products and services to those communities efficiently. They use government subsidy programs, participate in public–private partnerships, and collaborate with nongovernmental organizations. They also employ and train locals who have deep knowledge about the needs and aspirations of local communities as well as access to rural, lower-income consumers out of reach of

---

[2]   McKinsey 2015.   [3]   Pisani & Yoskowitz 2012.   [4]   IDB 2015.

modern retailers, thus contributing to job creation and MoP members' income and improved quality of life. In general, enterprises must identify customer requirements as well as understand the dynamics and specifics of geography, competitors, and end-consumers. Companies, therefore, require mastering multiple distribution schemes to meet the diverse requirements from low- and middle-segment customers. Only by having a multichannel strategy are companies able to optimally allocate resources, maximize revenues, and minimize costs.

In order to elaborate on the aforementioned opportunities and the accompanying challenges as well as innovative solutions enacted by successful companies operating in LAC middle-income markets, we first present details on the largely untapped opportunity present at the LAC MoP. We continue by highlighting the challenges shadowing these opportunities and presenting innovative business models used by successful companies as solutions to these challenges. We complete the chapter by providing constructive conclusions and recommendations for practitioners.

THE "TRADITIONAL POTENTIAL"

The traditional distribution channels bear critical importance in providing a living for LACs MoP entrepreneurs and their families and in serving their customers and, therefore, require special attention from every enterprise. A number of drivers explain the expansion of the traditional channel in LAC. Due to low overhead costs, traditional independent retailers do not have to serve a large consumer base. They are located where modern retailers have not ventured – rural areas and small cities – and fill in gaps around modern outlets in urban areas. Middle-income consumers make small and frequent purchases at these local stores because of their proximity and convenience. Sixty seven percent of the middle-income households in the region rarely venture to locations different from those they usually frequent.[5] They

---

[5]   Azevedo et al. 2015.

are often willing to purchase a second-best product rather than venture out of their communities or shop at new retailers.

Unlike the modern channel (big-box retail centers such as Wal-Mart, 7-Eleven in the US, Oxxo in Mexico, and so forth) for distributing goods and services to end consumers, the so-called informal channel, or the one not or insufficiently covered by formal tax and similar arrangements[6] (such as small neighborhood stores or so-called "tienditas"), has traditionally been very profitable in LAC. According to a McKinsey study in 2011,[7] these outlets across LAC represent 38% of the region's true GDP. In retail, traditional channels represent about 50% of all retail sales. They are also the most important channel for distributing goods to consumers, accounting for an estimated 50% of fast-moving consumer goods. According to IFC,[8] in 2007 the market shares of the traditional channel in Mexico, Argentina, Chile, and Colombia were approximately 48%, 71%, 40%, and 53%, respectively. In parallel, demographic changes, economic growth, and advances in technology enabled the escape of large portions of people from the base to the middle of the pyramid, increasing their financial status and purchasing power as incomes rose among the bottom 40 percent.[9] However, even with enlarged purchasing power, socio-cultural connections between the MoP entrepreneurs and customers remained. Entrepreneurs provide products that individual customers need – in the quantities they need and when needed – and provide trust-based credits enabling customers to purchase products and pay when in possession of sufficient funds without having formal financial histories or instruments such as credit and/or debit cards, or steady jobs. Services like these are practically impossible for large retailers to provide. In exchange, customers continued to display trust in their sellers and loyalty through everyday visits.

The traditional channel is not only important but also more profitable than the modern channel. Approximately 2 million

6	International Labour Organization 2003.	7	McKinsey Global Institute 2011.
8	International Finance Corporation 2007.	9	*The Economist* 2016.

tienditas in LAC that continue to grow in number confirm this.[10] The small store segment is strong and is meant to serve a large base of consumers while providing healthy margins for manufacturers, who apply higher prices to traditional retailers due to their small order volume. MNCs entering retail channels in developing economies need to keep in mind the dual commercial and social nature of mom-and-pop stores. Buying locally every day fosters personal relationships and trust between shop operators and regular customers. Proximity, access to trust-based store credit, convenience of smaller store size, and a social connection are just some of the basic MoP consumer needs that drive consumption in tienditas across the region in recent decades.

THE GEO-SOCIAL CHALLENGE

While the accessibility, flexibility, and trust of small shops are positive attributes valued by the region's middle-income consumers, the lack of logistics and technological infrastructure, the disparity in the level of income amongst the population, and the security issues impose significant complexity to the efficient distribution. One of the primary economic challenges for companies is to exploit economies of scale. LAC countries, as with many other developing nations, have seen increasing concentration of people in large urban centers. However, a fair portion of population remains living in rural areas. According to the World Bank,[11] throughout LAC, there are just under 124 million people living in rural areas, representing some 18% of the total population, which is the lowest urban–rural population ratio in LAC in the last two decades, with discrepancies for each country. However, this trend is expected to slow down and eventually stop due to engagement of the local population in traditional jobs such as farming and agriculture, which carry a significant role in the region's economy.[12] Hence, LAC's rural population still represents a large and attractive pool of customers for any company. However, businesses face severe challenges in tackling this

---

[10]   Azevedo et al. 2015.   [11]   The World Bank 2015.
[12]   The World Bank 2015.

opportunity, such as the distance from distribution centers to rural customers, which drives up transportation costs and, hence, results in higher total costs and prices. In addition, rural territories have smaller populations and lower volume deliveries, making it much costlier for companies to serve these customers. The absence of basic infrastructure such as paved roads, together with the slow pace of infrastructure investments, act as a barrier to economic activity. The poor development in infrastructure across LAC, especially rural areas, and the limited, sporadic, and uneven incomes have driven the growth of the small retailer format. The fact that traditional store formats dominate LAC's MoP makes it harder for these nations to exploit economies of scale as infrastructural limitations impose constraints on the efficiency of distribution systems. It is, therefore, clear that the large geographical distances along with poor transportation infrastructure result in low consumer outreach.

Moreover, socio-cultural barriers in the form of the lack of trust toward large corporations and lack of basic financial and overall business literacy necessary to conduct businesses efficiently further complicate the operations of traditional retailers.[13] The issue of illiteracy refers to not only basic but also financial, marketing, stock management and control, planning, and similar business skills.[14] Poor skills of MoP entrepreneurs weaken their business development potential on one hand while strengthening their distrust toward modern big-box retailers on the other, rendering possibilities of successful penetration to these markets even more difficult.

Customers as well as entrepreneurs in the middle-income market stratum rely on each other. Entrepreneurs provide the types and quantities of products that consumers demand, with the payment flexibility and credit terms they need. They do not require proof of formal financial histories or instruments such as credit and/or debit cards or steady jobs, a service that is a far cry from large retailers. In exchange, customers trust in their sellers and display loyalty through

---

[13]   McKinsey 2015.   [14]   OECD/ECLAC/CAF 2016.

every day visits. MoP buyers and sellers alike complain that large corporations largely ignore their lifestyle and needs. Moreover, language and cultural diversity of the middle-stratum communities further hamper these relations, making it very difficult for modern enterprises to operate in these markets.

STRATEGY ESTABLISHED

The broad reach of traditional stores represents a strategic and high-value distribution network for any company that wants to reach middle market segments. Recognizing this potential, successful companies have chosen to form partnerships with local institutions and nongovernmental organizations with local experience. They established scale-affording distribution networks through arrangements with distributors serving customers in rural areas as well as urban centers. Using market-based models, large corporations collaborate with mom-and-pop shops to upgrade the management and inventory-planning skills of their proprietors. Consequently, they gain valuable insights about these consumers that they previously lacked, which benefits the bottom line of both traditional channels as well as the larger corporation. Moreover, they engage lower-income, local workers by employing and training them as their sales force, thus contributing to job creation, access to remote communities, and establishment of trust-based relationships with customers.

In the following, we present a series of case studies depicting the innovative business models of companies whose practices effectively serve the MOP in the LAC.

Case Study 1: Virtual Market (Mexico)[15]

Andres Gonzales Cuevas and Jorge Espindola founded Virtual Market (VM) in 2013 with, as they say in VM, "a dream to help traditional store owners of Mexico to expand their businesses and improve their lives." This private,

---

[15]   For all particulars regarding numerical data in this case study please refer to Appendix 2.

for-profit company in its two years of existence has expanded from a small start-up to a company with presence in all the major Mexican cities. Their dream was to tackle a common threat to all traditional channel members: the fast rise and popularity of the modern convenience stores (Oxxo, 7-Eleven) and the superstores (Wal-Mart) as fierce competitors. Estimations show that for the opening of every new, modern retailer, five or six traditional "tienditas" experience a loss in their revenues of up to 40%. The latter's lack of business knowledge and modern retail best practices and technological and financial exclusion, combined with the new competition, has led to such a rapid decline. Consequently, tienditas' problems spilled over to suppliers who lacked access to traditional stores, lack of visibility of their products and low productivity within traditional channel and, congruently, to customers who enjoyed only a limited selection of products at higher prices.

Observing these problems, Virtual Market saw, in fact, a large business opportunity. Such opportunity was reflected in almost 1 million tienditas across Mexico, producing about 15% of the country's GDP. Placing a focus on these problems, Virtual Market forged their mission: "Become the largest traditional stores chain by affiliating independent mom & pop stores, providing them with modern retail best practices, education & technology, and a direct connection to suppliers & all traditional channel actors, with immediate positive spillover effects across the business ecosystem." Virtual Market, therefore, stands for the business model that, through use of technology, connects traditional stores, suppliers, and customers in a virtual retail chain and that, through training, empowers BoP and MoP micro-entrepreneurs to compete with larger convenience stores, and to grow sustainably and efficiently. In the words of the CFO, Isabel Molina:

> What we actually do is matchmaking. Entrepreneurs, customers, suppliers, financial institutions and the country itself are aware of the importance of the traditional channel, but have been unable to help in its survival and development. We do it in cyberspace. The benefits are in real space.

VM set out to realize such a mission by designing and implementing a highly innovative, robust business model intended to generate profits across the entire traditional retail market value chain. Such a model does not presume ownership of a single store. It actually presumes providing the small retailers with a friendly and all-inclusive solution in the form of innovative technological tools used in the modern retail channel, internet access, business training, and market data, which they can employ to increase revenue streams, maintain their clients' loyalty, and attract new customers. Accordingly, VM equips and modernizes the tienditas with the Integral

Store Management Tool Kit (ISMK), enabling them to incorporate the best modern retail management practices and help them grow profitably. Such a tool kit features a POS terminal, card reader, fingerprint reader (for the security purposes), receipt printer, and wireless internet connectivity router, all in a recognizable orange color with a promotional display for suppliers and a touch screen for owners or operators. Although there are similar platforms on the market, VM's ISMK is the only such platform focused on increasing sales for the entire business ecosystem, including both tienditas and suppliers while producing various benefits for the MoP customers at the same time.

Micro-entrepreneurs owning or working in the tienditas receive training in operating the terminals as well as in contemporary retail practices. They receive pricing consultations and are able to implement different promotions and exhibits on their own or in collaboration with suppliers. VM secures wireless internet connections for the terminals and actually pays for it so the store owners do not have any concerns other than paying Virtual Market's 150 MXP membership fee per month. This enables traditional stores to conduct different types of business analysis concerning aspects such as shopper's traffic, optimum portfolio of products and services according to the customer's purchases, and payments, new revenues, incremental sales, productivity, and stronger bottom line. In addition, the VM terminals deliver various options that allow these tienditas to gain a competitive advantage in comparison to larger chains. Such options include the possibility that customers pay their purchases with credit and debit cards, all at once or in limited monthly installments. Customers can also pay more than forty different types of utility bills (electricity, water, etc.) and mobile phone bills in tienditas through VM Kit. This is very important for tienditas as a means of defense against large retail chains who, until now, were the only retailers providing this option to customers.

Micro-entrepreneurs can also use the terminal to manage their inventory. The status of every item in stock is available in only "one or two clicks" and operators receive a message when certain items are low in stock, implying a necessity to reorder. Replenishing the stocks is also a few clicks away as the terminal connects stores with suppliers who are now able to submit an order directly to the supplier via their terminals. This shortens the time for delivery of the merchandise to the store as well as reduces the time in which the store is out of given products, which again has a positive effect on revenue and profit increase for both the store and the supplier. Although this option is in the implementation phase and not in use by every tiendita, it does provide a significant benefit for store owners, customers, and suppliers alike: Stores reduce the risk of stock-outs, customers find the products they need, and suppliers receive real-time orders, improving their time-to-market sales.

ISMK further enables the traditional stores to conduct different promotions (discounts on the basis of location and schedule, try-outs, exhibits) on their own and/or in collaboration with suppliers with whom they are now connected and in 24/7 real-time communication. Vendors and suppliers can also communicate by performing different surveys in order to identify, for example, best-selling products or what methods and/or times of delivery work best for stores and their customers. VM's integral system allows creation of various customer loyalty programs on behalf of the tienditas alone or in collaboration with suppliers. VM provides suppliers with the opportunity to offer various loyalty programs for entrepreneurs based on their purchasing and payment histories, thus allowing them to achieve lower prices, which they can transfer to their customers, again building and maintaining their loyalty. According to Virtual Market, the suppliers do not know what happens with their products at the point of sale. The sales point for them is a "black box." VM tackles this problem by enabling suppliers to gain accurate data about the time and value of sales of their products, promotions, and visibility of their products at the sales point, thus turning the black box into the "orange box." Through their innovative system, VM's ISMK enables suppliers to perform market intelligence activities, integrated advertising & promotional B2B and B2C solutions, product promotion, and sales monitoring. This enables efficient marketing budgeting and better decision making for more effective results in their balance sheets. In addition to working with store owners, suppliers, and customers, Virtual Market also builds on partnerships with credit card issuers to promote their use and attract more customers to tienditas – hence, absorbing another important member of the business ecosystem through increased credit card use.

The manner in which Virtual Market disseminates their business model is through direct sales. Their sales representatives, uniformed in recognizable orange shirts, perform an average of 150 daily visits (per sales representative) to tienditas in their area and present the store owners the VM business model by explaining the advantages and benefits as well as costs of implementing their business solution. According to the VM's sales representatives, the main barrier in their work is gaining the trust of the store owners. This is logical, as these individuals, due to poor levels of technological literacy, are reluctant to collaborate with high-tech companies they do not know, since their work principles tend to be relationship based. However, once they succeed in gaining their trust and establishing a relationship, they can focus on nurturing that store as a critical part of the company's value chain and work further to acquire new ones. As one of VM's employees says: "The trust is critical and most difficult to obtain. They (micro-entrepreneurs) all want help as they are aware of their own deficiencies, but they will not accept it until they can trust you, not even at the expense of closing their business. It is a process. Sometimes, it is a very long process."

Every sales representative has his/her area of responsibility as well as "his/her" store owners. The company pays for their fuel, car registration, and service expenses, and their paycheck is commission-based. Every VM's subsidiary has a supervisor, a tech-support officer, and sales representatives as the main sales model. They must be at their service at any given moment providing assistance by phone or onsite. Problems usually relate to technological issues, although this decreases over time when store owners gain sufficient amount of experience in handling the hardware delivered by VM.

Virtual Market's revenue model is, like their business model, highly innovative. Advertising, which connotes advertising places for suppliers and other interested parties on VM's ISMK to gain visibility in every tiendita under the VM umbrella, holds a 53% revenue share. Business intelligence & market lab have 12%, transactions (VM charges certain percentage from every transaction in agreement with credit card companies so as not to transfer this burden to the stores or customers) have 33%, and membership fees hold a mere 3% of company revenue share. This confirms the company's commitment to help and not exploit the vulnerable, increasingly threatened traditional stores. On the other hand, the company's cost structure is comprised of store owners training at 28%, hardware 21%, internet connectivity 17%, hotspot and promotional screen 13%, marketing & overheads 13%, and innovation & technology 8%.

Although Virtual Market has been operating their innovative business model for only two years, the results have been astonishing. On average, affiliated tienditas have experienced a 30% growth in sales volume, while suppliers have reported an increase in value and productivity ranging from 40% to 200%. They are also able to design and conduct more effective and efficient marketing campaigns based on the real-time feedback they receive from traditional stores though VM's innovative system. Suppliers such as Orbit (the chewing gum producer) have experienced a 15.2% increase in sales of their products in the traditional channel by being a part of VM's virtual network, while suppliers such as Trident experienced growth in sales of their products in traditional channel reaching up to 43.5%.

By 2014, VM had their orange virtual market boxes in 300,000 establishments, of which 90% are located in Monterrey. By 2015, 3,500 tienditas had joined the VM system, generating about 400,000 MXP in monthly sales with an average bill of 25 MXP. In 2015, the company had a gross annual revenue of USD 5.5 million and net annual revenues of USD 0.5 million. The company, currently worth about 200 million MXP, has invested about 18 million MXP and plans to invest an additional 20 million in 2016 in the further development of their business model, which reaches a USD 43 million investment in a two-year period. The company also plans to increase average monthly sales up to 1.125 million MXP in 2016 and 15.750 million in long term. VM is also planning to acquire 10,000 tienditas in 2016 and 14,000 in the long term. In comparison to their and tienditas' main competitors, such as, for example, the Mexican retailer Oxxo, by 2015 VM had in their network 35,000 tienditas, which equals one-third of Oxxo's number of outlets, while the company expects to surpass Oxxo's size by second quarter of 2017. Their strategy for future development focuses on the improvement of the value proposition for retailers to give them more incentives to become part of the VM's virtual chain and to adopt the continuous usage of VM's services in order to increase traditional channel sales and, consequently, suppliers' sales and customer satisfaction. VM is also planning to increase coverage in the most relevant cities for the suppliers to ensure their interest in being part of the network, keeping VM a sustainable business solution serving the entire MoP business ecosystem. Their CFO, Isabel Molina, considers their business model solid and likely to drive growth: "Indeed, we are growing fast but we are not afraid. Our business model was recognized by our clients as one focused to them, collaborative, inclusive and with mutual interest. We gained their trust and that is the reason of our growth. This gives us the right to dream about what is unthinkable for most companies – to be recognized as a company providing benefit for all the society and not just the company itself through sales to customers. That is our model and dream." Isabel Molina, CFO Virtual Market

By employing this type of business model, VM generates a high social impact by propelling, in a sustainable way, the development of small businesses that are the pillar of the Mexican economy, in terms of both jobs and income. With such a significant impact, the multidimensional value of their model gained international recognition. Virtual Market received the GIIRS[16] 2015 Platinum Certificate for high social impact. They also received

[16] Methodology used to estimate investment impact, conducted by "B Analytics" company.

recognition as one of the "Top 10 Most Innovative Companies of 2015 in LAC" by Fast Company magazine, "Startup of the Year 2015" by eShow México, "Top 10 Entrepreneurs" by Revista Expansión 2015, and one of the ten Companies with high social impact by I3 LATAM.

Case Study 2: SABMiller LAC

Founded in South Africa in 1895, SABMiller is the world's second largest brewing company, with more than 200 beer brands and some 70,000 employees in more than 80 countries on 6 different continents. It is also one of the world's largest bottlers of Coca-Cola drinks and produces a portfolio of wholly owned soft drink brands. Beer comprises 82% of its volume; the remaining 18% is non-alcoholic beverages. In fiscal year 2013, SABMiller's revenues exceeded USD 34 billion, with some 72% coming from developing markets. LAC and Africa account for 63% of EBITA and are two of the company's fastest-growing markets at 9% and 5%, respectively.

Even though it is a foreign company, SABMiller recognized the potential of LAC and has invested in it by purchasing local companies with a tradition stretching back for more than a century and established products with a firm customer base: Backus Brewery in Peru, Bavaria Brewery in Colombia, and Industrias La Constancia Brewery in El Salvador, respectively. Across these countries, the traditional retailer is a vital distribution channel, with small-scale retailers (store owners) representing approximately 40% of the company's total sales volume.[17] There are some 780,000 such retailers in the company's value chain in these countries, with 65% located in high poverty areas.[18] These outlets are located close to their customers in urban and rural areas that are often hard to reach, which makes them the ideal distribution channel for serving low-income communities. Micro-entrepreneurs, many of them women, own and/or operate many of these outlets, which again makes the traditional channel a key source of employment and income for millions, and thus a key source of nutrition, health care, education, and other benefits for their families. Traditional retailers also play a social role in their communities and tend to bring together people, forming social hubs. Store owners often provide advice and services beyond their business and are persons of reference in their communities. They get to know their customers well and allow customers to purchase on credit when times are particularly tight and reasonably expect repayment. Customers are their

[17]   SABMiller 2015.   [18]   SABMiller 2015.

neighbors and friends, and for the reasons mentioned they want them to be able to come back to these stores. Traditional trade is, thus, a promising channel for reaching low-income populations with the potential to improve businesses and standards of living.

However, the constraints for store owners are numerous. These micro-enterprises face significant challenges, such as access to finance and securing the necessary permits to operate. Outlets are numerous and small, often with working capital and storage space for just a few days' inventory. This limits their ability to negotiate with suppliers for better prices or payment terms and requires suppliers to make frequent deliveries of small quantities of product. Outlets also face stiff competition from one another and from big-box retail formats that are beginning to take hold. Many traditional retailers have low levels of financial literacy, do not understand how formal financial services could help them, and tend to mistrust the banking sector. As a result, they often stick with the informal lenders and tend to use only cash, adding to suppliers' transaction costs. While traditional retailers often have quite a bit of innate business sense, few have training in skills such as inventory management, accounting, marketing, and sales that would help them optimize their performance and, in turn, the incomes and opportunities they are able to offer their families and communities. Because their customers have low and unpredictable incomes, outlet revenues can be low and unpredictable as well. Combined with limited access to financial services, this makes it difficult to invest in technology, equipment, and other assets that could, over time, reduce operating costs and increase revenues.

Hence, SABMiller, through its LAC companies, realized that to maximize growth and development, products and services provided through traditional trade channels must include offerings that help outlets themselves to overcome these challenges. For SABMiller, empowering traditional retailers involved two distinct and mutually reinforcing activities: training them as business owners, heads of household, and even agents of change in their communities; and strengthening the business ecosystems in which they operate (building links with a range of companies, financial institutions, government agencies, academia, and other stakeholders). SABMiller had strong faith that empowering traditional retailers will increase their incomes; protect them from financial risk; enable them to provide better nutrition, health care, and education for their children; and expand access to valued products and services in their communities.

In 2012, with support from Fundación DIS, a nonprofit consulting firm serving companies and social enterprises, SABMiller LAC and its subsidiaries decided to consolidate, strengthen, and scale a consistent regional approach to supporting the small retailers and broader communities on which such a significant share of its sales depend. It was with this objective that the company launched its social program "4e Camino al Progreso" (The path toward progress). It mirrored the best practices and previous experiences gained from pilot projects run by SABMiller and its Latin American companies, such as the "Progresando Juntos" program in Peru (Backus) and El Salvador (Industrias La Constancia), focused on improving business skills, as well as the "Oportunidades Bavaria" project in Colombia (Bavaria), providing microcredit for small retailers. These projects eventually scaled up to the "4e Camino al Progreso" program, launched in August 2013. To create the program, SABMiller collaborated with specialist research firm MindCode, conducting an in-depth study on the aspirations, desires, and dreams of store owners in order to establish what would make them more fulfilled in their day-to-day lives. The answers provided were of two kinds: firstly, the store owners wished to have more successful and growing businesses; second, they wanted to improve the quality of their private lives and their self-esteem and secure better opportunities – such as education for their children or buying a home – and to help the communities around them. Building on these insights, SABMiller designed the 4e program with the objective of training store owners to not only be better business people by running more efficient and appealing shops but also to build leadership skills to take on responsibilities at the community level.

The 4e program aims to improve small retailers' overall business performance, quality of life, and capacity to play leadership roles in their communities, while at the same time strengthening SABMiller's retail network and sales.[19] As the shops become more efficient and appealing to consumers, income rises and thereby store owners have the opportunity to lead more fulfilling lives and even become community leaders. The program objectives are:[20]

I. Position SABMiller and its local companies as innovative organizations capable of getting a scalable impact in LAC through social development.
II. Responsibly meet the sales policy of the company.
III. Improve the quality of life of the shopkeepers and their families.
IV. Develop sustainable stores and improve the welfare and development of their own communities.

---

[19]   Jenkins 2014.   [20]   Jenkins 2014; SABMiller 2015.

The program has four main indicators: People (personal safety and private property, gender equality, diversity, combating the discrimination), Environment (employment generation, contribution to community), Economy (training for employment, health and safety at work), and the Company (budget execution, operational support for sustainability of the value chain). The program also has two innovative, high-impact features: (1) it is a social inclusion program aimed at the MoP populations, and (2) it combines business training with traditional components of LAC societies – personal and family well-being and community outreach.

In order to maximize the effectiveness of the program, SABMiller joined forces with Fundes, a civil society organization that works to bolster the competitiveness of micro, small, and medium enterprises in LAC. SABMiller LAC and Fundes are also working with the Multilateral Investment Fund (MIF) of the Inter-American Development Bank (IDB), which channels much of IDB's grant funding and technical assistance, particularly to companies and civil society organizations. These organizations have distinct drivers bringing them together around a common objective. Accordingly, main drivers for the 4e Program are visible in Fundes' desire to improve livelihoods and jobs, SABMiller's desire to accelerate growth and social development through its value chains, and IDB's desire to reduce poverty and inequality.[21] MIF provides expertise and advice, especially in the areas of financial and technological inclusion, as well as USD 3 million in grant funding. Fundes takes responsibility for program oversight and overall relationship management with SABMiller and IDB. Fundes recruits, deploys, and manages trainers and consultants to deliver the classroom training and in-store mentoring of the store owners. IDB's Multilateral Investment Fund in Washington, DC provides expertise and advice, especially in the areas of financial and technological inclusion, as well as USD 3 million[22] in grant support to Fundes to strengthen the impact of the 4e model. MIF's country offices liaise directly with SABMiller's subsidiaries and Fundes' country offices, providing expert advice and local connections on a day-to-day basis.

The backbone of the 4e program is a twelve-week cycle of recruitment, diagnosis, classroom training, in-store mentoring, monitoring, and awarding of certificates. Recruitment is an active process of store visits, group information sessions, and follow-up in person and over the phone. SABMiller teams jointly select recruits from their small retail customers according to a list of

---

[21]   Jenkins 2014.   [22]   Azevedo et al. 2015.

criteria, including personal characteristics, outlet sales, growth potential, and community poverty rate. SABMiller sales representatives then introduce recruits to the program on their next regularly scheduled visits and issue formal letters of invitation to attend group information sessions in their communities. Recruits receive phone calls reminding them of the sessions and asking them to confirm attendance. Fundes hosts the sessions and SABMiller sales staff and senior management are always present. Recruits who are unable to attend their information sessions receive follow-up visits from their sales representatives and Fundes consultants who tell them about the program and offer the opportunity to sign a letter of commitment to participate.

The diagnosis generates baseline information and an action plan for each participating retailer, in collaboration with that retailer. Fundes consultants visit the retailers in their stores to discuss their strengths and weaknesses, needs, and aspirations for improvement, noting a variety of baseline indicators. Afterwards, the consultants complete their diagnoses and design appropriate action plans. Classroom training (eighteen hours) and in-store mentoring (seventeen hours) introduce a wide variety of topics and help participating retailers implement what they have learned. Importantly, the curriculum covers two major areas. First, the business development area focuses on training in general business, finance, and marketing skills, intended to help participants improve their overall sales across all of the products they sell. Second, the health and well-being area covers responsible retailing of alcohol as well as life skills such as healthy lifestyles and prevention of and assistance with domestic violence, and covers the importance of separating the business and family finances and financing one's education. The curriculum has four stages, with each stage consisting of six modules taught in thirty-five hours. The phases range from "responsible tendero" to "sustainable tendero" to "excellent tendero" to "leader tendero." The modules, each lasting four weeks, cover sales (module 1), business administration (module 2), finance (module 3), household operations (module 4), SABMiller relations (module 5), and support and monitoring (module 6).

The financial literacy components of the program aim to build the confidence of the store owners to apply for and manage loans, open bank accounts, purchase micro insurance, and explore other formal financial services. The business management components help store owners to improve their business performance by, for example, tracking expenses and reducing costs or taking on new revenue generation opportunities such as qualifying to become branchless banking agents. The content of the courses is adapted in language and form to the social and cultural conditions of each of the six host countries. Monitoring determines how participating retailers' businesses have improved since beginning the program. Each retailer receives a visit from a Fundes consultant who assesses changes in key indicators from the baseline, including sales, number of customers, customers' average purchase, inventory rotation, and expenses. Certificates recognize participating retailers' investment and achievement. Finally, approximately 20% of participating retailers receive invitations to participate in a leadership module. The most outstanding program participants have the opportunity to present an action plan, with the support of SABMiller, enabling them to develop an initiative for social entrepreneurship to their communities.

The program's effectiveness has to receive evaluation along four dimensions using control groups:[23] the business dimension (sales, costs, and margin), the family dimension (income and well-being), the community leadership dimension (self-esteem or community organization), and permanence over time. These dimensions use a set of several Key Performance Indicators.[24] KPIs for the business of the Tendero focus on the increase in sales, reduction in costs, and improvement in quality, profit margin, and business assurance; KPIs for the tendero and his/her family focus on the increase in family revenue, family life plan, availability of leisure, and improvement in quality of life; KPIs for the Community focus on the social entrepreneurial initiatives, projection of the tendero's leadership, information and communication, and recognition; and KPIs for the company evaluate the compliance with responsible sales, reputation, etc. The company uses a Social Return of Investment (SROI) methodology to evaluate the effectiveness of the program, with a baseline of April 2014. The measurement process looks at the jobs created, income generated, and the change in life conditions on four levels: business, personal, family, and community.

The 4e program is still in its early days, with two years and five cycles of training completed as of August 2015. The program finished the first implementation phase with 3,614 tiendas. SABMiller increased its sales through the traditional channel by approximately 39%, while store owners achieved a sales increase of 17% and margin increase of 2%.[25] Tiendas are transforming into drivers of local development and there is an evident increase in customer loyalty. SROI (social rate of return on investment) is determined

[23]   Jenkins 2014.   [24]   Jenkins 2014.   [25]   SABMiller 2015.

at 30.43%, which implies that each peso invested yields 3.04 pesos in terms of benefits.[26] Effectiveness of the program is also visible in a profit increase of SABMiller of USD 105000 and in an increase of 11% of owners with an assigned salary for managing the business.[27] Participation of the families in the use of profits increased by 8 points, the value of new jobs generated USD 18000 a year.[28] Among the beneficiaries, 63.3% feel that the program fulfilled their expectations, especially in terms of the improvement of their businesses and the quality of life of their families.[29] For 80.8% of them, the program has a very high benefit because it raised their self-esteem, developed their competences, and created an interest in the community. Finally, in August 2015, *Fortune Magazine* recognized the 4e program by ranking SABMiller nineteenth out of fifty companies. It's editors, along with experts from the non-profit consulting firm FSG, described the Company as making a "sizeable impact on major global social or environmental problems as part of their competitive strategy."

Targeting 40,000 store owners across 6 LAC countries' base and MoP by 2018, and 200,000 by 2020, 25% of stores in the region, of which 20% are able to survive,[30] SABMiller believes that via this program, it could touch up to 10 million people in the same segments, directly and indirectly. Overall, SABMiller will invest USD 17 million[31] to benefit 200,000 store owners in that period. SABMiller's aspiration is that the project creates a model that can be replicated and improve people's lives across the globe. SABMiller intends to expand its scope in different ways. Firstly, the company's sales force database should play a critical role in ensuring continuous communication by tracking the project and trainees. This will help create a mentoring system to continue to work with the entrepreneurs after the training. Furthermore, the company intends to introduce technology into the training activities and will pilot a project in LAC this year.

Case Study 3: Bimbo (Mexico)

Grupo Bimbo is the largest baked goods manufacturer in the world, with more than 4% global market share in an industry valued at USD 339 billion in 2015. In 2015 alone, estimations for Grupo Bimbo's sales revenue were about USD 14.19 billion. Lorenzo Servitje, Roberto Servitje, Jaime Jorba, Alfonso Velasco, Jaime Sendra, and José T. Mata founded the Company on December 2, 1945,

[26]   SABMiller 2015.   [27]   SABMiller 2015.   [28]   SABMiller 2015.
[29]   SABMiller 2015.   [30]   Jenkins 2014.   [31]   SABMiller 2015.

with headquarters in Mexico City, Mexico. Its current CEO is Daniel Servitje Montull. At home, Bimbo's well-developed distribution infrastructure has enabled it to offer strong retail coverage across Mexico, reaching even small tienditas in remote towns and villages. Globally, Bimbo currently operates 165 plants, 1700 sales centers and 2 million retail outlets in 19 countries throughout Asia, Europe and the Americas, with more than 21,370 employees. Their broad product portfolio includes more than 10,000 products at affordable prices including fresh and frozen bread, pastries, cookies, crackers, and tortillas as well as salted snacks and other packaged goods. It is renowned for its 100 globally recognizable trademarks including Bimbo, Orowheat, Arnold, Marinela, Thomas' Barcel, Sara Lee, Rocolino, Tia Rosa, and others.

The company's sales and distribution networks are the world's largest, with more than 52,000 routes and 129,000 sales associates. Its exceptional design and execution represent a key competitive advantage of Grupo Bimbo in Mexico and abroad. Grupo Bimbo aims to maximize their distribution reach through scale, technology, and infrastructure. Some of the ways this is achieved is through pre-sales, mobile and onsite sales, daily deliveries, night-time stocking, shelf-space optimization, branded display cases, and specialized support for tienditas, as well as differentiated product offerings for each channel. In eighteen of the markets in which they operate, Grupo Bimbo is responsible for both production and distribution and products are highly customized to meet local consumer needs.

Bakery products have long played an important role in Mexican consumer's diets, whether it be corn tortillas or sweetened baked goods. In Mexico, from 2006–2012 alone the industry grew by nearly 10%, favored by both positive economic conditions and demographic growth. Households made most purchases, representing 91% of all industry sales in 2012 with bread, baked desserts, and fresh pastry representing 54% of the industry. Grupo Bimbo maintained a market share of 9%, producing bread cookies, pastries, and chips under the brand names Bimbo, Lara, Barcel, Marinela, Ricolino, and Tia Rosa. Its second largest competitor is a subsidiary of Pepsi Inc. called GrupoGamesa S de RL de CV, with a share of 5%. T Gamesa, Chokis, and Surtido Rico Gamesa are some of its well-known product brands.[32]

Historically, Bimbo has maintained a strong presence at traditional grocery retailers where its highly developed logistics and distribution operations represent a key source of competitive advantage. It is not alone; many

---

[32]   *Euromonitor 2016a.*

large, corporate food and beverage conglomerates such as Coca Cola, Pepsi, and Grupo Bimbo have historically provided an important source of sales revenue for the tiendita retailers throughout Mexico. According to the INEGI, one of every 110 Mexicans owns a tiendita. There are an estimated 975,760 total tiendita retailers throughout Mexico. Most are considered survival businesses, providing a point of sale of consumer goods to the community and a source of employment, but in fact are often poorly administered and barely profitable. For example, on average a small tiendita sells 40,000 pesos per month of goods with a net profit of maybe 8,000 pesos, divided among four or five family employees and requiring long store hours. These traditional retail channels represent 35% of the spending budget of 32 million Mexican families who on average visit one of these small stores 276 times per year. However, an important limitation is that only 10% accept forms of payment other than cash such as credit cards, debit cards, and electronic food voucher cards. Poor productivity due to lack of technology and modern sales techniques and persistent threats of aggressive competition from newer, more modern store formats have forced small Mexican retailers to adapt or perish. To survive, these small family retailers must modernize their stores as well as adopt sales techniques that allow them to increase their productivity, sales revenue, and profitability through a broader product portfolio and higher sales volumes.[33]

One way Grupo Bimbo successfully grew its business through traditional distribution channels is with the electronic platform Red Quibo, which allows for the acceptance of electronic payments in traditional and small retail stores. It was created by a joint venture between Bimbo and the electronic payment company Blue Label, in alliance with VISA. This platform, now available in 200 municipalities throughout Mexico, is a platform designed by Bimbo that essentially modernizes the traditional retail store by allowing small store owners to gain access to technology that promises important productivity gains. The initiative had its roots in "The Better than Cash Alliance" promoted by the United Nations representing an association of governments, companies, and international organizations united in their desire to speed up the transition from cash to electronic payments to both combat poverty and stimulate the economy through the financial inclusion of small family retailers. According to Hortensia Contreras, VP of Services at Bimbo, more than 700,000 small, Mexican retailers do not currently offer this payment possibility. Specifically, in 2013, Grupo Bimbo and Visa signed an

[33]   *Forbes* 2017.

agreement that would jointly promote the acceptance of electronic payments in the small stores that carry their products throughout Mexico. Specifically, the alliance allows consumers to make purchases using both credit cards and debit cards with the support of Red Quibo, the transaction platform that also allows for payment of utility services, purchase of cell phone minutes, etc. The only requirement is that the small stores pay a 600-peso onetime membership fee to the Quibo network and a daily usage fee of 1.50 pesos. The store owners receive a commission, calculated as a flat fee when consumers make payments through the network. In essence, the network allows the store owners to increase their competitiveness while allowing them to participate formally in the financial system. This inclusion is accompanied by basic financial education and business training provided by Bimbo. For 2015 alone, it was estimated that 150,000 small tienditas in Mexico would be given access to the VISA sales terminals. While in their initial launch phase Bimbo intended to focus on the middle- and upper-income segments; they expect to reach the base of the pyramid as this segment often receives subsidies of government transfers through bankcards.

The business environment of Mexico, like most LAC emerging markets, is chaotic, complex, and unpredictable. Mexican multinational Grupo Bimbo has skillfully demonstrated execution excellence to adapt its business model to the operational and distribution realities of Mexico and other emerging markets where it enjoys a presence. This is particularly crucial in the bakery business where optimal efficiency in production and distribution is critical given the low margins that plague the industry. Profitability depends on the bakery's capacity to deliver just the right number of perishable products to stores at the right moment at an affordable cost. These stores, in Mexico and other emerging markets, are mostly the tiendita-type retail stores widely dispersed across distances in both marginalized urban areas and inaccessible rural ones. For decades, Grupo Bimbo demonstrated a near relentless pursuit of operational efficiency. For example, at the time of acquisition of Sara Lee, the US food and beverage conglomerate had lost much of its execution excellence and Bimbo turned it around.

Grupo Bimbo achieves distribution excellence through a variety of means. For example, it owns its own huge truck fleet for physical distribution, while adopting tricycle delivery in urban areas where streets are too narrow for trucks. Meanwhile, all of its trucks are equipped with modern computer information systems to optimize delivery routes. Bimbo boosted profitability and achieved a 1% savings in distribution costs in 2014 by implementing Oracle Transportation Management Cloud Service. By allowing the distribution managers to visualize the national baked goods distribution network, they succeeded in eliminating manual processes, saving on fuel and freight-carrying costs and achieving optimal use of both its transport infrastructure and their human resources. This enabled Grupo Bimbo to reduce time dedicated to product distribution from ninety minutes using local spreadsheets to forty-five minutes using the Oracle Transportation Management Cloud Service, thereby ensuring the timely delivery of baked goods each day. In addition, they have reduced human resource costs by efficiently assigning routes to operators and trucks and accurately calculating trips and operator payments. The centralization of transportation costs and rate information has allowed them to make the rate negotiation process more transparent and efficient. Similarly, the systems are used to automate trip calculation and forecast the number of trucks needed for food transport and therein eliminating many common scheduling errors. They have also adopted Oracle's BPEL Process manager cloud service, which automates sales order creations nationwide, replacing the previous forms unique to each plant and optimizing transport efficiency. In sum, they have employed state of the art technology to create centralized scheduling, ordering, assigning, and distribution processes throughout the country needed to optimize scarce resources and boost productivity.

Case Study 4: Natura Cosméticos (Brazil)

Natura Cosméticos SA is a Brazilian manufacturer of natural beauty and personal care products. Natura sources many of its raw materials from the Amazon rainforest and promotes itself as an ethical, environmentally sustainable company. It is the sixteenth largest beauty and personal care company in the world and the third largest direct seller.

Since its founding in 1969, its success has been driven by "relationship selling" through the work of its more than 1.9 million Natura consultants in Brazil, Argentina, Chile, Colombia, Mexico, Peru, and most recently France, who together reach more than 1.37 million Natura customers globally a year. Their commitment to building sustained relationships is embodied in the company's vision statement that affirms "the quality of its relationships, its products and services, and its commitment to building a better world with the nature they are part of."[34]

---

[34]   Natura 2015.

Since its foundation in 1969, distribution has been exclusively through direct sales. This was supported by the company belief in relationship selling. At the time, department stores hardly existed and there were few employment and professional development opportunities for Brazilian women at the time. By 2015, the company could pride itself on the impact this network of consultants had had not only on company sales but also on their communities; its 1.4 million independent consultants in Brazil earned, on average, sixteen times the national minimum wage and participated in corporate profit sharing as well.

Natura faces an uncertain future that will include reevaluation of its predominant direct sales distribution strategy. According to *Euromonitor*, 98%[35] of its sales were from LAC alone and 76% from Brazil. Given the weak economic prospects for the domestic economy, Natura must prioritize growth in global markets as it faces ever stronger local (Botocário) and international competitors (Lóreal) at home. Natura sales outside Brazil have been robust, growing at 17% in 2015 in the rest of the Americas region compared to 3% in Brazil. In 2013, it acquired 65% of Aesop Natural, personal care brand from Australia, which included its international distribution outlets. Natura announced new store openings were concentrated in the United States, Japan, Canada, and Germany, with the remainder in Australia, Asia, the Americas, and Western Europe. This included entry into new markets, including Canada, Macau, and Italy. Similarly, times have changed and Natura must develop alternative distribution channels besides direct sales. Brazilian consumers are switching to store based retail and online retail and Natura will have to switch along with them or risk losing them. In April 2016, it opened its first brick and mortar stores in Sao Paolo and Paris and has recently launched an e-commerce platform called Rede Natura where Natura consultants hold virtual meetings with customers and run their business. Its products are now sold in 1,200 drugstores throughout Brazil. The brand is also sold at stand-alone sites in department stores as well as via high-end beauty boutiques. Ultimately, the success of Natura will depend upon its ability to build the company as a truly global, relationship brand capable of developing alternate distribution strategies reflective of its increasingly modern and global consumer base.

---

[35] *Euromonitor* 2016b.

CONCLUSIONS

Physical distribution of goods remains a seemingly insurmountable challenge for businesses in LAC looking to tap into the region's elusive, emerging entrepreneurial and consumer middle class. As of 2015, one-fifth of the LAC population was found in difficult-to-access rural areas and another one-fifth in marginalized urban slums, the latter an undesirable by-product of the region's massive rural–urban migration phenomenon of the past few decades.[36] Inaccessibility is complicated by the fact that on average, only 25% of roads in LAC are paved.[37] Moreover, many of the emerging-middle-class entrepreneurs across LAC's least accessible regions lack the financial literacy and resources, technological expertise, and business acumen to grow and connect their small business enterprises with established businesses of large urban metropoles. The cases presented in this chapter exemplify the possibility of targeting and reaching the region's MoP business and consumer segments through innovative distribution models that address head-on the challenges that traditionally have characterized the region while preserving the social connection with their consumer communities that has allowed them to thrive for so long. Virtual Market, SABMiller LAC, Bimbo, and Natura demonstrate that innovative distribution models in LAC focused on increased productivity gains through the adoption of technology and modern retail practices, having a powerful impact on retailers and their surrounding communities. VM and Bimbo achieved this with technology, such as the Integrated Stores Management Kit promoted by VM, the integration of the Quibo payment system established by Bimbo, and the newly implemented Rede Natura of Natura cosmetics. SABMiller achieved modernization of small informal retailers mostly through the implementation of modern administration practices complemented by household management skills and community leadership

---

[36]   The World Bank 2015.   [37]   Reyes & Sawyer 2016.

training. Table 11.1 provides an overview of challenges, opportunities, and the innovative solutions companies used to tackle those.

Similarly, SABMiller and Bimbo expanded their companies' distribution throughout LAC through heavy reliance on the preexisting small-scale retailers that represent an importance source of employment, goods, and community relations throughout LAC. The important alliances forged through the 4e program enacted by SABMiller and the Red Quibo implemented by Bimbo were mutually beneficial, enabling these multinational companies to reach retailers and consumer segments. At the same time, entrepreneurs and small retailers gained meaningful employment, livelihoods, much needed business training, access to technology, and the finance necessary to grow their business. In the case of Natura, the company relied on the recruitment and training of MoP women as independent consultants to distribute the products themselves through direct sales in their communities, and in that way circumvented the access barrier.

In the SABMiller and Bimbo cases, international nongovernmental organizations played a pivotal role in providing much needed seed capital and know-how to undertake initial initiatives. SABMiller depended on financial contributions and expertise from Fundes, an international development organization dedicated to promoting the competitiveness of micro and small business enterprises throughout LAC. In the case of Bimbo, The United Nations Capital Development Fund provided the resources for Bimbo to accelerate the transition to digital payments through Red Quibo at tiendita retailers throughout Mexico. Alliances have equally played an important role in the case of Virtual Market, who used technology to empower strong alliances between suppliers, customers, retailers, and participating credit card companies to increase their productivity and boost sales. In conclusion, the significance of these distribution innovations cannot be overstated; empowering traditional distribution forms, whether they be retailers or direct sellers, not only allows them to grow sales for themselves and the companies whose goods they sell but also generates employment and livelihoods that ultimately create more

Table 11.1 *Opportunities, challenges, and innovations for the poor distribution channels in LAC's MoP*

Company	Virtual Market	SABMiller	Bimbo	Natura
Opportunity	The size of the MoP segment (micro-entrepreneurs and customers)	Size of the MoP segment (micro-entrepreneurs and customers)	The traditional channel as a means of livelihood for MoP in rural, semi-urban areas	Large country. Growing population. Dispersed MoP consumers with growing demand for consumer goods such as cosmetics
	Socio-cultural aversion of the MoP customers toward modern retailers	Traditional channel as a principal means of employment for MoP families	Current administration practices of traditional retailers' limit operations productivity	
	Trust and loyalty of MoP customers toward traditional retail channel	Traditional channel as a cohesive factor in communities	Traditional retailers are an important point of sale for fast moving consumer goods such as bread	
	Economic convenience of MoP traditional retailers	MoP entrepreneurs strong desire for successful businesses		
	Traditional channel as a source of good margins for manufacturers/suppliers	MoP entrepreneurs strong desire to improve the quality of life, self-esteem, education, and to help the communities around them		
	Inability of the MoP to combat the emerged modern retailer threat			

Challenge	Socio-cultural aversion of the MoP entrepreneurs toward modern technologies. Lack of MoP entrepreneurs' business skills and technological literacy. Limited, uneven and sporadic income streams of the MoP. Low quality and non-existent communication with suppliers. High retail prices, low product range, late deliveries	Lack of business and financial literacy of the MoP retailers. Lack of access to financing opportunities for the MoP entrepreneurs. Limited negotiating power of entrepreneurs, due to small ordering volumes and frequent deliveries. Limited and uneven income of the MoP retailers preventing investments	Access. Traditional retailers located in rural, semi-rural and urban communities with difficult access. Traditional retailers lack training in store management, sales practices, finance, inventory management. Future sales growth limited by lack of technology, non-acceptance of forms of payment other than cash	No modern retailers nearby. Access hard to reach MoP consumers through direct sales
Innovation	User-friendly all-inclusive tools connecting retailers, suppliers, creditors into single value chain	All-inclusive social development program entailing MoP, environment, economy, and the company	Own transportation fleet. Innovation of vehicle types: truck, small truck, bicycle—. Centralize distribution decisions via cloud	Direct sales, mostly by women. Relationship selling particularly suited to LACn cultures who value trust.

Table 11.1 (*cont.*)

Company	Virtual Market	SABMiller	Bimbo	Natura
	Personal approach through direct sales and after-sale support fostering trust and relationships Training micro-entrepreneurs in technology and retail practices Revenue model minimizing financial pressure for retailers	Empowering traditional retailers through training businesspeople, heads of household and agents of change Building links with companies, financial institutions, government agencies, academia	technology to guarantee timely delivery of goods. Alliance between Bimbo, Visa and Blue Label provide for installation and training of small retailers in use of POS technologies, electronic payments	Face to face direct selling, now also online via Rede Natura.
Effect	Connecting retailers, suppliers in 24/7 real-time communication Promotions, loyalty programs for customers and entrepreneurs Optimized deliveries and inventory structure in the stores	Increased incomes, protection from financial risks, better nutrition, health care, education, Expanded access to products and services in communities through the	Distribute consumer goods too hard to reach retail outlets in emerging markets Financial inclusion of MoP retailers across Mexico Increased store sales. Greater store productivity through	Income and employment for 1.8 million Natura independent consultants. Satisfaction of MoP consumer needs.

Analytic options for retailers and suppliers

Lower prices, flexible payments, wider product range for customers

Higher revenues all

Mom-and-pop shops as a strong market competitor

empowerment of traditional retailers

Increased confidence of store owners to apply for loans, bank accounts, insurance

Improved retailer's business performance,

Store owner's and SABMiller's sales increase

Tiendas as drivers of local development

Increase in customer loyalty

Increase in participation of families and job generation

technology. Impact of greater store profitability on community.

Source: Authors

sustainable, viable communities in the region's emerging economic areas. One of the most important lessons to be drawn is how closeness to the customers in the middle of the pyramid helps businesses grow. Either connecting with the local people or using previously established relationships and distribution channels allows trust to flourish in the firms, so that their innovations are accepted and endorsed. In this sense, when the customers lack proper training or education regarding a specific aspect of the innovation, providing said training would be beneficial for both the clients and the firms in the long run.

REFERENCES

Azevedo, V., Baigún, A., Bouillón, C., Duke, D., & Gallardo, M. 2015. A Rising 750 million $ Market. Inter-American Development Bank. Accessed August 18, 2017. https://webcache.googleusercontent.com/search?q=cache:H0_-dmObzTYJ: https://publications.iadb.org/bitstream/handle/11319/6992/A_Rising_US%24750_ Billion_Market.pdf+&cd=1&hl=es-419&ct=clnk&gl=mx

Euromonitor. 2016a. Grupo Bimbo SAB de CV in packaged food Mexico. Euromonitor. Accessed August 17, 2017. www.euromonitor.com/packaged-food-in- mexico/report

Euromonitor. 2016b. Natura Cosméticos SA in beauty and Personal Care. Euromonitor. Accessed August 17, 2017. www.euromonitor.com/packaged-food-in-mexico/report

Forbes. 2017. Grupo Bimbo invertirá 700 mdd durante 2017. Forbes. Accessed August 18, 2017. www.forbes.com/companies/grupo-bimbo/ http://dx.doi.org/ 10.1787/leo-2017-en

Hussmanns, R. 2003. Guidelines Concerning a Statistical Definition of Informal Employment in: Seventeenth International Conference of Labour Statisticians (Geneva, November 3, December 2003), Report of the Conference; Doc. ICLS/17/ 2003/R; International Labour Organization. International Labor Office, Geneva. Accessed August 13, 2017. http://ilo.org/public/english/bureau/stat/download/ papers/def.pdf

Inter-American Development Bank. (2015). A Rising 750 million $ Market: Unlocking Opportunities at the Base of the Pyramid in Latin America and the Caribbean, Inter-American Development Bank. https://webcache.googleuser content.com/search?q=cache:H0_-dmObzTYJ:https://publications.iadb.org/bit stream/handle/11319/6992/A_Rising_US%24750_Billion_Market.pdf+&cd=1& hl=es-419&ct=clnk&gl=mx

International Finance Corporation. 2007. The Next 4 Billion: Market Size and Business Strategy for the Base of the Pyramid. International Finance Corporation. Accessed August 16, 2017. http://pdf.usaid.gov/pdf_docs/pnadl883 .pdf

International Labour Organization. 2003. Guidelines Concerning a Statistical Definition of Informal Employment in: Seventeenth International Conference of Labour Statisticians (Geneva, November 24 to December 3, 2003), Report of the Conference; Doc. ICLS/17/2003/R; International Labour Office, Geneva.

Jenkins, B. 2014. *Empowering Small Businesses in Corporate Value Chains: The Case of SABMiller's 4e Camino al Progreso Program.* Cambridge, MA: The CSR Initiative at the Harvard Kennedy School and Business Fights Poverty.

McKinsey & Company. 2015. Perspectives on Retail and Consumer Goods. September 2015. McKinsey Practice Publications. USA. Accessed August 16, 2017. www.mckinsey.com/industries/retail/our-insights/perspectives

McKinsey Global Institute. 2011. Building globally Competitive Cities: The Key to Latin American growth. McKinsey Global Institute. Accessed August 18, 2017. https://mobileservices.mckinsey.com/global-themes/urbanization/building-com petitive-cities-key-to-latin-american-growth

Natura. 2015. Natura Annual Report. *Natura.* Accessed August 18, 2017. http://natu .infoinvest.com.br/enu/5679/Natura_RA_2015_versao_completa_ENG_v2.pdf

OECD/ECLAC/CAF. 2016. Latin American Economic Outlook 2017: Youth, Skills and Entreclacpreneurship, OECD Publishing, Paris. Accessed August 18, 2017. www.oecd.org/dev/americas/E-Book_LEO2017.pdf

Pisani, M. J. & Yoskowitz, D. W. 2012. A Study Of Small Neighborhood Tienditas in Central America. *Latin American Research Review* 47/4, Special Issue: 116–138.

Reyes, J. & Sawyer, C. 2016. *LAC Economic Development.* New York: Routledge.

SABMiller. 2015. Annual Report 2015. *NYU.* Accessed August 18, 2017. http:// people.stern.nyu.edu/adamodar/pc/blog/SABAnnualReport2015.pdf

The Economist. 2013 Mammon's New Monarchs: The Emerging-World Consumer Is King. *The Economist,* January 5th. Accessed August 16, 2017. www.economist .com/news/business/21569016-emerging-world-consumer-king-mammons-new-monarchs

The World Bank. 2015. Urban Population as % of Total. The World Bank. Accessed August 18, 2017. http://data.worldbank.org/indicator/SP.URB.TOTL.IN.ZS/ countries/1W-ZJ?display=graph

12 Innovating for the Middle of the Pyramid in Emerging Countries
Doing Well by Doing Good

Alvaro Cuervo-Cazurra and Miguel A. Montoya

INTRODUCTION

A typical view of income distribution in emerging economies is of countries composed of two types of consumers, a tiny wealthy elite and a massive poor class. This was typified in the metaphor of "Belindia," which although used to describe Brazil as consisting of two countries, a wealthy one such as Belgium and a very poor one such as India in the 1970s,[1] it is still being applied to other emerging countries.[2] One outcome of this polar wealth distribution was managers of advanced economy multinationals directing their firms toward serving the wealthy classes with the same products they sold to consumers in their home countries. The introduction of the concept of the base of the pyramid[3] changed this attitude. Even though the large segment of the population at the base of the income pyramid could not afford the products offered by foreign multinationals, they were nevertheless a potentially profitable market if only multinationals would locally adapt and innovate their products to make them very inexpensive. The result was a reinforcement of the bimodal segmentation of consumers in emerging markets: a small wealthy segment that are global consumers, and a large poor segment that are local consumers.

However, such an enduring view of consumers in emerging markets no longer seems to be accurate because of the appearance of a new and growing middle-class segment, which we call the middle of

---

[1]   Bacha 1974 introduced this idea in a discussion of income distribution.
[2]   Wolf 2015.
[3]   This concept was popularized by Prahalad and Hammond 2002 and Prahalad 2005.

the pyramid. The integration of emerging markets in global trade and investment networks and the implementation of pro-market reforms that lowered regulations resulted in not only the transformation of global value chains but also the growth of emerging economies. This growth helped many people come out of poverty and join *en masse* a new market segment: the middle of the income pyramid in emerging economies.

These new middle classes are transforming not only their countries as economic growth shifts from export to consumption, but also the products and services that domestic and foreign firms can offer. The new middle classes have increasing disposable income and, more importantly, increasingly aspirational desires that result in demand for new products. They are no longer content with getting the ultra-low-cost with no features products that they bought when they were poor or the stripped-down version of the products from advanced economies that some multinationals are offering them. Instead, they want high-quality, innovative products that match their self-perception of no longer being poor but still demand the low prices they are willing to pay.

Thus, the middle of the pyramid in emerging economies has become a new market that requires local and foreign firms alike to innovate their offers to match the new needs. The innovative products have to fit two demands that seem to be incompatible. One is that they have to be new and high-quality products that match the aspirational desires of the new middle classes. Another is that they have to be priced low to match the lower levels of income that the middle of the pyramid has in comparison to the middle classes in advanced economies. This is not impossible. The companies analyzed in this book illustrate how achieving this is possible. They have created products and services that are both high quality and innovative, and at the same time, are affordable. Moreover, these products are truly innovative. They are not just simplified versions of existing products, but products created from the ground up. Firms consider the demands of the new middle classes and design products and services that meet these demands and that can be produced and distributed at a low price while still providing the companies with a steady profit. They illustrate how companies can do well by doing good, building profitable businesses that serve the new needs of the middle of the pyramid in emerging economies.

Thus, in this chapter, we explain how firms were able to design and introduce successful innovations for the middle of the pyramid across a large spectrum of industries. The main lessons are the following. First, the middle of the pyramid in emerging economies requires new products and services from the ones that are traditionally offered by domestic and foreign firms, given their new higher aspirational demands, but still low income.

Second, successful innovations for the middle of the pyramid tend to start with an understanding of these demands and are designed to provide as many features as possible while still being sold at a low price. Many of these innovations are not the result of large-budget research and development investments, but rather are the outcome of a creative understating of the new needs and the design of processes that enable the firm to create innovative products and services at a low cost. The innovations of the middle of the pyramid can be moved upmarket at a later stage to serve higher-income segments that appreciate the innovation and lower prices provided by the products. This trickle-up of the innovations can be combined with the international expansion of the firms that market the products to serve the needs of the middle-of-the-pyramid segments in other countries.

Finally, these innovations are designed to be sold profitably and help consumers improve their lives, thus fulfilling the conflicting demands of doing well by doing good. Some companies choose, as part of their social mission, to build innovations for the middle of the pyramid that are subsidized or supported by other sources of income, while other firms create business models that are self-sustaining with the sale of innovative products. The process of developing innovations are similar, with the difference in the firms being their view of the role of companies in society and the willingness to subsidize the innovations to serve a large segment of the population that includes not only the middle but also the lower segment of the income pyramid. Both types of firms help do good and provide most individuals in emerging economies with better products and services than before.

THE MIDDLE OF THE PYRAMID: THE NEW MIDDLE CLASSES IN EMERGING MARKETS

Discovering the Middle of the Pyramid in Emerging Economies

The middle classes in emerging markets have not been discussed much as a target market. This is partly because, until recently, this segment was relatively small and in some countries considered non-existent. In emerging economies, there tends to be a much higher disparity in wealth than in advanced economies.[4] Consumers tend to be polarized. On the one hand, there is a small upper class that has a very high level of wealth and is served with the products and services used in advanced economies. On the other hand, there is a large majority of very poor consumers that are usually served by local firms that produce simple and inexpensive products.

The ignorance of the middle classes in emerging economies is also partly driven by their differences with the middle classes of advanced economies in terms of their aspirations and income levels. The middle of the pyramid in emerging markets is not easy to identify in terms of the level of income. Although they are, by definition, those consumers who have an average or median income in the country, such a statistical approach is misleading as managers of multinationals from advanced economies tend to reflect on their experience with the middle classes in their home countries and assume that the middle of the pyramid in emerging economies has just a slightly lower income than the ones in advanced economies. This could not be more wrong. The level of income that qualifies as middle class in advanced countries would qualify as high income in emerging economies. Moreover, the middle classes in emerging

---

[4] For some discussions of inequality within and across countries, see De Ferranti et al. 2004, Lopez-Calva & Lustig 2010, Milanovic 1998, Piketty 2015, and Ravaillon 2001.

economies were until recently poor in terms of income and have only just become middle classes, with a different outlook on consumption and a willingness to pay for aspirational products and services.

Income Segments in Emerging Economies

Before discussing the middle classes in emerging economies, it is useful to dispel some myths on the three income segments: upper classes, the base of the pyramid, and the new middle of the pyramid. Although they are related in name across countries, their actual levels and patterns of consumption differ significantly between advanced and emerging economies.[5]

The upper class in emerging markets: Conspicuous, global consumers. The upper classes are self-made entrepreneurs who have created successful private companies, politically connected entrepreneurs and former government officials who control state assets and have used the connections to extract rents, or government officials who have used their position in power to become wealthy, in some cases as a result of bribery.

In many countries, this upper class has remained at the top of the country for generations, partly because they can educate their offspring in top schools at home and abroad, and partly because of the importance of family connections in establishing and maintaining relationships that facilitate business activities. This, of course, is not a pattern that prevails in all countries. Formerly communist countries do not have a tradition of private property until recently, and thus their upper classes are newly created, and are just experiencing a first inter-generational transfer of control in companies and the wealth associated with this.

---

[5] More detailed explanations of the middle classes in emerging economies that underpin the ideas discussed in this section are available in Banerjee & Duflo 2008; Dayton-Johnson 2015; Easterly 1999; Ferreira et al. 2013; Goodman & Robinson 2013; Kharas 2010; Lopez-Calva & Ortiz-Juarez 2014; Ravallion 2001, 2009; and Vidich 2016. *The Economist* 2009 provides an accessible summary.

Regardless of the source of wealth, these upper classes are, in many cases, obvious conspicuous consumers, with logos and brands being the primary driver of purchase and the associated exclusivity that being able to afford luxury products brings. This is especially the case when those luxury products are purchased on trips to advanced countries with the associated cachet of being able to take the trip and to buy what is perceived as a superior product because it is created in a more advanced country. Many of these upper classes have a much higher status and quality of life in emerging economies as a result of being able to hire a multitude of employees to cater to their needs, with in-house service and servants that are uncommon among all but the wealthiest consumers in advanced economies.

The lower class in emerging markets: feast and famine. The polar opposite in emerging economies are the lower classes, which constituted the majority of the population in many countries only a generation ago and are still the majority in many nations. This is the segment that, for the most part, has been outside much of the global economy and has been served by local entrepreneurs and domestic companies with low-quality, low-priced products and, in many cases, has been underserved.

These consumers are mostly underemployed and work in the informal sector, working for others and being paid at the end of the work or week. They tend to have very low levels of education, and in many cases left school to work as children or teenagers to support the family. They are also internal migrants within the country, moving from the countryside to the city and thus losing the support infrastructure of the extended family.

Their very low levels of income and the unpredictability of their income lead them to purchase products based on price. The result is bouts of feast and famine, in some cases literally, with consumers going on shopping sprees after being paid and then running on the purchased products until they are paid again.

The middle class in emerging markets: new high demands at low prices. The middle of the pyramid in emerging economies differs from both these two segments, as well as from the middle classes in advanced economies that most managers have in mind. Whereas managers in advanced economy firms might be coming from the upper- and middle-income segments, managers in emerging economies tend to be coming from the upper segment. Thus in both cases, they have a miss-perception of what the middle classes in their countries look like.

Although middle classes are definitionally those who have a level of income in the middle of the income pyramid, even their identification is tricky.[6] There are two main approaches, an absolute, global one, and a relative, local one. The global approach aims to identify the middle classes across countries to facilitate the comparison and identification of market opportunities on a global scale. The specific levels vary, but they tend to settle around individuals whose income is between the average GNI per capita of Brazil and that of Italy in power purchasing parity as a quick rule of thumb, which results in those whose incomes were between about USD 16000 and 42000.[7] Alternatively, there is a variation of cutoff points to use, such as defining middle classes as those with incomes of between USD 10 and USD 50 per day like what the Pew Research Foundation does, which results in much lower levels of between USD 3650 and USD 18250 per year;[8] or using the level of the USD 1.90 as the international poverty line the World Bank uses (or the Lower Middle Income Class Poverty Line of USD 3.20 PPP and Upper Middle Income Class Poverty Line of USD 5.50 PPP), which results in annual incomes of USD 600 per year[9] (USD 1168 and USD 2007 for the lower and middle income countries). Of course, this level of income is critiqued as not

---

[6]   See alternative approaches in Birdsall, Graham, & Pettinato 2000; Jayadev & Reddy 2018; Milanovic 2011; Milanovic & Yitzhaki 2001; and Ravallion 2009.
[7]   World Bank 2019.   [8]   Kocchar 2015.   [9]   World Bank 2019.

taking into account the large differences across countries, since, in the US, for example, an individual is considered poor with an income of USD 13000, which is not far from the threshold of the global middle class but would rarely be considered so,[10] while in a country such as China the government establishes that the middle class starts at CNY 60000 per year, or about USD 7250.[11] The relative middle classes take into account the differences in income distribution within the country and show a much higher level of variation, limiting the comparison across countries but facilitating the analysis of the evolution of income within the country. Thus, going back to the example of China, whereas the Chinese government identifies the middle class as those with income between CNY 60000 to CNY 500000 per year (USD 7250 to USD 62500), McKinsey prefers the levels of CNY 75000 to CNY 280000 per year (USD 11500 to USD 43000).[12]

A more challenging issue is that the middle classes differ not only by income but also by attitude. In many cases they were poor until very recently but have been progressing in their jobs and some have been able to obtain formal jobs that provide them with a more stable stream of income that helps them better plan for the future. Nevertheless, individuals in the middle of the pyramid do not have the excess income that enables them to withstand well the loss of a job. Finding and moving across formal jobs in emerging economies is challenging for individuals with limited training, as they face ample competition from the informal economy and its applicants' lower wages and higher flexibility.

The low income of the middle classes, in general, appears to mean that they are unable to purchase durable goods or are unable to finance them because they have low and irregular incomes. This opens the opportunity for firms to design business models that address these issues, establishing new ways of providing finance for

[10]   United Census Bureau 2019.   [11]   China Power 2017.
[12]   China Power 2017.

consumers that would be ostracized by the traditional banks and have typically relied on loan sharks or family support to be able to make large purchases. They either have to pay very high levels of interest to the loan sharks or have to limit the purchase to what the extended family can afford to save and share.

Another characteristic of the middle of the pyramid is that they are demanding of the products they purchase because they have aspirational levels and are willing to pay more for products that are perceived to provide them with a status. This is an important and distinctive difference between the poor and the middle classes. The middle of the pyramid were until recently considered poor by all standards. Nevertheless, they now have disposable income and a change in attitude toward the way in which they purchase products. They have a willingness to pay extra for products that are not only qualitatively better but can provide a measure of additional self-esteem and signaling of no longer being poor. This is not the conspicuous consumption of the upper classes who are willing to spend for the sake of spending to impress others, but it becomes a variation of this in which the middle-of-the-pyramid consumers are willing to spend extra to be able to show that they are no longer poor. Nevertheless, they do not have the level of excess income that would enable them to spend without caring for the price. On the contrary, they become very demanding consumers, and because they have a limited income, they require the best quality that their income can afford. Their excess income enables them to try new products that before were out of their reach and at the same time they are thinking about the cost of the products and the alternative value they could have obtained with the money spent elsewhere.

The middle of the pyramid is avid consumers as they are replacing products that they could barely afford when they were poor, and are first-time buyers of many products, especially durable goods and services. When they were poor, they purchased products for which they had the income, eschewing the purchase of many products that were deemed outside their reach. As they become middle of the pyramid, they have the additional income that enables them to replace products they purchased when they were poor for better quality ones. The extra income also enables them to purchase products and services for the first time, but they analyze these purchasing decisions carefully because they do not have enough income to try different products and compare their quality. At the same time, they do purchase products sequentially until they find the ones that meet their needs better.

They are also first-time buyers of services, not only the leisure services associated with being middle class but also services that are underprovided by the government, such as health care and education. One of the signs of being middle class is, in addition to having excess income, having excess time that can be used for leisure. These middle-of-the-pyramid consumers are able and willing to spend time in pursuit of relaxation and are willing to invest money in this, in some cases saving throughout the year to be able to splurge during a vacation or leisure activity, or enjoying the vacation or activity and then paying for this in installments during the rest of the year. As first-time consumers, they need to be educated on how the new products and services work. They are also more demanding with the new products as they are considering the personal cost of savings or future payment that the leisure activity will require.

The middle of the pyramid also comprises first-time buyers of goods that elsewhere are provided by the government, but that in emerging markets are underprovided. Public goods that tend to be taken for granted in advanced economies such as health care, education, or safety are in many emerging economies underprovided or not available from the government.

Thus, these middle-of-the-pyramid emerging economies require innovations that can meet their particular needs and still be delivered at a low price point. These are not just stripped-down versions of existing products but innovative products. Firms in emerging markets seem better positioned to understand and deliver on such needs.

INNOVATING FOR THE MIDDLE OF THE PYRAMID IN EMERGING COUNTRIES

Emerging economies have changed from being a destination for innovations created in advanced economies to becoming the source of new products and services sold there and eventually worldwide. Traditionally, emerging economies were the market for innovative products created in advanced economies or places in which these products are copied and mass produced. Instead, they are becoming the source of truly innovative products, some of which are being marketed in advanced economies. Traditionally there was an implicit assumption that innovations were created in advanced economies, which can rely on a supportive innovation system, educated workforce, and strong protection of intellectual property rights. As a result, the study of innovation in emerging markets tended to receive less attention. This is partly because the challenging innovation system of emerging markets leads many to assume that firms cannot create new products because they do not have a supportive institutional environment, highly educated workforce, or protection of intellectual property. Thus, many of the new products and services created by these firms were dismissed as imitations of existing products. This criticism misses the importance of understanding the sources of innovation that enable products to be adapted to the needs and income of poor consumers, or the sophisticated processes and business models that support the advantage of these firms.

The chapters in the book challenged these assumptions to reveal that firms in emerging markets can indeed innovate and do so to create new products and services that are effective at meeting the needs of consumers and that these are genuine innovations in the sense of being new to the world. Moreover, the analysis of innovations for the middle of the pyramid reveals that these are a new type of innovation from the traditional dichotomy between lavish and frugal innovation, as they fit a different type of need.

Traditional Types of Innovation: Lavish and Frugal Innovations

In broad terms, we can group our understanding of the types of innovation[13] into two broad types: what we call lavish innovations, which are the usual innovations created in advanced economies offering new features at a premium price for high income individuals; and frugal innovations, which are being developed in emerging economies and provide good enough products at a very low price for poor individuals. The innovations for the middle classes seem to fit in between these two archetypes, as they provide many features and an aspirational desire but are nevertheless marketed at a low price.

On one hand, lavish innovation is the typical innovation identified in most studies. The novelty and the ability to solve new and, in many cases, unknown needs of consumers are the main drivers of the creation of such innovations. These innovations are sold based on the novelty and on the additional features provided. The target market is wealthy individuals who are able and willing to pay a premium for the products, as they are early users of the technology and are looking for new products that can complement their image among their peers. These innovations usually go through short-term cycles in which improved and new versions are introduced to entice consumers to replace their previous products with more innovative ones. This is the case even if many of the changes are not providing much improvement over the previous version, and many of the features are not fully used.

On the other hand, frugal innovations are the common innovations that have been identified in recent times as being created in emerging economies. These innovations are targeting the base-of-the-pyramid market segment with products that are of very low cost.

---

[13] Deeper reviews of lavish innovations appear in the handbooks edited by Dodgson, Gann, & Phillips 2014; Fagerberd, Mowery, & Nelson 2005; Hall & Rosenberg 2010; and Stoneman 1995. Explanations of frugal innovations are available in Leadbeater 2014; Radjou & Prabhu 2015; Govindarajan & Trimble 2012, Govindarajan & Ramamurti 2011; and Prahalad 2005.

The innovations in these products come, in many cases, from their adaptation so that they can be purchased at a very low price, for example because they are being sold in small packages or are being leased rather than sold to consumers. The objective of the innovations is to lower the price point at which the products can be sold profitably, as cost performance is the main driver of the innovation. The products do not require the inclusion of the latest technology as the consumers are unable and unwilling to pay a premium for advanced features and instead they want products that are designed to meet their basic needs.

Innovations for the Middle of the Pyramid

Innovations for the middle of the pyramid combine two aspects that, in principle, do not seem to be compatible: highly innovative products with new features that at the same time are sold at a low price. The traditional marketing view is that companies have to choose between either introducing innovative products and charging a premium for them as consumers are willing to pay for the new features, or introducing simple products that are marketed at a low price as consumers purchase the product based on their price. The innovations for the middle of the pyramid have to solve these two conflicting approaches. They have to provide products that have new and high-quality features so that they become aspirational in the mind of the middle of the pyramid. At the same time, they have to be priced low so that they are within reach of these middle classes that, while having more disposable income, are still not wealthy.

Innovating for the Middle of the Pyramid in Emerging Markets

There are three processes for innovating for the middle of the pyramid: downmarketing top-of-pyramid innovations, upmarketing bottom-of-pyramid innovations, and creating innovations for the middle of the pyramid. In the downmarket approach, innovations created for high-income consumers are stripped of most features to reduce their costs of production and thus the sale price. In the upmarket approach, innovations developed for poor consumers are given more features and increased prices. In the true innovations for the middle of the pyramid, firms take the needs and desires of the new middle-income consumers and create products that meet such needs. The three types of innovation processes can yield products that meet such needs, but they do so with different outcomes. Table 12.1 summarizes these three processes.

First, the downmarketing of top of the pyramid innovations is relatively simple as these innovations use existing products that have been already created for a higher income market. The company relies on the innovations successfully introduced to satisfy the needs of high-income consumers. It takes the product and strips the features that make it not only appealing for high-income consumers, but also that can create additional costs of production and distribution. It then simplifies the product for the middle-income segment to the point at which it can price the product at a level that the consumers can afford, and the firm can make a profit. This process might require innovating the materials or the production process, as there are fewer features and the materials might not be as high-end as before. The middle-income consumers thus get an aspirational product that has been marketed and sold for the upper classes at a price they can afford. This process has the danger that it may undermine the senses of exclusivity among the higher-income consumers who see versions of their high-end products in the hands of lower-income consumers and are thus alienated from continuing to purchase the products. It also suffers from the potential problem of making the middle-class consumers feel cheated. They think they are buying what they consider a luxury product and learn that they are not getting the same features they were expecting from the product even if the price is lower than usual. One way to get around this potential cannibalization of the high-end products with the lower-level version is to market the products with a different brand and distribution system to ensure a clear separation between the high and middle end. Joint ownership maintains the connection and aspirational features of the products. This is

Table 12.1 *Alternatives for developing innovations for the middle of the pyramid*

	Downmarketing top-of-the-pyramid innovations	Upmarketing base-of-the-pyramid innovations	Innovating for the middle of the pyramid
Customer value proposition	Aspirational product at a lower price	Better product at a still affordable price	Product that matches needs and aspirational desires
Starting point of innovation	Existing sophisticated, high-quality products with multiple features sold at a premium price to high-income individuals	Existing simple, good-enough products with limited features sold at the lowest price to poor individuals	Identify functional and aspirational features of the products that match the needs and desires of the middle of the pyramid individuals
Innovation process	Reduce features and quality in materials of an existing product to lower costs to the level at which the price matches what the middle of the pyramid can pay	Add new features and use better quality materials to improve the product to the level at which the product matches the aspirational desires of the middle of the pyramid	Determine the price point that meets the willingness to pay of the middle of the pyramid and design the product with the quality and features that matches the needs and desires
Limitations of the approach	Undermine the perception of exclusivity among the top-of-the-pyramid individuals Creation of perception of being cheated out of high quality among the middle of the pyramid	Not match aspirational desires from a lack of clear separation of products for the middle and bottom of the pyramid segments	Achieve profitability from an innovation that leads to imitation by competitors
Potential solution	Separate brand and distribution channels to ensure coherence in image	Redesign product to reduce confusion of target segment	Rapid scalability and expansion beyond the middle of the pyramid market to reach profitability

Source: Authors

a typical approach among designers who start with the exclusive and high-priced brands and then create lower level brands that provide some aura and cachet but that are clearly targeted toward the middle-income consumers.

Second, the upmarketing of bottom-of-the-pyramid innovations follows a different process as it requires taking a product that initially has been created for the base of the pyramid segment and adding new features that make it attractive to the middle of the pyramid. The original innovation was created with a limited set of features to cover the basic needs of the base of the pyramid consumers. Once these products are created, the innovation comes from adding more features that match not just the basic needs but also the aspirational needs of the middle of the pyramid. Consumers might be familiar with the products and might have purchased them when they were poor, but they are now looking for products perceived to be better quality and more aspirational. Thus, the company needs to redesign products so that they appear to be different from those sold to low-income consumers. This provides middle-of-the-pyramid consumers with the sense that the products are better than before and thus worth the higher price. This upmarket innovation is typical of most products as the additional features tend to result in an incremental increase in costs, if the production process is well designed, while the increase in price can be substantially superior to the cost. It also helps improve the image of the product and move it from being sold only on the basis of price to becoming sold based on features. The challenge of going upmarket is that the middle classes may want to purchase products that have more aspirational features and image than the products they were previously purchasing when they were in a low class. They may prefer new brands over the upmarket version of the brand they used to buy.

Third, innovating for the middle of the pyramid starts differently from the downmarketing and upmarketing of existing products since the departing point is the identification of the needs of the middle of the pyramid rather than the use of an existing product that is modified. This does not mean that the products are completely new to the world but that the starting point is to gain a sense of what the middle-of-the-pyramid consumers desire in terms of unmet needs and potential features of the product and then create a product or service that matches such needs. The identification can be done from understanding the needs of the base-of-the-pyramid consumers and following these consumers as they increase their income and alter their preferences for better products and services, which not only are sold on the basis of a low price but also on the basis of new features and an aspirational image.

The aspirational needs of the middle classes are driven by two subprocesses, the upgrading of existing products and the purchase of new products. On one hand, these aspirational needs can be driven by the middle of the pyramid having disposable income that enables them to purchase products that signal such excess income to others. This is a process of upgrading in which middle of the pyramid consumers buy products that are of better quality and have more features than the products they used to purchase when they were in the base of the pyramid and had no excess income to splurge. The company that has previously been serving such consumers can keep track of how, as they gain more income, they want better products than those they bought previously. This was, for example, the case of the sale of balls for consumers, which were based on an initial base of existing balls, whereby the firm redesigned the production process to upgrade the quality of the balls with new designs and graphics that appealed to the middle of the pyramid.

On the other hand, the aspirational needs can also be driven by the disposable income enabling the middle of the pyramid to access products that were before out of their reach but that are common among the middle and upper classes. In this process, the middle-of-the-pyramid consumers are new buyers for some product categories that were out of their reach when they were considered poor. As new buyers, they do not have the experience with purchasing the products but may likely be aware of the products being offered elsewhere and may set their expectations on the quality of the product by the firm that offers them the new product. For example, consumers who were not able to have access to a medical facility when they were poor started seeing doctors when they were sick at the offices located next to the pharmacies in Famacias Similares, setting their new aspiration in terms of the quality and price of the service by the company.

From the understanding of the aspirational needs, the next step is to design the products and services that meet such needs. This design differs from the other process in that the design of the product is first based on a still-low price that the middle of the pyramid can afford and then requires adding new features that such classes are unaccustomed to receiving and will entice them toward such product. The middle-of-the-pyramid consumers are no longer considered to be poor because they have higher incomes and in some cases more stable sources of income than when they were poor. However, many are still not quite fully established with a formal employment and a continuous stream of income and can easily fall back into poverty, limiting their ability to purchase high-priced products. They might be able to afford higher-priced products but are still constrained in their purchasing ability, and the price is still a large determinant of whether they will purchase the products. Thus, the challenge for the company is to determine the price point at which they want their product or service to be sold and then design the product that can match such price point and be sold profitably. This initial price point is important, because in many cases it sets a target in the mind of the consumers and from which it is later difficult to move upward. The new product is then sold as being different from what consumers experienced when they were poor and thus entices them to repeat the purchase. For example, the marketing of generic medicines to poor consumers was done initially by determining the low price point of the medicines that would make them affordable to the new middle classes but the pharmacies were newly designed to be well lit and look modern, with employees dressed in white coats to signal that the service was superior to what many were used to previously.

Once the new product is tested and the market provides a good reception, the next challenge is to ensure the scalability of the distribution so that the consumers and the firm can benefit from the economies of scale that provide lower costs of operations and thus can sustain the lower prices while providing a profitable operation. The scalability ensures that the innovation is not only reaching the middle of the pyramid in one area but that others with similar needs are also benefiting. This scalability requires that the business model upon which the innovation is created is profitable so that it can fund the continued growth of the firm. Finance to support the growth of a firm, especially a new one with a new business model, tend to be scarce in most emerging economies. This limits the scalability of many good ideas beyond what the initial operation provides. The innovations we indentified are not supported by donations in a not-for-profit model but are actually driven by profits that can ensure the continued expansion. This was the case, for example, of the provision of microlending to the urban classes in Mexico by the bank Compartamos. This used to be a not-for-profit that was transformed into a for-profit bank with the notion that by going into an initial public offering and becoming a publicly traded firm, it would provide the funds needed to scale the business and offer the services to a much larger segment of the population than was possible as a not-for-profit dependent on donations for its operations. The scalability serves not only to ensure the support of the firm but also as a demonstration that the business model is refined to the point at which it can be replicated in other locations outside the direct oversight of the entrepreneurs. The initial innovation for the middle of the pyramid needs refinement, not just in the innovation but mostly in the process of creation and delivery, and its replication across geographies forces the entrepreneur to determine which features resonate with the customers and which ones are not working out. However, the scalability of the innovation also means that many more competitors become aware of the innovation and will start imitating the key features. This is facilitated by the replication of the business model in which the innovation is distilled and transferred to new locations. This replicability by the firm means that competitors can also learn how to imitate the innovation with their operations. Even if the firm is unable to benefit from the innovation fully because competitors rush in to imitate the innovation, such diffusion of the innovation can be nevertheless beneficial for the middle of the pyramid. They have more providers from which they can purchase new products and services. These give a wider access and at the same time better products and services from continued competition among providers.

The final stage in innovating for the middle of the pyramid seems to be the expansion beyond the current middle of the pyramid in the current market in two alternative directions: other middle-of-the-pyramid markets in foreign countries, and the move upmarket in a trickle-up process. On one hand, international expansion enables the transfer of the innovation to other countries in which there are also new and growing middle classes that can benefit from and desire the innovations created by the firm. This expansion can open a new, much larger market in which the innovation can be sold profitably and thus contribute to a further reduction of the cost of production and potentially the price at which the innovation is being sold, thanks to the economies of scale that internationalization affords. There are three types of economies of scale that internationalization provides. The first one is the traditional economies of scale in the manufacture of the product for those that can be exported, with the firm being able to make full use of the production capacity by selling at home and abroad and thus reducing the unit costs. A second one is economies of scale in innovation, in which the expansion to a foreign market provides a higher return on the investments in the creation of the innovation, given that once the innovation has been created, the additional knowledge for adapting it to the particularities of foreign markets tends to be lower. The third one is the economies of scale in learning, as the foreign expansion enables the company to learn from new and subtle differences in the markets and refine and adapt the products, continuously improving them from introducing new requirements that lead to better products. This process of foreign expansion is not always successful, however, as it requires not just the identification of the new market and the transfer of the innovation to the new foreign market, but also the establishment of the relationships and distribution in the host country and the efficient coordination of operations. Additionally, in some cases, there might be already local competitors in place that have either come up with similar innovations for the middle of the pyramid on their own or imitated the innovations. The newly entering company may be at a disadvantage, as it lacks an established presence with suppliers and distributors.

Social problems are always more difficult to solve than market problems, so social innovations in emerging economies need additional or special financing or funding. Companies with social businesses for the middle of the pyramid have more risks than regular businesses. The venture philanthropy funds that combine equity investments, providing mezzanine financing as well as grants geared toward capacity building of the company, are a possible solution. There are associations, such as The Aspen Network of Development Entrepreneurs or The Global Impact Investing Network, and organizations, such as Promotora Social México [which has funded part of this research], that are dedicated to venture philanthropy in Latin America.

The alternative expansion is the trickle-up of the innovation to serve the needs of higher-end consumers, both at home and abroad.[14] At home, the trickle-up innovation leads to the marketing of the innovation to upper segments of the market who can pay for the innovation, and even if more sophisticated products already serve them, they nevertheless appreciate the innovative features offered by the innovations. This requires changing some of the marketing as well as some of the features so that the product or service becomes more appealing to the upper levels while it maintains the innovativeness and low price of the target group. In so doing, the product might receive an implicit enhancement in the image that further supports

[14] For a classic discussion of the diffusion of innovations, see Rogers 2010.

the aspirational perception among the middle-of-the-pyramid consumers. For example, the provision of medical services next to the
pharmacies was one feature that initially was developed for the
middle of the pyramid who did not have access to affordable health
care. This became a selling point to the upper classes, who could go to
the doctor as soon as they did not feel well, perhaps on their way to or
from work, in a convenient and fast way instead of having to make an
appointment at their usual doctor. This realization of the potential for
the trickle-up led the firm to start opening outlets in higher-income
neighborhoods from the traditional low and low-middle neighborhoods in which they had been operating. The new locations led to
the refurbishment of the doctor and pharmacy locales, which were
then transferred to other locations to increase the desirability and
appeal of the operations to the middle classes. The company can also
aim to move upmarket abroad by expanding into countries that have a
much higher-income middle class that are not driven by the low price
offered but rather by the innovativeness of the product or service.
Thus, for example, the cinema firm expanded in the United States
to offer a new concept of cinema service to high-income consumers
who appreciated the higher quality services of a movie plus a meal and
drink. This process differs from the so-called reverse innovation, in
which firms from advanced economies innovate their existing products in emerging economies and bring these innovations back to the
home countries to serve their existing consumers there. In the case of
the trickle-up of innovations for the middle of the pyramid, firms from
emerging economies are the ones that create the innovations to serve
the middle classes in their home countries. They then use such
innovations to expand both in more advanced countries and to serve
wealthier consumers than those they normally serve.

DOING WELL BY DOING GOOD

The innovations for the middle of the pyramid can help firms do well
by doing good. These innovations are designed to be sold profitably
and help consumers improve their lives, thus fulfilling the conflicting

demands of doing well by doing good. However, achieving the balance between social welfare and economic profitability is not easy. Some companies choose as part of their social mission to build innovations for the middle of the pyramid that are subsidized or supported by other sources of income, while other firms create business models that are self-sustaining with the sale of innovative products. The processes of developing innovations are similar, with the difference in the firms being their view of the role of companies in society and the willingness to subsidize the innovations to serve a large segment of the population that includes not only the middle but also the lower segment of the income pyramid.

This tension between social purpose and profitability leads to a classification of the types of companies into two types, depending on whether addressing social needs is the primary focus of the firm or whether it is secondary. Some companies are created with the sole objective of serving some social needs that the founders perceive as existing in emerging markets. The social needs can take the form of a lack of provision of finance for entrepreneurs, a lack of provision of health care for poor people, or a limited provision of quality education for the masses. In these cases, the founder first perceives the social need and then thinks about creating an organization that can address it. In contrast, other companies are created to generate value for the owners and society and end up creating products and services that address a social need as a secondary objective. In this case, the solution to social needs in emerging markets becomes a business proposition as a result of the relatively large levels of the middle of the pyramid. Thus, even though in both cases we end up with companies that create innovations for the middle of the pyramid and in essence come up with similar solutions, how they arrive at these solutions differs.

The innovations for the middle of the pyramid that these firms create can also be separated into two main types depending on whether the innovations are solving imperfections in the provision of public goods by governments or are solving market imperfections.

Some companies are focusing on areas that are usually the realm of government intervention because they have some public good nature. Unfortunately, in the case of emerging economies, many of these countries have governments that have a limited capacity for providing such public goods in the amount and quality that citizens need and that would help the country develop. In these cases, companies create innovations to address the under-provision of public goods tradition-ally created by the government, such as health care or education. Other companies focus on innovating in areas that are commonly addressed by the market in more advanced countries but are still underserved even by the market in the emerging economies because of the underdevelopment of markets, for example as a result of the higher levels of information asymmetries and transaction costs of emerging markets. These market imperfections remain unsolved, both by traditional companies as well as the government, which in emerging economies lacks much capacity and opens the possibility for some innovative entrepreneurs to create new products, services, and business models that solve these needs.

The result of these two types of firms and needs is a typology of innovations for the middle of the pyramid based on whether the companies have a primary or secondary social objective, and whether the companies are addressing areas that tend to be the focus of the government or the focus of the market. Table 12.2 illustrates this classification and places in it the companies that we analyzed in this book. The four types that result from such classification are the developmental entrepreneur, the social entrepreneur, the develop-mental capitalist, and the social capitalist.

Developmental entrepreneurs are companies that create innovations whose primary goal is to address the lack of provision of public goods by the government and do so with the underlying social objective in mind. These are, in many cases, done by not-for-profit organizations that have a social mission and compensate for the weakness of the government, or by foundations that provide subsid-ized goods to low-income consumers who do not have access to

Table 12.2 *Types of innovations for the middle of the pyramid*

		Type of imperfection addressed	
		Governmental	Market
Social objective of the company	Primary	**Developmental Entrepreneurs** Benestare Clinicas Azucar Farmacias Similares Hospital Solidaridad Innova Schools Khipu Institute Zapopana	**Social Entrepreneurs** Asegurador Rural Bradesco Colceramic Compartamos CrediAmigo Cumplo Echale a tu casa Fondo Esperanza Lendico Oxxo-GNP Patrimonio Hoy Pro Mujer Profin Regalii
	Secondary	**Developmental Capitalists** Fundacion Universitaria María Cano UNITEC Universidad Continental Universidad Interamericana	**Social Capitalists** BCI-Rabie Bimbo Casas Bahía Elektra Farmacias Similares Natura Permoda Rokys SABMiller LAC Sanchez y Martin Topitop Tricot Virtual Market

Source: Authors

government services. Different from these, we found for-profit companies that had seen in the lack of provision of public goods such as education or health care an opportunity to step up and solve this need, and whose missions were primarily the achievement of social development in the country but, unlike not-for-profits, doing it profitably to continue scaling the provision of the goods and services to the middle classes.

Social entrepreneurs are similar in the sense of having a social objective as the main driver of the business model but focusing on addressing imperfections in the market that limit the access to needed goods and services for the middle of the pyramid. These entrepreneurs rethought the lack of provision of goods and services that was common in countries with more sophisticated markets and found ways to get around the market limitations. These market imperfections were associated with the limited information in the middle of the pyramid and the challenges of writing contracts that are typical of emerging markets, and that prevented the new consumers from accessing products and services even when they were willing to pay for them. These social entrepreneurs created new business models that got around the market imperfections and enabled the middle of the pyramid to access products such as insurance, finance, and housing.

Developmental capitalists are companies that create secondary business models to provide public goods that are usually delivered by the government. These tend to be existing companies that have already been working on the provision of goods for customers and realize that there is still an unmet need on the part of the government that can be addressed, nevertheless, with a new way of providing the service. Some of the provisions are initially subsidized by the main business line of the firm, but the new product eventually becomes an independent and self-sustaining business proposition that helps address the government under-provision.

Finally, social capitalists are companies that are primarily driven by the achievement of returns but that happen to find a market opportunity that is unmet by existing companies and proceed to create business models that can fulfill these needs profitably. Even if the social objective is secondary to the profit objective, these firms are nevertheless fulfilling an unmet need by creating innovations that enable the middle of the pyramid to access goods and services that were outside their reach. These social capitalists operate in a variety of industries, illustrating that the market imperfections typical of emerging markets can be solved with innovative business models that also have a large positive externality in enabling the middle of the pyramid access to new and better products and services.

CONCLUSIONS

We analyzed the development of innovations for the middle of the pyramid in emerging economies. The main message of the book is that the middle of the pyramid of emerging markets is different from others and requires innovative products and services that can be sold at a profit and enable firms to do well by doing good.

The middle of the pyramid in emerging economies provides firms with many potential opportunities as they are becoming the largest segment of the population in the world, but they are usually misunderstood. They are neither similar to the middle classes in advanced economies that have had a much higher level of income for decades, nor are they similar to the poor in emerging economies who can barely cover their basic needs. These middle-of-the-pyramid consumers have new and unique aspirational needs and desires that are underserved because of imperfections in the provision of public goods by the government and goods and services by the market from the typical limitations of emerging economies.

Firms can take advantage of these opportunities to serve the middle of the pyramid, but this requires innovative approaches. The firms need to gain a new understanding of the needs of these middle classes in emerging economies and provide features that make the product aspirational while still producing and marketing it at a low price, as the middle classes have limited disposable income. The innovations that meet this high aspiration and low-price mix become later the basis of a scalable business model that can help the firm expand into new market segments and internationalize. Innovation to solve the problems of emerging countries will most likely not come from the big players in the sector.

In so doing, these for-profit firms illustrate how social and developmental objectives, even if secondary, can help provide goods and services that improve the lives of the middle of the pyramid while offering a profitable market for the companies. The firms thus mix the social with the profit motive in a way that has been in many cases portrayed as being incompatible, as they are able to solve important social needs of a large and growing segment of the population in emerging countries. Innovating for the middle of the pyramid shows that profits and social causes are not in conflict but can be integrated with some creative and innovative effort.

REFERENCES

Asakawa, K., Cuervo-Cazurra, A., & Un, C. A. 2015. Frugality-Based Advantage. Paper Presented at the Academy of Management 2015 Annual Meeting.

Autocar India. 2019. Tata Nano. Accessed May 17, 2019. www.autocarindia.com/cars/tata/nano

Bacha, E. L. 1974. O rei da Belindia: Uma fabula para tecnocratas. Jornal Opiniao, Sao Paulo.

Banerjee, A. & Duflo, E. 2008. What Is Middle Class about the Middle Classes around the World? *Journal of Economic Perspectives* 222 3–28.

Birdsall, N., Graham, C., & Pettinato, S. 2000. Stuck in the Tunnel: Is Globalization Muddling the Middle? Working Paper 14, Brookings Institution, Washington, DC.

China Power. 2017. How Well-Off is China's Middle Class? Accessed May 17, 2019. https://chinapower.csis.org/china-middle-class

Dayton-Johnson, J. (ed.). 2015. *Latin America's Emerging Middle Classes: Economic Perspectives*. New York: Palgrave Macmillan.

De Ferranti, D., Perry, G. E., Ferreira, F., & Walton, M. 2004. Inequality in Latin America: Breaking with History? The World Bank.

Dodgson, M., Gann, D. M. & Phillips, N. 2018. *The Oxford Handbook of Innovation Management*. New York: Oxford University Press.

Easterly, W. 1999. The Middle Class Consensus and Economic Development. The World Bank.

Fagerberg, J., Mowery, D. C., & Nelson, R. R. 2005. The Oxford Handbook of Innovation. New York: Oxford University Press.

Ferreira, F., Messina, J., Rigolini, J., López, L. F., Lugo, M. A., & Vakis, R. 2013. Economic Mobility and the Rise of the Latin American Middle Class. World Bank.

Goodman, D. & Robison, R. 2013. *The New Rich in Asia: Mobile Phones, McDonald's and Middle Class Revolution*. New York: Routledge.

Govindarajan, V. & Ramamurti, R. 2011. Reverse Innovation, Emerging Markets and Global Strategy. *Global Strategy Journal* 1: 191–205.

Govindarajan, V. & Trimble, C. 2012. *Reverse Innovation: Create Far from Home, Win Everywhere*. Boston: Harvard Business Review Press.

Hall, B. H. & Rosenberg, N. 2010. *Handbook of the Economics of Innovation*. Volume 1 and 2. Amsterdam: North Holland.

Jayadev, R. L. & Reddy, S. 2018. The Middle Muddle: Conceptualizing and Measuring the Global Middle Class. In M. Guzman (ed.), *Toward a Just Society: Joseph Stiglitz and Twenty-First Century Economics*: 63–92. New York: Columbia University Press.

Kharas, H. 2011. The Emerging Middle Class in Developing Countries. OECD Development Center, Working Paper no. 285. OECD: Paris.

Kochhar, R. 2015. A Global Middle Class Is More Promise than Reality. Pew Research Center. Global Attitudes & Trends. Accessed May 17, 2019. www.pewresearch.org/global/2015/07/08/a-global-middle-class-is-more-promise-than-reality

López-Calva, L. F. & Ortiz-Juarez, E. 2014. A Vulnerability Approach to the Definition of the Middle Class. *Journal of Economic Inequality* 12(1): 23–47.

López-Calva, L. F. & Lustig, N. C. (eds.). 2010. *Declining Inequality in Latin America: A Decade of Progress?* Baltimore, MD: Brookings Institution Press.

Milanovic, B. 1998a. *Income, Inequality, and Poverty during the Transition from Planned to Market Economy*. Washington, DC: World Bank: 237.

Milanovic, B. 1998b. *Worlds Apart: Measuring International and Global Inequality*. Princeton, NJ: Princeton University Press.

Milanovic, B. & Yitzhaki, S. 2001. *Decomposing World Income Distribution: Does the World Have a Middle Class?* Washington, DC: World Bank.

Piketty, T. 2015. About Capital in the Twenty-First Century. *American Economic Review* 105(5): 48–53.

Prahalad, C. K. 2005. *The Fortune at the Bottom of the Pyramid: Eradicating Poverty through Profits*. Philadelphia, PA: Wharton Business School Press.

Prahalad, C. K. & Hammond, A. 2002. Serving the World's Poor, Profitably. *Harvard Business Review* 80(9): 48–59.

Radjou, N. & Prabhu, J. 2015. Frugal Innovation: How to Do More with Less. *The Economist.*

Ravallion, M. 2001. Growth, Inequality and Poverty: Looking beyond Averages. *World Development* 29(11): 1803–1815.

Ravallion, M. 2009. The Developing World's Bulging (But Vulnerable) "Middle Class." Washington, DC: World Bank.

Rogers, E. M. 2010. *Diffusion of Innovations.* New York: Free Press.

Rogers, E. M. 2010. *The Fortune at the Bottom of the Pyramid: Eradicating Poverty through Profits.* Philadelphia, PA: Wharton Business School Press.

Stoneman, P. (ed.). 1995. *Handbook of the Economics of Innovation and Technological Change.* Cambridge, MA: Blackwell.

The Economist. 2009. Burgeoning Bourgeoisie: A Special Report on the New Middle Classes in Emerging Markets. *The Economist*: 14.

United Census Bureau. 2019. Poverty Thresholds. Accessed May 17, 2019. www.census.gov/data/tables/time-series/demo/income-poverty/historical-poverty-thresholds.html

Vidich, A. J. 2010. *The New Middle Classes: Life-Styles, Status Claims and Political Orientations.* London: Macmillan.

Wietzke, F. B. & Sumner, A. 2018. The Developing World's "New Middle Classes": Implications for Political Research. *Perspectives on Politics* 16(1): 127–140.

Wolf, M. 2015. How South Africa Can Escape the "Belindia" trap. *Financial Times*, November 24. Accessed May 17, 2019. www.ft.com/content/9a3a4716-91cd-11e5-bd82-c1fb87bef7af

World Bank. 2019. GDP per capita, PPP (current international $). Accessed May 17, 2019. https://data.worldbank.org/indicator/NY.GDP.PCAP.PP.CD

World Bank. 2019. Poverty & Equity Data Portal. Accessed May 17, 2019. http://povertydata.worldbank.org/poverty/home

Index

Printed in the United States
By Bookmasters